## BERNARD WILLIAMS ON LAW AND JURISPRUDENCE

This book is the first collection of essays on Bernard Williams' moral and political philosophy to shed light on the nature of law, and key legal concepts. By the time of his death in 2003, Williams was widely regarded as the most important moral philosopher of his generation. Surprisingly, his work is still largely under-discussed in legal theory. This book aims to fill this gap with brand new discussions from scholars both from law and philosophy.

The first part of the book focuses on Williams' work on responsibility and regret and its implications for law. Drawing from Ancient Greek authors, Williams maintained that luck might play a key role in our practices of responsibility and that some dimensions of responsibility are tied to the notion of having a character. What we do – intentionally or not – might affect our understanding of ourselves and of our place in the world. How do those ideas help us in making sense of legal responsibility? How do broader concerns about our practices of responsibility impact the law? Those are some of the questions addressed by the authors in this part.

The second part looks at how Williams' understanding of philosophy can shape the way we do jurisprudence. Williams' work on the methodology of philosophy combines resources from analytical philosophy, continental authors, history, and literature. He understood philosophy as a humanistic discipline. The authors in the second part of the book draw from Williams' work, notably his innovative take on the genealogical method, to discuss how we could practise legal philosophy in this same spirit.

**Volume 18 in the series Law and Practical Reason**

## Law and Practical Reason

The intention of this series is that it should encompass monographs and collections of essays that address the fundamental issues in legal philosophy. The foci are conceptual and normative in character, not empirical. Studies addressing the idea of law as a species of practical reason are especially welcome. Recognizing that there is no occasion to sharply distinguish analytic and systematic work in the field from historico-critical research, the editors also welcome studies in the history of legal philosophy. Contributions to the series, inevitably crossing disciplinary lines, will be of interest to students and professionals in moral, political, and legal philosophy.



**Recent titles in the series**

**Volume 8:** Private Law and the Value of Choice
*Emmanuel Voyiakis*

**Volume 9**: Freedom and Force: Essays on Kant's Legal Philosophy
*Edited by Sari Kisilevsky and Martin J Stone*

**Volume 10:** The Nature and Value of Vagueness in the Law
*Hrafn Asgeirsson*

**Volume 11:** Law's Humility: Enlarging the Scope of Jurisprudential Disagreement
*Triantafyllos Gkouvas*

**Volume 12:** Rightful Relations with Distant Strangers: Kant, the EU, and the Wider World
*Aravind Ganesh*

**Volume 13**: The Making of Constitutional Democracy: From Creation to Application of Law
*Paolo Sandro*

**Volume 14**: New Essays on the Nature of Legal Reasoning
*Edited by Mark McBride and James Penner*

**Volume 15**: New Essays on the Fish-Dworkin Debate
*Edited by Thomas Bustamante and Margaret Martin*

**Volume 16**: A Dynamic Approach to Hans Kelsen's General Theory of Norms
*Monika Zalewska*

**Volume 17**: Moral Responsibility and Artificial Intelligence
*Maximilian Kiener*

**Volume 18**: Bernard Williams on Law and Jurisprudence: From Agency and Responsibility to Methodology
*Edited by Daniel Peixoto Murata, Julieta A Rabanos and Veronica Rodriguez-Blanco*

# Bernard Williams on Law and Jurisprudence

*From Agency and Responsibility to Methodology*

Edited by
Daniel Peixoto Murata
Julieta A Rabanos
and
Veronica Rodriguez-Blanco

•HART•
OXFORD • LONDON • NEW YORK • NEW DELHI • SYDNEY

HART PUBLISHING

Bloomsbury Publishing Plc

Kemp House, Chawley Park, Cumnor Hill, Oxford, OX2 9PH, UK

1385 Broadway, New York, NY 10018, USA

Bloomsbury Publishing Ireland Limited, 29 Earlsfort Terrace, Dublin 2, D02 AY28, Ireland

HART PUBLISHING, the Hart/Stag logo, BLOOMSBURY and the Diana logo are trademarks of Bloomsbury Publishing Plc

First published in Great Britain 2026



A catalogue record for this book is available from the British Library.

A catalogue record for this book is available from the Library of Congress.

ISBN: HB: 978-1-50997-613-3
ePDF: 978-1-50997-615-7
ePub: 978-1-50997-614-0

Typeset by Compuscript Ltd, Shannon
Printed and bound in Great Britain

For product safety related questions contact productsafety@bloomsbury.com

To find out more about our authors and books visit www.hartpublishing.co.uk. Here you will find extracts, author information, details of forthcoming events and the option to sign up for our newsletters.

# ACKNOWLEDGEMENTS

We would like to thank the Surrey Centre for Law and Philosophy at the University of Surrey, whose funding made possible a workshop on the theme of the book in April 2023, and to all the participants at that workshop for their remarkable contributions and discussions.

We are also grateful, for funding that enabled this volume, to the Horizon Twinning project 'Advancing Cooperation on The Foundations of Law – ALF' (project no 101079177) – financed by the European Union (Belgrade-Lisbon-Genoa) and UK Research & Innovation – UK-RI (Surrey).

Finally, we are thankful for the support of everyone at Hart Publishing, notably Kate and Verity, and to the *Law and Practical Reason Series* Editor, George Pavlakos, for his continued support.

# CONTENTS

*Acknowledgements* ........ *vii*
*List of Contributors* ........ *xi*

*Introduction: Bernard Williams as a Legal Philosopher* ........ *1*
**Daniel Peixoto Murata, Julieta A Rabanos and Veronica Rodriguez-Blanco**

PART I
RESPONSIBILITY, REGRET, AND THE LAW

1. *'The Idea of the Voluntary is Essentially Superficial': Bernard Williams on Responsibility and Political Freedom* ........ *23*
**Ulrike Heuer**

2. *The Politics of Civic Maturity v the Politics of Justice: Reflecting on Bernard Williams' Separation Thesis* ........ *41*
**Veronica Rodriguez-Blanco**

3. *Internal Reasons, Motivation, and the Proleptic Nature of Blame* ........ *67*
**Gerald Lang**

4. *Taking the Edge Off Professional Ethical Dilemmas* ........ *85*
**Emmanuel Voyiakis**

5. *Response-Norm Concepts in Law and Morality: A Qualified Defence of Moral Luck* ........ *103*
**Benjamin C Zipursky**

6. *Thinking about* Shame and Necessity *in Liberal Constitutional Theory* ........ *125*
**Emily Kidd White**

7. *Political Realism, Tragedy, and the Violent Foundations of the State: Reading* The Man Who Shot Liberty Valance *with Bernard Williams* ........ *141*
**David Owen**

PART II
WILLIAMS ON THE METHODOLOGY OF PHILOSOPHY AND JURISPRUDENCE

8. *Creon's Revenge: Lawfulness and the Genealogy of Law* ........ *161*
**Stephen Bero**

9. *Law and Lawfulness: Genealogy, Jurisprudence and the Thought of Bernard Williams* ....... 181
**Christopher Tollefsen**

10. *The Idea of Humanistic Middle-Range Theory* ....... 197
**Damian Cueni**

11. *Why Can't Law be More Like Morality?* ....... 219
**Christopher Kutz**

12. *An Unusual but Successful Philosophical Marriage in Bernard Williams: Nietzsche and Wittgenstein* ....... 229
**Ronaldo Porto Macedo Jr**

13. *Law as a Test of Conceptual Strength* ....... 249
**Matthieu Queloz**

14. *Practical Reasoning as Interpretation: Williamsian Remarks on Dworkin's Methodology* ....... 269
**Daniel Peixoto Murata**

15. *A Williamsian Account of Jurisprudence as Conceptual Morphology* ....... 285
**Miodrag Jovanović and Bojan Spaić**

*Index* ....... 303

# LIST OF CONTRIBUTORS

**Stephen Bero** is Assistant Professor, Department of Philosophy, Simon Fraser University, Burnaby, British Columbia, Canada.

**Damian Cueni** is an International Postdoctoral Fellow at the University of St Gallen, Switzerland.

**Ulrike Heuer** is Associate Professor in Philosophy at University College London, United Kingdom.

**Miodrag Jovanović** is Full Professor of Jurisprudence and the Head of the Department for Theory, Sociology and Philosophy of Law at the University of Belgrade Faculty of Law, Serbia.

**Emily Kidd White** is an Associate Professor at Osgoode Hall Law School, Canada.

**Christopher Kutz** is Maxeiner Distinguished Professor of Law, and Professor of Philosophy and Political Science (by courtesy) at UC Berkeley, United States of America.

**Gerald Lang** is Professor of Philosophy at the University of Leeds, United Kingdom.

**David Owen** is Professor of Social and Political Philosophy at the University of Southampton and, for 2024–25, SSS Visiting Professor at the Institute for Advanced Study, Princeton.

**Daniel Peixoto Murata** is a Professor of Law at the Mackenzie Presbyterian University, Brazil.

**Ronaldo Porto Macedo Jr** is Full Professor at the University of São Paulo Law School, Brazil.

**Matthieu Queloz** is an Ambizione Fellow of the Swiss National Science Foundation at the University of Bern, Switzerland.

**Julieta A Rabanos** is a Ramón y Cajal Fellow at the University of Girona, Spain.

**Veronica Rodriguez-Blanco** is Professor of Political and Moral Philosophy (Jurisprudence) at the University of Surrey Centre for Law and Philosophy, United Kingdom.

**Bojan Spaić** is Associate Professor of Introduction to Jurisprudence and Philosophy of Law at the University of Belgrade Faculty of Law, Serbia, and Director of the Center for Legal Fundamentals of the Institute for Legal and Social Sciences of the same faculty.

**Christopher Tollefsen** is Professor of Philosophy at the University of South Carolina, United States of America.

**Emmanuel Voyiakis** is Professor in Law at LSE Law School, United Kingdom.

**Benjamin C Zipursky** is James H Quinn '49 Chair in Legal Ethics and Professor of Law at Fordham Law School, United States.

# Introduction: Bernard Williams as a Legal Philosopher

DANIEL PEIXOTO MURATA, JULIETA A RABANOS
AND VERONICA RODRIGUEZ-BLANCO

## I. Bernard Williams: An Overview and Some Lessons for Legal Philosophy

Bernard Arthur Owen Williams is often considered one of the most prominent moral philosophers of the 20th century. Having studied *Greats* at Oxford, he was as comfortable discussing minutiae of contemporary philosophy as he was in discussing opera and Greek literature. His erudition and humanistic character were not the only traits that separated him from most analytical philosophers, however. Williams was also engaged in British political life. He took part in many royal commissions and committees, such as the drug abuse and the gambling ones, and famously chaired the Committee on Obscenity and Film Censorship (*The Times* 2003). In the academic realm, he held positions at the Universities of Cambridge, Princeton, Berkeley, and Oxford, among others. Williams was knighted in 1999 and passed away in 2003 after four years battling against cancer.

Also different from other great moral and political philosophers of his time, such as John Rawls, it is hard to identify a *Williamsian* way of doing philosophy. We can confidently say that Will Kymlicka and Samuel Freeman are *Rawlsians* (despite all the inherent distortions that such *isms* and *ians* entail). There are some traits that we can pinpoint, such as the use of a certain philosophical toolbox that distinguishes a thinker as Rawlsian. This is not as straightforward regarding Williams; however, as we will try to argue – or rather, gesture – in this Introduction, there indeed *is* a Williamsian way of doing philosophy, and legal philosophy has much to gain from it. Within the scope of this text, we can only hope to present in fairly schematic terms some of Williams' insights and their relevance to jurisprudence.[1]

One aspect of Williams' corpus that certainly plays a role in explaining why it is difficult for people to identify *the Williamsian way* is that much of his work,

[1] For the purposes of this Introduction, we will use 'jurisprudence', 'legal theory' and 'legal philosophy' as synonyms.

especially his most famous pieces, are devoted to criticism of traditional moral theories. Williams took issue with both utilitarianism and Kantianism (and, it is worth adding, his views on Aristotle were ambivalent, to say the least). The gist of his criticisms against both utilitarians and Kantians is that they both distort how we experience our ethical lives. Each in its own way, utilitarianism and Kantianism reduce ethics to a single, or supreme, value: they are instances of what Williams calls the *morality system* (utilitarianism being a 'marginal member' of it, as he says).

What is the morality system, according to Williams? It is the philosophical representation of 'a deeply rooted and still powerful misconception of life' (Williams 2011: 218). According to the morality system, life has only one sovereign, moral obligation. The morality system treats moral obligations as supreme, as being impossible to override in practical deliberation. Furthermore, moral obligations are also taken to be systematic, which means that there can be no real conflicts between moral obligations, and they also apply to everyone, regardless of their inclinations and the like (which is another way to say that every person is morally obligated, whether they recognise it or not) (Williams 2011: 194–201). This way of understanding moral obligations distorts our ethical experience since it either mistranslates other sorts of ethical considerations that are better thought of in different terms – think about considerations about virtue, or about love – into the language of obligation or takes us to the misguided conclusion that 'without its very special obligation, there is only inclination' (Williams 2011: 218). There is more to ethical experience than moral obligations, says Williams. If the morality system distorts ethical experience, why is it so appealing? How are we to explain how it has bewitched so many great philosophers? Here is what Williams has to say about this question: 'The purity of morality itself represents a value. It expresses an ideal, presented by Kant, once again, in a form that is the most unqualified and also one of the most moving: the ideal that human existence can be ultimately just' (Williams 2011: 217). As one of our contributors to this volume, Matthieu Queloz, puts it elsewhere, the morality system provides us with a form of 'shelter from luck' (Queloz 2022). As long as a person acts according to their moral obligations, claims the morality system, their life will have supreme value. The system also provides us with a very special picture of agency (that Williams refers to as a 'double-picture' of agency) (1999a). This special picture introduces a sharp distinction between the action on the one hand and the agent of the action on the other. 'There has to be, or so the myth goes, a point which is *me* as the ultimate author or gate-keeper', says Williams, '[a]nd this has to be the will' (1999a: 149).[2] This will of the agent must be something fundamentally distinct from the agent's desires and other idiosyncrasies, and it is this will that is the ultimate recipient of praise or blame. Because this will is independent of whom we contingently are, allocation of praise or blame to it would be *just* (Williams 2011: 216). Arguing that such

[2] See also Williams 1995a: 68–72.

purified conception of the will is an illusion is the goal of much of Williams' work (Williams 1995a).

Williams' criticisms of the morality system do not necessarily lead us to despair, nor to cynicism. There are many ethical resources we can still mobilise, from considerations of virtue to emotions such as shame, gratitude, and love to our own ground projects. Even obligations still play a role, although not the supreme role they had in the morality system, in our ethical lives. Williams invites us not to simply give up ethical life but to think hard and honestly about its demands. As he puts it in an interview, we can still 'make some sense of the ethical as opposed to throwing out the whole thing because you can't have the idealised version of it' (Williams & Voorhoeve 2004: 85). The same sort of consideration applies to legal philosophy. Take for instance the classical idea of the *will*. In most legal theorising (and practice) the will plays a crucial role in identifying the relevant action for the purposes of the law, usually in connection with the idea of the *voluntary*. However, if we follow Williams and put pressure on both ideas – the will and the voluntary – we are then faced with a different way of thinking about action, and are forced to rethink many of our legal categories. However, from the fact that some ways of thinking about the law are put under pressure, it does not follow that our legal categories cannot survive. In any case, we need now to address the question of how to make some sense of the ethical, and to Williams' views on the way of doing philosophy.

In his famous *Cogito* interview, Williams, when asked if there are any unifying themes in his work, expressed the idea that there are at least two recurrent concerns throughout his philosophy. The first concern is broadly about the methods of philosophy. Williams believes that something like a 'scepticism without reductionism' is the most fruitful way to engage with philosophical problems. The second concern is about how a person shapes themselves, that is, how they become the person they are. We are all in the business of shaping *ourselves*, and how we go on doing that is a central issue in Williamsian philosophy (1999a: 143–44). Let us elaborate a bit on each of those concerns, and in doing so, we will also revisit some commitments of much jurisprudence.

Regarding 'scepticism without reductionism', we can better understand what Williams means if we look at what he says in the essay 'Philosophy as a Humanistic Discipline'. This essay is Williams' clearest exposition of what he takes philosophy's business to be: 'part of a more general attempt to make the best sense of our life, and so of our intellectual activities, in the situation in which we find ourselves' (2006b: 182). Many philosophers, both canonical and contemporary, believed that philosophy's business was the crafting of grand theories.[3] This is doubly so regarding moral philosophy. If we may combine two different Williamsian ideas into a single explanation here, much of moral

[3] And indeed, one volume organised by Quentin Skinner intended to present an overview of some such contemporary philosophers. See Skinner 1990.

philosophy was both under the spell of 'the absolute conception of the world' (Williams 2011: 146–72) and of a tendency to be providential, some sort of gospel bringing good news in an unfair world (Williams 2006d). The latter was already explored when we discussed the morality system, so let us turn to the 'absolute conception of the world'.

The 'absolute conception of the world' can be understood as an ideal for scientific inquiry. It amounts to a conception of the world that is as independent as possible from local practices, concepts, and particularities. How does this work as a goal? Think about different ways we have for explaining the idea of *cold*. An explanation of cold could have the following form: 'cold is what we feel when we go out during winter'. Another way of explaining cold is this: 'the property of coldness consists in the relative absence of thermal energy'. The first explanation depends fundamentally on our sensorial capacities and on our cultural constructions and understanding of seasons. The second explanation, on the other hand, depends only on a more general capacity to understand how energy works. According to Williams, this second explanation is closer to the 'absolute conception of the world' since it is less dependent on the particularities of those engaging with it. Cruder forms of naturalism go hand-in-hand with the search for an 'absolute conception', as they attempt to *reduce* complex social, cultural, and normative aspects of life to less complex natural facts.

One might have doubts about the plausibility of such a conception in the hard sciences, but when practical philosophy – moral, political and legal – is practised under its influence, there are reasonable chances that its object – ethics, politics, the law – will end up distorted or poorly explained. This is so because the search for an absolute conception is antithetical to attempts to make sense of things as they appear to *us*, human beings that inhabit certain forms of life. In legal philosophy, for instance, a commitment to the absolute conception would make us blind to a very salient aspect of law, namely, that we engage with its directives not only from an external perspective but also from what H.L.A. Hart has called an 'internal point of view' (1994). Under the absolute conception, law could only be described as regularities of some sort, as some patterns of behaviour described externally. This amounts to an impoverished view of law (although one that might be correct depending on the purposes of the researcher) that fails to account for its normativity, that is, for how law appears in the agents' exercise of practical deliberation. In ethics, the search for an absolute conception sometimes takes people to implausible versions of moral realism, as if ethics were determined by moral facts in the same way that chemical properties determine the result of combustion. Alternatively, it takes people to vulgar forms of relativism: because it is not possible to 'objectively' determine what is right and what is wrong in the same sense that we can determine the nature of water, then there is no right and wrong.

Going back to Williams' understanding of philosophy's business, how do we make sense of ourselves? The Williamsian way to answer this question connects his subtle brand of scepticism (from the slogan 'scepticism without reductionism') to his second concern, about how a person becomes who she is. It is in *Shame and*

*Necessity* that we can find important clues. In the sixth chapter, Williams compares Plato's and Thucydides' underlying psychological views and, following Nietzsche, sides with Thucydides:

> Thucydidean "impartiality" should not be seen as an attempt to produce an entirely "value-free" account of human affairs, one that tries to reduce them to phenomena on the same level as physical transactions. *His aim is to make sense of social events, and that involves relating them intelligibly to human motivations, and to the ways in which situations appear to agents* (...). But Thucydides' conception of an intelligible and typically human motivation is broader and less committed to a distinctive ethical outlook than Plato's; or rather – the distinction is important – it is broader than the conception acknowledged in Plato's psychological theories. The same is true, if less obviously, in relation to Aristotle (1993: 161–62, fnn omitted, our emphases).

The quotation above provides a summary of Williams' views, and there are four items to it. *Firstly*, and connected to what has been previously said, we should not attempt to reduce human affairs to physical or natural facts. Again, it is not that such attempts at reduction would be in any sense wrong, but that they would fail as explanations of *human* action. As Williams puts it elsewhere, biological studies might provide us with useful information about why humans have a need for music. It will fail to provide us with an explanation, however, of how we came to have Beethoven (1995b).

*Secondly*, if we are to make sense of social events (and of human action more generally) we need to be able to relate 'them intelligibly to human motivations' (Williams 1993: 161–62). Williams has defended a version of reasons internalism regarding action that has been the subject of much discussion in the specialised literature. In his most mature version, Williams' internalism amounts to the following: 'A has a reason to φ only if he could reach the conclusion to φ by a sound deliberative route from the motivations he already has' (1995c: 35). For a given reason to be a reason for action *for me*, says Williams, this reason must somehow be reachable through deliberation that starts from *my motivations*. Two caveats here. Firstly, Williams does not assert that one cannot be mistaken in their deliberations (they can be, for instance, if they are provided with false information or when the reasoning becomes flawed due to wishful thinking). Secondly, his concern, as he clarifies later in an interview, was merely with the explanation of action: '[Williams' original essay on the matter] was only about *explaining individual action and in particular explaining individual action in terms of reason*' (1999b: 260, our emphases).

The preceding remarks also explain a *third* point from the quotation, namely, that Williamsian philosophy is mostly concerned with how 'situations appear to agents'. It is not a philosophy from a metaphysical point of view. Rather, its perspective is 'radically first-personal' (Williams 2011: 23); its starting point is our own condition in the world. Williamsian philosophy resists the attempt to present phenomena as they appear to theories, since its main concern is with understanding things (social events, actions and so on) as they appear to us, agents with certain psychological make-ups.

A *fourth* and final point is related to how we should understand what counts as 'an intelligible and typically human motivation'. Many moral philosophers seem to have confused at some level what counts as an intelligible and typically human motivation with *moral* motivation. This is particularly so with Kant, who saw a natural connection from rationality to freedom to morality.

Against moralised psychology, Williams invites us to ask 'what an experienced, honest, subtle and unoptimistic interpreter might make of human behaviour elsewhere' (1995a: 68). The more important characteristics here are honesty and subtlety. An interpreter must be honest about herself, about her own motivations, and about those of the people she is trying to make sense of. This takes us away from the moralised views on agency and closer to a realistic view. Subtlety is also relevant because it is too easy to overlook fine grained distinctions in motivations. There is an important difference between saving one's wife *because she is one's wife* and saving one's wife because *in such and such circumstances it is morally allowed to save one's wife* (Williams 1981b).

Williams invites us to think about who the agents underlying our theories are. Returning to legal philosophy, how are we to describe the persons presupposed in a certain jurisprudential theory? Are we operating under a plausible picture? Those are issues neglected by much contemporary legal philosophy. Those issues, however, are central if jurisprudence wants to say anything relevant about how law figures in the agents' practical reasoning, that is, an adequate account of legal normativity must be anchored in an adequate account of the agent that engages with the law.[4]

One important topic in this connection is *responsibility*. Williams states that 'in the story of one's life there is an authority exercised by what one has done, and not merely by what one has intentionally done' (1993: 69) and that 'Regret must be governed, in good part, by results that go beyond intention' (1993: 69). What he is pointing out is that attribution of responsibility, in a very relevant sense, does not depend on our good or ill intentions. It follows from this that if we are unlucky, our lives might be wrecked by our own actions even if we had the best intentions. We can see, once more, how Williams resists the allure of the morality system and its promises of an ultimately fair life. Williams' candid reflections about responsibility also help us to think about responsibility *in the law*. Williams helps us to make sense of legal distinctions such as the differences in punishment between attempted and successful crimes, as well as law's somewhat 'unfair' habit of treating less harshly people that were reckless but luckily caused no harm, in comparison to those that were equally reckless but caused harm.[5]

So, where does all of this take us? We believe it takes us to a distinct way of doing philosophy, and a distinct way of doing legal philosophy. Williamsian (legal)

[4] For a detailed analysis of how Williamsian philosophy can help with the understanding of legal normativity, see Murata (*forthcoming*).

[5] Indeed, as Williams himself points out, philosophy has a lot to learn from the life of the law. See Williams 1995e.

philosophy is radically first-personal, it takes *ourselves* as its starting point. The inherent messiness of agents implies that they are not necessarily systematic, leaving ample room for conflict. We are not, after all, worked out creatures. Finally, given that we are complex, cultural beings, Williamsian (legal) philosophy is open to inputs from other disciplines, such as literature and history. It is, in a nutshell, a 'humanistic discipline' (2006b).

## II. Summarising the Book

Our book intends to fill an important gap in the literature by providing insight on how the philosophy of Bernard Williams can help us in our understanding of the law. Our contributors draw from different parts of the Williamsian corpus and connect his ideas in some new and surprising ways in order to shed light on both law and legal theory. We have decided to split the book into two parts. The first part, *Responsibility, Regret, and the Law*, focuses on Williams' work on responsibility and regret and its implications for law. The second part, *Williams on the Methodology of Philosophy and Jurisprudence*, looks at how Williams' understanding of philosophy and of philosophical methods can impact the way we do jurisprudence. This is not to say, to be clear, that the chapters fall squarely within those parts, but to suggest an organised way of reading the material.

Regarding the general topics of the first part, drawing from Ancient Greek authors, Williams maintained that luck might play a key role in our practices of responsibility (e.g., see his work on moral luck) and that some dimensions of responsibility are tied to the notion of having a character. What we do – intentionally or not – might affect our understanding of ourselves and of our place in the world. How do those ideas help us make sense of legal responsibility? How do broader concerns about our practices of responsibility impact the law? These are the questions addressed by the authors in this part.

The discussions on regret emphasise the other side of the coin. Williams' pioneering work on agent-regret (e.g., *Moral Luck* and *Problems of the Self*) (1981a and 1973) can help us in understanding what it means for the agent to be the one that has caused a bad, harmful, or otherwise regrettable state of affairs. This sounds particularly true regarding those that must make difficult political or legal choices. One of Williams' favourite examples here comes from Greek tragedy: the case of Agamemnon at Aulis. Faced with two unpleasant options, one might end up picking the lesser evil, but that does not mean that there are no costs involved for the agent and those around him. The first part of the book looks at those considerations and at their upshots for our understanding of our engagement with the law.

The second part, in turn, focuses on what is usually called the methodological issues of contemporary jurisprudence and on how Williams can help us with them. For much of the second half of the 20th century, jurisprudence was dominated by the idea that to do philosophy is to do conceptual analysis. In general, this view meant that there was little attention paid to the ways in which concrete agents engage with the law, to the inherent contingence of legal institutions, and to the historical character of the law. Williams' work on the methodology of philosophy, notably in books like *Philosophy as a Humanistic Discipline* (2006a) and *Truth and Truthfulness* (2002) can bring fresh air to the field, and that is the purpose of the second part of the book.

Ulrike Heuer opens our first part of the book, *Responsibility, Regret, and the Law*, with her chapter, '"The Idea of the Voluntary is Essentially Superficial": Bernard Williams on Responsibility and Political Freedom'. Williams was famous for his writings on responsibility, for instance, he usually claimed that the idea of voluntariness was shallow, that there was no depth to it, but arguments such as this one are scattered among many works. In her chapter, Heuer aims at finding a unifying interpretation of Williams' views about responsibility. In *Shame and Necessity*, Williams describes four building blocks that any recognisable view of responsibility must incorporate: cause, intention, state, and response. But they are not necessary and/or sufficient conditions of responsibility. Their role is different. With these four elements in place, Heuer seeks to resolve a dilemma that Williams describes in *Moral Luck*: a) a person is only responsible for what she does intentionally, or b) we appear to be responsible for the actual results of what we do, whether or not they are intended. A lorry driver, for instance, who runs over a child, without fault is responsible for the child's death, and feelings of regret seem adequate and appropriate. Nevertheless, a) and b) appear contradictory. We are either responsible for our intentional actions only or are responsible for the results of our agencies; regardless of our intentions, we cannot have both.

Heuer aims to show that Williams reconciles both horns by developing two key interpretative ideas. First, Williams argues that voluntariness, understood as acting intentionally in a normal state of mind, is an essentially superficial concept. It doesn't allow for a metaphysically deep understanding, but it nonetheless serves an important function in certain institutional settings, for instance, in criminal law. The focus is on the role that voluntariness plays in securing that the state's actions and rulings are not arbitrary and unpredictable and are thus compatible with political freedom and fairness. The concept of voluntariness should be understood as serving this function and not as tracing a deeper notion of freedom. Hence, Williams can embrace the first horn of the dilemma: in certain contexts, we can be held responsible only for our intentional actions. Secondly, since this understanding of responsibility is restricted to a particular domain, the criminal law, Williams embraces the second horn of the dilemma too: a non-purified conception of agency underlies ordinary ascriptions of responsibility. Here too, the four elements of responsibility are present but not in the manner that the view of moral responsibility as control and intentional actions envisions. There are appropriate responses that would attribute responsibility to the agent if the agent did not act intentionally or was not in a normal state of mind.

Rodriguez-Blanco's chapter, 'The Politics of Civic Maturity v the Politics of Justice: Reflecting on Bernard Williams' Separation Thesis', takes issue with Williams' scepticism about the potential of practical deliberation. It is, in a sense, a chapter that connects Williams' famous defence of reasons internalism (mentioned in the previous section) to political philosophy, but that does so in a creative way, revisiting his theses and challenging them. Williams has argued in 'Voluntary Acts and Responsible Agents' (1995d) that practical deliberation can take us far, but not very far. Notably, we cannot change all of our desires, goals, attachments, and so on. 'Total control' is, as he puts it in his essay, a 'hopeless fantasy'. According to Rodriguez-Blanco, important consequences follow from this. Firstly, we have no reliable account of how we can 'reason out' of our desires. Secondly, and *a fortiori*, we have no account of how we can 'reason out' desires together, that is, we have no account of communal deliberation that is plausible. Thirdly, in any case, to be a mature agent demands that a person owns their actions. Thus, the public sphere demanding that the agent 'take responsibility' is either too soon or too late. It is too late if the agent is mature, since he already took responsibility. It is too soon if the agent is immature and fails to do so by themselves. Justice and maturity, it seems, are indeed separate.

Against this thesis, called the 'separation thesis', Rodriguez-Blanco argues that there can be a continuum between the politics of justice and the politics of civic maturity. To do so, she undermines the thesis that desires are a given in our deliberation. Williams seems to believe that practical deliberation merely makes our desires clear to ourselves and that then we act on those desires. Drawing on Iris Murdoch's ethical writings, Rodriguez-Blanco claims that 'our intelligent, open thinking changes our perspectives on matters such as our attitudes towards other people and who they are'. Our desires – as reasons for action – are not given things we merely identify. Through descriptions and redescriptions, our attitudes change. Equally important, as we go on living, we are presented with demands of justice we cannot in good faith ignore. To borrow an example from Simone Weil, if I am hurting someone and this person cries, 'Why am I being hurt?', I cannot in good faith ignore this question. I need to reply to it, and such a reply will demand an 'exchange of practical thoughts' between me and the person being hurt. As Rodriguez-Blanco puts this point, '"the demands of justice" are imposed on us, and we are forced to see the other in their practical thoughts and in our own practical thoughts'. As a result, the responsibility is on us to develop civic maturity.

Reasons internalism is discussed further by Gerald Lang, who writes a thought-provoking piece named 'Internal Reasons, Motivation, and the Proleptic Nature of Blame'. Lang shows us the advantages of a certain understanding of Williams' complex notion of internal reasons and its connection to the proleptic blame mechanism. Externalism on reasons for actions posits that what one has reason to do is settled independently of our motivation. Internalists, on the other hand, contend that reasons for action depend on the agent's motivational set. Lang provides the strongest possible interpretation of internalism in order to show externalists 'what they are up against'. Lang interprets the internalist claim in two ways. First, 'the procedural interpretation' establishes that we cannot rely on the actual motivations of the agent but rather on a sound deliberative route that ties the purported reason to the agent's motivational set. Second, the 'motivational interpretation' states that the agent's actual motivations are constitutive of the agent's reasons for actions. Lang demonstrates that the motivational interpretation has several advantages over the procedural interpretation. More importantly, Lang shows that the motivational interpretation of internal reasons enables us to make good sense of the role of proleptic blame in Williams' work.

The aim of Emmanuel Voyiakis' chapter, 'Taking the Edge Off Professional Ethical Dilemmas', is to critically discuss Williams' contribution to professional ethics. In 'Professional Morality and its Dispositions', Williams puts forward a controversial claim: firstly, he distinguishes different dispositions professionals might have regarding the relationship between their professional demands and the broader demands of morality (the term here is not to be understood in the pejorative sense of the 'morality system' in *Ethics and the Limits of Philosophy*). Secondly, he claims that (to quote Voyiakis' presentation of this claim):

> in somewhat paradoxical terms (…) we should be aiming to create professionals comfortable with experiencing genuine ethical discomfort when their professional ethical commitments and ordinary morality diverge. It follows that, depending how often they have to deal with ethical conflict, and on the nature of the competing ordinary and professional duties, lawyers who fit that profile may be ethically required to experience significant amounts of regret in their practice.

Voyiakis is happy to grant that Williams might be right in saying that there are benefits in this picture, notably that our professionals (especially legal professionals) will be able to reach better conclusions and have more resistance to self-deception and the like if they cultivate the dispositions to 'tortured co-existence'. However, he wants to complicate things a bit by adding that there are limits to the ethical pressure we should expose our professionals to. There might be good reasons to either alleviate or distribute ethical conflicts across the board. Unless we do so, warns Voyiakis, we run the risk of misrepresenting an important issue, namely, of pinning down an ethical failure that is institutional, about the design of our legal practices, to individuals.

The idea of moral luck, that is, that luck might interfere in our moral standing, became something of a trademark of Williams, and in his chapter, 'Response-Norm Concepts in Law and Morality: A Qualified Defence of Moral Luck', Benjamin Zipursky unpacks it and its relation to legal luck. Legal luck, Zipursky claims, is pervasive and deep. However, instrumentalist approaches to legal luck, such as law and economics theories, may justify *some* amount of legal luck but fail to justify its endemic presence. By contrast, the chapter acknowledges the endemic presence of legal luck and offers an explanation that is both non-instrumental and based on blame. Hence, Zipursky shows that the path to defending legal luck leads us to a defence of a specific kind of moral luck, namely, wrongful acts that result in injury. Zipursky demonstrates how legal theory has learned from ethics, but *vice versa* is also true. The result-inclusive structure of the law sheds light on moral inquiry. Like Heuer, Zipursky scrutinises Williams' recognition of the importance of institutional structures to illuminate and move forward the moral inquiry. The roots of moral luck scepticism stem from three key ideas. First is the idea of control over one's actions. Second, the notion of fairness is construed in terms of the view that equal actions should be reflected in equal blame. Third, respect for the different levels of culpability, namely blameworthiness for an act, cannot change unless the agent's level of culpability for the act differs. Thus, two identical acts under identical circumstances manifest the same level of culpability, regardless of consequences outside the agent's control. Similar ideas can be extrapolated to the domain of the law, where control, fairness, and respect for the different levels of culpability are the core of our practices of legal blame and liability. Zipursky uses the example of two drivers, Fate and Fortune, who both drive negligently, but only Fate runs over Hurt. We say that Fate's negligent driving caused the accident. Thus, Fate could have avoided injuring Hurt by driving carefully. Zipursky uses the outcome theory of responsibility developed by Honoré and Perry to defend the result-inclusive structure of the law of negligence. Like Perry and Honoré, Zipursky invites us to pay attention to the way we describe the *legal* action. In the case of negligence, it is not only that Fortune's and Fate's actions were different because Fortune negligently injured Hurt, but also that Hurt had a legal right not to be injured and Fate had a legal duty not to injure Hurt. This legal institutional structure shed light on moral luck and blame. Thus, according to Zipursky, blameworthiness belongs to 'response-norm concepts' that function in different ways, including the use of blame in the context of attribution of responsibility for what the person *did*.

Emily Kidd White's chapter, 'Thinking about *Shame* and *Necessity* in Liberal Constitutional Theory', provides us with thought-provoking connections between Williams' *Shame and Necessity* and constitutional theory. This might sound surprising at first, since *Shame and Necessity* is mostly about Greek poetry and what we can learn from it regarding action and responsibility. As Williams himself highlights in many bits of the book, it has direct relevance for how we think about torts or criminal liability, but Kidd White's arguments shed light 'on the way that a series of philosophical assumptions about the components of the mind and their relation to ethical activity are reflected in the foundations of liberal constitutional theory, which rely on (narrow) conceptions of intention and will'.

How so? Most liberal constitutional theory is in continuity with a certain Kantian view on morality, a view that presupposes a historically contingent philosophy of mind, which centres notions of a purified will and a theory of moral obligation that casts the will as superior to desires, emotions, personal commitments, contingencies, character traits, and so on. In moral philosophy, this peculiar philosophy of mind serves to place the domain of the ethical beyond history and contingency, but the price it pays for doing so is a radically distorted ethical experience. In constitutional theory, the effects are similar. As Kidd White points out, the high-minded philosophy of mind that Williams attacks, if underlying constitutional theory, ends up glossing over 'certain constitutional politics that should otherwise be heavy and pressing'. Not blind impartiality, but a close regard to history and to contingency might be – ironically – the right path forward if we want our constitutional theory to straightforwardly address the manners in which liberal constitutional theory has 'long supported expropriation, exploitation, and exclusion'.

In tandem with Williams' own approach to philosophy as a humanistic discipline, David Owen uses Ford's *The Man Who Shot Liberty Valance* to show that Williams' criticism of the morality system and his early work on ethics, namely his reflections on Greek tragedy that centred on excellence and honour, cannot be isolated from his political realism articulated prior to his death. In his piece, 'Political Realism, Tragedy, and the Violent Foundations of the State Reading *The Man Who Shot Liberty Valance* with Bernard Williams', Owen argues that citizens' ethical outlook and narratives, including the foundational myths of the city, are not independent of the political relationship of truthfulness and myth in liberal politics. According to Owen, there is always a moral cost to the transition into a political society in the form of a state. Owen shows how, for Williams, there are inevitable disagreements on what counts as liberty and what the costs of liberty are. By contrast, the morality system tells us a different story. It promises the possibility of a unifying view on values, including liberty. Learning how the narratives in transition operate enables us to illuminate the way conflicts in transition occur and how these conflicts shape the self-understanding of the people who live in the modern state. Owen tells us, 'Taking political opposition in such contexts seriously matters because it has implications for how we see ourselves as people'.

Stephen Bero is the first author in our second part, *Williams on the Methodology of Philosophy and Jurisprudence*. Bero's contribution, 'Creon's Revenge: Lawfulness and the Genealogy of Law', looks at the methodology of jurisprudence. In a thought-provoking chapter, Bero takes issue with the way that the genealogical method was traditionally deployed in jurisprudence, notably Hart's way of using it and its further developments in Philip Pettit's work. According to Bero, what we are lacking is an account that explains our 'disposition of lawfulness', that is, a sense of commitment or attachment that we have towards law. Why do we need to explain this disposition, that some might take as primitive or simply not relevant from a moral point of view? We need to explain it because it plays a central role in how we understand our own relationship with the law and its particular kind of authority.

Bero focuses on the differences between Bernard Williams and Philip Pettit in how they account for the internalisation of norms. Pettit's view is arguably thinner. He relies heavily on reputational considerations an agent might have to not free-ride and on the endorsement such agents might have, in the game-theoretical sense of the term. Williams, on the other hand, takes as his starting point the fact that real agents 'have, and are understood by one another to have, a range of motivations', cares, attachments, values and the like. We are all messier than theory (a point important to Bero's paper and that Williams himself recognises time and time again). According to Bero, the general issue with an account like Pettit's is a *non sequitur*. Pettit's account boils down to a choice between different norms, but the relevant, practical question, is a choice between different actions (i.e. to comply or not with a given norm). Bero's ultimate aim is to add some blood (in a literal sense) to the genealogy of law: commenting on Hartian genealogy he claims that we should expect 'Law's emergence out of a system of primary rules to be troubled, a site of struggle and contestation'. Law's survival, in such a scenario, would fundamentally depend on the disposition of lawfulness.

Christopher Tollefsen's chapter, 'Law and Lawfulness: Genealogy, Jurisprudence and the Thought of Bernard Williams', in a sense forms a pair with Bero's contribution. Tollefsen's chapter discusses Williams' seminal book *Truth and Truthfulness* and its connection to an important, although overlooked, virtue, namely, lawfulness. Following Williams, Tollefsen begins by pointing out a tension between our commitment towards truth and our suspicion of its very possibility. A similar tension affects law: if Hart is right and there is nothing (really, or necessarily) valuable about law, then a disposition to lawfulness, that is, a disposition to recognise in law something worthy of respect, is not in itself a virtue. That will depend on the merits of the legal system in particular. This, of course, is a problem for anyone that wants to argue that law is normative in a thicker sense. Williams' own project in *Truth* is to use the genealogical method to provide us with vindicatory genealogies for the virtues of Truth, Sincerity and Accuracy, that is, genealogies that would enable us to see how those virtues came about but that at the same time would be compatible with naturalistic commitments broadly conceived.

Tollefsen contends that if something like that could be made regarding lawfulness, this would be an important advance in legal philosophy. To see how this can be done, he looks to Williams' later writings on political philosophy. Placing himself as a continuator of the traditions of Thucydides and Hobbes, Williams intends to provide an account of the political that does not reduce it to the moral. Williams' starting point is the existence of a basic demand for legitimacy. The institution of a political order cannot be simply one group of people terrorising another, since such situation would be precisely what the political was supposed to alleviate to begin with. Law, understood as comprising some important notions of the Rule of Law, emerges as part of a solution here, as it helps to address the basic demand for legitimacy. If there is this connection between law and demands for legitimacy, then it is also the case, claims Tollefsen, that

> law as having the kind of intrinsic value such as to demand respect, and lawfulness as a multifaceted virtue of the law-respecting, both among the ruled and the ruling and contributing to a form of reciprocity between them, can be said to be 'constructed' in Williams's sense.

Tollefsen's arguments, surprisingly, approximate Williams to a thinker very different in temperament, namely John Finnis.

Damian Cueni, in his chapter 'The Idea of Humanistic Middle-Range Theory', proposes a novel reading of Williams' more 'methodological' arguments, notably his idea that philosophy should be practised as a humanistic discipline, that is, that it should move beyond conceptual analysis and engage with other areas of inquiry such as history, the arts, psychology, and literature. His main argument is that Williams is better understood as a 'middle-range theorist' along the lines of someone like Robert K. Merton. By presenting connections between those projects, one mostly philosophical and another mostly sociological, Cueni's chapter, like Owen's, is in itself a piece of philosophy as a humanistic discipline. Cueni intends to make three distinct contributions. Firstly, in the second section of the chapter, Cueni intends to clarify what is distinctive about humanism in Williams' writing, contrasting it with both scientism and moralism. Secondly, in the third section, he explains the sense in which Williams is a middle-range theorist. Cueni does so by drawing on the work done by Peter Hedström Lars Udehn to explain the notion of middle-range theories in Merton's work and then, in the fourth section, he brings those ideas back to Williams, through discussions of what Williams has said about truthfulness, blame, and voluntariness. Thirdly, to deploy the philosophical framework developed throughout the chapter to finally understand law as a humanistic discipline, Cueni uses the doctrinal distinction that appears in many jurisdictions, between infringement of a right and its violation, as his privileged example.

Christopher Kutz, in his chapter 'Why Can't Law be More like Morality?' argues that Williams provides us with philosophical tools that are useful in moving us beyond some of the perplexities that plagued the positivism versus anti-positivism debate in legal theory. Given that law seems to be, at least *prima facie*, the result of contingent social facts (i.e., the sovereign's will at a given time), it might lack the power to create genuine, moral obligations. Anti-positivists insisted, against this, that legal obligations should be understood as a peculiar set of moral obligations and/or that legal obligations are ways we have to give shape to our moral obligations. However, once we follow Williams and deflate morality we can find a way out from those debates. Legal concepts such as 'due process' and 'proximate cause' combine both factual and evaluative aspects, they function like Williamsian thick concepts. As Kutz puts this point, 'These concepts are as thick as they come, guided by patterns and facts, transformed by arguments. The normativity inheres holistically in the practice of argument'. Much of Williams' effort in moral philosophy can be seen as an attempt to cast aside the presuppositions of the *morality system* (which he famously called a 'misconception of life') while retaining faithfulness to our ethical experience. Kutz's chapter attempts something similar for law: it is an attempt to cast aside the presuppositions of a debate that misconceives our legal experience while retaining faithfulness to that experience itself.

Ronaldo Porto Macedo Jr's chapter, 'An Unusual but Successful Philosophical Marriage in Bernard Williams: Nietzsche and Wittgenstein', brings to the fore two of Bernard Williams' most important influences, Nietzsche and Wittgenstein.

Both authors are traditionally regarded as hard readings, unsystematic and even anti-philosophical to a certain extent. Both were also interpreted in diverse and conflicting ways. Nietzscheans and Wittgensteinians, furthermore, seem divided by the unhelpful chasm between analytical and continental philosophies, a chasm that Williams himself once compared to a distinction between a Japanese car and a front-wheel drive (2002: 201). Macedo Jr explains, through rigorous textual analysis, how Williams managed to combine the philosophical toolboxes of both Nietzsche and Wittgenstein in order to further some of their (and Williams') key ideas.

The invocations of Wittgenstein in moral and political philosophy are often conservative, as if the Austrian thinker were defending some philosophy of the folkways and the primacy of tradition. Macedo Jr points out why Williams believes this to be a mistake and why it is possible for someone to be a Left Wittgensteinian. It is a mistake because, among other things, such views gloss over the historical aspect of our concrete communities and how, in the circumstances of modernity, the criticism of our practices became in itself a practice that belongs to us. Nietzsche, on the other hand, is much harder to recruit to any political or moral philosophy (which is not to say that his ideas were not appropriated, distorted and even butchered by thinkers left and right). His toolbox, however, was successfully used by Williams in many creative ways (the genealogical method, the suspicion towards ethical theories, the claim that we need a subtler moral psychology, and so on). Macedo Jr's chapter provides us with a cartography of those uses.

Matthieu Queloz's chapter, 'Law as a Test of Conceptual Strength', draws attention to one of the most intriguing short pieces written by Williams: his postscript to David G. Owen's collection on tort law, *The Philosophical Foundations of Tort Law*. Williams's piece was called 'What Has Philosophy to Learn from Tort Law?', which means to imply that, contrary to what most philosophically minded people would think, not only does law have to learn from philosophy, but philosophy can also learn from law. Notably, it can learn 'the difference between practical reality and philosophical frivolity'. Queloz's chapter unpacks this idea by developing, among other topics, Williams' metaphor of microwave-resistant concepts, that is, concepts that are tested time and time again by the argumentative pressure they come under in courts and judicial procedures.

As Queloz highlights, however, Williams distinguishes himself from J.L. Austin by not sharing the latter's confidence in common sense. For Williams, common sense is neither consistent nor free of ideologies. More importantly, says Queloz, the concepts coined by common sense cannot validate themselves: they need to be validated by something other than common sense. By what? By the 'practical reality' in which we find ourselves. Our ethical, political and legal realities can put pressure on commonsensical concepts, and not all of them can survive such pressure. Queloz presents in a clear and systematic way why Williams believes that tort law is especially well-suited for testing the concepts that form the currency of common sense. Tort law systematically combines hard questions about ordinary situations with a pressure to arrive at clear-cut answers. As a result, the ordinary concepts we use anyway elsewhere instructively come under special pressure when subjected to legal scrutiny. Queloz then shows how the lessons that Williams draws from tort law align with some of his signature claims in moral philosophy – about the essential superficiality of voluntariness (a topic also discussed by Heuer in this volume) and the authority of what one has done, notably. Queloz concludes that 'Williams's foray into jurisprudence' proves 'surprisingly programmatic in relation to his own work in philosophy', thus raising the question of how much Williams himself originally learned from the law.

Daniel Peixoto Murata's chapter, 'Practical Reasoning as Interpretation: Williamsian Remarks on Dworkin's Methodology', vindicates a Williamsian view on practical reasoning through a comparison to Dworkin's model developed in *Justice for Hedgehogs* (2011). The chapter is built around the idea that moral conflicts are inevitable and inherent in who we are. When we make a decision, there is always the possibility of a remainder, a regret, or of loss of a good or value. Against this, Dworkin proposes an interpretative theory to solve practical conflicts and genuine disagreements in both law and morality. Dworkin's theory ultimately treats practical conflicts – and practical reasoning – in pretty much the same way it treats conflicts between beliefs and theoretical reasoning. In a sense, this theory comes as a kind of good news as it protects us from loss in the practical realm. However, the theory ends up dissolving conflict at the expense of disregarding the structure of our desires and character in our thinking and action. This should come as no surprise once we realise that the motivations, values, dispositions, projects, and the like that an agent has are not as malleable and flexible as Dworkin purports to show. Thus, Dworkin's model is a theoretical form of reasoning that falls short of explaining our agency in action and practical conflict: we are messier than theory. Murata's goal is to offer 'a reminder of the importance of taking seriously the point of view of a concrete practical agent when doing philosophy'.

Miodrag Jovanović and Bojan Spaić agree, in 'A Williamsian Account of Jurisprudence as Conceptual Morphology', with Bernard Williams's criticism of conceptual analysis as a limited method for a discipline like philosophy, including legal philosophy and ethics, which are typically humanistic disciplines. Conceptual analysis, even the modest type, presupposes that there are necessary and hence, 'metaphysical' features of law regardless of the historical circumstances that have shaped the respective concepts. In other words, it presupposes an 'absolute conception of reality' and an abstract view that renders agents' ethical and juridical experiences strange and alienating. In this way, conceptual analysis and its counterpart, naturalised methodologies, are mirrored images of each other. Naturalised methods believe that there are essential features of our natural and/or empirical world that determine the truth of our concepts, whereas conceptual analysis believes that the task is to determine via analysis the basic vocabulary that refers to the essential features of our concepts. By contrast, the focus of a humanistic discipline is the agents' self-understanding within their respective historical contingency. Consequently, the agents' engagement with both each other, including their needs, concerns, and emotions, and the world, shapes their concepts. Thus, Williams' genealogical method, as opposed to conceptual analysis or naturalised methodologies, seems the most appropriate method to unveil some of our key concepts, for instance, human rights.

The core idea is that an understanding of their contingent conditions enables us to better grasp the nature of the concept. But Williams is also aware of the importance of analytical philosophy and its focus on clarity. Hence, Jovanović and Spaić tell us, 'the main preoccupation in Williams' late work was to develop a philosophical methodology that would incorporate historical inquiry into a specifically understood analytical style of philosophising'. Jovanović and Spaić argue that this method that combines analytical tools and genealogy is 'conceptual morphology'. This is not a method explicitly endorsed by Williams, but they think it can be derived from his approach to legal and political problems. It maps concepts formations, and conceptualisations through a hermeneutical perspective. Thus, the content of a concept is determined by its use in the context of historical changes in society, emphasising the diachronic and synchronic conceptions of a concept. In spite of not being a full alternative to conceptual analysis, it offers a) philosophical analysis that is conducted for the sake of clarity without technicalities, and b) the possibility of genuine dialogue – dialogue without dialectics – with past philosophers of law to understand changes, practices and problems. There is no 'absolutization of the development of concepts'. Finally, it also offers c) a historical approach to locate our practices, ethical and juridical experiences; however, this does not mean that history determines our cultural and social phenomena.

Let us conclude our Introduction. Williams' philosophy is much rooted in the classical tradition, as it is the Humean tradition. This blend makes it challenging to understand the implications and originality of his ideas. From the classics, he learnt not only the emphasis on the contingency and particularity embedded in tragic choices and luck but also the importance of desire as the motive of action and the complexity of understanding the content of one's desires. Williams introduced a number of ideas that are unfamiliar to the modern philosopher. He emphasised the importance of looking at the phenomenon as it is presented to us in the richness of our experience, as well as attempting to undermine any artificial category or metaphysics that will prove alien or do violence to the ethical experience. He problematised the category of voluntariness, blame, intention, reasons for actions and the way we ought to think about intellectual history.

Williams resisted frivolity and, with Nietzsche and Austin, shared the view that philosophy cannot be seen as a set of simplistic formulations and frivolous abstractions, 'thoughts on a Sunday afternoon'. In this sense, law emerges as a domain where accountability for 'making sense' is more robust. In the law, says Williams, there is a constant struggle to 'make sense' of public conceptions and their connections; in the law, the parties involved will pay special attention to the conclusions.

Only well-formulated and concrete arguments will fulfil the required task. It is our hope that the essays in this volume also manage to fulfil what is demanded from them. All of them have tried to engage with both Williams' 'down-to-earth' methodology and his commitment to think about the phenomenology of responsibility, agency and legal method from the experience of us, human beings with specific needs, concepts, values, emotions and traditions, struggling to confront a reality full of contingencies and tragic choices.

## Bibliography

Dworkin, R (2011) *Justice for Hedgehogs* (Cambridge, Massachusetts, The Belknap Press).
Hart, HLA (1994) *The Concept of Law*, 2nd edn (Oxford, Clarendon Press).
Murata, DP (*forthcoming*) *Reasons, Respect, and the Law* (Oxford, Hart Publishing).
Queloz, M (2022) 'A Shelter from Luck: The Morality System Reconstructed' in M Talbert & A Szigeti (2022) *Morality and Agency: Themes from Bernard Williams* (Oxford, Oxford University Press).
Skinner, Q (1990) *The Return of Grand Theory in the Human Sciences* (Cambridge, Cambridge University Press).
*The Times* (2003) 'Professor Sir Bernard Williams – Times Online Obituary' 14 June 2003. Archived from the original on 13 May 2011. Retrieved 3 February 2024.
Williams, B (1973) *Problems of the Self* (Cambridge, Cambridge University Press).
—— (1981a) *Moral Luck* (Cambridge, Cambridge University Press).
—— (1981b) 'Persons, Character and Morality' in B Williams, *Moral Luck* (Cambridge, Cambridge University Press).
—— (1993) *Shame and Necessity* (Los Angeles, University of California Press).
—— (1995a) 'Nietzsche's Minimalist Moral Psychology' in B Williams, *Making Sense of Humanity* (Cambridge, Cambridge University Press).
—— (1995b) 'Making Sense of Humanity' in B Williams, *Making Sense of Humanity* (Cambridge, Cambridge University Press).
—— (1995c) 'Internal Reasons and the Obscurity of Blame' in B Williams, *Making Sense of Humanity* (Cambridge, Cambridge University Press).
—— (1995d) 'Voluntary Acts and Responsible Agents' in B Williams, *Making Sense of Humanity* (Cambridge, Cambridge University Press).
—— (1995e) 'Afterword – What Has Philosophy to Learn from Tort Law?' in DG Owen (ed), *Philosophical Foundations of Tort Law* (Oxford, Oxford University Press).
—— (1999a) 'Interview' in A Pyle (ed), *Key Philosophers in Conversation – The Cogito Interviews* (London, Routledge).
—— (1999b) 'Seminar with Bernard Williams' 6 3–4 *Ethical Perspectives* 243.
—— (2002) *Truth and Truthfulness* (Princeton, Princeton University Press).
—— (2006a) *Philosophy as a Humanistic Discipline*, edited by AW Moore (Princeton, Princeton University Press).
—— (2006b) 'Philosophy as a Humanistic Discipline' in B Williams, *Philosophy as a Humanistic Discipline*, edited by AW Moore (Princeton, Princeton University Press).
—— (2006c) *The Sense of the Past*, edited by Myles Burnyeat (Princeton, Princeton University Press).

—— (2006d) 'The Women of Trachis: Fictions, Pessimism, Ethics' in B Williams, *The Sense of the Past*, edited by Myles Burnyeat (Princeton, Princeton University Press).
—— (2010) 'Professional Morality and its Dispositions' in B Williams, *Making Sense of Humanity* (Cambridge, Cambridge University Press).
—— (2011) *Ethics and the Limits of Philosophy* (London, Routledge).
Williams, B & Voorhoeve, A (2004) 'A Mistrustful Animal: Bernard Williams Interviewed (by Alex Voorhoeve)' 12 1 *The Harvard Review of Philosophy* 81.

# PART I

# Responsibility, Regret, and the Law

# 1

# 'The Idea of the Voluntary is Essentially Superficial'[1]: Bernard Williams on Responsibility and Political Freedom

ULRIKE HEUER*

## I. Introduction

Much of the recent philosophical discussion of responsibility has evolved in the shadow of P F Strawson's 'Freedom and Resentment'. But there is another voice which rejects the preoccupation with freedom of will, exploring the phenomenology and practice of responsibility in a different way, namely Bernard Williams'. Like Strawson, Williams is not concerned with free will in the sense in which it is excluded by the truth of determinism. His work on responsibility focuses on a distinctive range of questions, in particular, those raised by moral luck cases. He often approaches these issues from the first-person perspective of someone who holds themselves responsible, rather than the third-personal concern with blame and other responses that has become the focus of much of the discussion in the wake of Strawson. Williams' contribution is scattered over several papers and there isn't, as far as I'm aware, any attempt yet to see those as part of a larger picture. Filling this gap, or beginning to do so, is the purpose of this chapter.

Bernard Williams famously introduced the notion of moral luck into the discussion of responsibility. The issue of moral luck is typically thought to be bound up with the question whether we can be responsible only for what is under

[1] Williams uses this phrase repeatedly (eg 1993a, 1997).

* For helpful comments and suggestions, I'm grateful to our lockdown discussion group, in particular to Joseph Raz, Ezequiel Monti, Jed Lewinsohn, Maria Alvarez, Veronique Munoz-Darde, and Felix Koch. I also benefitted immensely from the opportunity to discuss the paper with the authors in this volume at a workshop in Surrey. Michael Moore invited me to discuss the paper with his students – I learned much from the discussion and Michael's comments. Finally, I'd like to thank Victor Braga Weber and John Hyman for their insightful, searching comments on an earlier draft.

our voluntary control. If we focus on the ways in which we actually hold ourselves responsible or identify with features or outcomes of our agency the answer is no. Is it then just a mistake to think that voluntariness matters for questions of responsibility? In a lesser-known essay, 'Moral Responsibility and Political Freedom' (1997), Williams argues that it is not a mistake. However, the claim that voluntariness is a condition of responsibility has been vastly over-generalised. It has its proper place in the criminal law, at least in our time, the time of political liberalism.

But if there are different understandings of responsibility at work in different contexts and at different times, why even insist that they concern the same concept? After all, it is a philosophical stock in trade to distinguish different 'senses' in which an expression can be used. Theories of responsibility have delivered their fair share of attempts to draw such distinctions, starting perhaps with H.L.A. Hart's (1967/2008) 'Postscript' and Gary Watson's (1996) 'Two Faces'. 'Recognising Responsibility' (Williams 1993a) holds the key to Williams' reply. Williams claims that there is something in common among different ways of understanding responsibility. They are all part of a broader, but also fuzzier, idea.

In this chapter, I first try to substantiate this sketch, as an interpretation of Williams' writings on responsibility. I then look at the arguments for those claims. Finally, I raise some questions about the emerging view.

## II. Three Ideas

### A. Moral Luck

Williams' most influential contribution to discussions about responsibility is through his paper 'Moral Luck' (1976). He coined the term 'moral luck' which has since become a household word and the focus of an ongoing, prolific discussion.[2] In one of its guises, the moral luck debate concerns the question whether agents can be responsible for the results of their agency. After all, often the outcomes of our actions, even when they are intentional, don't depend only on us or our agency, but also on compliant circumstances. Things might have turned out otherwise. If we accept responsibility for the results of what we do, we accept that our responsibility is not limited to what we think up at the drawing board. As Williams puts it, 'my involvement in my action and its results goes beyond the relation I have to it as an *ex ante* rational deliberator' (1993b: 256). The *ex ante* deliberator intends or foresees the results of possible actions and rationally decides what to do on the basis of the available information. A view of responsibility taking its cue from this remark might claim that a person is responsible for what she does insofar as it was intended or foreseen (alternatively: foreseeable). According to Williams, our

[2] 'When I introduced the expression moral luck, I expected it to suggest an oxymoron' (Williams 1993b: 251).

involvement with our own agency is not limited in this way. It extends to outcomes and results that have been neither foreseen nor intended. I will say more about the argument in 'Moral Luck' in section III.

## B. The Four Elements

In 'Recognising Responsibility', Williams argues that it is a mistake to think that there is 'just one correct conception of responsibility' (1993a: 55). Our understanding of who ought be held responsible for something and in what way varies at different historical times and in different cultures. But any recognisable conception of responsibility has to speak to the relation of four features, which he calls cause, intention, state of mind, and response:

> [W]e have four ideas: [i] that in virtue of what he did, someone has brought about a bad state of affairs; [ii] that he did or did not intend that state of affairs; [iii] that he was or was not in a normal state of mind when he brought it about; and [iv] that it is his business, if anyone's, to make up for it. We might label these four elements cause, intention, state, and response. These are the basic elements of any conception of responsibility (1993a: 55).
>
> These really are universal materials. What we must not suppose is that they are always related to one another in the same way or, indeed, that there is one ideal way in which they should be related to one another. There are many ways of relating them, in particular of relating intention and state to response (1993a: 56).

The four elements are the materials of views held by the Ancients just as much as of Kantian or contemporary theories. The claim is not that, when a person is responsible for what she does, all four elements must be present. Williams suggests that cause needs to be present, at least as a default.[3] But the four-elements-claim doesn't preclude the possibility of being responsible for something one didn't intend to do. When a person causes something unintentionally, the appropriate response tends to be different from what it would have been had the action been intentional, not least because the resulting action is of a different kind. Telemachus, who unintentionally left the door to the weapons store open allowing the suitors to get in, acts very differently from someone who would have left the door open intentionally for them to enter. But the absence of intention doesn't show that Telemachus is not responsible: 'no one else is to blame. I left the door of the room, which can close tightly open at an angle. One of them was a better observer than I'.[4] Similarly, if a person doesn't act in a normal state of mind – if she is drunk or drugged, say – this typically modifies the appropriate response, or furnishes an excuse, but it doesn't

[3] There are some exceptions which concern marginal cases, e.g., vicarious responsibility as when someone occupies a particular role (parent, pet-owner) or responsibility in an institutional context. A larger exception that Williams doesn't discuss are omissions. However, according to some at least, a person who omits doing something causes an outcome by her omission (see e.g., Sartorio 2016: ch 3).

[4] Homer, Odyssey, quoted from Williams 1993a: 50.

deny responsibility (at least not in general). We need to consider the first three of the four elements to determine the appropriateness and the shape of the fourth, but not in a mechanical, uniform fashion.

Williams sees the four-elements view supported by his interpretations of ancient texts, considering in particular Homer, Antiphon's Tetralogies, and the Tragedies. The Ancients don't use the word 'intention', but they nonetheless interrogate aspects of a person's agency which concern its intentional character when they seek to establish the appropriate response. Some of the ways in which responses are related to cause, intention and state of mind may strike us as somewhat alien in the ancient literature. Which of the many things that Oedipus did unintentionally and unknowingly is he responsible for? What is an appropriate response? Isn't the blinding he inflicts on himself at the very least excessive? Williams shows that such doubts and questions are already present in the Tragedies themselves.[5]

The difference between us and the Ancients is not that they neglected intention or state of mind, but rather that, according to them, the absence of intention or the presence of a non-normal state of mind can modify the appropriate response in ways which can be different from the ones we tend to regard as fitting.

## C. 'Moral Responsibility'

While he acknowledges that there isn't one correct way of thinking about these issues, Williams insists that any conception of responsibility must incorporate the four elements. However, there is a view which doesn't sit easily with this kind of variability. It is sometimes traced back to Kant and is, at any rate, familiar from current discussions: the view that we can be responsible only for those aspects of our agency that are done voluntarily. Proponents of a Kantian view may see this as an enlightened and therefore superior view which should also be the basis of any more specific form of assessment as, e.g., of legal responsibility. Williams uses 'moral responsibility' as the name of such conceptions of responsibility which put voluntariness centre stage[6]. I will follow him in this. But it is important to bear in mind throughout that 'moral responsibility' is used idiosyncratically here: its meaning cannot be gauged from its use by other writers, and it is, in Williams' usage, not an honorific.

One reason in favour of 'moral responsibility' is that holding people responsible for what they do involuntarily or unintentionally can seem unjust or unfair.[7] Thus, the focus on voluntary agency can be seen as part and parcel of what responsibility is. Williams doubts that moral responsibility has the special status it accords

[5] 'I suffered those deeds more than I acted them'. Sophocles, Oedipus at Colonus, quoted from Williams 1993a: 68; Williams comments: '[w]hat has happened to him, in fact, is that he has brought it about' (1993a: 70).

[6] Williams (1997) as well as (in a slightly different way) Williams (1990) develop this view.

[7] On responsibility practices and fairness, see for instance Wallace 1996.

itself. '[W]hat we must not suppose is that we have evolved a definitively just and appropriate way of combining those materials [i.e., the four elements]' (1993a: 56).

Whether or not the Moral Responsibility View (henceforth MRV) provides a uniquely correct combination of the four elements, it can easily be characterised in those terms: according to it, a person is responsible for something, X, if she causes X intentionally in a normal state of mind, and that in turn justifies certain responses (depending on the character of X).[8] On Williams' approach, MRV is clearly recognisable as a conception of responsibility. But it ossifies one way of relating the basic elements, the one where all four elements must be present if a person is responsible for an action: the first three are individually necessary and jointly sufficient for the fourth.[9]

# III. The Lesson from Moral Luck

## A. The Argument

Williams's writings on moral luck (1976, 1993b) provide his strongest argument against the hegemony of MRV. The basic thought is that MRV is at odds with our ordinary understanding and practices of responsibility (also 1990). We do hold ourselves and others responsible for results of our agency even when they are not intended. In 'Moral Luck' (1976), Williams discusses the case of Gauguin, the (somewhat fictionalised) painter, who hopes to develop his artistic talent when he leaves his family behind in Paris to set off for Tahiti.[10] We praise Gauguin for his paintings, even though he couldn't have intended to become a great artist. Praising is one of the salient responses (the fourth element). We blame people when they negligently or recklessly cause harm or damage, blaming being another such response. We feel terrible for inflicting pain on others even when we didn't mean to do so, self-directed blame (or agent-regret) being yet another such response. When these responses are appropriately tailored, taking the other elements into account, they are warranted.

Let's take a closer look at Williams' argument. Gauguin, when he decides to leave Paris and his family behind, could neither rationally foresee nor intend that he would become a great artist. Foreseeing lacked an evidential basis; intending would have been similarly preposterous. And yet, it seems that he

[8] This assumes Williams' view that acting voluntarily is equivalent to doing something intentionally in a normal state of mind. I will say more about this later in section IV.

[9] There are of course theories of responsibility, which claim that we need a much stronger free-will condition in addition to intention and state.

[10] Williams (1990: 1 ff) discusses a whole range of different counterexamples to MRV, e.g., actions that occur under conditions of somnambulism or post-hypnotic suggestion, where the agent may well be responsible, but not criminally liable for what they do. I don't have space in this chapter to discuss these issues in detail.

can take pride in his achievements. But taking pride in one's work is justified only if one is responsible for its results. Similarly, if we, the museum visitors, who enjoy the work, admire his achievement, it had better be an achievement as well as his.[11]

Williams casts the question in terms of Gauguin's justification for leaving his family behind. Their dependence on him gives him strong reasons not to pursue his calling. At the time of deliberation (from the *ex-ante* deliberator's perspective), he cannot point to his future paintings as reasons for his action. This is not because they haven't materialised yet, but because they cannot, at this stage, count as its foreseeable or intended outcomes (1976: 24 ff). Therefore, he is left only with reasons *against* embarking on the journey. So the *ex-ante* verdict seems clear: he should stay. However, from the *ex-post* perspective, it seems that there is at least something to be said for the course of action he has taken. (Williams is not concerned with adjudicating whether it is all-things-considered right or justified.)

Situations of this kind are not rare. We often embark on courses of action whose results we can only hope for but cannot rationally intend because they depend on too many factors unknown. Many career decisions as well as other life-changing decisions are of this kind.[12] (The argument that follows is not tailor-made to address proponents of MRV, since it predates Williams' discussion of it. I'll come back to MRV at the end of the section. Bear with me.)

Williams' discussion of moral luck is not about 'resultant luck' in Nagel's (1976) sense. The worry is not that the outcomes of our actions are never fully under our control. This is now often regarded as the focal point of the moral luck discussion.[13] Williams' question is different. One way of asking it would be this: how can a person be responsible for features of her agency that aren't and couldn't have been rationally chosen?

This question arises even when one isn't exercised by the notion of control that underlies Nagel's worry. It arises for those who think that what we are responsible for are those actions, or aspects of actions, for which we could offer reasons or which are done for reasons, in particular, so-called answerability views of responsibility.[14]

But even if Gauguin couldn't rationally intend or foresee the outcome, didn't he nonetheless have reasons for his journey? He hoped to become a painter, and he strongly desired to pursue his vocation. Aren't these reasons? On a view of rationality that Williams doesn't reject and that he even invokes expressly

[11] Of course, a parent can be vicariously proud of what their child achieves without presupposing that the child's achievements are their own. But a person can be proud of their own work only if they are responsible for it. If it is (say) plagiarised, or mainly the work of one's co-author, pride seems inappropriate.

[12] For further discussions of such cases and the rationality of the decisions, see Paul 2014 and Callard 2018.

[13] See e.g., Zimmerman 2002.

[14] See e.g., Gardner 2003 and Smith 2015.

(1993b: 256), the answer turns on the role of Gauguin's ability to rationally assess the probabilities.

*Gauguin, modified*. To make the problem clearer, let's modify the case a little, and grant that Gauguin had some reasons for his action (other than hope and desire). Let's assume for instance that he had some evidence that he could become a painter of some repute and standing, based perhaps on having tried his hand at painting while still being in Paris. Perhaps he produced some works that held sufficient promise. This evidence would have provided some reason for Gauguin to take the plunge. If so, he might have been justified in making his decision. Even so, Williams' concern comes back in a different form. If we assume that Gauguin had reasons to leave (i.e., that the likelihood of success was non-negligible and he was able to know that), this wouldn't be enough to show that he can justifiably take pride in his paintings. Imagine (counterfactually) that, despite having some justification for taking the risk, he failed as an artist. After all, this is a possibility even in cases where there is a reasonable prospect of success. In this case, the question would be how to assess the, in fact, valueless pursuit he embarked on vis-à-vis the evidence that had informed his decision. *Modified Gauguin* makes a rational decision to leave but his project fails. These kinds of comparison – deciding rationally and failing vs deciding rationally and succeeding – are sometimes invoked to show that the agent doesn't have ultimate control over the outcome (Nagel 1976; Zimmerman 2002). But that is not my point here. What I want to show is that the actual outcome, whatever it is, determines the appropriate reaction (in addition to the other elements). Hence, the modified case shows that the force of the Gauguin example does not depend on whether or not Gauguin had reasons for leaving. Even if he did, the assessment of his action does not depend only on them.[15] As Williams sees it, the *actual outcome* carries weight in assessing Gauguin's action as justified.[16] He argues against those who claim that there is only one thing that matters for justification, namely the reasons (or the evidence) the decision is based on. Rather, both the available evidence at the time of the decision and the actual outcome are relevant.

This may sound like a departure from Williams' own account of practical reasons (1981, 1995). After all, according to that account, a person has a reason to do something if there is a 'sound deliberative route' from their given motives (Williams 1995: 35) to the conclusion that they have a reason. If *modified Gauguin* had sufficient evidence that he might succeed, then, on this view, there was a sound

[15] In recent writings on rationality (Kolodny 2005; Raz 2005), the case would look different: while modified Gauguin was rational in leaving, rationality depending only on the available evidence, he didn't have a reason to do so, since only the actual, not the prospective, value of his action would have provided a reason. On such a view, despite the fact that he would have relied on evidence, and therefore would have made a rational decision, what he did was wrong. While this is a by now familiar way of explaining the relation of reasons and rationality, it is not Williams'. Williams doesn't countenance the sharp distinction between being rational and having reasons that it relies on.

[16] Williams (1990: 3) points out that the outcome determines the description of an action.

deliberative route to the conclusion that he has reason to leave. And if only reasons justify, it is unclear what additional role the *actual* outcome could play. According to the view Williams canvasses in 'Moral Luck', it doesn't matter whether Gauguin has no relevant evidence, or whether there is some evidence that the action could turn out to be successful (as in my modified case). What matters is that, either way, the assessment of the action will depend, at least in part, *on the actual outcome* – which is not a reason for the action since it doesn't contribute to the rationality of the decision.

Perhaps the best way of reconciling these claims with Williams' reasons internalism is this: the assessment of what a person does is not solely based on reasons for or against their action. Reasons must indeed be gauged from the *ex-ante* deliberator's perspective.[17] So 'justification' must be understood in a way that cannot be cashed out in terms of reasons alone. If so, Williams would reject the common view that whether a person's actions are justified depends on her reasons or rationality.

On this interpretation, Williams champions an idiosyncratic use of 'justification'.[18] It can be avoided if we abandon Williams' claim that justification is the issue here. Plausibly, what Williams discusses under the heading 'justification' really belongs under 'responsibility':[19] the reasons for which a person acted are not sufficient to assess what they are responsible for. That responsibility and reason-responsiveness come apart in this way is a much less surprising claim. It takes issue with a substantive theory of responsibility – the view that responsibility depends on reason-responsiveness – but it doesn't involve a conceptual revision as the provocative notion of 'retrospective justification' perhaps does. Understanding the argument of moral luck as being concerned with responsibility rather than justification salvages the basic point of Williams' discussion that we can be responsible for outcomes that we hadn't and couldn't have anticipated. Acting for sufficient reasons and on justified decisions is not a condition of responsibility for outcomes – be they welcome (as in Gauguin's case) or unwelcome (as in my case of modified Gauguin when he fails). On this interpretation, Williams' main target in the moral luck discussion are reason-responsiveness views of responsibility.[20]

Reason-responsiveness views may be related to MRV, but they are not the same. However, Williams' argument shows that responsibility is not (solely) based on assessing the rationality or justifiability of what a person intended to do and, as we'll see in section IV, Williams identifies voluntary agency – the core notion of MRV – with a certain kind of intentional agency.

[17] This is not a consequence of reasons internalism, by the way, but of the generally accepted assumption, by externalists alike, that the reasons for an action must be able to guide the agent.

[18] I take it that this is indeed the point of Williams' introduction of 'retrospective justification' (1976: 24).

[19] I discuss this issue in more detail in Heuer 2022.

[20] This is particularly clear in Williams 1993b.

## B. The Dilemma

What we are responsible for is the basis of assessing our agency. The question is in what way its actual results matter. They certainly seem to inform our judgments when we admire Gauguin's work. As Williams sees it, this leads to a dilemma:

> [R]eflection can go only in one of two directions: either in the direction of saying that responsible agency[21] is a fairly superficial concept, which has a limited use in harmonizing what happens, or else that it is not a superficial concept, but that it cannot ultimately be purified – if one attaches importance to the sense of what one is in terms of what one has done and what in the world one is responsible for, one must accept much that makes its claim on that sense solely in virtue of its being actual (1976: 29 ff).

On the first horn of the dilemma, a person can be responsible only for what she does intentionally (or rationally). On the second horn, people are considered (and consider themselves to be) responsible for the actual results of their agency – for what they actually do. But if those results are not intended and couldn't be rationally foreseen, then the second claim contradicts the first. Similarly, the other way around: if we embrace the first horn, then much of what we ordinarily and in fact appeal to as a basis for assessing a person's actions shouldn't be considered at all. Therefore, according to the first horn the concept of responsibility is superficial, and according to the second, responsibility appeals to aspects of the person's agency 'which cannot be purified'.

In the following, I will argue that Williams attempts to reconcile the two horns of the dilemma, at least if one takes a synoptic view of his various writings on the topic. This may sound surprising to those who take 'Moral Luck' as Williams' main contribution to the discussion. The moral luck discussion pushes us towards rejecting the first horn and embracing the second. Williams' choice of language, describing responsibility on the first horn as a superficial concept of limited use seems to indicate this direction. But these remarks notwithstanding, Williams offers another argument.

In 'Recognising Responsibility' (Williams 1993a), we learned that there is not one correct way of combining the four elements despite MRV's insistence that there is. However, MRV, the claim that we can be responsible only for what we do voluntarily, has undeniable force.[22] But we also partake in a practice where our responses to our own agency and that of others far exceeds those limits. Replacing our ordinary practice with MRV would not be an easy feat. Hence the dilemma.

Williams suggests a way of reconciling the horns by putting MRV in its place, revealing its limited use, thereby making space for a broader understanding of responsibility. There are indeed contexts in which questions of responsibility

[21] Note that Williams himself here switched from discussing justification to 'responsible agency', perhaps vindicating my interpretative suggestion in the previous section.

[22] As Nagel puts it: 'Prior to reflection it is intuitively plausible that people cannot be morally assessed for what is not their fault, or for what is due to factors beyond their control' (1976: 138).

are determined by MRV. But it is not the basis of ordinary assessments of what a person does.[23] MRV is one of the legitimate ways of understanding responsibility. Under certain conditions, the notion applies, but these conditions include features which are external to the question of responsibility itself. As Williams puts it, a bit enigmatically, the notion of moral responsibility doesn't guarantee its own application. Whether the concept applies depends not only on its content, but on features which are only contingently related to it. But that does not undermine its usefulness.

## IV. Voluntariness and Political Freedom

Williams defines 'voluntary' as: A does X voluntarily if and only if A does X intentionally in a normal state of mind (1990: 4, 1993a: 66, also 1993b, 1997). It combines three of the four elements of responsibility: cause, intention and state. This definition is certainly not uncontested[24] and one should put a question mark here as to whether this tilts the scales. But it is also not outlandish (see Hieronymi 2022).

But why is the use of the concept, in this sense, limited and in what sense is it 'superficial'? Williams supports his claims in two stages:

i. If voluntariness is understood as the basis of all responsibility, the concept is asked to do too much. The approach leads to scepticism.
ii. But we have an explanation of how voluntariness made its way into the discussion of responsibility which reveals both its use and proper place, and its limitations.

Let me explain both in turn.

### A. The Road to Scepticism

As proponents of MRV see it, the voluntariness condition is crucial because it guarantees that we don't hold people responsible for aspects of their agency that are not under their control.

But on reflection, it turns out that the voluntariness condition can't achieve what it promises. After all, which intentions a person forms depends on their understanding of their reasons which in turn is presumably shaped by their education and upbringing and various other limitations of their circumstances. These

[23] By 'assessment', I don't mean assessing whether an action is right or wrong – that may well be independent of voluntariness even for proponents of MRV, but whether the person is to praise or to blame for the action, or whether any of the responses that Williams groups together as the 'fourth element' will be appropriate.

[24] For a critical discussion of this view of voluntariness, see Duff & v Hirsch 1997; for a view of voluntariness that contrasts sharply with Williams', see Hyman 2015.

are all features which are not under their control. Thus, restricting responsibility to what we do voluntarily does not secure control. Instead, it leads to the free will discussion. And that's the way scepticism lies.

As Williams puts it:

> [T]here is a further question of why he is someone who can want to do such things, whether it is in his control that he is such a person, and so on (1997: 101).
>
> It is not that [questions about free will] get a favourable answer, as free-will libertarians suppose, nor that they get an unfavourable answer which puts moral responsibility out of business. Nor again is it, as some reconcilers perhaps suppose, that there is a transparent rationale for construing the voluntary within certain limits that exclude those questions. It is simply that the voluntary is an inherently superficial concept which should not be asked to do too much (1997: 101 ff).

In the quote, Williams explains that his choice of words calling the voluntary 'essentially superficial' should be taken seriously. The philosophical projects he briefly hints at all rely on the possibility of 'deepening' our understanding of the voluntary, but

> the idea of the voluntary … is essentially superficial. It is a mistake to suppose that the notion of the voluntary is a profound conception that is threatened only by some opposing and profound theory about the universe (in particular, to the effect that determinism is true). That supposition underlies the traditional metaphysical problem of the freedom of the will. … Just as there is a 'problem of evil' only for those who expect the world to be good, there is a problem of free will only for those who think that the notion of the voluntary can be metaphysically deepened. In truth, though it may be extended or contracted in various ways, it can hardly be deepened at all. What threatens it is the attempt to make it profound, and the effect of trying to deepen it is to put it beyond all recognition (1993a: 67 ff).

## B. The Role and Importance of the Superficial Concept

But while the concept is superficial, it is not therefore useless.[25] Williams shows that it has an important role to play by exploring how MRV enters the scene. The importance of voluntariness becomes apparent once we focus on a particular kind of response, namely punishment under the criminal law. It is perhaps the most severe way in which the state interferes with the freedom of its citizens. A common justification of such punishment is *deterrence*.

Bentham (1789: Ch XIII) claims that the deterrence justification itself suffices to show that punishment must be restricted to voluntary actions since the threat of punishment cannot deter a person from doing what they bring about

[25] Queloz (2022) offers detailed support, arguing that the concept couldn't serve its function if it weren't taken as superficial. This is how I too interpret Williams's remarks, but Queloz explains in greater detail what the superficiality consists in, contrasting it with a 'deepened' understanding of the voluntary.

involuntarily or unintentionally. Williams sides with Hart in rejecting this argument.[26] Punishment could be an effective deterrent even if those who are punished do not satisfy the conditions set by MRV – that is, even if we punish people for what they do involuntarily or unintentionally (Williams 1997: 98). Granted, the person who involuntarily harms another cannot be deterred by the threat of punishment. But since punishment is public, others may well be deterred. In fact, such punishment might have a considerable chilling effect.

Thus, we need a different reason for restricting criminal punishment to voluntary agency.[27] Hart's principle of political freedom offers such a reason.[28] In Williams' rendering, it is 'the principle that citizens should be able to conduct their affairs so far as possible without the state's power being unpredictably directed against them' (1997: 98).[29]

In punishing the person who causes harm involuntarily, the state would violate this principle.

> The argument implies … a particular responsibility of the state with respect to the use of its own power, a responsibility which, I take it, will be claimed by any version of liberalism. (Williams 1997: 98)
>
> The condition of being politically free in a certain regard is not, in the first instance, that of being unaffected by what the state does; it is, rather, *a condition in which the state's intention does not forcibly become one's own intention* (Williams 1997: 99 – my emphasis).

Thus, holding people criminally responsible for doing X only when they do X voluntarily makes violating the law and being potentially subject to the state's power a matter of choice. The state's intention of preventing crime can become the citizen's own intention by choice, as long as the threat of punishment is restricted to voluntary agency. Since the citizen knows that certain actions are punishable by imprisonment, they can choose to avoid the punishment by not performing those

[26] Hart 1957/2008: 40–44. As Hart puts it, whenever a person commits a crime, the threat of punishment has failed to be effective. But could he have been deterred? This, as Hart sees it, concerns the question whether the criminal belongs to a class of persons whose punishment could deter others (possibly himself on other occasions). This 'seems to destroy the entire notion that in punishing we must be just to the particular criminal in front of us' (1957/2008: 43). Furthermore, it is a '*non sequitur*' that a punishment that could not deter a particular criminal, is therefore inefficacious. 'It may well be that, if the law contained no explicit exemptions from responsibility on the score of ignorance, accident, mistake, or insanity, many people who now take a chance in the hope that they will bring themselves, if discovered, within these exempting provisions would in fact be deterred' (1957/2008: 43).

[27] 'The fundamental point is that insofar as we do deal differently with criminal responsibility under the law [compared to the Ancients], this is because we have a different view, not of responsibility in general, but of the role of the state in ascribing responsibility … [I]n liberal societies … a citizen shall not have the punitive power of the state fall upon him unless he puts himself in jeopardy by what he intentionally does' (Williams 1993a: 65).

[28] See Hart 1957/2008: 46: 'we can regard [the] function [of excusing conditions within the criminal law (which might be summarized as establishing lack of voluntariness)] as a mechanism for … maximising … the efficacy of the individual's informed and considered choice in determining the future and also his power to predict that future'.

[29] For Hart's own formulation see 1957/2008: 46–48.

actions. It is the mark of political freedom that the state allows for this kind of choice. The point of introducing the voluntariness condition is not that it secures that the agent is 'truly' responsible for their action (as theories which attempt to deepen the notion may have it), but it is to secure political freedom, i.e. the state's respect for individual liberty.

Williams tries to show that *retributivist theories of punishment* are relevantly similar: retribution, understood as the expression of an appropriate emotional response, needn't be constrained by the voluntary.

> The reason why we still need the argument for moral responsibility is that retribution does not have to be directed to voluntary acts. This is easily overlooked, because the presence of intention on the part of the agent is important to the psychology of retribution. Yet voluntariness cannot be strictly necessary, since retributive feelings easily extend to a reckless agent with respect to the actual outcome, and not simply to the recklessness itself (1997: 100).

The view of retribution that Williams considers here is one which sees punishment as the deserved or appropriate expression of emotions.[30] For this kind of punishment, the restriction to voluntary acts must rely on the principle of political freedom as an additional premise just as much as the deterrence justification because our emotions by themselves are not so restricted (and they are not, for that reason, inappropriate).

Williams argues that retribution in this sense is impossible in a modern liberal state. The retributivist faces a problem: retributivist punishment requires that only the guilty may be punished. Only they deserve to face the expression of the emotion. But establishing, in a court of law, who the guilty party is takes time. Emotions, however, wane over time. What is more, it is a condition of their rationality that they do (Marušić 2022). By the time guilt is established, the expression of the emotion (i.e., the punishment) would often not be appropriate anymore. Retribution in this sense is impossible in a legal system which allows to devote time to a proper investigation of the facts.

## V. Summary of the Argument

I have tried to square three of Bernard Williams' contributions to the discussion of responsibility: 'Moral Luck' (1976), 'Recognizing Responsibility' (1993a), and 'Moral Responsibility and Political Freedom' (1997). The three sources are not obviously compatible, but I have offered a unifying interpretation. As I see it, Williams' argument is, in outline, this: according to MRV, agents are responsible only for their voluntary agency. It is also deemed to be the basis for criminal responsibility. In that its proponents are right, but it is of limited use for understanding

[30] Williams has Michael Moore's (1993: 253 ff) view in mind.

responsibility outside of the criminal law. Far from being a necessary condition of responsibility generally, voluntariness is relevant mainly to criminal responsibility, and even that is true only if we assume liberalism and its commitment to political freedom. The restrictions on responsibility that proponents of MRV seek to impose are therefore external and not required by the concept of responsibility itself. With this in hand, Williams can solve the dilemma:

**Regarding the first horn:** MRV relies on a superficial concept, that of the voluntary. Voluntariness does not establish control over outcomes or true responsibility in any deep sense. But that does not undermine the concept's usefulness within the law, because it secures political freedom, i.e., the freedom of citizens from undue state interference. Political freedom is superficial because it secures only that being subjected to a criminal sanction depends on the agent's choice. It does not presuppose free will in a deeper sense. In particular, it is not concerned with the metaphysical possibility of free will.

**Regarding the second horn:** When political freedom and the constraints on the power of the state are not in the picture, the four elements needn't be combined in the way MRV suggests. Their role in modifying the appropriateness of responses in ordinary contexts is different. A person can be responsible when they didn't act intentionally or when they weren't in a normal state of mind, but the appropriate response would be tempered by these features.

Therefore, it is possible to embrace the second horn of the dilemma as well and allow that there can be responsibility for what one brings about unintentionally or involuntarily. Exploring the ways in which those results of our agency affect us isn't precluded by allowing MRV its limited role.

## VI. In Lieu of a Conclusion

In this final section, I want to begin to explore some objections to the view.

### A. 'The State's Intention does not Forcibly become One's Own Intention'

Is there really a choice to avoid the state-sanction if it is restricted to voluntary agency? After all, the criminal who voluntarily commits a crime does not normally choose the crime *qua* crime. But they could have been aware of the consequences: the law and its threat of punishment are public. In that sense, if someone responds to the threat of punishment and forms the intention the state wants them to have, it is not by force that they do so. However, if someone decides not to kill another (say) because there is a threat of punishment, this doesn't seem a model case of being unforced. An unforced intention would be the intention not to kill because it is wrong, because it harms another person etc., in short: an intention that responds to the reasons against killing *other than* the threat of punishment. But forming the intention not to kill on that basis would not be a way of adopting the state's intention by choice. It would be a moral choice which, coincidentally, also lines up with the state's intention. Thus, in the good case, it is not the 'state's intention' that becomes one's own, if the state's intention is that its citizens should respond to the threat of punishment.

## B. The Criminal Law, Actually

The criminal law as we know it does recognise crimes which are not committed voluntarily or intentionally, e.g., in cases of recklessness or negligence. In those cases, the agent might be criminally liable for the results of their actions or omissions, even if those results are not intended.[31] Might Williams simply reply that the law oversteps its boundaries in those cases? That is: should recklessness and negligence not be part of the criminal law, but only of tort law (as in most cases they are anyway)? Thus, the question is whether criminal punishment (i.e., imprisonment) with its adherent infringement of the agent's freedom in some cases of recklessness and negligence is compatible with the understanding of political freedom in a liberal state.[32]

## C. Political Freedom

Even if we grant that restricting criminal justice to voluntary agency is necessary for political freedom, is it sufficient, even just in the area of criminal justice? Imagine the state declares certain areas within a city as 'safe areas' where killing a person would be treated as murder, whether or not it is done intentionally. This doesn't violate the voluntariness restriction because it is up to everyone to simply avoid going to these areas, and thus not putting themselves in danger of accidentally killing someone.[33] But it seems that a criminal justice system which allows for such 'safe areas' violates the liberal understanding of political freedom and oversteps its boundaries in a way akin to the one Williams' discussion is concerned with. It seems therefore that there must be more to political freedom – again, even just in the area of criminal responsibility. The powers of the state have to be restricted in ways that go beyond Williams' suggestion. This objection, while valid, doesn't look overly damaging to me. Williams attempts to find a place for MRV and its emphasis on voluntariness, not to provide a comprehensive theory of political liberalism.

[31] Duff and v. Hirsch (1997) raise this objection in their response to Williams.

[32] John Hyman pointed out to me that there is a considerable difference between negligence and recklessness here. While decriminalising negligent behaviour is at least worth thinking about, the same is not true of recklessness, as becomes obvious if one considers, e.g., the case of a rapist who recklessly disregards the risk that their victim does not consent.

[33] This example was given to me by Ezequiel Monti.

## D. Responsibility Beyond MRV

While Williams offers an explanation *cum* justification of the criminal law's reliance on MRV, his view of responsibility beyond MRV does not have a clear shape. The arguments for it are mainly negative, rejecting certain views of responsibility (in my interpretation, in particular reason-responsiveness views). But it is much less clear what the resulting view is. What are *its* foundations? So far, we have been offered some examples of our existing practice which are deemed to show how non-intentional aspects and results of our agency affect our self-understanding and the ways in which we go forward on the basis of what we have done. However, we are presumably not responsible for just anything that we happen to bring about. In 'Moral Luck', Williams sets out to establish a distinction between mere luck and the kinds of unintended results that an agent is responsible for by introducing a distinction between the internal and external conditions of success and failure – this is perhaps the beginning of an answer.[34]

However, what affects our self-understanding and the ordinary view of responsibility can come apart. In 'Moral Luck', one of Williams' examples is of a lorry driver who kills a child when she runs into the path of the lorry. The accident happens despite the fact that the lorry driver is neither reckless in his driving nor negligent in maintaining the safety of his lorry. While the killing is an unintended and unforeseen result of the driver's agency, it will affect his life and the way in which he sees himself deeply, as well as the way in which he is seen by others. But is a case like this usefully discussed under the heading of responsibility? Well, the driver killed the child. The fact that the killing is unintentional modifies the appropriate responses. The relevant responses – the fourth element – depend in their appropriateness on the other three. It would be inappropriate to blame the driver or to hold him criminally liable. But it is appropriate that he feels what Williams calls 'agent-regret'; it may also be appropriate that he should make amends, as far as that is even possible. In all these regards, the lorry driver is an Oedipus of our time. Even if there isn't a uniquely right response, the path the agent chooses will determine their lives, going forward,[35] acknowledging that 'in the story of one's life there is an authority exercised by what one has done, and nor merely by what one has intentionally done' (Williams 1993a: 69).

# Bibliography

Bentham, J (1789) 'Cases in Which Punishment Must be Inefficacious' in J Bentham, *Principles of Morals and Legislation*, Chapter XIII.

Callard, A (2018) *Aspiration* (Oxford, Oxford University Press).

[34] I develop this answer in Heuer 2022.

[35] As Victor Braga Weber reminded me, Williams took great interest in a notion of 'ethical freedom' (Fricker 2020) which, in this context, could be the freedom to take responsibility and mould the relevant responses.

Duff, A & v. Hirsch, A (1997) 'Responsibility, Retribution and the "Voluntary": A Response to Williams' 56 1 *Cambridge Law Journal* 103.
Fricker, M (2020) 'Bernard Williams as a Philosopher of Ethical Freedom' 50 8 *Canadian Journal of Philosophy* 919.
Gardner, J (2003) 'The Mark of Responsibility' 23 2 *Oxford Journal of Legal Studies* 157.
Hart, HLA (1957/2008) 'Legal Responsibility and Excuses' in HLA Hart *Punishment and Responsibility*, 2nd edn (Oxford, Oxford University Press).
—— (1967/2008), 'Postscript: Responsibility and Retribution' in HLA Hart *Punishment and Responsibility*, 2nd edn (Oxford, Oxford University Press).
Heuer, U (2022) 'Luck and Responsibility According to Bernard Williams' in A Szigeti & M Talbert (eds), *Morality and Agency: Themes from Bernard Williams* (Oxford, Oxford University Press).
Hieronymi, P (2022) 'When is an Action Voluntary?' in U Maoz & W Sinnott-Armstrong (eds), *Free Will: Philosophers and Neuroscientists in Conversation* (Oxford, Oxford University Press).
Hyman, J (2015) *Action, Knowledge and Will* (Oxford, Oxford University Press).
Kolodny, N (2005) 'Why Be Rational?' 114 455 *Mind* 509.
Marušić, B (2022) *On the Temporality of Emotions* (Oxford, Oxford University Press).
Moore, M (1993) *Act and Crime: The Philosophy of Action, and its Implications for Criminal Law* (Oxford, Oxford University Press).
Nagel, T (1976) 'Moral Luck' 50 *Proceedings of the Aristotelian Society* (Suppl).
Paul, LA (2014) *Transformative Experience* (Oxford, Oxford University Press).
Queloz, M (2022) 'The Essential Superficiality of the Voluntary and the Moralisation of Psychology' 179 *Philosophical Studies* 1591.
Raz, J (2005) 'The Myth of Instrumental Rationality' 1 1 *Journal of Ethics and Social Philosophy* 2.
—— (2011) *From Normativity to Responsibility* (Oxford, Oxford University Press).
Sartorio, C (2016) *Causation and Free Will* (Oxford, Oxford University Press).
Smith, A (2015) 'Responsibility as Answerability' 58 2 *Inquiry* 99.
Strawson, PF (1962) 'Freedom and Resentment' 48 *Proceedings of the British Academy* 187.
Wallace, RJ (1996) *Responsibility and the Moral Sentiments* (Cambridge, Mass., Harvard University Press).
Watson, G (1996) 'Two Faces of Responsibility' 24 2 *Philosophical Topics* 227.
Williams, B (1976) 'Moral Luck' 50 *Proceedings of the Aristotelian Society* (Suppl) 115. Cited from B Williams 1981.
—— (1981) 'Internal and External Reasons' in B Williams, *Moral Luck* (Cambridge, Cambridge University Press).
—— (1990) 'Voluntary Acts and Responsible Agents' 10 1 *Oxford Journal of Legal Studies* 1.
—— (1993a) 'Recognising Responsibility' in B Williams, *Shame and Necessity* (Berkeley, University of California Press).
—— (1993b) 'Postscript' in D Statman (ed), *Moral Luck* (Albany, State University of New York Press).
—— (1995) 'Internal Reasons and the Obscurity of Blame' in B Williams, *Making Sense of Humanity* (Cambridge, Cambridge University Press).
—— (1997) 'Moral Responsibility and Political Freedom' 56 1 *Cambridge Law Journal* 96.
Zimmerman, M (2002) 'Taking Luck Seriously' 99 *The Journal of Philosophy* 55.

# 2

# The Politics of Civic Maturity v the Politics of Justice: Reflecting on Bernard Williams' Separation Thesis

VERONICA RODRIGUEZ-BLANCO*

## I. Introduction

The objectives of this chapter are twofold. First, I aim to explain Williams' challenge to the idea that self-knowledge and civic maturity are inevitably embedded in the politics of justice. Williams' argumentative path to ground this challenge is elusive; however, what is clear is that he aims to defend the idea that there should be a stark separation between the politics of civic maturity, self-knowledge and the politics of justice. I will call this thesis Williams' separation thesis. In this chapter, I reconstruct Williams' sceptical position concerning the possibility of control of one's deliberation from the first-person point of view, together with the idea of the pervasive presence of moral luck in our agency, to scrutinise the key implicit arguments of his separation thesis. This reconstruction provides the strongest version of Williams' separation thesis.

The second goal of this chapter is to demonstrate that when we, as philosophers, ask how the demands of justice in terms of rights and duties *actually* enter into ordinary citizens' practical reasoning, our explanations tend to look at self-knowledge and maturity. In other words, civic maturity and self-knowledge make intelligible the demands of justice advanced to us by others. I show that when I present you with the demand that 'I have a right to x', you cannot help but be presented with my thoughts, which are engaged with my ends as value-based. But *vice versa* is also true when I demand that 'I have a right to x'. I cannot help

* I would like to thank audiences at the Durham Centre for Law and Philosophy and the Amsterdam Centre on the Legal Profession and Access to Justice for their feedback. Thank you to Amalia Amaya, Hrafn Asgeirsson, Eric Boot, Rene Brouwer, Ken Ehrenberg, Noam Gur, Anthony Hatzistavrou, Ulrike Heuer, Gerald Lang, Ambrose Lee, William Lucy, Daniel Peixoto-Murata, Ronaldo Porto Macedo, Chris Taggart, Christopher Tollefsen, Iris van Domselaar and Kara Woodbury-Smith for their comments on earlier versions of the chapter.

but be presented with your thoughts connected to your ends as value-based. This exchange of 'intelligible practical thoughts' is possible, I will argue, because both you and I possess self-knowledge and strive for maturity and transformation, or at least have this capacity. Consequently, if this argument is correct, Williams' strongest version of the separation thesis is put under pressure. Williams' argument is ingenious but flawed. Finally, I consider some objections to my criticism of Williams' separation thesis.

## II. The Illusion of Control Over Our Knowledge when We Deliberate

Williams' separation thesis is mainly defended in his paper, 'Voluntary Acts and Responsible Agents' (1995). The arguments of the paper are elusive, and there is a set of implicit premises that needs to be untangled in light of Williams' other texts, namely his arguments advanced both in 'Moral Luck' (1981) and *Ethics and the Limits of Philosophy* (1993). According to Williams, *ex-ante* deliberations neither of utilitarian style nor of deontological type can help us determine the answer to the question, 'What shall I do?' (1993). The question 'What shall I do?' arises in everyday situations, e.g., when we are deliberating whether to invite friends for dinner next weekend. But the question also arises in less than ordinary situations, e.g., when the artist Paul Gauguin had to decide whether to stay with his family or pursue his life as an artist in Tahiti (Williams 1981).

The question, 'What shall I do?' should be distinguished from the question, 'How Should One Live?'. Williams names the latter 'the Socratic question' (1993: 1–21). It requires that one live an examined or reflective life, and therefore requires self-knowledge, i.e., knowing the place of our desires and values in our internal economy. The former is essentially practical and radically first personal, whereas the latter invites us to abstract and generalise from our particularity and our own circumstances of deliberation and action. An answer to 'the Socratic question' presupposes that there is a *locus* where I am detached from my ends, goals, character, passions, and desires and *from which* I can provide an answer to the question, 'How (One) Should Live?' that illuminates the answer to the question, 'What shall I do?'. This not only presupposes the existence of formulaic solutions, such as deontological or utilitarian ones, to impose order on the messiness of our lives, but it also disregards the agent's ethical perspective. Consequently, the first-person perspective or deliberative stance disappears.

However, Williams' criticism not only aims to problematise the abstract – 'view from nowhere' – conception of practical deliberation, but he also wants us to be aware of the problem of the diachronicity of agency. Our agency's evaluation changes *ex-ante* and post-events. The example of the painter Gauguin illustrates Williams' point. The painter abandons his wife and children to pursue a painting career. We cannot separate his success as a painter, which involves giving a unique artistic legacy to the world and attempting to define the way human existence is meaningful, from any justification of his actions. Nevertheless, neither he nor anyone else could have foreseen his success at *the moment of deliberation and action*. If Gauguin fails, he has done the wrong thing; if he succeeds, his actions might be justified (Williams 1981: 23). Of course, this justification is not moral, but it is part of a life that adheres to certain values, i.e., a life that is meaningful through aesthetic experience. Williams recognises that, this justification is not directed at others, i.e., his children will still have grounds for reproach, but the justification will operate retrospectively. Williams' point is that *at the moment of action*, Gauguin cannot act in light of all the relevant rational considerations that apply to him (1981: 24), because much of the justification of his actions will depend on his talents, deliberative capacity (1981: 25), character, and how *he* successfully develops these talents.

This is what Williams calls 'intrinsic luck' (1981: 26). He tells us, 'the locus of intrinsic luck, largely lies in him – which is not to say, of course, that they depend on his will, though some may' (1981: 26). He recognises, however, that the *locus* of intrinsic luck can lie outside the agent. Williams seems to hint at the idea that agency continues once we have performed our actions; when we look back and ponder over the consequences of our actions, we can see these consequences as part of our actions, *in spite of the fact that we may have had no knowledge of the action and did not intend it*. For Williams, it would be an insane conception of rationality if we expected people not to feel they own the consequences of their actions, or if we expected them to detach themselves from the unintended aspects of their actions (1981: 29).

However, let us recall that for Williams, this evaluation is not in terms of moral blameworthiness, as one cannot make clear judgements of liability and moral blameworthiness. He concludes that agency cannot be purified of contingencies in the world; therefore, any sound account of rationality and responsibility needs to consider this impure conception of the self.

Williams' argument can be summarised as follows:

1) If control is through knowledge of the action, and our knowledge of the action *ex-ante* is necessarily limited due to intrinsic luck, then we are less in control of our actions than we usually think, and as theories have so far presupposed.

This is a well-rehearsed and carefully examined set of arguments, discussed brilliantly by a number of contemporary authors (Enoch & Marmor 2007; Heuer 2022; Kutz 2009; Lang 2019, 2021; Walker 1991). However, Williams' diagnosis of the failure of the Aristotelian conception regarding control in practical deliberation, or at least the version defended by Terence Irwin (known as the Aristotelian-Irwin theory), receives less discussion in the Williamsian literature.

I will scrutinise Williams' criticism of the Aristotelian-Irwin theory because it displays the implicit premise of his defence of the separation thesis. In other words, he aims to demonstrate that *not only is* 1) *true*, but that *any* attempt, including a sophisticated and complex Aristotelian theory of practical reason, *cannot rescue reflection within practical reason.*[1] This will have significant implications for comprehending Williams' conception of maturity and self-knowledge, and it forms the pillar of his belief that there ought to be a stark separation between the politics of civic maturity and the politics of justice.

According to Aristotle, we could say that we are responsible for our voluntary actions if a) we know what we are doing when we are doing it, i.e., we are able to give a description of our action; and b) we are not subject to force or coercion when we are acting. In contemporary terminology, these are the two key conditions of responsibility, which we call a) the 'epistemic condition'; and b) the 'free will' condition. According to Irwin, from Aristotle's *Nichomachean Ethics*, we can infer that if the agent's action fulfils conditions a) and b), then we can say that the agent is responsible. Irwin calls this the Aristotelian 'simple' theory of responsibility. Thus, if I pour you a cup of hot tea with the intention of pouring it over your hand and pretending that it is an accident because I want to take revenge on you, then I would be responsible for intentionally burning your hand. However, Irwin argues that the Aristotelian 'simple' theory of responsibility faces difficulties as it entails that certain immature or not fully rational agents are responsible when, in fact, we usually, in our everyday normative practices, do not attribute responsibility to these agents. Thus, the Aristotelian 'simple' theory not only includes mature agents but also mentally disabled people and children as responsible for the wrong that they have committed. According to Irwin, this is counter intuitive. Imagine a five-year-old toddler taking a cup of hot tea and pouring it over your hand. She is upset and sees it as an act of revenge. She fulfils conditions a) and b). However, our intuitions tell us that she is not *fully* responsible in the way that mature agents are.

Irwin argues that this 'simple' theory of practical deliberation ought to be modified through the addition of a third condition c), according to which an agent is responsible if they engage in deliberation, or at least, that the agent has the capacity to deliberate. This means that to be *fully* responsible, an agent needs to fulfil a), b), and c).

In this chapter, I will not concentrate on whether Williams characterises Aristotle's and Irwin's interpretations correctly. I will only focus on Williams' understanding of the Aristotle-Irwin model of responsibility.[2] Williams tells us that the Aristotlian-Irwin model requires that we 'reason' out our desires and manage our desires in light of our ends and values. Williams (1995: 27) states that Irwin's model is inspired by other models of responsibility, where deliberation or reflection are key, e.g., Frankfurt or Watson,[3] or even Taylor's model of strong

[1] For a criticism of Williams' conception of practical reason as 'internalism' and his desire-belief moral, see Teichman 2018.

[2] Williams calls it the 'complex' model of responsibility.

[3] Williams states that Irwin acknowledges a debt to Frankfurt and Watson. See Frankfurt 1971, Watson 2004. See also Irwin 1980.

evaluation (Taylor 1985a, 1985b). The general idea of the Aristotelian-Irwin model is that we can transform our desires if we apply reason to our ends and values, as well as to other, more deliberative desires. In the previous example, according to the Aristotelian-Irwin model, the five-year-old toddler is not responsible because she could not 'reason out' her *immediate* desire and her anger towards the adult.

Williams has tried to undermine this account, which he calls the ideal-bearing account, on the basis of one key argument. If we are responsible for our desires, character, and passions because we can reason about them, then there is an act that brought them about. This must be an act of reason, which we should be able to trace back to the initial act of thinking about the matter when it actually happened. However, this initial act of reason and deliberation that produced certain desires might not be connected to my current acts of reason when I engage in current deliberations. Williams observes that the problem is just pushed back. For example, imagine that when I was a teenager, I deliberated on my initial desire to always hate or take revenge on my enemies. I performed many actions aligned with this deliberation and consequently developed a stable character characterised as that of a vengeful person. At this present time, there is not much I can do about my vengeful character, passions, and desires, prompting Williams to question, 'Why should the feckless acts of long ago be blamed for everything we now do as a result?' (1995: 27). According to Williams, Irwin could argue that the power of reason to shape our characters is always present; however, this position would have unpalatable implications in terms of the belief that we have 'total deliberative control of one's disposition' (1995: 27). For Williams, this is a hopeless fantasy (1995: 27).

The general view advocated by Irwin and other authors is that we can 'reason out' our desires, and this view is named by Williams 'the mature agency view'. The mature agency conception presupposes that there is an ideal-bearing account. This means that there is the possibility of human growth, of learning to be good (Burnyeat 1980) and engaging with what is right, dutiful, and good. The puzzle, according to Williams, is that the possibility of reflecting on my desires, of shaping them, of transforming myself into a mature agent seems implausible when we face the everyday question, 'What shall I do?'. According to the mature agency view, maturity is essential to being responsible for oneself. This account appears to link self-knowledge through deliberation, transformation of one's immediate desires, and self-responsibility. This means that to be a mature agent, we need a sense of reality, of the place of our desires in our inner thoughts and lives.

In this chapter, I will argue that Williams appears to believe that our desires refer to a substantive reality that can be grasped and 'pinned down' using our reasoning capacities and reflective insights. However, a closer look at the philosophical tradition of the mature agency conception, which encompasses authors such as Socrates-Plato, Aristotle, Murdoch, and Taylor, allows us to question this presupposition of a substantive reality that can be grasped by self-knowledge and self-reflection. I will demonstrate that by dismantling the myth of the substantive reality of desires, or the 'given' nature of this substantive reality of desires, we can gain a deeper understanding and appreciation of the inextricable relationship between the mature agent and the agent involved in justice-related matters. The separation thesis between the politics of civic maturity and the politics of justice seems implausible. But first, let me explain Williams' key argument that grounds the separation thesis.

Williams problematises any possible reconciliation between the mature agency conception and the fact that we are responsible when we answer the everyday question, 'What shall I do?'. In the latter case, I am purely and simply responsible for my acts. For example, if I pour hot water over you as an act of revenge, I am responsible for what I have done because I can deliberate and sustain a minimal level of control. This means that I know that hot water can cause burns, if I approach you with a cup of hot water and pour it on your hand, I will injure you. When I act according to minimal deliberation and sustained control, this is the *first starting point*, as Williams tells us. But when I reflect, know myself, have insights into the place of my desires, and aim to grow and mature, then this is the *second starting point*. Williams, however, asks the following:

> But if we are addressing the ideas of being held responsible or regarded as a responsible agent, it is not clear why such an ideal should be relevant. The ideas of responsibility developed from the first starting point are rather a matter of what is involved in a set of persons, not necessarily known to each other or specially important to one another, *living under a common system of justice* (1995: 29 – the emphasis is mine).

In this paragraph, Williams makes a move that I think should be interpreted as follows. Within the phenomenology of deliberative practice and practices of responsibility, we say that 'x is responsible for her action y' because x has a minimal deliberative capacity and sustained control of her action. When we are dealing with strangers, we do not care whether the person has a capacity for reflection or self-knowledge, or whether she knows the place of her desires within her internal economy and is capable of being a mature agent. The key question is about justice. That is, whether you have complied with the objective standard, norm, or rules of conduct. It does not matter whether you have special insights into your desires, or whether you are especially virtuous, reflective, and mature and always know how to 'reason out' your desires, but on this occasion have failed to do so. Arguably, we could also say that the law addresses the citizens of a state in terms of norms and rules that they must comply with and obey. However, Williams also emphasises that the relationship between legal authority and the citizen is not one-sided; it also encompasses individuals 'capable of deliberating together about what the law should be' (1995: 29).

Consequently, he recognises three levels of politics: control, acknowledgment, and communal deliberation. From the point of view of agency, the first level, the politics of control, is the most basic. Williams provides an example involving an interaction with slaves, best expressed as the simple statement 'the slave did it'. The second, the politics of acknowledgement, entails a dispositional capacity to shape actions according to social expectations. The third, the politics of communal deliberation, presupposes a general capacity for long term practical thinking, and the ability of the individual to 'consider the relation of his life to that of others' (1995: 29). We are talking about citizens at the second and third levels.

However, Williams argues that even within the last model of politics, the politics of communal deliberation, it is not sound to think that the mature citizen coincides with the responsible citizen. Any hope of reconciling civic maturity, justice, and responsibility as self-knowledge is doomed to fail because we are transposing the way of thinking in terms of ideal-bearing and deliberative control by 'reasoning out' desires at the individual level to the larger and communal level. Society cannot reasonably hope that 'its citizens will be like coincides with what they would ideally want to be like: that freedom, rationality, virtue, citizenship, and individuality can ultimately coincide' (1995: 31). The reasoning of the 'reconciliation' strategy lies in the mistaken idea that there is such a possibility of 'reasoning out' one's desires, passions, and characters *not only at the individual level, but also at the communal level, i.e., when we deliberate together on the question 'What shall we do'?*. Furthermore, the mature agency view cannot clearly show how, *from* this reflective stance, we can 'reason out' our desires when we are immersed in deliberation and trying to address the question 'What shall I do?' *from* a particular and contingent action.

According to Williams, it is not only the impossibility of luck-free actions (the truth of statement 1)) that is the main obstacle towards any plausible view that will reconcile the politics of justice and the politics of civic maturity. A further obstacle to a reconciliation strategy between civic maturity and justice is the impossibility of advancing a stable philosophical position that is both psychologically realistic and explains how we 'reason out' desires when we are immersed in acting and answering the question, 'What shall I do?'. Therefore, at the individual level, we cannot give a plausible and psychologically realistic explanation of how we 'reason out' desires; *a fortiori*, we cannot provide a plausible and psychologically realistic explanation of how we reason out desires *together* when we are immersed in action and answering the question 'What shall we do?' *together.*

Williams concludes his thoughts on the separation thesis with a final argument. To be mature is to own what we have done. However, it would be contradictory to assert that you are responsible if, in the public sphere, someone tells you that 'you have to take responsibility'. This clearly demonstrates that you are a non-mature agent, as you need to be told to take responsibility. According to Williams, this seems paradoxical. Arguably, within this view, not only the politics of justice and civic maturity/self-knowledge should remain separated, but also the public and private spheres should remain severed. In the next section, I will touch briefly on this argument, as a proper treatment of this crucial point deserves a more careful analysis.

I will divide Williams' arguments that ground the separation thesis into three key statements:

**Statement A:** There is no plausible and sound conception that explains how we 'reason out' desires when we are immersed in answering the question, 'What shall I do?'.

**Statement B:** There is no plausible and sound conception that explains how we 'reason out' desires *together* when we are immersed in answering the question, 'What shall we do *together*?'

**Statement C:** To be mature is to own responsibility for our actions, i.e., 'to take responsibility'. If someone in the public sphere demands that 'we take responsibility', then this means that we are not mature. Maturity, therefore, cannot be relevant in the public sphere.

I will demonstrate that statement A relies on the myth that desires are substantive and 'given'. I will also show that we learn about our desires through our own thinking, and that we gain diverse perspectives when we think with others. If this is correct, then statement B will be directly undermined. Statement C is also false, or so I will argue, because it presupposes that there are only two types of agency: mature and non-mature agency. It overlooks that we are constantly transforming ourselves and that we are essentially learners of the good, the right, and the dutiful.

## III. The Demands of Justice: Undermining Williams' Key Statements Concerning the Separation Thesis

Let us go back to our initial example. You are serving hot tea with the intention of pouring it on my hand, causing me to burn. You see this as an act of revenge for the rumours I have spread about you among our colleagues in the office. The challenge that arises is how the demands of justice are presented to practical reasoners when they are addressing the question, 'What shall I do?'. In this example, when the injurer completes the deed, the injured person may demand the following from the injurer: 'I have a right to be respected in my physical integrity, and you have a duty to respect me in my physical integrity'. We will refer to this as 'the basic demands of justice'.

The crucial question is how 'the basic demands of justice' enter into both the injured person's and the injurer's practical reasoning. Williams' answer would be something along the following lines: 'The injurer has behaved below the objective standard of a norm of social conduct'. Williams would tell us that this is sufficient to ground the separation thesis, which states that the politics of justice should remain separate from the politics of self-knowledge/civic maturity. There is nothing else to say, Williams would add. Thus, we expected the injurer to conform to certain norms, but she has failed to do so. The injured person does not and cannot care whether the injurer has acted according to self-knowledge and reflectively or has capacity for self-knowledge and is able to 'reason out' her desires. The injurer, according to Williams' separation thesis, will only state: 'I have breached an objective standard of conduct, and it is only just for the injured person to make some demands on me'. But we must pause here. After reflecting on Williams' answer, we can still ask two key questions: a) how does the injurer know that she has breached an objective standard of conduct; and b) how can the injurer assess whether 'it is just that the injured person makes some demands on me?' Not surprisingly, Williams cannot provide any reasonable answer to questions a) and b). Let us suppose that Williams' replies to a) and b) are along the following lines. The injurer knows that she cannot hurt others, and she has learned this through social conventions. She has also learned through social conventions that when one hurts people, the injured person has a claim against the injurer. This is not a robust conception of the term 'just', Williams would assert. Rather, the term 'just' derives its meaning from a social convention.

However, I suspect that this response would be unpalatable for Williams. This would mean that there are *ex-ante* conventions that are socially constructed, and that we can guide our conduct according to these *ex-ante* conventions. This would contradict the truth of 1). Furthermore, Williams' separation thesis cannot make a more robust account of the demands of justice in terms of rights and duties intelligible. This would mean that when the injured person claims that she has a right to be respected for her physical integrity and the injurer has a duty to respect that right, the 'basic demands of justice' will be seen only as a matter of 'adjusting social expectations'. The injurer should adjust to the expectation that when she hurts someone, the injured person will demand something from her. But this does not realistically capture the robust meaning of the notions of 'right' and 'duty' within the context of 'the basic demands of justice'. If, at the general level, we say that citizens ought to respect the physical integrity of others and that everyone has a duty to respect this right, we expect people to behave accordingly, not just because it is a social expectation or a convention, but because they are *persons*. It would neither be ideal nor stable for a society if most of its citizens stated, 'I respect the physical integrity of my fellow citizens because I adjust my expectations'. On the contrary, we would expect that most citizens would say something like this: 'I respect the physical integrity of my fellow citizens because they are *persons*', and perhaps we would want a robust conception of *persons* to be part of the content of their thoughts when they are addressing the question, 'What shall I do?'. Let us recall again how Williams ended up in this strong and unintelligible position. Statement A states: There is no plausible and sound conception that explains how we 'reason out' desires when we are immersed in answering the question, 'What shall I do?'. According to statement B, there is no plausible and sound conception that explains how we 'reason out' desires *together* when we are immersed in answering the question, 'What shall we do *together*?'.

I will argue that the mistake lies in thinking that our desires are substantive and 'given'. This means that reason's role is to 'pin down' substantive desires and then shape them. Conversely, I will demonstrate that our thoughts shape our desires. However, desires are neither substantively given nor do they refer to a reality. Their content, or perhaps 'reality', so to speak, is present in our thoughts only. However, our interactions and engagement with others transform the thought-dependent desires that count in immersive deliberation such as when we answer the question, 'What shall I do?'. This model of deliberation is neither 'from nowhere', nor general and reflective in an abstract way. It considers actual, tangible individual, thereby providing a level of psychological realism for the mature agent. This model of mature agency can also account for the ideal-bearing feature within a realistic moral psychology and explain the way 'the basic demands of justice' appear in the mature agents' practical reasoning. In the upcoming section, I will scrutinise the arguments that refute the notion of desires as given substantive reality and explore their thought-dependent nature, thereby shedding light on how we learn about our desires from our thinking and interactions with others.

## IV. Maturity and Learning to be Good

As Cavell observes, *learning and maturation* are not too different (1979: 171). Our deliberations and experiences enable us to mature into the depths of our values. But at some point, in our lives, we also become teachers, and we need to take responsibility for this (1979: 178). We learn forms of life in which charity, benevolence, and justice, for example, acquire deeper understandings, and we unveil new layers through experiences. But we also learn about greed, ambition, resentment, and hatred, and these negative traits reveal their depth as part of our different experiences. The identification of error means looking anew at oneself through one's activities, deliberations, thinking, and engagement with the world, whether caring or not, through avoidance or recognition. The direction we take in our deliberations is crucial, and this chapter addresses how the possibility of inhabiting a mature perspective is possible within a moral and psychologically realistic picture.

However, this does not mean that the deliberator is engaged in an abstract, top-down deliberation such as when a 'grand end' of our lives is either explicit or implicit.[4] Nor does this conception of reason and deliberation assume that our deliberations pin down given desires and shape them. The focus on language-games helps us see that some things gain salience from our interactions with others and our environment. Through language-games, we inherit salient features to carve the world, and this is the background of deliberation. We cultivate a

[4] Williams describes the 'grand end' or 'grand vision' view as representing 'one's life as a rectangle, so to speak, presented all at once and to be optimally filled in' (1981: 33).

'form of life', which serves as the background and foundation for transformation (Anscombe 1958; Vogt 2017: 15).

Our concepts concerning ends or values are learned through language-games, and engagement with them reveals a multiplicity of ways of looking at them, considering them, and learning them. 'Forms of life' shape our evaluative outlook. There is no passivity; there is activity as long as there is thought, because when we deliberate, we engage with the particular circumstances that demand action, and thought is required to see and settle *what* we need to do.

If I ask the question, 'What shall I do?' as if there were a unique, correct end, value, or grand vision that can be grasped as an image, then the language-game is dragged out (Wittgenstein 2009: §370) This is precisely what Wittgenstein warns against. The language-game of deliberation, so to speak, both immersive and aspirational, or mature, can only be shown. The teaching and learning never end. When I settle the question, 'What shall I do?' the settling is what happens. There is no misrepresentation or misidentification.

One important lesson of the language-games approach is that the external/internal or inner/outer dichotomy is a metaphor that, if taken seriously, leads to philosophical confusion. We realise that one aspect of an experience hides other aspects through our forms of life and language-games. *To learn means displacing one aspect of an experience to let another in.* The result is not a simple replacement but an enrichment of what we could see before; it is also the connection between two aspects of an experience.

We deliberate in everyday matters, but also our everyday experience of deliberation shows us another face or aspect of deliberation. Looking back at our own lives, we can see that we have larger goals, values, or ends; we can see the failure of some of our projects and the success of others. Looking into the future, we envisage a number of medium- and long-term projects.

The problem that now arises is the following: if thinking in terms of narrow deliberation is immersed or substandard, how can we correct our thoughts within an immersed vision? Immersive deliberation is when we are trying to answer the question, 'What shall I do?' (what Williams calls the '*first starting point*' *of deliberation*) (1995: 29). Furthermore, if our thoughts are able to transform our desires and character, we need to make sure that our thoughts are directed towards what is right, good, or dutiful in order to transform our desires towards the right desires[5] and form a character that approximates excellence. Williams would say that we seem, nevertheless, trapped within the limited vision of our own narrow deliberations. The position from *here and now*.

Let us consider Neurath's boat metaphor and say that we would need to bracket the question of whether the end was good, or, rather, take as hypothesis that the end to be pursued is good, as we repair one plank at a time whilst navigating rough

[5] It is not correct to think of practical truth as *closely* related to theoretical truth. Practical truth is clarity and coherence in choice, and we should emphasise the disanalogy with theoretical truth (Broadie 1991: 226–27 and 230).

seas. The other planks remain untouched and stable, and in a similar fashion, the conception of the end as good remains stable. However, we see ourselves not only immersed in short-term goals but also in medium- and long-term projects, goals, and plans. Neurath's boat metaphor allows us to envision ourselves standing on the shoreline, witnessing the dismantling of the entire boat, seeing it fully repaired and admiring its entirety.

It is not just a matter of establishing a bridge between digestible particulars and more abstract rules or principles. It is rather that answering the question, 'What shall I do?' can involve medium- and longer-term projects and plans without losing the practical knowledge and insights of narrow deliberation and replicating the depth of that *knowledge* on a larger scale.

One potential answer is to say that we need to reflect on our medium- and long-term goals. We could present the modern conception of reflection as a potential answer.[6] But how should we understand reflection without losing the immersed perspective? *Losing the immersed perspective is precisely what Williams warns us against.*

Contemporary philosophy tends to focus on reflection, and one difficulty that arises when thinking about reflection in the practical domain is that we are both object and subject. This means that we must pay attention and think intelligently about our actions before, during, and after acting. When we are confronted with the question, 'What shall I do?', we need to engage in an investigation of the particulars and circumstances of the action to determine the 'What?' and the 'How?' of the act. At the same time, we are subjects of our actions because, while investigating and deliberating what to do, we transform our desires and character, and these desires and character change our vision of the *what*. We are not only subjects of our actions, but also objects.

The challenge now lies in achieving the correct understanding of reflection when we are simultaneously the subject and object of our actions. On the other hand, however, self-knowledge seems inevitable and imperative as we need to adjust to the world. We need to know our current desires and beliefs so that we can adjust (Bobonich 2007).

I will examine a conception of reflection that prioritises looking at features of our relationships with others, looking carefully at our desires and aims over time, and examining how shifts in our thinking alter our view of the subject matter, such as our relationships, the features of others, and conceptions of good and right. Although there is a change in our thinking and vision, there is no action that mirrors these changes. This is a model advanced by Iris Murdoch, and she illustrates it with her well-known example of the mother-in-law, whose thinking about her daughter-in-law changes with time, though there is no external action that

[6] The problematic character of reflection in the Aristotelian corpus is recognised by McDowell; see McDowell 1998. For him, our values are subject to reflection. Reflection, however, does not mean 'stepping outside' (Williams 1995).

reflects her thinking. Let me quote the example, as its detail will become crucial in our analysis:

> A mother, whom I shall call M, feels hostility to her daughter-in-law, whom I shall call D. M finds D quite a good-hearted girl, but while not exactly common yet certainly unpolished and lacking in dignity and refinement. D is inclined to be pert and familiar, insufficiently ceremonious, brusque, sometimes positively rude, always tiresomely juvenile. M does not like D's accent or the way D dresses. M feels that her son has married beneath him. Let us assume for the purposes of the example that the mother, who is a very 'correct' person behaves beautifully to the girl throughout, not allowing her real opinion to appear in any way. We might underline this aspect of the example by supposing that the young couple have emigrated or that D is now dead: the point being to ensure that whatever is in question as happening happens entirely in M's mind. This much for M's first thoughts about D. Time passes, and it could be that M settles down with a hardened sense of grievance and a fixed picture of D, imprisoned (if I may use a question-begging word) by the cliché: my poor son has married a silly vulgar girl. However, the M of the example is an intelligent and well-intentioned person, capable of self-criticism, capable of giving careful and just *attention* to an object which confronts her. M tells herself: 'I am old-fashioned and conventional. I may be prejudiced and narrow-minded. I may be snobbish. I am certainly jealous. Let me look again.' Here I assume that M observes D or at least reflects deliberately about D, until gradually her vision of D alters. If we take D to be now absent or dead this can make it clear that the change is not in D's behaviour but in M's mind. D is discovered to be not vulgar but refreshingly simple, not undignified but spontaneous, not noisy but gay, not tiresomely juvenile but delightfully youthful, and so on. And as I say, *ex hypothesi*, M's outward behaviour, beautiful from the start, in no way alters (Murdoch 1950d: 312–13).

Like us, Murdoch believes that language-games provide the framework for our ends, values, and experiences and that words acquire their meaning through context. However, the way we experience language and describe matters enriches and modifies our shareable concepts. 'The concept does not give us an experience with immediately self-contained unambiguous sense' (Murdoch 1950b: 54).[7] However, values, ends, desires, and sensations can be described in an infinite number of ways, and therefore the meaning, initially given by context and our language-games, is shaped by our multiple descriptions of values, ends, desires, and sensations (Murdoch 1950b: 44–46).[8] Our thoughts depend on our concepts and we can think because we have learned concepts; however, contrary to some interpretations of Wittgenstein's criticism of private language, this does not mean that thoughts and our inner life do not exist. It is rather that (if we follow a reading

[7] Murdoch (1950f) also shows us that between 'everything is public' and 'everything is an internal event', there is an intermediate position. There are our thoughts that work with concepts as mediators of reality, but our own perspectives that constantly change and give us a vision and clarity on the matter to be considered do not depend on our behaviour, or the behaviour or interpretation of the behaviour of others. This is what the example of the mother and daughter-in-law aims to show. Murdoch also refers to forms of life (1950f: 97) and see also 1993: 'Living is making distinctions and indicating order and pattern'.

[8] See also the discussion in my book: Rodriguez-Blanco 2025: Ch 5.

of Wittgenstein's arguments against private language) our psychological concepts like desires, beliefs, intentions, thoughts, or imagining, do not refer to an internal state or private event. On the contrary, they need to find their expression in a language-game.

Privileged access does not capture the phenomenon of privacy. There is no substantive or particular event that constitutes a reference to our psychological concepts. There is, however, a thinking that we engage with, where our learned and shareable concepts acquire shape, colour, and depth. An example of the changes that the mother-in-law experiences in relation to her daughter-in-law are elaborations and re-elaborations of her thoughts.[9] The attitudes, actions, and general behaviour of the daughter-in-law have not changed. The way the mother-in-law describes and re-describes her thoughts about herself has changed.

Thus, changes in our thinking are characterised by three key features. First, there is no correspondence with a substantive or empirical reality, a referent that determines the shape of our thoughts. Thus, the daughter-in-law has not changed her behaviour or attitude; everything remains the same. The changes are based on the mother-in-law's level of thinking and perspective. Second, there is no act of will that explains the changes in the mother-in-law's descriptions and re-descriptions of her daughter-in-law. The descriptions and re-descriptions seem to force themselves upon us. The language blends seamlessly with the object. One could argue that the object we encounter is transparent, and the meaning and the event are inseparable. Language-games are intermediaries and define the contours of our experiences, but our elaborations and descriptions give them shape. Simultaneously, the object, such as the character and attitudes of the daughter-in-law, undergoes changes due to shifts in our perception, focus, and appreciation. The more we focus on the object and think about it, the sharper our vision becomes, and we obtain clarity on the object. In parallel, the concept becomes more exact (Murdoch 1950b: 54). If we focus on the empirical matter only or the essential properties of the world – what Murdoch calls the substance of the world – (1950a: 66),[10] then we stop being reflective, and Murdoch conceives of reflectivity as this process of describing, re-describing, elaborating, and re-elaborating our own thoughts on the matter. For Murdoch, reflection is not detachment; rather, it is looking carefully and paying attention (with all our conceptual apparatus and language resources) to the content of our beliefs, desires, and thinking. In this way, we exercise our freedom and learn to see the world differently (1950a: 70–73). We don't confine our thinking to a particular time or space, but it constantly evolves, leading us to perceive things and relationships in unique ways.

Third, the emphasis is on respecting truth and avoiding fantasy that distorts our thinking; we need to give careful attention to the object. Fantasy is opposed

[9] Murdoch calls it 'inner experiences' to emphasise that it does not depend on our will nor on the conduct that we manifest outwardly.

[10] Murdoch reiterates that moral concepts do not move about within a hard world separated by science and logic (1950d: 320).

to imagination.[11] Fantasy resists changes of thought and resists attention. It could be said that fantasy focuses on our experiences for our experiences' sake, and consequently, while fantasising, our attention is removed from the object. Our sensations, or inner thoughts, are the object of fantasy. Fantasy, as opposed to imagination, is a 'barrier to our seeing "what is really there"' (Murdoch 1950c). By contrast, the object of our imagination is outside us; it is the subject matter of our attention. We direct ourselves towards the object and are open to its features and different presentations of it.[12]

Imaginative thinking means going beyond the facts, but it also means being close to the subject matter through its consideration, description, and re-description. Changes in our thinking generate new moral visions and concepts through careful and imaginative thinking, and proper attention to the subject matter.[13] Therefore, we minimise the notion of choice as the determination and exercise of the will.[14] Ethical differences and ethical disagreements are presented as differences and disagreements in visions and perspectives (Murdoch 1950f: 93).

To conclude, for Murdoch, reflection entails seeing beyond mere facts and the substance of the subject matter. Ethical reality is not there for every observer to determine its nature.[15] It is not an inner mental state that is projected onto the world, nor is it an inner shadow of our thinking (1950d: 304), describing, elaborations, and re-elaborations (1950d: 304). Ethics is about thinking clearly, and *this entails shifting our perspectives and vision*. Ethical action is not the movement of our will away from an independent reality in our thoughts. Murdoch suggests that our thoughts and imaginative thinking can change, but there is no external manifestation of those changes.

I believe she is correct when she asserts that our perspectives on others shift, resulting in both *open and closed ways of seeing others*. However, it's important to note that these shifts do not reflect the ethical reality as if our language can capture it. Nevertheless, *it is implausible*, or so I will argue, that our intelligent, imaginative, and open thinking about matters, including the people in our lives and their visions of goals, ends, and desires, has no repercussions for our actions.

[11] Murdoch defines imagination as follows: 'Imagination as restoration of freedom, cognition, the effortful ability to see what lies before one clearly, more justly, to consider new possibilities, and to respond to good attachments and desires' (1993: 322). The particular can be brutalised, not respected, and absorbed into private fantasy (1993: 340).

[12] This openness is characteristic of the human power of indefinite and extended rational capacity (Murdoch 1950e: 216). She also claims that love is knowledge of the individual (1950d: 320).

[13] For Murdoch advances in ethics are insights generated by thinking (1950f: 83).

[14] Murdoch criticises Kant's notion of the will and also the notions of the will of existentialists, like Sartre. For a criticism of her interpretation of Kant, see Bagnoli 2003, for a criticism of her interpretation of Sartre's existentialism, see Moran 2017.

[15] The example is powerful and illustrates this. M's thinking is an activity, but there are no observers. The activity is hard to characterise, not because reality is hazy but because it is moral (Murdoch 1950d: 317). In this context, M is striving to discern what is justifiable and what is loving. M's activity is perfectible as she is engaged in an endless task. For Plato and Aristotle, thinking is activity.

Let us go back to the example of the mother-in-law's changing attitudes towards her daughter-in-law. The example presents several issues. The illustration begins by portraying M as a correct person who behaves beautifully towards the daughter-in-law, keeping her thoughts hidden from her. If this is the case, then the example is not truly realistic and believable. From our own experiences of relationships with in-laws, it is more likely that at the start of the relationship – when the mother-in-law thinks that the girl is vulgar, lacks dignity, and is unpolished – there will be some manifestation of her attitude. It is true that the mother-in-law can behave beautifully, but there is always a wrong gaze, a guarded conversation, a long silence, and cues that betray our best possible intentions and efforts. The mother-in-law, inevitably, becomes reserved or on guard in her conversations or interactions with her daughter-in-law. When she changes her opinion and sees her as gay and delightfully youthful, then something in her conduct must have changed – some openness and being less guarded in her conversations and interactions with her daughter-in-law must be visible.

Furthermore, the setup of the example begs the question. Murdoch tells us that for the example to work better, we can imagine that the young couple have emigrated, or D has died. However, this last requirement is puzzling, as the point of the example is to demonstrate that our actions and interactions with others do not affect our thinking about them. However, the example instructs us to assume the absence of any interactions. The example works only if we isolate the mother-in-law from the daughter-in-law. Murdoch's point is important, but it needs softening; our thinking and perspectives towards others change, but our actions and interactions with them are not irrelevant.

What Murdoch highlights is that our intelligent, open thinking changes our perspectives on matters such as our attitudes towards other people and who they are. We can extend this analysis to desires, and, therefore, to the development of our character. In order to decide what to do, we need to settle on what to desire and what to believe, but we do not look at our psychological concepts, beliefs, or desires as if they were internal events. On the contrary, we need to look at the features of the world and pay careful attention to goals, ends, values, and other people and their moral vision as presented in particular contexts and circumstances. It is true that we change perspectives and our ways of thinking about specific matters. It also seems inevitable that we will act according to what we have learned through our thinking. We move our thoughts in specific directions, paying attention or not, to subject matters that may or may not become part of our narrow deliberation. The changes in our thinking are important and might lead to action. Murdoch's point is that action does not follow immediately from thoughts. It can be argued that our thoughts, and any changes in them, are a part of our narrow or immersed deliberation, and they can contribute to it at any point during the exercise of narrow or immersed deliberation (the first starting point).

Thus, imagine that the couple in Murdoch's example did leave town 10 years ago and that the mother-in-law meets the daughter-in-law in her new home after all these years and after the death of her son. She sees her now as gay, delightful, and dignified. She engages in narrow deliberation and puts careful thought into making a nice meal and making the encounter a special moment for her daughter-in-law. We now observe that her actions are informed by her new perspective concerning her daughter-in-law's qualities.

Let us recall that our initial problem was how to maintain the insights of our immersed or narrow deliberation while locating ourselves within a wider perspective that includes medium- and long-term goals, ends, values, projects, and plans. However, we recognise that they are indeterminate and uncertain. Furthermore, we are faced with the challenge of whether it is possible to soundly grasp medium- and long-term goals, ends, and values and become good without losing sight of the immersed perspective. The latter defines our empirical reality and how we deliberate. As a corollary of this, the question is whether we can engage in non-immersed deliberation without losing the immersed perspective.

I will show that it is possible to grasp medium- and long-term ends and values and become good without losing our immersed perspective, and therefore also that we can engage with deliberation that is non-immersive. I will argue that we can inhabit an aspirational or mature deliberative perspective, that this is what is required when we are learning about the good and the right, and that this is sufficient to show that there is a possible trajectory towards the specification of the '*what*' *of* action that embraces medium- and long-term ends and values.

I have already shown that our thinking can change, and this entails a change of perspective and thinking about the subject matter, which includes the content of our desires, goals, beliefs, and other psychological concepts. For Murdoch, the mother-in-law is a well-intentioned person, and this seems to be sufficient to occupy a critical space for our thoughts. It is not the case, however, that there is an internal mental event that we are trying to grasp and represent or refer to (correctly) when we think about the content of our attitudes or desires; rather, it is *our perspective or vision* of the subject that changes. However, it is difficult to believe that individuals in paradigmatic examples are self-critical and self-reflective in this way. Furthermore, in her example, Murdoch downplays the role of time and the fact that the mother-in-law has become more mature. This pertains to the transformation of her desires and character; encounters with other couples and young people, for instance, led to a shift in her perspective, and she likely observed positive changes in her son. Potentially, she has become a grandmother, leading to an adjustment in her view regarding her daughter-in-law. She has experienced illnesses or hardships that have altered her perspective on her daughter-in-law. We pay attention to the subject matter and look carefully, but this might not be sufficient. Something richer is missing in the experience. Furthermore, fantasy, distractions, and self-deceptions can all hinder our vision and intelligent thinking. We acknowledge that in Murdoch's example, the mother-in-law has been active in her thinking but not infallible. Murdoch tells us that she is self-critical and returns to the matter of her daughter-in-law to give it her full and careful attention. 'I am old-fashioned and conventional. I may be prejudiced and narrow-minded. I may be snobbish. I am certainly jealous. Let me look again.'

The question that arises is precisely how the mother-in-law can see herself as 'old- fashioned, narrow-minded, snobbish, and jealous'. This is an important question that Murdoch does not address. Perhaps other experiences have made her reflect on the person that she is. For example, prior to changing her views concerning her daughter-in-law, maybe she developed a friendship, with a young person and paid attention to how she interacted with her and how the young lady acted with others. Through this friendship, she learned that her way of looking at life is rather old-fashioned and narrow-minded. She has also become friends with people of a different social status who have made remarks about her snobbish attitudes. In general, my point is that her change of perspective *does not occur merely by thinking*. There are experiences and relationships that the mother-in-law has engaged in that have forced her to 'look again' at her views on her daughter-in-law (Murdoch 1993: 331).

I will argue that narrow or immersed deliberation and reflection on our narrow deliberations interact in a manner that illuminates the path for transforming our thinking, desires, and character, as well as how we engage with our medium- and long-term goals and projects. In my transparent self-knowledge and self-reflection, I focus on the subject matter's features and try to understand its particularities. The mother-in-law forced perspective informs the learning. The emphasis is on the fact that deliberation occurs not only when the *how* determines the *what* of an action, but also when we experience relationships, think about others, and consider their myriad ways of thinking and acting, thereby gaining knowledge and engaging in rich interactions with them. This is something that human beings do. We also learn to see and think about ourselves as we deliberate and interact with others, and what happens *between* each discrete, narrow, or immersed deliberation is equally crucial.

Cavell interprets the denial of the fantasy of private language advanced by Wittgenstein's *Philosophical Investigations*, as denying the existence of mental events when we use psychological concepts like desire, belief, intention, imagining, and so on. However, he tells us, this denial does not entail that there are no inner thoughts. Inner thoughts acquire a different character, and if we reject the 'mental event' or 'referent' model, then what is the inner thought about? For Cavell, they are *about perspectives and different layers of perspectives* (1979).

Let me explain. When I say, 'I am in pain', I demonstrate that I want to tell you something about my soul and body, but I am also presenting myself, telling you something about myself. However, the fantasy of private language is pernicious, as it leads to a conception of mysterious mental events and mental entities. This leads, consequently, to confusion, as if there is something that uniquely refers to your pain and that I cannot grasp; something mysterious that will always be inscrutable for me, the other.

If we deny the fantasy of the private language account, the fact that I express another desire or intention after deliberating and acting reveals simply a change in perspective in my deliberations or actions, or perhaps both. Murdoch's mother-in-law, for example, can now see that her daughter-in-law is not as undignified as she previously thought, and that she is gay and polite. There is no new mental state present for her, nor is there a unique referent that corresponds to her past or current thoughts. The mother-in-law has changed perspective.

Imagine that I am a very close friend of the mother-in-law (let us call her Sylvia) and that I knew her prior to her changed perspective. Sylvia tells me about the ways her views of her daughter-in-law have changed. It would be wrong to infer that others are inscrutable to us or that there are mysterious mental events that I need to interpret and reinterpret in light of others' actions and my interactions with them. Rather, from our conversations and Sylvia's actions, I assume that Sylvia is struggling to take the right perspective and that she is trying to make herself intelligible to both herself and to me.

More interestingly, like Sylvia, we often struggle to have coherent perspectives and can either avoid or recognise some of our perspectives or visions as being in tension with some of our other perspectives or visions. These changes in perspectives or visions and their recognition or avoidance are clearly illustrated by Cavell's example of the slave owner (1979: 376–78).

The example is as follows, though I have slightly modified it to emphasise my point. Imagine a slave owner who allows his slaves to eat with him, who goes hunting with them, who lets his children play with those of the slaves, and who allows his slaves to call him by a nickname, which pleases the slaves. For the slave owner, the slave is a good man, he is a good hunter, a good father, and a humorous person; however, the only space that the slave owner does not recognise for his slaves is the space of justice. He thinks that it is right that his slaves do not have freedom or autonomy (Cavell 1979: 353). Cavell emphasises the capacity to make connections. We do not share inner thoughts, but we share connections embedded in language-games. Imagine that this relationship between the slave and slave owner occurred at the end of the 19th century in a certain country, and that parliament recently enacted a new statute abolishing slavery. Furthermore, abolitionist movements have for some time articulated their views and propagated them to this country's population. Our slave owner might remain unmoved by their arguments, but Cavell asks, for how long can he continue to avoid taking a new perspective and depriving his slaves of the space of justice? How consistent is this with his other perspectives and thoughts about his slaves, i.e., being good men, good fathers, and humorous human beings? Can he still deny his slaves justice and dignity?

But how does inhabiting this mature or aspirational, so to speak, perspective enable us to also engage with medium- and long-term goals and ends, without losing the immersed or narrow deliberative perspective? We have learned that changing our perspectives through both thinking and experience does not involve contemplating our inner experiences and thoughts as if they were mere events or objects, and we reject the view that we can be impartial or detached from our experiences without losing something important. We advocate for a transparent model of self-reflection, where the agent not only settles the question 'What shall I do?' but also engages in careful thinking about considerations and features of the subject matter, such relationships, what is good, and what is right. When the agent notices deficiencies in her interactions with others, she can use this realisation as the material for further narrow deliberations. When we are confronted with others through relationships and experiences, we are invited to avoid or recognise, and when we pay careful attention to features of the world and our relationships, we are able to aspire to medium- and long-term goals and ends within the narrow or immersed deliberative perspective. The depth and richness of the latter enable us to better understand if or how our current position is lacking. Grasping these medium- and long-term goals is possible because there is a path from the immersed perspective to the deliberative-aspirational perspective. However, since we have absorbed the wisdom gained through prior deliberations, grasping medium- and long-term goals is still within the confines of the immersed perspective.

We have said that we can occupy or inhabit a higher ethical position – the aspirational-mature perspective – if we think of our current position as deprived or lacking. This is one of the roles that regret and shame play in our lives. They make us aware of our deprived or lacking position. Regret and shame force us into another perspective. We can avoid or recognise the particularity of the *what*, and our failure to achieve it with all our thinking, including our thoughts on our emotions, shame, and regret. If the slave owner or Sylvia (Murdoch's mother-in-law) recognises their deprived perspective, then they might shift to the aspirational or mature perspective, transform their emotions, and rethink their goals, ends, values, and desires.

If we take the denial of the fantasy of private language and extend it to our deliberations and thoughts on what is good, worthwhile engaging with, or right, we see that there cannot be a private vision of the good. We cannot have a private space where our referent to the good is only intelligible to us and inscrutable to others. If I feel, through shame and regret, that my perspective is deprived or lacking, I cannot find refuge in a special notion of good or right, which I myself only inhabit.

## V. The Demands of Justice, again

In our previous example concerning what I called 'the basic demands of justice', the injured person demanded from the injurer the right to be respected for her physical integrity. We have asserted that Williams' response to 'the basic demands of justice' might be along the following lines: 'the injurer has behaved below the objective standard of a norm of social conduct', and Williams could add, the injurer could even assert: 'I have breached an objective standard of conduct, and it would be just for the injured person to make some demands on me'. The term 'just' in the sentence is learned as a mere convention. However, two key questions arise: a) how does the injurer know that she has breached an objective standard of care; and b) how does the injurer assess whether 'it is just that the injured person makes some demands on me'. In other words, how are 'the demands of basic justice' presented to the practical reasoner who engages in an act that has caused injury? We have observed that Williams' responses are unpalatable and, furthermore, rely on statements A, B, and C, which we have found to be unsatisfactory.

Arguably, statement A is mistaken if we transpose our analysis of Murdoch's mature agent, whose new outlook or vision is acquired through the process of learning and changing perspectives through descriptions and re-descriptions of the subject matter, to the case of the practical reasoner who is confronted with 'the basic demands of justice'. Within Murdoch's model, there is no substantive and 'given' desire that I, as an agent, can refer to and 'pin down' by reason and therefore be subject to shape and change. The descriptions and re-descriptions of my desires do not refer to a mental phenomenon or substantive matter. Thoughts are concept-dependent and are learned publicly. However, this does not mean that our inner lives do not exist. On the contrary, the lesson that is conveyed by the idea of Wittgenstein's language-game and Murdoch's account of change of vision and perspective is that our psychological concepts like desire, thought, and imagining are not internal or private. Rather, they navigate their expressions through concepts created by our language-games. They do not represent any empirical reality.

Thus, the example of the mother-in-law illustrates that: a) desire does not correspond to a substantive empirical reality; b) there is no act of will that explains the changes of the mother -in-law; and c) within the Murdochian mode, there is a strong emphasis on respecting truth, being open to imagination, and avoiding fantasy. We must pay careful attention to our thoughts and descriptions of our attitudes and desires. This is a basic capacity that all human beings possess. Fantasy focuses on sensation and inner thoughts, whereas imagination focuses on the outside world and the subject of our attention. Arguably, we could add that there is neither an act of reason nor a specific *locus* for an act of reason that makes possible the changes in the mother-in-law's desires and attitudes towards her daughter-in-law. Our attitudes and desires towards an object, including the ends of our actions, change due to our attention and appreciation. We describe and re-describe what we desire and aim for.

The idea that we learn concept-ends and concept-values in language games also problematises statement B, which states that there is no plausible and sound conception that explains how we 'reason out' desires together when we are immersed in answering the question, 'What shall we do together?'. Individual agency, construed as a process of deliberation isolated from language-games, and specific 'forms of life' where concept-ends and values-ends play a key role are not the starting point to answer the question, 'What shall we do together?'. We are already immersed with others in trying to characterise, specify, and determine, 'What shall we do?'. The adjective 'together' does not add anything special to what we are already doing. 'Together' is not a specific or additional way of doing actions. The agent responds to the question, 'What shall I do?', but the answers she gives at this particular moment rely on a myriad of ways in which she has already described and re-described the matter and the collective thinking of her community and conceptual traditions.

Presenting 'the basic demands of justice' to the injurer forces her to pay attention and gather a description of the injured person's suffering. The injurer is also forced to both re-describe her attitudes and desires and shape them in light of her thinking about the matter. The question prompts her to contemplate the precise description or re-description of the specific 'right' and 'duty' that arise from the action and its outcome.

The idea that her thinking can be characterised by the statement, 'I have breached an objective standard of duty, and it is just (in conventional terms) that the injured person makes some demands on me' now seems implausible within the moral and psychologically realistic picture that Williams is so eager to demonstrate in his work. Rather, the injured person presents the demands of justice to the injurer, as well as a) the injured person's pain and suffering, and b) the injured person's thoughts on her diminished capacity to achieve specific ends and values. In our example, the injured person will be impeded from doing many of the things she values due to the burns on her hand. The injurer is forced to 'see' the injured (Rodriguez-Blanco 2022) as a *person, i.e., who is engaged in ends and values*. There is an 'exchange of practical thoughts' between the injurer and injured person, and this exchange requires both injured person and injurer to give attention to and have a vision of how to characterise 'the basic demands of justice'.

Using Cavell's example, let us think about the case of the slave owner. His children play with the slave's children; he thinks the slave is a good hunter and a good man. However, he deprives him of the space of justice and freedom. The 'basic demands of justice' of the slave in terms of freedom to vote, the right to decide his own destiny, his right to be part of a political community, and so on, are presented to the slave owner as a set of ends and values. The slave owner may avoid recognising the slave's freedom and justice while also recognising him as a good man. However, Cavell asks, up to what point does this situation cease to be possible? The slave owner's avoidance of inhabiting an aspirational or mature perspective will reach a limit due to the imposed 'exchange of practical thoughts'.

We have problematised statements A and B and have thereby shown that Williams' separation thesis cannot be sustained.

Statement C establishes that if we are asked to 'take responsibility' within the public sphere, then we are not mature agents. Therefore, a tension appears between mature agency and agency exercised at the collective level, where we interact with strangers and questions of justice are central. However, statement C presupposes an artificial dichotomy, i.e., that there are two kinds of agency: mature and non-mature. In the former, we take responsibility for our actions, whereas in the latter, we ask other people to take responsibility. But so far, the lesson from our discussion is that we are constant learners of what is good, right, and dutiful through the avoidance or recognition of different perspectives. We are the kind of creatures that can pay attention and engage in sound descriptions and re-descriptions of our values, ends, desires, and beliefs when we are addressing the question, 'What shall we do?'. However, this happens within our agency's diachronicity and within the only possible space, the public sphere.

According to Murdoch's proposal, reason is not an abstract or detached exercise that opposes a 'given' and substantive reality of desires. On the contrary, our learning of new visions and perspectives is in continuity with immersive deliberation.

We can recognise or avoid a mature or aspirational perspective,[16] but this does not entail that reflection operates *from nowhere* and we are veiled in the darkness of what we have absorbed and learned from previous ethical visions and experiences, including our descriptions and re-descriptions of our desires and attitudes.

A potential objection to our proposal might be as follows. Williams would agree with us that there is no reference to substantive and given desires and, furthermore, that our thoughts and descriptions might define the contour of our desires and deliberations. However, the idea that through our descriptions and re-descriptions we can attain a mature perspective in the practical domain is precisely the illusion or fantasy of control that our thoughts and concepts can exercise over our desires. Desires are more indomitable, Williams would say, and it will depend on luck whether you achieve the right thoughts and descriptions to develop a mature ethical vision or perspective.

But with this potential reply, Williams would be overlooking the key point that I am trying to make, namely that 'the demands of justice' are imposed on us, and we are forced to see the other in their practical thoughts, *and* in our own practical thoughts. We are forced to see their vision, encompassing their descriptions of desires and ends. In this way, their thoughts impose their maturity or immaturity, inviting the recognition or avoidance of an aspirational or mature agency to the issue at hand. My point is not so much about the control of our desires, as about how 'the demands of justice' are presented to us and, therefore, the way 'the basic demands of justice' are forced on us. We are forced to see the other from her own vision or perspective. This inevitably compels us to take a position towards her vision and, therefore, towards our own way of describing and re-describing the subject matter or object, which encompasses our desires and attitudes. Through our descriptions and re-descriptions, we transform our desires.

## VI. Conclusions

I have shown that Williams' separation thesis between the politics of civic maturity and the politics of justice is an ingenious argument. However, I have also tried to show that it is flawed. We started by reconstructing Williams' position in the strongest possible way to clarify the three statements that ground his separation thesis, and from here, we showed that Williams' separation thesis is untenable. I demonstrated this by advancing the view that: a) our psychological concepts, including desires, have no substantive and 'given' reality; b) there is no act of reason that 'pins down' desires; and c) we necessarily engage in either the recognition of or avoidance of an aspirational or mature perspective. I have also argued that we start with concepts-ends, and values that we learn together through our language-games. The result is that 'the basic demands of justice' require the 'exchange of

[16] For further details of this account, see Rodriguez-Blanco 2022.

practical thoughts' and therefore justice is necessarily implicated in our taking a mature or aspirational perspective. Therefore, inevitably, under 'the basic demands of justice', as injurers, we are forced to re-describe or describe not only the thoughts of the injured person but also her suffering and pain. We are forced to either avoid or recognise an aspirational or mature stance. As a result, we cannot separate the politics of justice from the politics of civic maturity.

Indirectly, we have also problematised the idea that the 'Socratic question' – 'How Should One Live?' – is formulated from *nowhere*, from the special and privileged *locus* of an examined life. According to Williams' reasoning, the 'Socratic question' appears to exist at a different level from our everyday actions, where we are addressing the question, 'What shall I do?'. By contrast, we have defended the view that we start with the question 'What shall I do?' (what Williams has called the starting point of deliberation), and we learn new visions and perspectives that expand towards a mature or aspirational perspective. The changes occur gradually, with the ambition to addressing the Socratic question once we are ashore in our lives. However, arguably, there is no need to do this because we might by then already know the answer to the question 'How Should One Live?' from the myriad of responses to the question, 'What shall I do?' in particular and specific actions in one's life.

## Bibliography

Anscombe, E (1958) 'On Brute Facts' 18 3 *Analysis* 69.

Bagnoli, C (2003) 'Respect and Loving Attention' 33 4 *Canadian Journal of Philosophy* 483.

Bobonich, C (2007) 'Plato and Akrasia and Knowing Our Own Mind' in C Bobonich & P Destrée (eds), *Akrasia in Greek Philosophy: From Socrates to Plotinus* (Leiden, Brill Publishing).

Broadie, S (1991) *Ethics with Aristotle* (Oxford, Oxford University Press).

Burnyeat, M (1980) 'Aristotle on Learning to be Good' in A Oksenberg Rorty (ed), *Essays on Aristotle's Ethics* (Berkeley: University of California Press).

Cavell, S (1979) *The Claim of Reason: Wittgenstein, Scepticism, Morality and Tragedy* (Oxford, Oxford University Press).

Enoch, D & Marmor, A (2007) 'The Case Against Moral Luck' 26 4 *Law and Philosophy* 405.

Frankfurt, H (1971) 'Freedom of the Will and Concept of a Person' 68 1 *Journal of Philosophy* 5.

Heuer, U (2022) 'Luck and Responsibility according to Bernard Williams' in A Szigeti & M Talbert (eds), *Morality and Agency Themes from Bernard Williams* (Oxford, Oxford University Press).

Irwin, T (1980) 'Reason and Responsibility in Aristotle' in A Oksenberg Rorty (ed), *Essays on Aristotle's Ethics* (Berkeley: University of California Press).

Kutz, C (2009) 'Against Political Luck' in D Callcut (ed), *Reading Bernard Williams* (London, Routledge).

Lang, G (2019) 'Gauguin's Lucky Escape: Moral Luck and the Morality System' in S Chappell & M van Ackeren (eds), *Ethics Beyond the Limits: New Essays on Bernard Williams' Ethics and the Limits of Philosophy* (London, Routledge).

—— (2021) *Strokes of Luck: A Study in Moral and Political Philosophy* (Oxford, Oxford University Press).
McDowell, J (1998) 'Some Issues in Aristotle's Moral Psychology' in J McDowell, *Mind, Value and Reality* (Cambridge, Massachusetts, Harvard University Press).
Moran, R (2017) 'Iris Murdoch and Existentialism' R Moran, *The Philosophical Imagination: Selected Essays* (Oxford, Oxford University Press).
Murdoch, I (1950a) 'Metaphysics and Ethics' in I Murdoch, *Existentialists and Mystics. Writings on Philosophy and Literature* (London, Penguin).
—— (1950b) 'Nostalgia for the Particular' in I Murdoch, *Existentialists and Mystics. Writings on Philosophy and Literature* (London, Penguin).
—— (1950c) 'The Darkness of Practical Reason' in I Murdoch, *Existentialists and Mystics. Writings on Philosophy and Literature* (London, Penguin).
—— (1950d) 'The Idea of Perfection' in I Murdoch, *Existentialists and Mystics. Writings on Philosophy and Literature* (London, Penguin).
—— (1950e) 'The Sublime and the Good' in I Murdoch, *Existentialists and Mystics. Writings on Philosophy and Literature* (London, Penguin).
—— (1950f) 'Vision and Choice in Morality' in I Murdoch, *Existentialists and Mystics. Writings on Philosophy and Literature* (London, Penguin) 76–98.
—— (1993) *Metaphysics as a Guide to Morals* (London, Penguin).
Rodriguez-Blanco, V (2022) 'Ways of Inhabiting the Deliberative-Aspirational Point of View: Practical Reason and Objective Goods' 67 2 *American Journal of Jurisprudence* 1.
—— (2025) *Responsibility for Negligence in Ethics and Law: Aspiration, Perspective and Civic Maturity* (Oxford, Oxford University Press).
Taylor, C (1985a) 'Self-Interpreting Animals' in C Taylor, *Human Agency and Language* (Cambridge, Cambridge University Press).
—— (1985b) 'What is Human Agency?' in C Taylor, *Human Agency and Language* (Cambridge, Cambridge University Press).
Teichman, R (2018) 'How Should One Live: Williams on Practical Deliberation and Reasons for Acting' in S Chappell & M van Ackeren (eds), *Ethics Beyond the Limits: New Essays on Bernard Williams' Ethics and the Limits of Philosophy* (London, Routledge).
Vogt, K (2017) *Desiring the Good* (Oxford, Oxford University Press).
Walker, M (1991) 'Moral Luck and the Virtues of Impure Agency' 22 1/2 *Metaphilosophy* 14.
Watson, G (2004) 'Free Agency' in G Watson, *Agency and Answerability* (Oxford, Oxford University Press).
Williams, B (1981) 'Moral Luck' in B Williams, *Moral Luck* (Cambridge, Cambridge University Press).
—— (1993) *Ethics and the Limits of Philosophy* (London, Fontana Press).
—— (1995) 'Voluntary Acts and Responsible Agents' in B Williams, *Making Sense of Humanity* (Cambridge, Cambridge University Press).
Wittgenstein, L (2009) *Philosophical Investigations*, 4th edn (Oxford, Blackwell).

# 3

# Internal Reasons, Motivation, and the Proleptic Nature of Blame

GERALD LANG*

## I. Introduction

In one of his most famous and intensively studied – but still oddly elusive – essays, Bernard Williams sets out to defend an 'internalist' conception of reasons for action, and deride an 'externalist' conception of reasons for action (Williams 1981a). He subsequently revisited the topic, offering clarifications, some responses to his critics, and further thoughts about the connection of reasons internalism to moral blame and other relevant phenomena in the conceptual vicinity (Williams 1995a, 1995b: 186–94).

I want to take another look at this material in order to recover an interpretation of his position that makes better overall sense of what he actually says about it. Arguments that can seem lacklustre, puzzling, or even question-begging under a standard interpretation may deserve fresh consideration if they can be pressed into the service of an alternative interpretation to which they are better fitted. Now I should say that, when all is said and done, internalism convinces me in none of its versions. But the point, for those of us who sympathise with externalism, is to see what we are up against. And the point, for those whose sympathies lie with internalism, is to help pinpoint what their options are. No attempt to refute internalism will be offered here. My purposes are primarily interpretive. What should we make of Williams' contributions to these issues? What, for him, made reasons

* For highly useful comments on more rudimentary versions of this material, I thank the audiences at the Dianoia/Leeds Normativity Workshop in Rome, the Bernard Williams: From Responsibility to Law and Jurisprudence Workshop at the University of Surrey, and a workshop on Bernard Williams at the University of Edinburgh. I am grateful for all the many probing and illuminating comments I have received, and thank, in particular, Jeremy Fix, my assigned commentator in Edinburgh, for his written comments. I also thank the members of the Leeds home audience at a CAMP retreat in April 2024 for their comments on a later, lengthier version. I am especially grateful to Pekka Väyrynen for his advice on more than one iteration of this material, and to Jessica Isserow for her exceptionally detailed comments on the penultimate version. Thanks also to this volume's editors for their comments on a penultimate draft.

internalism true? As we shall see, we are forced to go beyond what he explicitly says if we are going to find satisfyingly deep roots for his commitments.

This essay unfolds as follows. In section II, I report, with minimal critical intervention, the essentials of his position, drawing freely on both his major articles about the topic. In section III, I sketch a broad externalist reply. In light of these criticisms, I distinguish, in sections IV to VI, between two interpretations of Williams' account, and argue that one of them has more going for it than first impressions may suggest. The essay concludes, in section VII, with some more abstract speculations concerning the fundamental motivations for internalism, construed in the way I suspect Williams probably meant it to be understood.

## II. Internal versus External Reasons for Action

I start, then, with 'internal' reasons for action. Williams characterises an internal reason as follows: '*A* has a reason to $\phi$ only if he could reach the conclusion to $\phi$ by a sound deliberative route from the motivations he already has' (1995a: 35). A few things need to be unpacked here.[1]

First, the 'motivations [*A*] already has' constitute what Williams calls *A*'s 'subjective motivational set' (hereafter 'S-set'): what *A* cares about or is interested in (1981a: 102). Williams delineates the S-set in broad fashion: it may comprise 'dispositions of evaluation, patterns of emotional reaction, personal loyalties, and various projects … embodying commitments of the agent' (1981a: 105).

Second, internal reasons are reached from an agent's S-set via a 'sound deliberative route'. The sound deliberative route is roughly instrumental in character: if '*A* has some motive which will be served or furthered by his $\phi$-ing' (1981a: 101), then $\phi$-ing can be reached by a sound deliberative route from *A*'s S-set. Williams urges a flexible approach to what counts as a sound deliberative route. Though instrumental or means-end reasoning clearly lies at the heart of sound deliberation, deliberative processes can also take the form of

> thinking how the satisfaction of elements in [an agent's S-set] can be combined … where there is some irresoluble conflict among the elements of [the S-set], considering which one attaches most weight to … or … finding constitutive solutions, such as deciding what would make for an entertaining evening, granted that one wants entertainment (Williams 1981a: 104).

External reasons can be defined in contrast with internal reasons: any reason that does not count as internal is external. Williams is an internalist about reasons: reasons for action are all internal. There are no external reasons. Why so?

[1] The 'only if' bit of the formulation will be dealt with in section IV.

Reasons for action stand at the crossroads of two dimensions: the explanatory and the normative. They purport not just to explain action, but to guide or justify it. Williams' internalism aims to accommodate both dimensions of action, and it is internalism's superior accommodation of them, relative to externalism, which steers it to victory in this debate. Or so Williams contends.

The first condition that an account of reasons for action should meet, then, is the *explanation condition*, according to which a reason must be capable of explaining why an agent acts as she does when she acts on it. As Williams says: 'If there are reasons for action, it must be that people sometimes act for those reasons, and if they do, their reasons must figure in some correct explanation of their action' (1981a: 102). The second condition that must be met by an adequate account of reasons for action is what I shall call the *rational deliberation condition*: a reason for action must be such that it can be reached as a result of an agent's rational deliberation.[2]

Of course, these two dimensions can come apart, and such cases have much to teach us about the commitments of any account of reasons for action. Williams gives us a simple case to illustrate how these dimensions can diverge. In the '*Petrol*' case, an agent – I will call her Sarah – desires to have a gin and tonic, believes that the glass in front of her contains gin and tonic, and thus desires to consume the contents of this glass (1981a: 105, 1995a: 36). Unknown to Sarah, however, the glass contains petrol and tonic, not gin and tonic. Now we can understand, in *Petrol*, why Sarah is motivated to drink from this glass. The action is rationalised in the right kind of way by her beliefs and desires. There is nothing *puzzling* about Sarah's behaviour, as long as we know that she was ignorant of the contents of the glass. Thus, the explanatory dimension is provided for. But the normative or justificatory dimension has gone missing. Unless Sarah is after a trip to the emergency room and a difficult encounter with a stomach pump, she lacks a reason to drink it. If someone intervened, whisking the glass away from her, and explained what would have happened had she consumed its contents, Sarah would presumably accept that she has been saved from action for which she had no reason. No item in her S-set is served by her drinking the contents of this glass. In fact, she would presumably accept the stronger claim that she had an overwhelming reason to refrain from drinking it.

*Petrol* appears to teach us that, for the internalist, actual motivation is neither a necessary nor a sufficient condition of the existence of a genuine reason for action. The internalist is entitled to insist on moderately idealised conditions, consisting at least in factually adequate information, before what the agent is actually motivated to do can be certified as demonstrating the existence of a reason on which she acted. In this way, the *normative force* of reasons ascriptions is provided for: '*A* has a reason to $\phi$' is non-equivalent to '*A* is presently

[2] What does Williams have to say about the ontology of reasons? Does he think of them as facts, or mental states, or something else? It is difficult to recover an answer to these questions from his texts, though my suspicion is that he regarded them as basically propositional. Hopefully we can thread a path through these issues without having a definitive answer to the ontological question.

disposed to $\phi$' (1995a: 36). If reasons ascriptions retain normative force, then they are qualified to function as advice. We can advise others not to act on the reasons they take themselves to have, or reconsider the reasons they take themselves not to have.

Why does Williams dismiss externalism? He takes as his test case Henry James' story about Owen Wingrave. Though Owen 'hates everything about military life and what it means' (1981a: 106), he is nonetheless being badgered to respect family tradition and join the army. Williams writes:

> His family might have expressed themselves by saying that there was a reason for Owen to join the army. Knowing that there was nothing in Owen's [S-set] which would lead, through deliberative reasoning, to his doing this would not make them withdraw the claim or admit that they made it under a misapprehension. They mean it in an external sense (1981a: 106).

Williams uses this example because externalists are committed to the reality of certain reasons even if they do not motivate the agent to act on them. Stated as minimally as this, the point does not apply only to externalists. Think of Sarah and her glass of petrol and tonic. But the Owen Wingrave story is crucially different from the *Petrol* case. For in this situation, unlike *Petrol*, there is nothing, in the relevant sense, that Owen is kept in the dark about, and yet externalists will not be deterred from insisting that he may still have a reason to do what he steadily refuses to do. Hence this case, on Williams' view, usefully exposes the limitations of externalism.

Williams appears to advance complaints about externalism on both fronts already identified: in terms of explanation, and in terms of rational deliberation. I shall take these in turn. If Owen has a reason to join the army, then that reason must explain why he does so, if he does so. Suppose Owen initially resists this pressure to join the army, but then folds and signs up for the military life. At *that* point, Williams believes the reason can no longer be external:

> When the reason is an explanation of [an agent's] action, then of course it will be, in some form, in his [S-set], because certainly – and nobody denies this – what he actually does has to be explained by his [S-set] (1995a: 39).

Thus, the only way of meeting the explanation condition will require that Owen acts on a consideration that can be rationally related to something in his S-set.

There is also a problem with the rational deliberation condition, because 'there is no motivation to deliberate *from*, to reach this new motivation' (Williams 1981a: 109). Williams has less to say about this second condition, but his central point seems to be that it takes more for the rational deliberation condition to be satisfied than for an agent to be steadily confronted by a would-be reason and then, at some point, to be motivated to act in response to it. We must be able to point to something that looks like guidance or reasons-sensitivity, not just action that is better interpreted as a protective response to browbeating, even if it means that this agent is not genuinely acting on her reasons.

## III. A Quick Reply

Is this too fast? Critics of Williams' internalism will have an alternative account of what has transpired if we assume that Owen does join the army:[3] while Owen initially resisted the (external) reason, he then comes to *accept* it. And his acceptance of that reason is what, in turn, explains his acting on it. That is the standard explanatory route for all reasons for action, however proximately or remotely connected they are to the agent's immediate motivational concerns.

Of course, in this imagined extension of the story, the fact that Owen joins the army does not show that he responded to a genuine reason for him to join the army. Perhaps, after all, he was simply browbeaten into it. He folded under pressure, though he would have been truer to his reasons by standing his ground. But this is not a hill on which sensible externalists will have to die. For externalists will not concede that Owen has an *external* reason for joining the army merely because he strongly desires *not* to join the army. An external reason is not conjured out of an agent's mere refusal to accept the reason-giving credentials of some course of action. Externalists contend only that whether Owen has a reason to opt for the military life has to be settled independently of what he is motivated to do. The point is that whether, and how, Owen is motivated cannot tell us anything very much about his reasons to act. And that much seems to have been conceded by Williams' treatment of *Petrol*: we cannot tell from Sarah's actions alone whether she had a reason to drink this stuff. In determining what our reasons are, we can therefore disregard an agent's actual behaviour. While it would be unwise to disregard the broader lineaments of an agent's subjective situation – her interests, capacities, and circumstances – in enumerating her reasons for action, we can set aside the narrower and more specific question of what she happens to be motivated by on any particular occasion. Now Williams wishes to distinguish between the idealisation associated with the correction of Sarah's empirical beliefs in *Petrol* and the more complete idealisations which he imputes to critics of internalism. He thinks that, while every agent has a generic interest in being adequately informed about their environment, externalists owe us an explanation of why agents are assumed in advance to have a reasons-sensitive attunement to prudential and moral considerations (1995a: 36–37). Again, sensible critics of internalism can agree. These issues require further patient argument, not hasty opportunistic raids into territories that are supposedly now ripe for capture because *Petrol* demonstrates a gap between motivation and reason. But the result is not just a stalemate between internalists and externalists. For the accusation against Williams will be that he has failed to show why externalism is false. As Korsgaard puts it: 'the motivational analysis of the case *depends* upon your views of the content of rational principles of action, not

[3] My treatment here will be quick and dirty, but it is meant to echo familiar criticisms. Korsgaard (1986) is of particular importance here, though I have McDowell (1995) in mind as well.

the reverse' (1986: 16).[4] As far as the content of rational principles of action is concerned, it all depends on what happens next. Perhaps we will adopt a relatively ambitious account of the content of rational principles of action, and thus often find ourselves interpreting agents' actual behaviour as evidence of their failure to act on the reasons they had. Or we might settle for a less ambitious account of the content of rational principles of action – perhaps a form of the sound deliberative route – and note a generally higher degree of practical success. But at this point, before the relevant arguments are prosecuted in detail, externalists are no worse off than internalists, and Williams-style internalism does not appear to offer any distinctive resources for settling the issues in its favour.

## IV. Two Interpretations of Internalism

To see how Williams may respond to this line of argument, I shall now outline two different interpretations of what he is up to: the *Procedural Interpretation* and the *Motivational Interpretation*. These interpretations turn, at bottom, on divergent responses to *Petrol*.

The Procedural Interpretation accepts that the lesson of *Petrol* is that we cannot be guided by an agent's actual motivations in imputing reasons to her. We figure out her reasons by finding out what antecedently lies in her S-set, and in seeing whether the putative reason can be reached from one or more of the items in that set through a sound deliberative route. More fully:

> *Procedural Interpretation*: Whether *A* has a reason to $\phi$ need not appeal explicitly to any facts about *A*'s motivation. The existing contents of *A*'s S-set can determine whether A has reason to $\phi$, as long as we can recover instrumental or other procedural antecedent connections between those facts and $\phi$-ing.

A few more words about the Procedural Interpretation. We are rarely, of course, in possession of adequate information about an agent's S-set. We are complex creatures, and know even ourselves only imperfectly, let alone others. We may thus be guided, on occasion, by facts about an agent's motivations as a source of *evidence* about her reasons. If someone continuously refuses to practise the piano, despite having ample opportunity to do so, then we might conclude that there is nothing in her S-set that could give her a reason to do so. But nothing is settled by actual motivation, strictly speaking. To test the genuineness of any putative reason to act, what matters is whether the agent's S-set is populated by items that can be reached by sound deliberative reasoning. As we have seen, Williams is also

[4] Korsgaard notes that we do not have to abandon internalism. What she calls the 'internalism requirement' demands only that 'rational considerations succeed in motivating us *insofar as we are rational*', not 'that rational considerations always succeed in motivating us' (1986: 15 – my emphasis). But Korsgaard's defence of the internalism requirement need not be in tension with the spirit of most externalist replies. Like them, she is targeting *Williams*' form of internalism.

permissive about what counts as sound deliberative reasoning. The basic shape of it is instrumentalist, but it is not restricted to means-end reasoning. For that reason, I describe the interpretation as 'procedural' rather than 'instrumentalist'. The elements of rational deliberation may be fuzzy and contextually sensitive, but they are enumerable in principle.

The Motivational Interpretation, by contrast, makes an agent's actual motivations, in at least some circumstances, constitutive of what reasons she has. Of course, and bearing *Petrol* in mind, we cannot run this interpretation in a wholly unfiltered way. But the process of idealisation stops squarely at the correction of factual errors. Thus:

> *Motivational Interpretation*: Whether *A* has a reason to $\phi$ will depend on whether *A* is in fact motivated to $\phi$ when *A* is placed in circumstances in which *A* is adequately empirically informed.

Now the Motivational Interpretation must accept an immediate challenge.[5] One central explanation of why reasons do not have to issue in motivation to qualify as reasons is that Williams is not dealing with only conclusive or all-in reasons. His usual concern is with *a* reason. The indefinite article here is of key importance. Reasons can be defeated or outweighed by other reasons without ceasing to be genuine. Assume, then, that I seek entertainment for the evening: I might read a Maigret novel, or re-watch *The Apartment*. Imagine that I choose to read the Maigret novel. It does not follow that I had no reason to re-watch *The Apartment*. The film-watching reason, on this particular occasion, has simply been defeated. In this case, non-motivation does not impugn the existence of the reason.

There are two responses to this challenge. First, the Procedural Interpretation and the Motivational Interpretation might accept a certain division of labour. Most of the time, the Procedural Interpretation will take the lead, since we do not accept that an agent's actually being motivated to $\phi$ following her possession of empirically adequate information is the acid test of whether she had a reason to $\phi$. But this is not always the case, and this means, in turn, that the Motivational Interpretation has distinctive work to do. Sometimes the test of whether the agent has a reason to $\phi$ will indeed depend on whether she is motivated to $\phi$. The view I want to commend is that, for Williams, reasons cannot always be *silent*: they need to sustain certain patterns of actual motivation. If I spend other evenings watching films, then I will have film-watching reasons, even if I do not spend every evening watching them. Films will take their place among my reason-giving deliberative options, even if these reasons are sometimes defeated by other reasons. But if I never watch films – if I always decide against watching them to get on with other things – then there are substantially weaker grounds for supposing that I do have film-watching reasons. This will be true even if there is a nearby possible world in which I do come to enjoy watching films, because I have made a habit of watching

[5] I thank Jeremy Fix for making this challenge plain to me.

them.[6] It is this intermediate position which is captured by the Motivational Interpretation.

There is some textual evidence for the Motivational Interpretation, which brings me to my second response. Williams explicitly offers his internal procedural connection as only a necessary condition on reasons for action, not a necessary and sufficient condition (1995a: 35). The internal procedural connection states an 'only if' condition. Why 'only if', and not 'if and only if, or just 'if'? Why isn't the procedural connection sufficient? Reasons are cheap, after all, at least in their *pro tanto*, non-conclusive form. If $\phi$-ing furthers or serves one of the items in *A*'s S-set, why isn't this enough to say that *A* has a reason to $\phi$? On the face of it, Williams seems to be thinking about reasons in a more robust or stringent sense than merely *pro tanto* reasons. Yet he is not concerned with only conclusive reasons. So what does he have in mind? At this stage, it is not wholly clear. I offer further arguments below for thinking that actual motivation may matter to him – and how it may matter to him – and why purely procedural connections may not always be enough to certify a reason as genuine.

If the Motivational Interpretation is on the right lines, there is the possibility of principled resistance to the externalist line of argument sketched in section III. Williams would no longer have to accept that what Korsgaard calls 'motivational scepticism' can have no independent bearing on 'content scepticism' (Korsgaard 1986: 6). I now go over this territory more carefully, noting advantages and challenges as I go along.

## V. Why Favour the Motivational Interpretation?

I will now round up some considerations favouring the Motivational Interpretation. Some of these considerations are yielded by principles of interpretive charity and dialectical advantage, and others are more directly suggested by Williams' primary arguments for internalism.

First, what Williams says about needs, in particular, strongly suggests the Motivational Interpretation:

> There is a further question … about the content of [an agent's S-set]: whether it should be taken … as containing *needs*. It is certainly quite natural to say that *A* has a reason to pursue *X*, just on the ground that he needs *X* … I take it that insofar as there are determinately recognisable needs, there can be an agent who lacks any interest in getting what he indeed needs … If an agent really is uninterested in pursuing what he needs;

[6] See also Williams 1995b, when he is replying to the externalist challenge issued by McDowell (1995): 'The fact that listening to twelve-tone music can be a worthwhile activity surely does not give everyone a reason to engage in it' (1995b: 191). Why the 'surely'? Williams's point must be that listening to twelve-tone music will be reason-giving to those who have to come to enjoy listening to twelve-tone music. Those who would find twelve-tone music worthwhile, were they to invest the time and energy into it, but who have not done so, may lack such reasons.

> and this is not the product of false belief; and he could not reach any such motive from motives he has by [sound] deliberative processes … then I think we do have to say that in the internal sense he indeed has no reason to pursue these things (1981a: 105).

Williams puts up no great opposition in this passage to the inclusion of needs in an agent's S-set. He does not omit them in cases where they fail to lead to reliable patterns of motivation. But if they are in the S-set, there will be ordinary means-ends connections to certain acts that will promote or uphold them. As far as the Procedural Interpretation is concerned, that should settle matters: the agent will have reasons to perform these acts and thereby satisfy her needs. It is only the Motivational Interpretation which tells us that we will have to wait and see what the agent does in conditions where she is adequately informed to determine whether she has reasons to satisfy her needs. We may have a grip on rational processes in outline, but whether they can be connected to reasons is disclosed, in turn, by the further test of whether the agent is actually motivated to pursue them.

Note also that there may be no particular privileged moment at which a course of action is either confirmed as reason-giving (by inspiring motivation), or disconfirmed as reason-giving (by not inspiring motivation). What Williams seems interested in is a *pattern* of motivation: an explicit *motivational tendency*. If a putative need – to stay fit and healthy, for example – does not lead to appropriate motivation in Rebecca at any particular moment (to go for the early morning run on Monday), it does not follow that she lacked a reason to do it. If Rebecca raises her game on Tuesday morning and goes for the run, we may say both that she is now acting on a reason to go for the run and that she was failing to be motivated by the same type of reason on Monday. It will rarely be the case that there is any particular decisive moment at which a putative needs-based reason, through its failure to motivate, is disconfirmed as a reason for Rebecca. Yet if she *never* goes for a run, we plausibly have an example of a need which, for Williams, is not reason-giving.

Second, the Motivational Interpretation can retain what seemed essential to the concessions Williams makes about the 'normative force' of reasons ascriptions. Internal reasons, even on the Motivational Interpretation, possess requisite normative force insofar as agents are required to be adequately informed before acting. That condition is not met in *Petrol*, but it is comfortably met by the Motivational Interpretation.[7]

Third, the Motivational Interpretation makes sense of what, on the procedural interpretation, would have to be deemed a puzzling riposte of Williams to Korsgaard in his later essay:

> Somebody may say that every rational deliberator is committed to constraints of morality as much as to the requirements of truth or sound reasoning. But if this is so, then the

[7] To be clear, there is no pretence here that the Motivational Interpretation performs better than the Procedural Interpretation on this front: the claim is only that the Motivational Interpretation holds its own.

> constraints of morality are part of everybody's [S-set], and every correct moral reason will be an internal reason. But there has to be an argument for that conclusion. Someone who claims the constraints of morality are themselves built into the notion of what it is to be a rational deliberator cannot get that conclusion for nothing (1995a: 37).[8]

On the surface, this passage may strike you as non-puzzling, because Korsgaard *does* owe us such an argument. That much is true. What is puzzling about it is that Korsgaard never pretended otherwise. Korsgaard's critical target in this article is Williams' version of internalism rather than to set out an alternative view.[9] Her central contention is that Williams' arguments do not establish that agents lack moral or prudential reasons simply because these agents fail to be motivated by moral or prudential considerations. If the Procedural Interpretation were correct, then Williams would have conceded this point already. His business would then be to establish that our reasons are tailored to our S-sets, but not to prudential and moral considerations more generally. That particular burden of argument is not discharged when it is pointed out that externalists have to argue their way as well. On this way of setting up the debate, internalism is not the default victor. This passage, on the interpretation it must bear if we operate with the Procedural Interpretation, makes Williams seem curiously flat-footed, since it must depict him as ignoring Korsgaard's focus on the question of whether Williams has established the truth of his form of internalism. On the Motivational Interpretation, by contrast, Williams' points carry a heavier critical punch: his point will be that, for some agents, prudential and moral considerations carry no motivational force. This is what distinguishes them from the elements of these agents' S-sets that do carry motivational force. If Williams is committed to this motivation-dependent 'wait and see' approach, then what he says to Korsgaard will be more forceful, since some agents are plainly unmoved by prudential and moral considerations. Korsgaard assigns no intrinsic significance to that fact, but Williams does, and he thinks he can exploit it against her.

Fourth, the Motivational Interpretation makes it easier to explain why Williams is so relaxed about both what lies in agents' S-sets, and what counts as sound deliberative reasoning (1981a: 104–105, 110; 1995a: 38). Of course, it is not Williams' style to seek artificially neat lines and hard edges in moral philosophy. He is generally tolerant, indeed encouraging, of loose ends, hard choices, mess. But there have to be limits to this open-endedness if internalism is not to risk theoretical laxity. The Motivational Interpretation can help to relieve Williams from this critical pressure, and in two ways. First, it points to an additional resource for determining an agent's reasons: these reasons are partly revealed, in some circumstances, in what an agent is actually motivated to do. If the proof is in the pudding, and we can count on the pudding to rise, then the pudding's precise ingredients

[8] Williams adds in a footnote that he has 'no basic disagreement' with Korsgaard's argument (1995a: 44, n 3).

[9] For a development of that fuller, neo-Kantian view, see Korsgaard (1996).

may be less important. Second, the Motivational Interpretation seeks to certify reasons as reasons without having to play an all-in role or without being merely *pro tanto*. Again, what matters to Williams, as I see it, are patterns of motivation rather than particular instances of it. Thus an agent's failure to be motivated by a putative reason on any particular occasion will rarely amount to decisive evidence that she lacks this reason. This feature will provide a principled reason for a certain vagueness in truthful reason ascriptions.

Fifth, the Motivational Interpretation also makes good sense of Williams' insistence that the S-set is not 'statically given' (1981a: 105): elements of it can come and go, and its contents can be affected by the very processes of deliberation. This fluidity will be less welcome to the Procedural Interpretation, because that interpretation needs a relatively fixed picture of the combination of agents' S-sets and sound deliberative route in order to identify what reasons we have. Once again, the Motivational Interpretation can afford to be more relaxed on this front. It will be less important what was determinately part of an agent's S-set prior to the issuing of the bit of advice if we are waiting to see what, on the motivational front, will actually happen. If the agent is motivated, it will turn out in some sets of circumstances that she had a reason to do what she did. If she is not motivated, then that may be compelling evidence for her not having had a reason – at least if the non-motivation belongs to a general pattern of non-motivation. If we are waiting to see what happens, what was true of her S-set up to that moment will be less important.

There is one important further consideration, which I will discuss in the following section. We will also be re-encountering the Owen Wingrave case.

## VI. Blame, Bluff, and Owen Wingrave

A further advantage of the Motivational Interpretation is that it makes good sense of Williams' treatment of blame and the proleptic mechanism. Williams thinks, in short, that internalism nicely dovetails with the function of 'focused' blame in moral discourse. This is what he has to say in the later discussion, where the issue is given more sustained attention:

> [B]lame consists of … a proleptic invocation of a reason to do or not do a certain thing, which applies in virtue of a disposition to have the respect of other people. To blame someone in this way is, roughly, to tell him he had a reason to act otherwise, and *in a direct sense this may not have been true*. Yet in a way *it has now become true*, in virtue of his having a disposition to do things that people he respects expect of him (1995a: 41–2 – my emphases).

The proleptic mechanism served by blaming practices can conjure reasons into existence: by *pretending* that $A$ has a reason to $\phi$, the moral critic can *make it true* that $A$ has a reason to $\phi$. We get from 'bluff' or an 'optimistic internal reason claim' to actual reasons (1981a: 111). These proleptic considerations are a good fit for the

Motivational Interpretation. If *A* was not motivated to $\phi$ *before* the blaming, but was motivated to $\phi$ *after* the blaming, then we are free to say that *A* lacked a reason to $\phi$ beforehand, but did have a reason to $\phi$ afterwards. Blaming practices have indeed *created* a new reason for *A*. The existence of the new reason is constituted by the inauguration of a new pattern of motivation which *A* now exhibits.

If Williams thinks that it is an advantage of internalism that it can accommodate such proleptic reason-creating mechanisms, then the Motivational Interpretation is perfectly placed to deliver this form of accommodation. The Procedural Interpretation, by contrast, struggles to demonstrate the requisite sensitivity. If blame gives rise to *A*'s $\phi$-ing, then we can ask whether or not *A* already had a reason to $\phi$. If she did, then the blaming exercise is an exercise in reasons recovery: the function of the critic is basically to get *A* to see that she had a reason to $\phi$ all along. If, by contrast, *A* did not previously have a reason for $\phi$-ing, then the blaming exercise must qualify as browbeating, even if we actually then manage to talk *A* into $\phi$-ing. The fact that *A* may be motivated to $\phi$ does not definitively establish that she had any reason to $\phi$. Since Williams plainly wishes to leave open the possibility that the blaming exercise has indeed *created a reason* for *A*, he has to appeal to what *A* is actually motivated to do. This package of commitments is more easily honoured by the Motivational Interpretation.

At this point, however, we must re-enrol the Owen Wingrave case. For the dialectical significance of this case in Williams' original discussion was to expose the externalist as tilting at windmills. If Owen holds out, then the imputation to him of a reason to join the army is revealed to be just bluff. Owen's reasons for action are not the reasons his family would choose for him. But if he caves into family pressure and allows himself to be recruited, then the proleptic mechanism appears to enjoy application here as well: even if he did not have a reason beforehand, he apparently has one now. The fact that he is motivated to join the army reveals that he has gained this reason. The potential problem here is that there is nothing special about *moral* critics in the internalist picture containing the proleptic mechanism. *Anyone* whose respect an agent wishes to gain can thereby generate reasons for that agent. Williams' original discussion suggested something rather different. His point seemed to be that, without something in his S-set to deliberate *from*, Owen's acceptance of a reason to join the army will reflect merely his suggestibility or repose of trust in some authority figure (1981a: 107). As far as they went, these considerations actually counted in favour of internalism by making internalism seem better grounded in the agent's interests. They allowed internalists to register the nuisance value of browbeating, hucksterism and manipulation as sources of distortion in the story of how we come to discover what reasons we have. But the proleptic blame considerations risk reversing confidence on this score. It turns out that *anyone* with a pushy agenda and a persuasive manner will be able to muscle in on the reason-creating action. A morally unscrupulous huckster can earn his promotion into something like a legitimate influencer, if he gets his way. I will call this the *Promiscuous Influence Problem*.

The Promiscuous Influence Problem must be dealt with. Another and more general worry with the Motivational Interpretation consists in its non-alignment with our self-conception as deliberators and practical agents. Williams tells us, in his original discussion, that '[w]hat we can correctly ascribe to [an agent] in a third-personal internal reason statement is also what he can ascribe to himself as a result of deliberation' (1981a: 103). On the Motivational Interpretation, we wait and see whether the agent is motivated before coming to conclusions about her reasons for action. But is that view of her reasons shared by the agent herself? In putting to herself the question whether she has a reason for $\phi$-ing, does this agent *wait and see* whether she will be motivated to $\phi$? This picture seems deeply unsatisfactory, due to the fact that judgments about what reasons an agent has must be reached before those judgments are manifested in action. The degree of passivity apparently implied by the Motivational Interpretation cannot be accepted by any tolerable picture of agency and action. We require no expansively Kantian conception of agency in order to be suspicious of it. It falls at the first hurdle. I will call this the *Agency Problem*.

## VII. Reasons, Self-Understanding, and Non-Enforcement

Where does this leave us? We need to take a step back in order to attend to the fundamental motivations for Williams' internalism, or a reconstructed version of it. This will also permit us to deal, along the way, with the Promiscuous Influence Problem and the Agency Problem.

In a summary statement of his commitments in the later discussion, Williams identifies two motivations for internalism (1995a: 38–40). The first of these concerns the relationship between the explanatory and the normative: Williams' verdict is that internalism integrates these dimensions more convincingly than externalism. The second, related, motivation is that internalism can distinguish between the ascription of reasons to agents and other evaluations we can make about them. We can, for example, describe a man who serially mistreats his spouse as 'ungrateful, inconsiderate, hard, sexist, nasty, selfish, brutal', but without having to ascribe a reason to him, if he proves entirely unresponsive to these entreaties (1981a: 110, 1995a: 39). My view is that we are forced to go beyond these considerations if we want to identify satisfactorily deep commitments for Williams to embrace. For externalists have robust replies to these particular points.

With respect to the first of the motivations, it is still far from clear why externalists are left with nothing to say. An agent comes to see why this reason should carry force with her: nothing stops her from explaining why that is so, and she can intelligently speculate as to why she was previously unresponsive to it. She was initially blocked from seeing the force of the reason, but now she sees it. That is schematic, to be sure, but it is a schema she can do business with. She can fill in the details and arrive at a more lucid view of how she has come to see things more clearly. It is hard, in truth, to see what quarrel Williams can have with this schema. It is a kind of learning curve we are all familiar with. We make mistakes, which we then correct. The details may vary, but the structure is a recognisable one, and should not arouse suspicions as long as not too much is asked of it.

With respect to the second of the motivations, why can't externalists simply say that this man refuses to acknowledge the genuine reasons for improving his behaviour towards his wife – reasons which hold due in good part to these other evaluations which can be aptly made of him?[10] Williams simply does not give us enough to work with here. It is not clear why this man's reasons do not stretch all the way to what we can permissibly enforce in his behaviour, and to reflect what truthful negative appraisals we can make about him.

To remedy these lacunae, I will conclude this chapter by advancing a couple of thoughts. These go beyond anything Williams explicitly says, but I offer them in a constructive spirit. My hope is that Williams might have welcomed them as a way of making sense of his various commitments, even if they did not occur to him in the exact forms I am declaring here.[11]

What value is gained by keeping reasons ascriptions separate from these 'aretaic' evaluations or morally loaded descriptions (nasty, selfish, brutal, etc.)? There are two sides to the story. One part of it turns on the reflexive nature of agency and our practical lives. I will call this first line of thought the *Self-Understanding Thesis*. Reasons are what we can ascribe to ourselves: we will cite them in explanation of our conduct. They also contribute to our self-understanding. To do that, they need to be intelligible to us, and they will usually be intelligible to us if they serve to promote in some way the myriad of concerns and interests we have already accumulated. But in order to truly *own* these reasons, we also have to put them into operation, at least sometimes. We have to see what difference they make to us when their pursuit is fully incorporated into our lives, and our other cares and commitments are made to adjust to them. The connections to our concerns and interests will help to make our motivational attunement to them intelligible to us, but if these connections do not transpire in actual motivation, their significance to our self-understanding will be typically blunted.

Now we do not have to wait and see *whether* we are motivated, when we are deliberating – but we do know that *being* motivated will make a difference to the significance of this consideration in our lives. If we are motivationally unwilling to respond to a consideration, then we will have less self-knowledge. That point can be made without betraying the basic character of our agency. It is not being denied that, when we act intentionally, we *decide* what to do; we do not *wait and see* what we will do. Thus this picture is committed to no gross violation of our common ideas about agency. This heads off the Agency Problem.

[10] See Scanlon (1998: 363–73), for an illuminating discussion.
[11] But see Williams (1981b) for possible points of connection.

However, an echo of the Agency Problem still persists. For in deciding what to do, we may be committing ourselves to a course of action which establishes a reason for us to act in this way. Is there an element of bootstrapping about all of this? A reflective agent who is worried about what she should do does not want to be told that whatever she decides to do will turn out to be correct, because reasons are settled by motivation. She wants to be motivated by her reasons; she does not want her reasons to be determined by her motivations. The practical phenomenology places reasons before motivation, but the motivational interpretation of reasons internalism inverts this conceptual ordering.

This worry can be assuaged. The particular bullet to bite with respect to the Motivational Interpretation is that motives do help to establish an agent's reasons. But there is no commitment here to any worryingly imperious form of *infallibility*. The agent might have taken a different course, and responded to other considerations available to her. Perhaps her life would in some ways have been better had she embarked on this other course, even if the antecedent procedural connections would have been satisfied either way. She need not lose interest in *the reasons she might have had*, even if she establishes through her actions *the reasons she has*. In establishing the reasons she has, she comes to own them, but she also has to live with them. Agents' regrets, or at least agents' what-ifs, are not ruled out.[12]

A further advantage of the Self-Understanding Thesis, as I see it – though perhaps Williams himself might give this point only qualified support – lies in its implication that morality does not need our acknowledgement of its authority for it to enjoy enforceable authority over us. But this does mean, according to the Self-Understanding Thesis, that it may not always be *our* reasons which morality is enforcing.

The Self-Understanding Thesis may also help to explain why Williams insists on only partial idealisation: once the agent has adequate information, we wait and see what she does next, and that is going to teach us something about her. Imagine, in a variant of *Petrol* (*Petrol 2*), that Sarah is informed that the glass contains petrol and tonic (unlike *Petrol*), but she still goes ahead and drinks the liquid (like *Petrol*). The Motivational Interpretation, unlike the Procedural Interpretation, will have to register Sarah's response in *Petrol 2* as a reason for her, since she has already satisfied the relevant idealising constraints. There is definitely a bullet to bite in *Petrol 2*, but it will be easier for the Motivational Interpretation to bite it if we can discern internalists' larger purpose of waiting to see what agents do in figuring out what reasons they have. When Sarah reacts in this way, and accepts the implications of her action, and where she is not merely uninformed about factual matters, she takes a view about the relevance of what she cares about, and gives it a new twist. We may worry about these hostages to fortune, but I think Williams will

[12] There are echoes here of Williams' treatment of agent-regret and moral luck: see Williams 1981c. For a detailed examination of the main line of argument in this other famous and elusive essay from this period of Williams's career, see Lang 2021: Ch 5.

be less perturbed. This, for him, is what taking agents seriously requires.[13] They have their reasons, even if these are not always the reasons we think they should acknowledge. For these agents have their foibles and idiosyncrasies, too. Another inconvenient truth may be that, in discovering what these reasons are, we are indeed open to all sorts of influences. Advice does not have to pass through a prior critical filter, whereby only morally respectable critics are entitled to advise us, with everyone else being discounted. We are indeed open to all-comers. Morality simply has to take its place in the cultural queue, though most of us will hope that it can make its points vividly and persuasively against its counter-moral competitors. This deals with – perhaps by simply biting the bullet on – the Promiscuous Influence Problem.

The same goes for Owen Wingrave. If he caves in to family pressure and joins the army, then he may have gained a reason to do so. If he holds out, then he may also tell himself that he had no reason not to hold out. I do not think Williams has any principled reason for rejecting these implications, even if it exposes his dependence on the Wingrave case in pursuing his quarrel with externalism in the original article as strategically unwise.

Self-understanding is only one part of this story. I shall call the second line of thought the *Non-Enforcement Thesis*, and it is particularly concerned with the status of the recalcitrant husband.[14] In any mature social morality, we need to stand in relations of answerability to other moral agents. Reasons stand at the centre of these interpersonal relationships. The moral community that houses each of us has to achieve some form of equilibrium between the reasons that we ascribe to ourselves and the reasons that others impute to us. Entreaties that fall upon deaf ears, such as the reprimands we make to the brutal husband, may be considered to be *failed* reason ascriptions if they do not, in fact, make any difference to what these agents are voluntarily motivated to do. Reasons, on this line of thought, serve in a functional role: they form part of the common critical currency that can, without violence or physical coercion or unwilled enforcement, inspire agents to act in the way we think they should. This functional characterisation of reasons can help to explain why their actual efficacy in exercises in advice or condemnation is relevant to their classification *as* reasons.

The Non-Enforcement Thesis tells us that, if we cannot persuade the brutal husband to treat his wife better, then we should withdraw the view that he has a reason to do so. In this case, the ascription to him of a reason has failed the basic test of interpersonal efficacy. And that test of interpersonal efficacy is worth being on the books, because most elements of our moral lives need to unfold without

[13] Does this mean that, according to this conception of the internalist view, it would be wrong to prevent Sarah from drinking the petrol and tonic? That is less clear. We may continue to think that her conclusions are fragile, and that she could be persuaded to change her mind with just a little more reflection. We may think, with warrant, that she may thank us afterwards, and that her retrospective endorsement of our intervention also serves to justify it.

[14] For some other suggestive work in this broad vicinity, see Isserow 2023; Manne 2014; and Woods 2019.

active enforcement. We have to keep on the right side of morality out of voluntary commitment or personal discipline. There are not enough enforcers to go round – at the very least, there is only so much active third-party enforcement we can all put up with if we are going to have a tolerably non-claustrophobic social morality.

Even given the Non-Enforcement Thesis, other critical resources are still available to us: we can continue to *describe* the brutal husband in these ways, and we can protect other people's interests. We may be entitled to intervene on behalf of his wife. We can advise her to leave him. We can perhaps prevent him from going anywhere near her. But the alignment between these other critical resources and this agent's *reasons*, in particular, has to be achieved by something more: something that represents the outcome of a process in which we make our case to him and then he makes his response. If we have our say and he proves recalcitrant, then little is achieved by continuing to insist that he still has *his own reasons* for doing what we are beseeching or indeed forcing him to do. We should concede instead that this particular device of interpersonal interaction has failed in its deployment. We might still be within our rights to enforce his compliance with his moral obligations, but we should probably stop pretending that we will be enforcing what he would also accept, if only he would open his eyes, to be his own reasons. He has failed that test. These standards are simply not internalised in him to an adequate degree. We cannot count on him to implement them in his ordinary dealings in a robust way.

Even if *we* have our reasons to get the brutal husband to act in a morally better way, it may not be determinately the case that *he* has the same reasons. This is an odd juxtaposition, to be sure. Externalists will be suspicious of it. But I think Williams could live with it. His arguments point to it, or at least – in that characteristic Williamsian way – circle it. It makes sense of what he says, of what he half-says, and of what he leaves unsaid.

## Bibliography

Isserow, J (2023) 'Naturalizing Moral Naturalism', 25 3 *Journal of Ethics and Social Philosophy* 608.

Korsgaard, CM (1996) *The Sources of Normativity* (Cambridge, Cambridge University Press).

—— (1986) 'Skepticism about Practical Reason' 83 1 *Journal of Philosophy* 5.

Lang, G (2021) *Strokes of Luck: A Study in Moral and Political Philosophy* (Oxford, Oxford University Press).

Manne, K (2014) 'Internalism about Reasons: Sad But True?' 167 1 *Philosophical Studies* 89.

McDowell, J (1995) 'Might There be External Reasons?' in JEJ Altham & R Harrison (eds), *Ethics, Mind and World: Essays on the Ethical Philosophy of Bernard Williams* (Cambridge, Cambridge University Press).

Scanlon, TM (1998) *What We Owe to Each Other* (London, Harvard University Press).

Williams, B (1981a) 'Internal and External Reasons' in B Williams, *Moral Luck* (Cambridge, Cambridge University Press).
—— (1981b) 'Persons, Character, and Morality' in B Williams, *Moral Luck* (Cambridge, Cambridge University Press).
—— (1981c) 'Moral Luck' in B Williams, *Moral Luck* (Cambridge, Cambridge University Press).
—— (1995a) 'Internal Reasons and the Obscurity of Blame' in B Williams, *Making Sense of Humanity* (Cambridge, Cambridge University Press).
—— (1995b) 'Replies' in JEJ Altham & R Harrison (eds), *Ethics, Mind and World: Essays on the Ethical Philosophy of Bernard Williams* (Cambridge, Cambridge University Press).
Woods, J (2019) 'Footing the Cost (of Normative Subjectivism)' in J Suikkanen & A Kauppinen (eds), *Methodology and Moral Philosophy* (Oxon, Routledge).

# 4

# Taking the Edge Off Professional Ethical Dilemmas

EMMANUEL VOYIAKIS*

## I. Introduction

In 'Professional Morality and its Dispositions', Bernard Williams explores situations of conflict between ordinary or everyday morality, on the one hand, and 'professional' morality, on the other (Williams 2010: 192). The idea of professional morality, as he understands it, comprises ethical norms developed and applied within particular professions, such as that of a lawyer, a priest, or a police officer. His working premise is that sometimes professional morality will allow and occasionally even require a person to perform an act which a non-professional would regard as morally distasteful, e.g. a lawyer issuing speculative legal threats towards weaker parties, prying into the private life of a witness, failing to disclose the truth about the client's crimes or intentions, or playing all sorts of hardball with legal process. Williams believes that some of these conflicts are real, and that we cannot smooth them over by appealing to the fact that the profession itself is morally justified (e.g. by saying that if the profession itself is just, then acts carried out in compliance with the rules of the profession will be just too),[1] or that professional and ordinary morality address different acts (or acts 'under a different description') (Anscombe 1957: §26). In his view, such attempts to defuse or eliminate the relevant conflicts are 'casuistic' because they pay little heed to the psychological realities of a person's exposure to both sets of moral norms (Williams 2010: 196–97).

Williams then invites us to think about conflicts between ordinary and professional morality by focusing less on which decisions we would want professionals to reach in particular situations and more on which *dispositions* we would want them to have when deciding. He discusses three generic profiles of such dispositions

* I am grateful to the editors and to conference participants for their useful comments on an earlier draft and the presentation out of which this chapter grew, with particular thanks to David Owen and Matthieu Queloz, and to my colleague Jacco Bomhoff.

[1] See references below at n 17 at seq. in relation to the 'standard conception' of the legal advocate.

(2010: 194–95). The first involves 'specific professional adaptation' and describes professionals who have become disposed to regard certain professional acts (e.g. overly aggressive cross-examination, or the withholding of crucial information from the court) as morally justified, and in consequence have lost the countervailing ordinary moral dispositions. The second profile, which Williams leaves nameless but which might be called 'tortured co-existence', fits those professionals who feel perpetually torn between the demands of ordinary and professional morality and therefore remain conflicted about the justification of the professional acts that ordinary morality judges to be problematic. The third profile is 'non-specific professional adaptation' and fits professionals who have become disposed to believe that *every* act allowed or required by their profession is justified, and have lost all of the countervailing ordinary dispositions.

Williams considers several problems with the first and third options and settles on the second as the most promising. The punchline of his discussion is that, as a society, we should aim to create the kind of professional who is disposed to hesitate and struggle when confronted with a real ethical conflict. He thinks that this plan has several related benefits when applied to legal professionals:

> [O]ne can see quite a few reasons why some conflict, qualms, and moral unease might be usefully encouraged – or perhaps merely left – by a legal education. An education that properly allows for such things, and not just in the spirit of the padre's hour, will straightforwardly encourage lawyers to question the reality of what they are doing and to ask whether certain practices that cause suffering or (in at least an extra-legal sense) injustice are necessary. It will help them to ask how in detail the justifying arguments for the profession as a whole apply to this or that practice. It will provide some antibodies against absorbing a mystifying conception of the dignity of the profession. It will neutralize some of the mechanisms of self-deception, and so not only increase the human appeal of lawyers, but perform a social service, since lawyers are often powerful people with a strong interest in success, and it is a good idea that their self-image should leave them with inhibitions about how their armoury is being deployed (Williams 2010: 199).[2]

Williams does not use the language of 'roles' and 'role-related obligations', but the three profiles that he sketches and the conclusions that he reaches could be easily re-described as three alternative conceptions of the relevant professional roles and their relation to the demands of a person's non-professional identities.[3] For my present purposes, the similarity between disposition-focused and role-focused descriptions matters more than their points of divergence, so I will assume that these are different ways of climbing the same mountain.

[2] Or, in the beautifully succinct way that Williams has put it elsewhere: 'a habit of reluctance is an essential obstacle against the happy acceptance of the intolerable' (1981a: 63).

[3] See, e.g., Fried 1976: 1060. Williams (1981b) discusses Fried's account at 63–64 and remains unconvinced by Fried's analogy between lawyering and friendship, largely because one is not paid to be another person's friend. David Luban has voiced more general doubts about whether legal ethics is best understood as role-related; see 1986: 667. For a classic statement of role obligations, see Bradley 1876/2012: 145.

One could query several aspects of the way Williams describes the ethical quandary he wants to explore. Utilitarians and other ethical monists will insist that conflicts between ordinary and professional morality are more apparent than real and that, once we have attended carefully to the weights of the respective ethical considerations, those conflicts will disappear.[4] Those that Isiah Berlin described as 'hedgehogs' will take a broadly similar view.[5] They will point out that 'foxes' like Williams are too ready to diagnose ethical conflict, and miss the extensive potential of reaching a reflective equilibrium between our considered ethical intuitions, including those that come from different roles or aspects of our ethical life.[6] General ethical theory aside, one could also raise objections at the level of first-order judgement. An obvious possibility is to deny that professional practices create genuine ethical norms in the first place. For example, Arthur Applbaum has defended a 'practice positivist' account according to which professional norms, and role requirements more generally, could simply not 'mint moral permissions to do what otherwise would be morally prohibited' (Applbaum 1999: 3, 45 ff). On that account, professional rules are no different from the rules of a game, and have no greater power to justify exceptions from what ordinary morality requires or allows. Another possibility is to question whether the considerations that run against the grain of ordinary morality are best described as a *professional* morality. Robert Cover's study on judicial attitudes towards the United States Fugitive Slave Acts of 1793 and 1850 provides a case in point (Cover 1984: 226 ff). Judges conflicted between their ordinary moral duty not to return a person to slavery and their institutional duty to abide by legislative Acts that required them to do so ended up adopting very different attitudes towards that divergence, each attitude casting their ethical dilemma in a different light. Some judges chose to retreat into what Cover describes as 'mechanistic jurisprudence', but others treated the dilemma as a conflict between ordinary morality and the rule of law, or as a problem about the separation of powers between the legislature and the judiciary. The first of those attitudes seems a close match for the profiles of 'adaptation' that Williams discusses and rejects. The other two are harder to construe in the same way, as the norms that pull against the demands of ordinary morality, namely the norms of the rule of law and the separation of powers, are not obviously specific to the legal profession. A lay citizen could feel their weight just as much as a legal professional in deciding what to do, e.g. which party to vote for, which civil society initiatives and organisation to join or oppose, and so on.[7]

[4] See, e.g., Hare 1972: 168–69.

[5] Berlin 1957: 7, describing 'a great chasm between those who relate everything to a single central vision, one system more or less coherent or articulate, or a single, universal, organizing principle' (the 'hedgehogs') and those 'who pursue many ends, often unrelated and even contradictory, connected, if at all, only in some de facto way and not in accordance with some general organizing idea' (the 'foxes'). For a discussion of the different philosophical uses of Berlin's metaphor, see Lukes 2001: 43.

[6] See, e.g., Dworkin 2001: 73.

[7] Another way to put the point is to say that laypersons too can function as officials in respect of their role as citizens.

I have some sympathy for these objections, but for present purposes I will assume that none of them is fatal to the way Williams sets up the ethical problem. More specifically, I will grant that the conflicts that Williams describes are genuine, and that attempts to find a reflective equilibrium between the competing ordinary and professional moral intuitions will not always alleviate the ethical pressures experienced by the professionals exposed to that conflict.[8]

The aspect of Williams' argument that I want to explore concerns the specific profile of professional that he thinks we ought to favour and promote, and which I have dubbed 'tortured co-existence'. To express the point in somewhat paradoxical terms, Williams argues that we should be aiming to create professionals comfortable with experiencing genuine ethical discomfort when their professional ethical commitments and ordinary morality diverge. It follows that, depending how often they have to deal with ethical conflict, and on the nature of the competing ordinary and professional duties, lawyers who fit that profile may be ethically required to experience significant amounts of regret in their practice.

I am willing to grant that designing legal education so as to produce lawyers who have this disposition is likely to yield the social and individual benefits that Williams lists. His conclusions in that regard certainly seem to dovetail with Bernardo Zacka's seminar account of the relation between bureaucratic functions and moral agency. Whereas Williams thinks that habituating professionals to ethical conflict in hard cases is desirable insofar as it can dispose them to reach better decisions in easier cases, Zacka places more emphasis on the fact that sensitising bureaucrats to conflicts between their professional and their ordinary moral duties allows those persons to 'own' their ethical responses reflectively, and therefore reduces the risk that they may become alienated from their work.[9]

At the same time, I believe that Williams and Zacka do not take sufficient account of the costs that their preferred profiles entail for the ethical life of the professionals in question. My guiding intuition is that there is only so much ethical pressure that we may legitimately aim to put a person under.[10] Sometimes the cost of experiencing such pressure will be high enough that a person may reasonably require our institutions to put in place systems and structures that alleviate rather than heighten the relevant ethical dilemmas and their significance for that person's agency. Applied to the present topic, this thought suggests that sometimes we owe it to professionals to take the edge off conflicts between ordinary and professional morality. Using legal advocacy as an illustration, I pursue that intuition by

[8] Williams 1981b: 74–75, pointing out that seeing those conflicts as apparent would be 'to misplace the source of the agent's trouble, *in suggesting that what is wrong is his thought about the moral situation*, whereas what is wrong lies in his situation itself … In this, as elsewhere in these areas, … theory has to be responsive to what a reflective agent feels he needs to say' (emphasis added).

[9] Zacka 2017: 225: 'Instead of increasing what is at stake in the options that are available to the agent, one can increase how much a choice between these options means to the agent'. To cut through to the problem of conflict, Williams assumes that the alienation problem will not arise (2010: 195).

[10] In previous work, I have argued that our intuitions about what we are responsible for as individuals have no priority over our intuitions about a fair division of moral labour between us and our institutions, see Voyiakis 2021: 283–85.

distinguishing between different profiles of legal professionals according to the costs that each of them faces when processing conflicts between ordinary and professional morality. My main contention is that our thoughts about the ideal disposition of a legal professional should be sensitive to the variety of those costs. To illustrate what such sensitivity might amount to, I use an example of a rule that aims to deal with the risk of conflict between ordinary and professional morality by taking certain ethical dilemmas out of a legal professional's hands: the 'cab rank' rule for barristers.

My discussion proceeds in two steps. Section II tries to situate within legal ethics certain questions about the degree of protection that legal professionals might reasonably demand against the various cognitive and psychological costs of processing ethical conflict – I call these collectively 'internal' costs. It then lays out two pairs of different profiles of legal professional, ordered by the severity of internal costs that each faces, and outlines a general account of the various complaints that persons occupying those profiles might have against Williams' preferred approach. Section III turns to the cab rank rule for barristers and discusses whether we should regard it as a promising strategy for lowering such internal costs.

## II. Ethical Conflicts and their Costs

Williams approaches the issue of conflict between ordinary and professional morality from a collective point of view. He asks what sort of person we, as a society, would want a lawyer to be and which dispositions to have. That question is obviously important when we think about legal education and professional training, but it is not the only question we should raise. We should also ask how much ethical labour we can reasonably demand of legal professionals who may be exposed to hard conflicts between the demands of ordinary and professional morality, and what we might owe to such professionals in return.

This question seems to me a natural, if underexplored, counterpart to the central debate about the merits and limitations of what Bradley Wendel has called the 'standard conception' of legal ethics. According to that conception, a lawyer ought to be partisan to their client, neutral as to the appraisal of their client's person and actions, and non-accountable for the legal outcomes that they help secure for them (Postema 1980: 63; Wendel 2011: 548).[11] There is no mystery about why legal ethicists have tended to focus on the ethical duties that lawyers owe, rather than

[11] For a critical summary of different justifications of the standard conception, see Herring 2023: 167–76. For a classic statement of that conception see Lord Brougham's defence of Queen Caroline against the charge of adultery: 'An advocate, by the sacred duty which he owes his client, knows, in the discharge of that office, but one person in the world, that client and none other. To save the client by all expedient means to protect that client at all hazards and costs to all others, and amongst others to himself-is the highest and most unquestioned of his duties; and he must not regard the alarm, the suffering, the torment, the destruction, which he may bring upon any other', *Proceedings in the House of Lords* (1820) 7.

on the ethical duties that we, and our institutions, might owe to them in return. Both defenders and opponents of the standard conception see legal professionals as persons invested with considerable institutional *power*, the exercise of which has a serious impact not only on particular individuals but also on the fabric of social relations. Debates over the standard conception are, in that sense, debates about ethical limits in the use of that power.[12]

There are several indications that Williams takes that view. The passage I quoted in the Introduction notes not only that legal professional practices can 'cause suffering or (in at least an extra-legal sense) injustice', but also that 'lawyers are often powerful people' who ought to have certain 'inhibitions about how their armoury is being deployed' (Williams 2010: 199). An even clearer indication of how Williams associates the legal profession with the exercise of power comes from his essay on 'Politics and Moral Character'. In that essay, Williams puts forward an account of the ethical disposition that politicians, the paradigm of persons endowed with institutional power, ought to have. To get that discussion going, he draws a rather close analogy between the position of politicians and the position of legal professionals under a conception that is more or less a restatement of the standard conception of legal ethics (Williams 1981b: 64–65).[13] The analogy makes sense precisely because both legal professionals and politicians enjoy considerable institutional power.[14]

Seeing legal ethics as a constraint on institutional power also suggests an explanation for why the notion of 'professional morality' tends to be associated with professions such as that of lawyers, doctors, religious, military or police officers. Those professions are not distinguished simply by the fact that their codes of conduct sometimes demand or allow actions that ordinary morality regards as objectionable or odious. Helpline staff, security guards, cleaners, salespersons and countless other categories or professionals, both in the public and the private sector, encounter similar conflicts in their practice, and for broadly similar reasons. The differentiating factor seems to be institutional power coupled with better conditions for deliberation. Compared to those other professions, lawyers or doctors enjoy not only a greater degree of discretion in the discharge of their institutional tasks and duties, but also comparatively more favourable material conditions for giving deep and extensive consideration to ethical questions about its proper exercise. That is why 'you didn't

[12] See, e.g., Dare 2004: 25, who defends the standard conception by noting that the expertise of lawyers entails that 'they are better placed than any other group of citizens to work in, and with, our legal and political institutions. The principle of neutrality recognises this power and its potential for abuse. It guards against the possibility that someone might be denied rights allocated by a legal system because its lawyers find those rights or their allocation to that person morally objectionable'. For a defence of the standard conception as a requirement of democratic pluralism, see Markovits 2008.

[13] Williams formulates that conception as follows: '(1) In any complex society (at least) the enforcement of some legal rights involves morally disagreeable acts; (2) It is bad that legal rights which exist should not be enforceable; (3) Enforcement of many rights of the kind mentioned in (1) requires lawyers; (4) Any lawyer really effective in enforcing those rights must be fairly horrible; ergo (5) It is good that some lawyers are fairly horrible'.

[14] The main difference Williams finds between politician and legal professionals is that the institutional powers of the latter are more clearly circumscribed (1981b: 65–66).

need to make that decision', or 'you did not need to take that case', or 'you should not have raised that particular argument' or 'you could have reflected on the matter more deeply' sound more plausible as ethical admonitions to a lawyer or to a doctor than they do to members of those other professions.

At the same time, the view of legal ethics as a constraint on the use of institutional power should not blind us to the costs that legal professionals can face when exposed to ethical conflict. The most obvious such costs are social or *reputational*. For example, the fact that a lawyer represents an odious litigant can sometimes be used to cast the lawyer in a very poor light, especially when their choices and other practical decisions in the course of litigation become exposed to public scrutiny and debate in professional circles or social media. Lord Neuberger had such costs in mind when he described the 'cab rank' rule for barristers as a device that does not simply aim to guarantee competent legal representation for unpopular litigations but also to protect lawyers against criticism:

> The requirement that a properly qualified advocate cannot refuse instructions presented on the basis of a reasonable fee to represent an individual in court is the means by which we guarantee robust and independent representation for all, even those accused of the most heinous crimes. *It protects the lawyer from adverse influence, from public opinion, from improper pressure from the media or the State itself* (Neuberger 2013 – emphasis added).

I believe that the case for giving legal professionals, regardless of their specialisation (barristers, solicitors or other legal officials), a measure of protection against social or reputational costs is relatively uncontroversial. I want to focus instead on what I will call the *internal* costs of dealing with ethical conflict. These costs can be both cognitive (i.e. related to the difficulty of reaching the correct ethical decision in the circumstances) and psychological. To get a better view of the character and variety of those internal costs, and the degree to which legal professionals may require a measure of institutional protection against them, I would like to canvass four different professional profiles, arranged in pairs according to their dispositions towards ethical conflict. I will assume that all four profiles meet the basic requirements of Williams's account, i.e. that they describe persons with a measure of institutional power who are disposed to regard situations of conflict between professional and ordinary morality as occasions that require serious ethical introspection and may sometimes not admit of an ethically satisfactory answer. Moreover, while some of those dispositions may be problematic, I will assume that none of them is obviously pathological, in the basic sense that none of them has features that clearly would not belong in the description of a decent ethical agent. Finally, I will make no assumptions as to whether the dispositions in question reflect general ethical traits of the persons involved or adaptive responses to the specific nature and challenges of professional legal work.[15]

[15] Zacka (2017: 66 ff) distinguishes three profiles of street-level bureaucrats (the indifferent; the caregiver; and the enforcer), and treats them all as (pathological) adaptive responses to the pressures of bureaucratic systems.

Consider, then, the following profiles of legal professional:

- The *skilful ethicist* does not relish the prospect of negotiating ethical conflicts, but they take themselves to be good at imagining and empathising with the perspectives of different persons whose interests are at stake, and with identifying ethically material differences between alternative scenarios and courses of action.
- The *overthinker* is committed to grasping the ethical nettle and to expending considerable time and energy to work out the appropriate course of action. However, they are reluctant to trust their own ethical intuitions and their circumspection sometimes leads them to raise the alarm for potential ethical conflicts where their more experienced peers see none. This spiral of self-doubt further undermines their confidence in their intuitions.
- The *blasé lawyer* displays neither of the above dispositions. They see all ethical conflict, including conflict between norms of ordinary morality, as an annoyance and try to handle it as best they can without expending too much energy on it. Whenever possible, they will deflect hard ethical questions to another professional or agency.
- The *squeamish lawyer* finds hard ethical conflicts psychologically taxing. They consider themselves capable of appreciating the force of the competing ethical considerations, but they are tortured by the fact that in some cases they will end up doing wrong no matter what they do. This takes a toll on their sense of self-worth and their relations with fellow professionals and clients.

Professionals who fit the first two profiles will generally be psychologically more comfortable with ethical conflict. The skilful ethicist comes closest to the ideal disposition that Williams describes. Their internal costs will therefore tend to be low, at least as long as their cognitive ability is not severely tested (I return to this possibility in the next section). Overthinkers are a less straightforward case, inasmuch as their self-doubt sometimes leads them to detect or suspect ethical conflicts where there are none. Persons who fit that profile lie at the other end of the spectrum that Williams describes, so it is no surprise that his discussion does not raise any special concerns about them. But while those persons are not cutting ethical corners and would not appear to run the risk of tolerating great injustice in easier cases, the cognitive overload that they experience in the face of ethical conflict still seems problematic. Being preoccupied with hard cases, the overthinker risks losing ethical grip on what constitutes an easy case.

The second pair of profiles is interesting for different reasons. The third is a fair match for the profile of general or 'non-specific' professional adaptation that Williams discusses. Its problematic aspect is that blasé legal professionals are disposed to bat away conflicts between ordinary and professional morality and are therefore much more at risk of ignoring intolerable injustices committed right before their eyes. The fourth, which Williams does not contemplate, raises similar issues from the opposite direction. The squeamish professional is already sensitised to ethical conflict. The problem from their point of view is that processing such conflicts takes a serious psychological toll on them.

The variety of these internal costs obviously matters to the extent that it tracks the variety of ways in which a person's professional disposition can fall short of a given ideal. But I believe that it also has moral significance, i.e. that it bears on what we and our institutions may require of such professionals, and what we owe to them in return. That is particularly obvious in respect of the two profiles that struggle with ethical conflict: the overthinkers, who struggle cognitively, and the squeamish, who struggle psychologically. The former profile invites questions about how far our institutions might be required to help overthinkers focus their ethical energies on the right sort of case, or at least protect them against the downward spiral of self-doubt. The latter invites questions about how far squeamish legal professionals could reasonably require our institutions to make their ethical life less psychologically taxing. But the point could be plausibly extended to the other two profiles as well. There is a limit both to how much sensitising our institutions may legitimately require blasé lawyers to undergo, and to how much ethical labour we may reasonably require skilful ethicists to undertake. I will not try to offer a general account of where exactly those limits lie, though I will make some concrete suggestions in the next section. My point is that unless we acknowledge the existence of such limits, and try to design professional work with them in mind, we risk locating the ethical problem in the wrong place, by presenting what is an institutional or collective failing as a personal ethical shortcoming.[16]

The challenge, then, is to hold onto two thoughts at the same time. On the one hand, we must attend to Williams' insight that the refusal to deal with situations of conflict can lead professionals to lose sensitivity to ethical concerns in easy cases, just like not training a muscle can cause it to stiffen and atrophy. On the other hand, we must attend to the variety of costs for legal professionals of dealing with ethical conflicts, and consider different ways in which our institutions might be able to reduce those costs. It seems to me that an appropriate way to register and process those two concerns is to ask whether persons that fit one or the other of the profiles I have outlined could reasonably *object* to arrangements of professional legal work that leave them exposed to serious conflicts between their ordinary and their professional ethical duties.[17] Since the profiles differ, we should expect the content and the force of relevant objections to vary accordingly.

The objections of those persons to particular ways of designing professional legal work will not, as a general matter, be defeated because it is generally desirable, for the reasons Williams gives, that lawyers should face certain ethical conflicts head on. While ethical skills are intrinsically connected to our agency in a way that some other professional skills may not be, a person may have a duty to grasp the ethical

[16] See Voyiakis 2021: 284, cautioning against 'the impulse to regard ourselves as responsible' for the harmful outcomes of our conduct 'as a ground to reverse-engineer a virtue out of the absence of institutional alternatives for dealing with those outcomes'.

[17] For variations of this contractualist approach, see Darwall 2009; Scanlon 1998.

nettle and still be entitled to a measure of protection against the costs that doing so would involve for them. Similarly, the relevant objections will not be defeated by the fact that this person will typically have made a free and voluntary choice of professional occupation. Having a choice of professional orientation may sometimes affect the range of objections that a person can raise against particular features of the profession of their choice. Furthermore, a professional cannot reasonably demand total protection against internal costs. Just as firefighters cannot object to having to become involved in emergencies, surgeons cannot object to having to see blood when operating, and criminal lawyers cannot object to being exposed to graphic and gruesome detail of alleged crimes, none of those kinds of professionals can object to being required to process at least *some* ethical conflicts. At the same time, the availability of choice in that regard does not amount to a general forfeiture of complaints against the way professional work is designed, or the conditions under which legal professionals are called upon to grapple with difficult ethical dilemmas. One can reasonably want a job, even a job that involves the exercise of institutional power, and still raise legitimate complaints about the job specification. To flip the familiar saying on its head, if you cannot stand the heat in the kitchen, maybe we should open a window, or turn on the air-conditioning.

The next section explores how far this idea could function as a general justification for institutional measures that aim to take certain decisions out of the hands of legal professionals. The more specific question it raises is whether such measures could find an acceptable balance between Williams' insight about the importance of confronting ethical conflict, on the one hand, and protecting certain profiles of professional against internal costs that they can reasonably believe they are not well-placed to meet, on the other.

## III. The 'Cab Rank' Rule as Protection against Internal Costs

In March 2023, a group of UK-based lawyers concerned about global inaction in the face of rapid and catastrophic climate change issued a Declaration titled 'Lawyers Are Responsible'. In that Declaration, they pledge that they will withhold their professional services in respect of legal work that aims to support new fossil fuel projects, or action against climate protesters exercising their democratic right of peaceful protest.[18] In an accompanying statement, they write:

> The signatories to the declaration are convinced that at the present time offering their services in support of new fossil fuel projects or action against peaceful climate protesters would not serve the greater good. At present, our laws cause climate injustice and set society on a course with consequences so dire that they ultimately threaten the Rule

[18] The Declaration is available at www.lar.earth.

> of Law itself. By taking on these types of case, the signatories are of the view that they would be personally facilitating these consequences.[19]

The authors of the Declaration also note that the conflict between 'what their individual consciences tell them is the right course of action and the rules of their profession' is particularly sharp in relation to barristerial work. The most directly relevant professional rule, applicable to barristers practising in England and Wales, is the so-called 'cab rank' rule. The Bar Standards Board articulates the rule as follows:

> If you receive instructions from a professional client, and you are:
>
> 1. a self-employed barrister instructed by a professional client;
>
> ...
>
> and the instructions are appropriate taking into account the experience, seniority and/or field of practice of yourself or (as appropriate) of the named authorised individual you must ... accept the instructions addressed specifically to you, irrespective of:
>
> a. the identity of the client;
> b. the nature of the case to which the instructions relate;
> c. whether the client is paying privately or is publicly funded; and
> d. any belief or opinion which you may have formed as to the character, reputation, cause, conduct, guilt or innocence of the client.[20]

I reproduce most of the text of the rule in order to illustrate the extent of the ethical conflict as perceived by signatories to the Declaration. In fact, the signatories' reasons for refusing to act for litigants that support fossil fuel projects, or action against climate protesters, appeal to more or less every single one of the considerations that the Rule c29.1(a)-(d) explicitly excludes.

As discussed above, the dominant justification for this restriction in the range of reasons that a barrister can take into account in deciding whether to accept a brief, namely that this ensures competent legal representation for unpopular litigants.[21] The soundness of this justification is not without its critics. While professional legal bodies have so far stood firm behind the rule as a requirement of justice,[22]

[19] Available at www.lar.earth/press/statement-in-response-to-media-coverage.

[20] Bar Standards Board (BSB) Handbook, Rule c29. Rule c30 lists a number of exceptions from the relevant duty, none of which are relevant to my present concern.

[21] See, e.g., *Medcalf v Mardel* [2003] 1 AC 120 per Lord Hobhouse at [51], calling the rule a 'constitutional safeguard' of the independent advocate's duty to secure justice. Or, as Thomas Erskine put it: 'If the advocate refuses to defend, from what he may think of the charge or of the defence, he assumes the character of the Judge; nay, he assumes it before the hour of judgement', *R v Paine* (1792) 22 State Trials 357, 412.

[22] See, e.g., Statement by the Four Bars (England and Wales, Ireland, Northern Ireland, and Scotland), calling the rule 'a bedrock obligation for the independent referral Bar'. See also the Statement by the Chair of the Bar Council, Nick Vineall KC, in response to the Declaration: 'I would be profoundly unhappy if a climate change activist accused of a public order offence were ever to be precluded from obtaining the services of the barrister of their choice because their chosen barrister happened to disapprove of the particular way in which they had been protesting'.

several commentators regard it as outdated, as it applies only to barristers and in respect of only part of their work,[23] and unnecessary, as the idea that legal professionals should not be identified with their clients and their causes is adequately reflected in other professional norms.[24]

I will leave aside whether the cab rank rule could be justified as a requirement of justice towards litigants.[25] I want to focus instead on whether the rule, or at least some version of it, can be justified as protecting legal professionals against the internal costs of dealing with ethical conflict. As discussed in the previous section, I will approach that question by asking whether professionals occupying the different profiles I have described could reasonably object to the rule's central requirement that a barrister not take account of the client's identity, character, source of funding, or the nature of their cause in deciding whether to accept a brief.[26]

Blasé lawyers would obviously welcome this requirement. The distinguishing feature of that profile is that professionals who fit it see ethical conflict as an annoyance and are keen to deflect its resolution. The cab rank rule delivers handsomely for them on that score, as it asks blasé barristers not to take account of several considerations that ordinary morality deems to be ethically significant.

At first blush, the position of overthinkers and squeamish lawyers looks similar. The exclusion of those considerations promises to help overthinkers avoid getting lost in the thicket of ethical considerations, and to protect the squeamish against the psychological burden of having to negotiate the relevant ethical conflicts. The idea is that the rule turns a complex ethical question into a simpler one, namely whether overthinkers and squeamish lawyers have sufficient reason to believe that following the rules set out by the Bar Standards Board is more likely to lead them to correct ethical behaviour than working out a solution to the ethical problem on their own.

The logic of this argument may have resonances of Joseph Raz's service conception of authority, but that conception also highlights the argument's limitations (1988: 53 ff).[27] For the cab rank rule to be able to perform the promised service of lowering internal costs for overthinkers and the squeamish, it must either be the case that the Bar Standards Board has greater expertise in resolving the ethical conflicts in question, or that it can help barristers who fit those profiles to lower their internal costs by coordinating their responses

[23] See particularly Flood & Hviid 2013, concluding that '[w]hile the Bar is captivated by the rule and has promoted it as a shibboleth, we have no evidence as to its efficacy nor that it is understood within the legal marketplace'; Happold 2021: 19; Zander 1990: 558.

[24] O'Connor (2023) notes that Principle 18 of the United Nations Basic Principles on the Role of Lawyers ('Lawyers shall not be identified with their clients or their clients' causes as a result of discharging their functions') contains this guarantee for all lawyers, not just for barristers.

[25] For the view that the rule can be justified as promoting, within certain limits, a universal obligation to provide legal services, see Higgins 2017: 201.

[26] This requirement sets the cab rank rule apart from general norms that purport to protect lawyers against being identified with their clients or their causes.

[27] See also Raz 2006: 1033–34.

to such conflicts. Neither option is free from difficulty. The problem with the expertise option is that it is not obvious that the Bar Standards Board has any greater expertise than individual barristers as regards conflicts between ordinary and professional morality. The coordination option is problematic because the internal costs that a barrister experiences may be independent of how other barristers respond to similar ethical challenges, so requiring all lawyers to respond in the same way may not make much difference in that regard. The effectiveness of coordination will therefore depend heavily on the particular cause of the internal costs that overthinkers and squeamish barristers incur. If that cause is fear of 'sticking out from the crowd', coordination may indeed lower internal costs for those persons. But if the cause is fear of doing the ethically wrong thing, no matter what others do or think about the matter, coordination provides no help at all. Barristers falling in the second group would therefore have a clear objection against the rule.

Introducing a deliberative element would not be a clear improvement in that regard. Suppose that instead of a flat cab rank rule, the Bar Standard Board allowed overthinkers and squeamish barristers who feel ethically compelled not to represent a client could appeal to a competent professional body for its authoritative advice. That rule would still not necessarily reduce the relevant internal costs for either class of lawyer. What it would do is add to the list of considerations that those professionals would need to take account of in deciding how to deal with that conflict. Should they refer a given case to the body, or should they decide what to do by themselves? And should they follow the professional body's advice when it comes through, even if they disagree with it? Answering these questions is likely to be a complex task depending on the starkness of the conflict, the magnitude of the ethical stakes, the professional body's expertise and track record in dealing with similar cases, and so on. More to the point, it is not clear that this task will be cognitively and psychologically any less taxing than the task of figuring out what to do in particular situations of ethical conflict. At best, it suggests that providing overthinkers and squeamish barristers with appropriate protection against internal costs is likely to require a host of different regulatory and institutional measures of which that alternative deliberative rule will be only part.

Consider, finally, the position of the skilful ethicist. As a general matter, that person faces low internal costs when having to deal with a conflict between their ordinary and their professional duties, so they could not reasonably object to the cab rank rule on the ground that it puts them in that position. In fact, as far as the skilful ethicist is concerned, the presence of the rule does not remove any option from the table. Like signatories to the Declaration, that person may still decide that, all things considered, they ought to follow their ordinary ethical judgement over their professional duty and refuse to obey the rule. This reflects a questioning disposition that Williams would presumably applaud. However, a closer look reveals a more complex picture. Suppose that the skilful ethicist is one of the few top specialists in their field, that litigation in that field has considerable potential for conflicts between ordinary and professional morality, and that the nature of such litigation is such that it will usually be the party whose interests are suspicious from the point of view of ordinary morality that gets to pick their legal representative first. Various forms of so-called 'SLAPP suits' (Strategic Lawsuits Against Public Participation), especially suits in defamation, are a case in point.[28] A skilful ethicist who specialises in SLAPP suits may well find themselves in constant demand by the enemies of free expression and public accountability, not least on matters pertaining to climate change and environmental protection.[29] Extended over time, that pattern may cause them to entertain reasonable fears that they cannot both pursue their practice and live up to their non-professional ethical beliefs. So while our skilful ethicist may not require protection against the risk of having to process ethical conflicts on any given occasion, it seems to me that they can reasonably want a degree of protection against the risk that, applied to their specialisation, the cab rank rule can lock them into a pattern of practice that stands at odds with their ordinary ethical commitments.

Let us take stock. I have argued that while the cab rank rule reduces internal costs for some profiles of legal professional, it arguably fails to do the same for others and, in certain cases, it may even increase such costs further. This suggests that, whatever its merits as a measure for protecting unpopular litigants, the cab rank rule does not, in its current form, pass moral muster as a measure for protecting legal professionals against the internal costs of dealing with ethical conflict. By the same token, that conclusion also points to a way forward. While the particular modalities are beyond the scope of my present argument, I believe that a version of the rule that took seriously the objections of skilful ethicists, on the one hand, and overthinkers and squeamish barristers, on the other, should count as clear improvement. One option in that former regard might be to cut the Gordian knot by prohibiting SLAPP suits altogether.[30] Another might be to exempt specialists from the requirements of the rule by showing that their practice is not only occasionally punctuated but effectively dominated by a type of litigant that they have legitimate ethical qualms representing. More general responses might include allowing every barrister to refuse a small number of briefs each year, or giving barristers who face a conflict between their ethical commitments and the cab rank rule the opportunity to ask the Bar Standards Board for reassurance that their judgement about the appropriate course of action is in line with that of their more experienced peers.[31]

[28] The locus classicus is Canan & Pring 1988: 506.

[29] This is a point also raised by O'Connor (2023).

[30] For recent developments in that regard, see Farrington & Zabrocka 2023; Young 2022: 186.

[31] The BSB currently provides a confidential Ethical Enquiries Service for barristers and associated professionals, accessible at www.barcouncil.org.uk/support-for-barristers/ethics.html. The service, which does not amount to 'guidance' for the purposes of the BSB Handbook, is provided on the following understanding: 'you must reach your own conclusion on what your professional obligations and ethics require of you in any particular situation'.

# IV. Conclusion

I have agreed with Williams that our societies should aspire to create lawyers disposed to treat conflicts between their professional and their ordinary ethical duties as occasions for circumspection and reluctance. Even when they act within the limits of their profession, lawyers wield considerable institutional power, the justified exercise of which falls to be judged not only within the norms of their profession but also before the tribunal of ordinary moral and ethical intuitions. As we have seen, Williams also believes that legal professionals who are disposed to struggle when faced with conflicts between ordinary and professional morality are also less likely to commit more easily avoidable injustices. I have not deliberated much on that claim, which strikes me as plausible, because it is not essential to his central claim. We would have reason to want legal professionals to display the disposition that Williams favours even if that made no difference to how they approach easy cases.

My aim in this chapter has been to press a claim that I regard as a necessary companion or corrective to Williams'. The ethical labour that Williams asks legal professionals to undertake can carry significant costs for them, both of the social or reputational and (what I called) the 'internal' kind. I have focused on internal costs and argued that, while every professional will be exposed to such costs at some point in their practice, there is a limit to how much cognitive and psychological stress we can reasonably ask them to undertake in the process, even when they occupy positions of institutional power by choice. In particular, sometimes we owe it to those professionals to design their work in ways that lower those internal costs, either by reframing the terms of the ethical dilemma, or by putting in place less taxing ways of managing the relevant ethical conflicts. I have not said much about the proper characterisation of the duty that we owe to legal professionals, though I believe that it could be plausibly described in terms of distributive justice. My aim has been, rather, to emphasise the variety of the complaints that different professionals can have against a system of work that did not make sufficient space for such a duty.

Accommodating those complaints in practice is, of course, no straightforward matter. Ethical dilemmas do not admit of technological solutions in the way that other practical problems sometimes do. As my discussion of the cab rank rule has tried to illustrate, we cannot resolve them cleanly through rules that prohibit lawyers from taking certain considerations into account in the exercise of their professional duties. This is not simply because those dilemmas have an ethical subject-matter, but also because of the variety in the internal costs that different types of lawyers may face in the process of dealing with them. The prohibition in the cab rank rule works to lower internal costs for professionals who fit some profiles, but it might raise them for others. While my argument has been short on specific suggestions for improvement, I hope I have done enough to show that a defensible design for legal work must do more than dispose legal professionals to grapple with hard ethical conflicts, as Williams urges. It must also provide them with suitable 'protective gear' when the occasion calls for them to do so, and that gear may well differ from one type of professional to another.

# Bibliography

Anscombe, GEM (1957) *Intention* (Cambridge, Massachusetts, Harvard University Press).

Applbaum, A (1999) *Ethics for Adversaries: The Morality of Roles in Public and Professional Life* (Princeton, Princeton University Press).

*Bar Standards Board Handbook*, version 4.7 (Sep 2023), available at www.barstandardsboard.org.uk/the-bsb-handbook.html

Berlin, I (1957) *The Hedgehog and the Fox* (New York, The New American Library).

Bradley, F (1876/2012) 'My Station and its Duties' in F Bradley, *Ethical Studies* (Cambridge, Cambridge University Press).

Canan, P & Pring, G (1988) 'Strategic Lawsuits against Public Participation' 35 *Social Problems* 506.

Cover, R (1984) *Justice Accused: Antislavery and the Judicial Process* (New Haven, Yale University Press).

Dare, T (2004) 'Mere-Zeal, Hyper-Zeal and the Ethical Obligations of Lawyers' 7 *Legal Ethics* 24.

Darwall, S (2009) *The Second-Person Standpoint* (Cambridge, Massachusetts, Harvard University Press).

Dworkin, R (2001) 'Do Liberal Values Conflict?' in R Dworkin et al (eds), *The Legacy of Isaiah Berlin* (New York, New York Review of Books).

Farrington, F & Zabrocka, M (2023) 'Punishment by Process: The Development of Anti-SLAPP Legislation in the European Union' 24 *ERA Forum* 519.

Flood, J & Hviid, M (2013) 'The Cab Rank Rule: Its Meaning and Purpose in the New Legal Services Market (Report for the Legal Services Board)' *U. of Westminster School of Law Research Paper* 13-01, available at http://dx.doi.org/10.2139/ssrn.2229235

Fried, C (1976) 'The Lawyer as Friend: The Moral Foundations of the Lawyer-Client Relation' 85 *Yale Law Journal* 1060.

Happold, M (2021) 'The Cab Rank Rule: English Barristers in Foreign Courts' 171 *New Law Journal* 19.

Hare, RM (1972) 'Rules of War and Moral Reasoning' 1 *Philosophy & Public Affairs* 166.

Herring, J (2023) *Legal Ethics*, 3rd edn (Oxford, Oxford University Press).

Higgins, A (2017) 'Rebooting the Cab Rank Rule as a Limited Universal Service Obligation' 20 *Legal Ethics* 201.

Lawyers are Responsible, 'Declaration' (27 March 2023), available at www.lar.earth/

—— 'Statement in Response to Media Coverage' (n.d.), available at www.lar.earth/press/statement-in-response-to-media-coverage/

Luban, D (1986) 'The Lysistratian Perspective: A Response to Stephen Pepper' 11 *American Bar Foundational Research Journal* 637.

Lukes, S (2001) 'An Unfashionable Fox' in R Dworkin et al (eds), *The Legacy of Isaiah Berlin* (New York, New York Review of Books).

Markovits, D (2008) *A Modern Legal Ethics: Adversary Advocacy in a Democratic Age* (Princeton, Princeton University Press).
Lord Neuberger (2013) 'Tomorrow's Lawyers Today – Today's Lawyers Tomorrow', Speech delivered at the '80 Club' Association of Liberal Lawyers, 19 February 2013, available at www.supremecourt.uk/docs/speech-130219.pdf
O'Connor, P (2023) 'Is it Time to Reassess the Cab Rank Rule?' *Counsel Magazine* (10 July 2023), available at www.counselmagazine.co.uk/articles/is-it-time-to-reassess-the-cab-rank-rule-
Postema, G (1980) 'Moral Responsibility in Professional Ethics' 55 *New York University Law Review* 63.
*Proceedings in the House of Lords, Trial of Queen Caroline* (1820) vol 2.
Raz, J (1988) *The Morality of Freedom* (Oxford, Oxford University Press).
—— (2006) 'The Problem of Authority: Revisiting the Service Conception' 90 *Minnesota Law Review* 1003.
Scanlon, TM (1998) *What We Owe to Each Other* (London, Harvard University Press).
*Statement by the Chair of the Bar Council, Nick Vineall KC*, Press Release, 24 March 2023, available at www.barcouncil.org.uk/resource/the-cab-rank-rule-and-legal-representation.html
*Statement by the Four Bars (England and Wales, Ireland, Northern Ireland, and Scotland)*, Press Release, 26 May 2023, available at www.barcouncil.org.uk/resource/cab-rank-rule-statement-of-the-four-bars.html
Voyiakis, E (2021) 'Moral Luck, Responsibility, and Systems of Tort Liability' 27 *Res Publica* 271.
Wendel, B (2011) 'Three Concepts of Roles' 48 *San Diego Law Review* 547.
Williams, B (1981a) 'Politics and Moral Character' in B Williams, *Moral Luck* (Cambridge, Cambridge University Press).
—— (1981b) 'Conflicts of Values' in B Williams, *Moral Luck* (Cambridge, Cambridge University Press).
—— (2010) 'Professional Morality and its Dispositions' in B Williams, *Making Sense of Humanity* (Cambridge, Cambridge University Press).
Young, H (2022) 'Canadian Anti-SLAPP Laws in Action' 100 *Canadian Bar Review* 186.
Zacka, B (2017) *When the State Meets the Street: Public Service and Moral Agency* (Cambridge, Mass., Harvard University Press).
Zander, M (1990) 'The Myth of the Cab Rank' 140 *New Law Journal* 558

# 5

# Response-Norm Concepts in Law and Morality: A Qualified Defence of Moral Luck

BENJAMIN C ZIPURSKY

## I. Introduction

Is the blameworthiness of one's conduct ever affected by contingent happenings outside of one's control? When Bernard Williams answered 'yes' in his 'Moral Luck' article published almost 50 years ago, he acknowledged the tension between this conclusion and the perspectives of moral thinkers from the Stoics to Kant and present-day Kantians (Williams 1981). Williams' article (and Thomas Nagel's equally brilliant companion article by the same name) triggered a flood of writings in moral theory over the past half century (Nagel 1979; Nelkin 2023). The Williams and Nagel articles observed that even if in principle it seems intuitively correct to exclude matters of luck from determinations of responsibility, when we shift our intuitions to particular examples, we often permit such contingencies to factor into our judgements. A prominent portion of their inquiry concerns what is called 'resultant luck': the difference between cases in which wrongful conduct fortuitously does not turn out to cause injury and those in which it does. A speeding driver who injures no one faces no liability or at most a speeding ticket, but the speeding driver who seriously injures a child who leaps out from behind a parked car faces substantial tort liability for having injured the child. The legal case matches a difference in moral intuitions too. The driver's feelings of guilt for having acted wrongfully and the blame of third parties will differ dramatically in the two cases, and this will be true even if we are quite sure that the speeding driver in the first case *would not have been able to avert causing a serious injury had a child similarly jumped out in front of her car.*

Williams and Nagel flipped comfortably between the domains of morality and law in providing examples; this chapter begins by distinguishing between luck questions in the domain of critical morality and luck questions in the domain of interpretive legal theory. Some terminology will help. A key question in the moral domain is whether the common inclination among ordinary people to regard the injurer as more blameworthy than the would-be injurer is morally justifiable. I will call those who answer yes 'moral luck defenders' and those who answer no 'moral luck sceptics'. The legal domain presents a similar scenario. The legal liability of the driver who actually injures someone is typically greater than for the one who does not; indeed, in the law of torts (my principal focus here) it is systematically so. There is, however, a question about whether the law, in treating them differently, is sometimes justified. I shall call those who answer yes 'legal luck defenders' and those who answer no 'legal luck sceptics', opting for verbal symmetry over terminological precision.[1]

A common tack among legal theorists is to be moral luck sceptics and instrumentalist legal luck defenders (or at least remain open to the possibility that legal luck is justifiable). Doing so typically involves acknowledging, as David Enoch and Andrei Marmor do, that the moral blameworthiness of an actor is not the only consideration that properly enters into the justification of the existence or magnitude of legal liability; there may be reasons independent of blameworthiness for results to bear on liability (Enoch & Marmor 2007). If the putatively or seemingly moral parts of tort law were viewed as strictly analogous to the moral domain, then a consistent moral luck sceptic would be a legal luck sceptic too. However, once it is acknowledged that the considerations of deterrence, compensation, and a variety of issues of administrability and evidence enter into the proper appraisal of law, there is no inconsistency in combining these two positions. These acknowledgements typically constitute a strongly *instrumentalist* turn in interpretive legal theory. Instrumentalist interpretations downplay the appearance that various deontological-sounding legal terms are what they appear to be. They analyse such legal terms as instruments for the achievement of various welfarist goals.

This chapter ultimately takes what might be viewed as the opposite tack: it offers a defence of legal luck that is not instrumentalist and not based largely in concepts that are independent of notions of accountability. Rather, I argue that there are features of the law that are analogous to moral responsibility and that the law incorporates accountability concepts in this way. Legal luck in certain areas is thus defended on (what might be called) its own terms.

While the view advanced is compatible with moral luck scepticism, it also suggests a path towards being a moral luck defender. Far from allowing the alleged unacceptability of moral luck to support the eradication of legal luck, the reasons

[1] In the moral case, it is plausible to ask the question of whether the putative moral luck is real (i.e., the moral judgements of differences in blameworthiness are true), and it is therefore coherent to arrive at the answer 'no' (as, for example, David Enoch and Andrei Marmor do; Enoch & Marmor 2007). That position would be more precisely labelled a 'moral luck denier' and its antithesis 'moral luck affirmer'. Conversely, there is no question that the legal phenomena described in the 'legal luck' scenarios are as described, and the 'legal luck' sceptic I have in mind does not deny the correctness of those descriptions as a matter of positive law. In this sense, 'legal luck sceptic' is misleading as a label, and 'legal luck critic' would perhaps be better. The text of the chapter makes clear enough what is meant in both cases, and the rough symmetry is illuminating enough to warrant the choice of labels, notwithstanding the potential for confusion.

for accepting legal luck allow us to illuminate why moral luck is real and defensible.[2] Drawing not simply from Williams and Nagel, but also from P.F. Strawson's deeply suggestive 'Freedom and Resentment' and a range of prior work linking tort theory and moral theory, I advance a *qualified defence of resultant moral luck* (Strawson 1962).

A bit of overstatement will help in introducing the core of the qualified defence. I suggest that what might be called 'the idea of moral blameworthiness' utilised in everyday moral thinking includes two different strands, each of which is cogent and legitimate. For one of these, results that are outside the control of the agent should not and do not make a difference, but for the other, results should and do make a difference. So while it is in one sense true that the two actors who behave identically are equally blameworthy regardless of outcome, in another sense the one whose conduct ripens into injury is more blameworthy. The word 'blameworthy' is ambiguous, and indeed – quite apart from language – more than one blameworthiness concept plays a justifiable role in moral thought. For one of these, the question is whether a certain kind of negative appraisal of a person in light of his or her action is warranted from a detached perspective; for the other, the question is whether the kind of critical resentment toward someone that is characteristic of someone wrongfully injured by another is appropriately directed toward a person in light of his or her action. These are two different kinds of blaming, each answering to different standards; for one of them, results matter, which is why I claim to be providing a defence of moral luck. Because results do not matter to the other, it is only a qualified defence.

A more detailed preview of the chapter is provided below: for now, it will help to preview the role played by legal theory. Philosophers are familiar with those who pretend to solve problems by the mere fabrication of new conceptual categories, and the distinction between forms of blameworthiness may seem to be just another effort at such trickery. But knowledge of the law blunts this response. Moral blameworthiness, like moral responsibility, is a species of a much broader genus of concepts of *accountability*, and the law is all about accountability. And when we look at accountability in the law what we see is many different forms, each with a well-developed set of conditions and criteria that aspire to capture critical normative distinctions. My own area of legal expertise – the law of torts – is one in which there has been a great deal of analysis of when results matter to accountability and why, even though there are areas of law in which results do not matter. So our understanding of why results do matter and should matter in tort law allows us to ask the right questions about whether they matter to accountability in morality, and if so when and why.

In suggesting that the phenomena of causal luck in the law of torts can actually illuminate *moral* luck, I draw upon another and more pervasive theme in Williams' work. Williams regularly questioned the supposedly 'purer' nature of stripped down analytic moral philosophical inquiry; he himself proposed that the

[2] Parts of the view of resultant moral luck advanced here were sketched in Zipursky 2007b.

added institutional history and factual detail that lawyers, judges, and law professors confront could illuminate moral inquiry (Williams 1986; 1995). This chapter aims to move that effort forward.

Section II sets forth the challenge of resultant luck in morality, offering what Williams and Nagel appeared to regard as the challenges of moral luck. Section III offers a parallel problem in tort law, and it explains how instrumentalist legal theorists who are moral luck sceptics have tended to respond to the problem and why theoretical debates on this legal issue are of significant practical importance. The folly of instrumentalist tort theory is exposed in section IV, which explains resultant luck in tort law on non-instrumentalist terms that jibe with the deontological character of the language and reasoning of the law. Section V introduces the idea of 'response-norms concepts' and explains in what sense both legal liability and moral blameworthiness include response-norm concepts. The analysis of sections IV and V is used to construct a qualified defence of resultant moral luck in section VI.

## II. Moral Luck in Resultant Luck Cases: The Sceptic's Challenge

A control principle has remained the starting point for moral luck sceptics:

- **General Control Principle:** A person is not more blameworthy for an act that injures someone than for an identical act under the identical circumstances that does not injure anyone, if the reason for the differential outcome depends entirely on circumstances outside of the person's control.

Two arguments support the General Control Principle:

- **Fairness Control Argument:** A person is not fairly subject to blame for an event whose occurrence or non-occurrence was outside of their control. If a person's acts had more serious results than another person's identical acts or than their own act would have had but for events outside of their control, it would be unfair to subject her to more blame because of the results.
- **Culpability Manifestation Argument:** Two identical acts under identical circumstances express or manifest the same level of culpability even if they happen to have different consequences for reasons outside the person's control. Blameworthiness for an act cannot vary unless the agent's level of culpability for the act differs. An agent's act cannot be more blameworthy because of consequences that differed for reasons outside the person's control.

A word of explanation on what is meant here by the term 'culpability': I do not mean the term to be limited to any particular conception of what aspects of a person render them culpable or deserving of blame, but rather to be a stand-in for any number of different 'attributes' or 'properties' of the person, in the content-neutral sense of those terms. Some might think it is character or virtue, others qualities of the will, or other moments of certain intention or attitude toward others. Part of the reason that moral luck phenomena present such a deep and broad challenge is that they seem to present themselves compellingly with *any* of these accounts.

I will leave aside for the moment the question of whether the Fairness Control Argument and the Culpability Manifestation Argument are in the end distinct or independent. If, as I propose, neither one is sound, nothing turns on whether they are independent.

The problem is that the General Control Principle appears to be true and well justified, but ordinary moral thinking – as Williams famously suggested – seems to deviate from its implications. People commonly do in fact regard someone as more blameworthy if their negligent driving seriously injures someone than if it ends up harming no one. And we do in fact regard the successful killer as more blameworthy than someone whose sincerely and competently aimed bullet turns out not to hit anyone for reasons of chance (e.g., a random loud noise caused the target to flinch).

Moral luck sceptics are in a sense revisionists; they believe the General Control Principle really is true and ordinary moral thinking should change to conform to its implications. They reject the paradox, insisting that it is simply not true that the fortunate driver is less blameworthy (Enoch & Marmor 2007). Because both the Fairness Control Argument and the Control Manifestation Argument appear to be sound, the moral luck sceptic seems to have a strong position.

## III. Legal Luck in Torts and its Instrumentalist Defenders

In Jeremy Waldron's classic presentation of the legal luck problem in tort law, he imagined two drivers, 'Fate' and 'Fortune', who drive in an identically careless fashion on a city street, and one of whom (Fate) hits a motorcyclist (Hurt), while the other (Fortune) hits no one (Waldron 1995). Fortune faces no liability. Fate, on the other hand, incurs liability to the tune of five million dollars. Waldron grants that it is intuitive to suppose that Fate should face some liability. But, he continues

> [i]t is difficult … to go beyond this intuition and explain exactly why it is fair that Fate should be expected to come up with a sum of money this large. … The difficulty is exacerbated when we consider the other driver, Mr. Fortune. … No one would think it appropriate to require him to pay Hurt five million dollars; yet his behavior, morally speaking, was indistinguishable from that of Fate' (Waldron 1995).

Let us simplify the point: in law, Fate will face substantial tort liability and Fortune will face none, yet their conduct appears criticisable to exactly the same extent. Waldron understandably suggests that this is unfair and, further, that the charge of unfairness attaches to the common law of torts as a whole, because this is but a prototypical example of how it operates. More generally, Waldron and a range of other eminent scholars in both law and philosophy have suggested that the asymmetry of liability for equally culpable actors in tort law renders this field unjustifiable. In these respects, legal versions of the Fairness Control Argument and the Culpability Manifestation Argument have led to legal luck scepticism about the law of torts.

Here is how the critique might go. Let us begin with an assumption (which instrumentalist tort theorists end up rejecting) that tort law's treatment of result asymmetries is justifiable only if impositions of liability can be coherently interpreted as a justifiable system of attributing *accountability* to tortfeasors, where *accountability* is part of a family of 'responsibility' concepts to which *blameworthiness* belongs, and that it properly operates in parallel fashion. This would lead us to a tort-adapted version of the General Control Principle, defended by a tort-adapted version of the Fairness Control Argument and the Culpability Manifestation Argument.

- **General Control Principle for Tort Law:** A person should not face greater legal accountability for an act that injures someone than for an identical act under the identical circumstances that does not injure anyone, if the reason for the differential outcome depends entirely on circumstances outside of the person's control.

Two arguments support the General Control Principle for Tort Law:

- **Fairness Control Argument for Tort Law:** A person is not fairly held accountable for an event whose occurrence or non-occurrence was outside of their control. If a person's actions had more serious results than another person's identical acts or than their own act would have had but for events outside of their control, it would be unfair to subject her to greater accountability because of the results.
- **Culpability Manifestation Argument for Tort Law:** Two identical acts under identical circumstances express or manifest the same level of culpability even if they happen to have different consequences for reasons outside the person's control. Accountability for an act cannot vary unless the agent's level of culpability for the act differs. An agent's act cannot warrant greater accountability because of consequences that differed for reasons outside the person's control.

The conclusion to be drawn if one accepts either the Fairness Control Argument for Tort Law or the Culpability Manifestation Argument for Tort Law is that tort law's treatment of result asymmetries is unjustifiable.

Notably, there are numerous thinkers who take intermediate views of the justifiability of tort law's asymmetrical treatment of injury-causing and non-injury causing negligent actors: among moral luck sceptics, there are legal luck defenders. More precisely, many instrumentalist defences of legal luck do not require that one be a moral luck defender. These views will be sketched below. None of them reject the arguments above or purport to provide direct rebuttals of those arguments. Rather, they all implicitly reject the premise that tort law's treatment of result asymmetries is justifiable only if impositions of liability can be coherently interpreted as a justifiable system of attributing *accountability* to tortfeasors for wrongs, where *accountability for wrongs* is part of a family of 'responsibility' concepts to which *blameworthiness* belongs, and that legal accountability properly operates in parallel fashion. All are indeed happy rejecting the view that impositions of liability can be coherently interpreted as a justifiable system of attributing accountability for wrongs to tortfeasors.

Many scholars believe that even if the culpability level of the two actors does not differ, this symmetry does not necessarily yield the conclusion that the system is unjustifiable. The justification of the differential treatment may turn on matters other than culpability, and indeed may survive scrutiny even where the culpability is equal. Because one of the purposes of the legal system is to ensure that those who are injured receive compensation, requiring a payment by the injury-causing actor serves a purpose that is quite different from allocating blame. As there is no injury in the other case, forcing a payment would not be justifiable by reference to that purpose, even if the blameworthiness is the same.

On the question of whether it is permissible to visit this consequence on the injury-causing actor although no such consequence is visited upon others, the compensation theorists have an interesting theoretical answer: it is precipitous to assume the imposition of financial liability is itself a form of sanctioning or blaming such that the permissibility of a distinction turns on culpability level. To compare with another part of civil law, forcing residents of a town to pay for the water they consume is not *sanctioning or blaming them*, it is requiring them to pay money for a different sort of reason; culpability is beside the point. Tort liability may not be like compensation for resources used, but that does not entail that it *is* like punishment or sanction. It may well be that there are social benefits that arise from structuring the law such that the ones whose actions result in these injuries are forced to pay for them. Those favourable social consequences of drawing this line justify the legal requirement of paying a certain amount under these circumstances, and culpability is immaterial. On this view, we are not actually holding defendants *responsible for what they have wrongfully done (in any non-circular sense of 'responsibility')*, we are – for a variety of regulatory and welfarist reasons – imposing certain costs on them in a pattern that (to some extent) mimics, but is not actually, responsibility attribution.

An apt rejoinder at this juncture from the legal luck sceptic is this: if it is just an instrumentally justified arrangement, why do we even ask if the defendant driver was driving negligently? Here, again, 20th century scholars have supplied a number of ingenious answers. The answer underlying Richard Posner's famous law-and-economics theory of tort law is that a robust set of social advantages flows from providing shelter from financial liability to those injurers who take the rational level of precautions and act non-negligently (Posner 1972). This turns out to incentivise precaution-taking at just the socially optimal level.

Many scholars (like myself) reject the Posnerian account at an interpretive level because of the mismatch between the language and concepts of the law (on the one hand) and the normative grounds purportedly underlying it (on the other) (Zipursky 2007a). Another plausible intermediate option is available, however. One could argue that the reason 'negligent' conduct needs to be shown is that the social meaning of tort liability is more complicated than the pure instrumentalist supposes. This sort of 'mixed' theorist acknowledges that there is a sense in which defendants forced to pay for another's injury – even if insured – are being subjected to an onerous and negative consequence by the legal system and worry about whether it is justifiable for the legal system to put this whole burden on them, even if it is socially beneficial to do so. One answer is that it is not unfair to do so if the potentially liable parties are permitted to stay free of liability for injuries they cause by acting non-negligently; if they have, so to speak, a safe harbour from liability. On this view, the liability is not a sanction and therefore is not principally warranted by considerations of culpability, but by consequentialist, welfare-based reasons that pick out those who have in fact caused injury. Nonetheless, 'eligibility' for being subjected to this welfare-based system *does* turn on whether one acted wrongfully (i.e., negligently). So the parties are treated similarly insofar as both are eligible for liability, should they cause injury. Since the function and social meaning of liability is not sanction or blame, it is justifiable to distinguish in imposition of liability among those who are eligible, imposing liability on the ones who really do cause injury.

It is worth mentioning, finally, that some instrumentalist defences of legal luck in tort law focus on *institutional* considerations that distinguish questions about tort law from questions about morality. For example, some scholars believe that as an evidentiary matter, the occurrence of injury actually casts light on the question of whether the defendant was in fact negligent; they are not prepared to assume adequate evidence of equal blameworthiness independent of whether injury actually occurred, or at least they are attentive to the additional costs of an evidentiary system sure enough about negligent conduct even where no injury occurred. Similarly, once we include concerns about predictability, evidence, insurance premium setting, and legal practice, a variety of instrumental reasons arise that warrant a legal distinction between the injuring and non-injuring defendant, even if the critiques of moral luck are sound (Enoch & Marmor 2007).

One cannot overestimate the real-world significance of the tort theory debates rehearsed above (although typically without express reference to 'moral luck' or 'legal luck'). Two broad sets of reasons will have to suffice for now. One might be called 'the specific causation challenge'. Over the past 75 years, there has been a vast number of cases in which plaintiffs and their lawyers are able to prove negligent conduct of a company that makes certain products or emits certain toxins *and* they are able to prove that they have suffered serious injuries, but they are not able to provide sufficient evidence that the negligent conduct of the party whom they have brought before the court actually caused their injury. If tort liability is not exactly about holding people *responsible* for injuring others, but about the value of compensation to those injured and the value of deterrence to those who create risks of the sorts of injuries that occurred, the absence of specific causation proof should not necessarily stand in the way of recovery. Perhaps we should change our tort system to open up liability. This is tempting because, if the negligent conduct was proved, then the eligibility constraint that appears to confront fairness objections has been satisfied (*Sindell v Abbott Labs* 1980; *Hymowitz v Eli Lilly & Co* 1989; Rosenberg 2002). It is doubly so because the reasons for the inadequacy of the evidence are often unconnected to the deservingness of the injured persons or the risk-creators' need for deterrence, and the deterrence level appears to decrease dramatically to the extent that holes in evidence block liability for the risk creators.

A second might be called 'the fault challenge'. If the point of requiring proof of negligence is not that tort liability is all about holding people accountable for wronging one another, but simply to make sure that there is a safe harbour for our instrumentally justified imposition of costs for losses, then perhaps proof of negligence should not be required. There are other ways to create safe harbours. One kind of safe harbour is simply staying out of the area of risky activity altogether. More generally, the importance of a safe harbour turns on many considerations, including whether there is a background right to engage in the activity without standing ready to pay damages, whether it is the kind of activity in which risks of injury and liability are properly assumed, whether it is something the state plausibly licenses, and so on. This means that the allegedly principled moral grounds for not having strict liability may be far thinner than has conventionally been acknowledged. Needless to say, the combination of the fault challenge and the specific causation challenge create the opportunity for a remarkably robust world of tort liability.

## IV. Rethinking Luck in Tort Law

This section explicitly challenges the legal versions of the General Control Principle and our two core arguments against moral luck as applied to tort law. Consider, first, the Fairness Control Argument as applied to Tort Law. It begins with the statement that: (a) A person is not fairly held accountable for an event whose occurrence or non-occurrence was outside of their control. It then moves to the conclusion that (b) If a person's actions had more serious results than another person's identical acts or than their own act would have had, but for events outside of their control, it would be unfair to subject her to greater accountability because of the results.

There are two quite different accounts of why (a) justifies (b). One is that a person should not be held accountable for bringing about a result they lacked the control to avoid bringing about. This follows from an ought-implies-can kind of principle: one ought to have avoided causing a certain result (injury) only if one was able to avoid bringing it about (Zimmerman 1987). Let's call this the 'Unavoidability Justification (of the Fairness Control Principle)'. A second is that there is no relevant difference between the scenario in which it comes about and the scenario in which it does not come about, if the difference was unrelated to the agent's exercise of volition. Let's call that the 'No-Agential-Difference Justification (of the Fairness Control Principle)'. It should be clear that the No-Agential-Difference Justification is just a repetition of the Culpability Manifestation Argument.

Let's focus on the Unavoidability Justification then. Is it true that Fate could not have avoided hitting Hurt, in Waldron's example? Clearly not. It is part of why there is tort liability not just that Fate caused the accident by driving, but that Fate caused the accident by *driving negligently*. It is part of our understanding of the finding that Fate was driving negligently that Fate was driving less carefully that he could have been and should have been. Finally, it is also part of what Hurt needs to prove to prevail that *if Fate had been driving non-negligently – which Fate could have been doing – then the accident would not have occurred and Hurt would not have been injured*. The Unavoidability Justification of the General Control Principle thus actually fails in the case of Fate and Fortune. That does not mean that the General Control Principle is untrue or even that the Fairness Control Argument is unsound. It just means that if the Fairness Control Argument is sound, it is because of the No-Agential-Difference Principle. But, as acknowledged above, the No-Agential-Difference Principle – if it is true – is true for just the reasons that would support the Culpability Manifestation Argument.

The point seems small, but it is not. Both Tony Honoré (1988) and Stephen Perry (2002) put forward important theories of tort law based in significant part on the notion of outcome responsibility they developed. Perry argued, in particular, that if an agent has the capacity to act non-negligently and if the outcome in question was foreseeable and would have been averted through non-negligent conduct, then the outcome was avoidable. Because of that, a certain kind of control argument simply fails to block the attribution of responsibility for certain losses (Honoré 1988; Perry 2002; Zimmerman 1987). It is notable that Nagel's arguments in 'Moral Luck' vacillated between complete lack of control over outcomes and partial lack of control. In laying out the resultant luck problem, he set forth

> the idea that one cannot be more culpable or estimable for anything than one is for *that fraction of it which is under one's control*. It seems irrational to take or dispense credit or blame for matters over which a person has *no control, or* for their influence on results over which he has *partial control* (Nagel, 1979: 28)'.

However, partial lack of control, as in the case of Fate, is insufficient to support the Unavoidability Justification of the Fairness Control Argument.

Turn now to the Culpability Manifestation Argument. It relies on the assertion that an agent's act cannot *justifiably* generate greater accountability based on different outcomes unless the different outcomes express or manifest a different level of culpability. The argument that it is unjustifiable turns on the idea that accountability of the sort that belongs to the family of concepts that includes blameworthiness is not merely a matter of paying for results, it is accountability for *what one has done*. And the problem is that the conduct of Fate and Fortune, their acts, what *they have done* … appear to be the same: they have driven negligently.

Part of what was important in Williams' and Nagel's *Moral Luck* articles – and is indeed important of Williams' philosophical corpus generally – is the focus on *agency*. Consider Williams' example of a truck driver who – although driving carefully – runs over a child on the street who ran out unexpectedly from behind a parked car. Williams thought it mattered that *running over a child* was something the truck driver in his example had *done*, just as, for example, becoming a great artist and producing truly great art are among the things that Gauguin had done in his life. There is, Williams claimed (as did Nagel), something philosophically artificial about supposing the only proper objects of moral assessment are the acts stripped of their results.

With this in mind, it seems we might deem Fate to face greater accountability than Fortune because Fate's acts *were* different than Fortune's: Among the acts of Fate, but not Fortune, is the negligent injuring of Hurt. It is true (by hypothesis) that the acts of negligent driving, abstracted from results, are identical. The greater accountability is not for those identical acts, but rather turns on accountability for a different act – a negligent injuring in Fate's case, but not in Fortune's.

Philosophers from Nagel to Enoch and Marmor have of course recognised that acts can be described (and, indeed, individuated) differently, but that has not necessarily led them to any greater philosophical comfort with resultant moral luck (Enoch & Marmor 2007; Nagel 1979). Their understandable worry is that (at least in the moral case, and perhaps in the legal one) one must have reasons for selecting the broader, result-inclusive individuation of action that do not simply beg the question. Since none of the differences between the result-inclusive act and the non-result-inclusive act are under the agent's control, the choice of the result-inclusive act seems less to solve the problem than to beg the question (Enoch & Marmor 2007).

Within tort law, however, there *is* a non-question begging reason to focus on an act that Fate performed that Fortune did not, and, in particular a reason to focus on Fate's negligent injuring of Hurt and the absence of such an act by Fortune. The reason is that Fate's negligent injuring of Hurt was a violation of Hurt's legal right not to be negligently injured and a breach of Fate's legal duty not to negligently injure him. A key question in a tort case is whether the plaintiff is entitled to a right of action against the defendant, and it is overwhelmingly a requirement of tort law that the plaintiff must have endured a rights invasion by the defendant in order to have such a right of action. Hurt *is* legally entitled to hold Fate to account for the wrong of negligently injuring him because Fate committed that legal wrong to Hurt and (correlatively) violated Hurt's legal right. Hurt cannot hold Fortune accountable for negligently injuring him because that is not among the acts that Fortune did and, correlatively, Fortune violated no legal right of Hurt.

More than two decades ago, Arthur Ripstein and I (and, shortly thereafter, John Goldberg and I) argued that Fate breached a legal duty to Hurt not to negligently injure him, and the legal system deems Fate accountable for that breach of duty, which is correlative to Hurt's right (Goldberg & Zipursky 2002; Ripstein &

Zipursky 2002). We called that the breach of a duty of non-injury. Fate's act is complex; in negligence law, it is not just an injuring, but an injuring of another through failure to take care towards the other (which we called the breach of a duty of non-injuriousness). In this way, Fate also breached a duty of non-injuriousness. Negligence law actually conditions Hurt's entitlement to use the courts to hold someone accountable on whether that person has breached this qualified duty: a duty not to injure Hurt through breach of a duty not to act carefully toward them. Fortune breached the embedded duty of care, but did not breach the legal duty for which negligence law provides legal redress. That is why he cannot be held legally accountable to Hurt. Because there is no one to whom he breached a legal duty of non-injury, he faces no accountability in tort law whatsoever (although he might get a traffic ticket for speeding or for driving dangerously).

The interpretive claim that tort law is about empowering those whose rights have been invaded to have courts hold the rights-invader accountable is, at this stage, neither novel nor underdeveloped. That is today the leading position among Commonwealth tort scholars (Stevens 2007; Weinrib 1995); it has arguably been the traditional common law position since Blackstone; and it has returned to the mainstream in American legal theory (Keating 2023). A large body of prior work explains why the rights-based account offered above is neither circular nor vacuous.

A central point of emphasis in this account is one that will admittedly cause us some trouble when we return from torts to the topic of moral luck: accountability in tort law is plainly relational; it is a question of whether a defendant is properly held accountable *to* a plaintiff for what he or she did to that plaintiff. The events that constitute *the ripening of an act that is wrongful in part because of its harmful potentiality* turn out to be important because they are injurings and rights violations that provide private parties with legal standing. This is important, in turn, because the proper vulnerability to being held to *account* is being held to account for *what one did to the plaintiff.* As a kind of accountability that is *to someone whose legal rights one invaded*, tort liability builds in principled reasons for outcomes to make a difference.[3]

[3] Those who remain suspicious should note that the account presented here is, at least on its face, not especially well suited to explaining other troubling kinds of legal luck, such as the extra criminal punishment visited upon one who succeeds in committing a homicide (compared to the fortuitous shooter who misses). Because the state's standing to prosecute does not turn solely upon its own rights having been invaded, but (at least in part) on a much broader regulatory capacity, no legal luck explanation here seems forthcoming. Whether such legal luck in the criminal law is justifiable remains a difficult question. I have elsewhere sketched a preliminary answer to what such a justification might look like, arguing that – as an interpretive matter – legal luck in criminal law reflects the view that part – but not all – of the state's power to punish those who have committed criminal wrongdoings upon others derives from its obligation to vindicate the dignity of the victim by holding the wrongdoer to account for what they did to the victim (Zipursky 2007b). Nonetheless, the criminal case is far less straightforward than the tort case, and it is fair to say that moral-luck-sceptical critiques of a punishment differential in criminal law have met with greater success in changing the positive law than comparable critiques in tort law.

The analysis above is largely interpretive, and it therefore does not necessarily mean that tort law should stay the way it is or that the toxic tort-based challenges sketched at the end of section III must simply be rejected for a more traditional position. They do, however, suggest that alleged conceptual incoherence of such resultant legal luck should not be deemed a reason to eliminate the rule. Moreover, no weight should be put on the putative success of instrumentalist approaches in rationalising legal luck phenomena that allegedly haunt non-instrumental approaches to understanding the positive law. To the contrary, the relational non-instrumentalist approaches appear to have far greater interpretive power with respect to the resultant-luck features of the positive law than the instrumental approaches (Goldberg & Zipursky 2002). One can be a resultant legal luck defender without being an instrumentalist.

The foregoing account of the justifiability of resultant luck in tort law has been embraced and elaborated by a number of scholars since it was introduced more than two decades ago. The intellectual roots of this analysis can be found in Ernest Weinrib's insistence on the distinctive character of tort law as a form of *private law*, not *public law* (as many leading scholars of the 20th century had insisted). For now the point is this: some forms of public law – regulatory law, and to some extent criminal law – are plausibly understood as systems of rules with corresponding sanctions attached, and the nature and magnitude of the appropriate sanction is typically taken to relate to the nature of the wrongdoing conceived in a particular way. The critical attributes of the wrongdoing with respect to which the appropriateness of punishment and its proper magnitude are gauged are ones that are subjectively accessible to the agent. And that is because – as is commonly conveyed in the examination of criminal culpability – the sanction is closely linked to an appraisal of the agent in acting. If one tries to squeeze tort law into this public law model, its extraordinary result-sensitivity is anomalous or calls for some elaborate instrumentalist rewrite. That is all the more reason to see that tort law is an entirely different kind of accountability. The state is not assigning sanction based on a certain kind of appraisal of the actor at the moment of action. It is rather judging that an individual is entitled to hold another accountable *for having wrongfully injured him or her.* Tort law has a different structure than criminal law or regulatory law (as traditionally conceived), but each offers its own structure of accountability. That accountability in tort is properly result-sensitive does not undercut the viability of result-insensitive forms of accountability in other parts of the law.

## V. Response-Norm Concepts

The return to blameworthiness and the topic of moral luck is important not only for the fulfilment of an undertaking at the beginning of the chapter. It is also important because the claim to have solved a parallel 'legal luck' problem in tort law, above, turned in part on the assertion that the concept of 'accountability' in the tort case belongs to a family of 'responsibility' concepts to which blameworthiness also belongs. Without follow through on at least that point, readers might be entitled to think the tort domain is not genuinely analogous.

*Blameworthiness* belongs to a family of what I call 'response-norm' concepts.[4] When we ask if someone is blameworthy for something they have done we are typically asking if they are, in at least certain respects, appropriate objects of appraisals or reactions that include the negative affect of blaming or verbal and non-verbal negative sanctioning (of certain sorts). One can concede this largely semantic point without taking a position on what sorts of blaming reactions are appropriate or when or why, and, indeed, without taking a reductive or operationalistic definition of 'blameworthy'. In the same way, acknowledging that the term 'creditworthy' connotes warranting a loan or credit line does not involve taking any substantive position on what standards of banking should be or whether there are or are not fundamentals to creditworthiness. Similar terms – 'despicable', 'desirable', 'adorable', 'trustworthy', 'laughable', 'pitiable', 'impeachable', 'indictable' – all of these express response norms in this sense too. They are commonly used to ask whether certain attitudes, actions, activities, or dispositions are appropriate to a person or entity or their acts. So too, I suggest, are the terms 'accountable', 'liable', and 'responsible', and many of the concepts that they connote. R. Jay Wallace's important book *Responsibility and the Moral Sentiments* (Wallace 1988) may be understood to include an analysis of the concept of responsibility as a response-norm concept, conjoined with a general normative account of what it is that certain characteristic emotional responses to others' conduct to be fair. Like Wallace – whose work has influenced mine – I see my model as an extension of some of Strawson's key insights.

It appears that different response-norm concepts function in different ways. Some pertain to the appropriateness of affective responses ('adorable'), others to actions ('creditworthy'), others to legal procedures ('indictable'), others to judgments ('reliable'), and some to combinations ('trustworthy'). Some pertain to whether a certain response would be permissible or whether the actor in question is eligible for a certain response, while others connote that a certain response is not only permissible but appropriate and perhaps mandatory. 'Fittingness' is probably different from either of these. To say of someone that they are creditworthy is to say something about their proper eligibility for credit, not to give an affirmative indication that they *should* be given credit; rather it rules out that they should not. By contrast, to describe someone as 'despicable' tends to suggest that they ought to be despised (or least that despising them would be fitting). Additionally, some concepts build in a sort of relativity to a set of persons who would be so responding; 'impeachable' is an example of this, picking out members of Congress; whether a conclusion is 'debatable' appears more general. Finally, some concepts are not simply about a person, but rather about a person in connection with some thing, action, or event (or simply about a kind of

[4] These ideas, and the distinction between detached-appraisal and patient-resentment conceptions of blameworthiness, were previously developed in connection with the analysis of blameworthiness for inadvertent negligence (Zipursky 2021).

thing). Whether lying in a grand jury about one's sex life is an *impeachable* offence is an example of an action as a focus; whether someone's wardrobe is *enviable* focuses on the person and the thing.

When one asks, in tort law, if a driver (Fate or Fortune) is accountable to an accident victim (Hurt) for having negligently injured him, one is utilising a legal response-norm concept that is both eligibility-based and relational. The legal question is whether an effort by Hurt to hold Fate accountable legally for having injured him should succeed. One part of the answer, in our actual law, is whether the events described by Hurt, including the vehicle colliding into him or running him over, did in fact occur. Another is whether the driver was acting negligently, and another still whether the negligent conduct caused the injury. All of these – including the results – are relevant to the accountability.

As indicated in section IV, there are other parts of the law – to be simple here, traffic tickets – where results do not matter. If we are trying to figure out whether there was a legal infraction committed by the drivers for which the state should be imposing accountability via a financial penalty whose proceeds go to state revenue – the result of the conduct makes no difference. The legal system contains a variety of rules and principles that address the question of how to respond to wrongdoing. Different parts of the law do it in different ways for a wide variety of reasons.

## VI. Moral Luck and Forms of Blameworthiness

Reconsider Fate, Fortune and Hurt, now from a moral point of view. Is Fate more blameworthy than Fortune for what he did? If we are allowed to consider all of the things that Fate and Fortune did with their respective automobiles that afternoon, we will answer that there is a blameworthy action Fate did that Fortune did not do: negligently running over Hurt. The moral luck sceptic will object that Fate's negligently running over Hurt is no more blameworthy than Fate's negligent driving, and by hypothesis Fortune's negligent driving was equally blameworthy. The tort example leads me to reply that Hurt could not blame Fortune for running him over (since Fortune did not in fact do that), but could blame Fate for running him over. To the extent that one is willing to entertain answers that refer to the permissibility of a blaming attitude by Hurt against each of the two actors for *what they have done*, one can indeed see a distinction between them. The moral luck sceptic maintains that, while those words can be spoken, the real blameworthiness question concerns only the drivers' actions abstracted from their results (Enoch & Marmor 2007).

A qualified defence of moral luck, as I call it, acknowledges that both the moral luck sceptic and the moral luck defender are using recognisable and cogent conceptions of blameworthiness. Our practices of blaming and holding responsible, even apart from the law, are complex and contain numerous different strands. One could say that the term 'blameworthy' can be used in more than one way, and, indeed, there is a variety of related concepts that fall under the general heading of blameworthiness, just as in law, there are a variety of kinds of liability and accountability. If one wishes to use the term 'blameworthy' to refer to attributes of the actor that were expressed by his or her actions, then one will likely want to abstract away from the results. Here evaluating blameworthiness of an actor is a kind of appraisal *of a person* (Scanlon 2010). The actions of the person are relevant to the appraisal as evidence, but the actions of the person are not otherwise the object of evaluation. There are many contexts in which this manner of appraising others is valuable, and in these contexts, resultant luck may be justifiably ignored in determining blameworthiness. I have elsewhere called a 'detached appraisal' conception of blameworthiness (Zipursky 2021, 2007b), and it may be seen as a variant on what several moral philosophers have denominated a 'moral record' view (Coates & Tognazzini 2012). While speakers commonly use it in connection with particular acts, their evaluation is done in the context of maintaining an overall evaluation of the person.

Acknowledging the value of utilising the concept of blameworthiness in this way, however, leaves open the possibility that the language of 'blameworthiness' is often used differently and justifiably so. Indeed, we commonly ask the question of whether to blame someone for what they *did* and, if so, to what extent and why. The object of the question is not simply the person, but the person *as an agent who did something on a certain occasion*. 'You can't blame her for *refusing to come to the wedding*'. 'You can't blame him for *disappointing the voters*'. Beyond that, we often ask the question of whether to blame someone for something that occurred or something someone else did. 'You can't blame him for *the failure of the restaurant*'. 'You can't blame him for *his daughter's crazy aggressiveness on the soccer field*'. These are all statements that invite debate: we know what the other side, in favour of the argument that one *can (or 'may')* blame the person for this, would look like. As in (many) tort cases, they would be a combination of statements about the wrongfulness or faultiness of the actions chosen (in a restricted sense of 'action'), statements about the causal link between the action in the restricted sense and the action in the less restricted sense (or the action in the restricted sense and the event in question), and statements about the actions of others and the circumstances more generally. The appropriateness, permissibility, or mandatoriness of certain kinds of responses will typically turn on a combination of these (Zipursky 2007b).

A salient version of the kind of inquiry outlined above involves persons who have suffered an injury, a misfortune, or an untoward event in their lives. It is a platitude that people vary in how prone they are to blame others for their injuries or misfortunes. This is not to say, however, that all instances of such blaming are equally justifiable. To the contrary. If Hurt were to blame Fortune for his injuries, he would not be justified in doing so; if he were to blame Fate he would be. Needless to say, such questions can become nuanced in any number of ways: perhaps Hurt was himself driving carelessly; perhaps Fate was driving a bleeding child to the emergency room; perhaps Hurt's injuries cleared up in two days and

Fate was extraordinarily kind in helping him and transforming his life. Notably (as modern urban drivers, bikers, and cyclists know), people sharing the road sometimes resent and fault other drivers for almost hitting them, or for driving in ways that display inadequate attention to their own physical well-being. Perhaps some resentment and condemnation of Fortune would be justifiable. But Hurt's blaming Fortune for his injuries would not be justified, and blaming Fate would be. It should also be noted that the justifiability of resenting others does not always entail that *not resenting them* would be *un*justifiable. There is of course a broad swath of moral thinking that emphasises the virtue of being forgiving.

The foregoing describes what might be labelled a 'victim-resentment' or – utilising an older, agent/patient model of relational wrongdoing – a 'patient-resentment' conception of the blameworthiness of agents, as opposed to the detached appraisal conception outlined earlier. The patient-resentment conception is eligibility-based: the question is typically not whether one *must* or *should* blame someone but (like creditworthiness), whether one *may*. It is also, at least as I have set it up, responder relative rather than general. Strawson famously distinguished third-party responses (indignation) from second-party responses (resentment) and first-party responses (guilt), and he focused on the second-party (Strawson 1962). Likewise, Stephen Darwall, who has worked substantially on the tort-morality connection, has emphasised the second-person standpoint (Darwall 2006). One need not take a position on whether appropriate responses actually differ across these parties to acknowledge *the possibility that they differ* in setting out a framework. Needless to say, the fact that elaborate legal institutions providing a privileged place to the second party – the victim or patient – have been created and sustained for centuries is another reason to leave open this possibility. Finally, the response of directed resentment and directed anger is different than that of a negative evaluation of the values, virtues, and goodness of someone as a person, which is most commonly what appraisal is said to concern.

Notwithstanding these three differences on responses – eligibility versus mandatoriness or fittingness, patient-relativity versus generality, and resentability/anger versus appraisal of quality – there are crucial similarities in how these response norm concepts work. First, both involve responses that are mental states (not actions). Second, in both cases they are propositional attitudes and they are directed at least in part *at someone*. Third, in both cases, the use of the language we are deploying pertains to the question of whether we are considering reactions that may or may not be justified, and the response norm(s) (standards of blameworthiness) address the normative status of the responder's actual response: whether it is justified, permissible, appropriate, fitting, mandatory under the circumstances. Each, taken separately, satisfies what some philosophical scholars have plausibly designated as a desideratum of a philosophical account of blameworthiness: they allow for a distinction between *blaming* and *judging blameworthy* (Coates & Tognazzini 2012). Fourth, and relatedly, reasons can be offered and articulated for why a response does or does not have that normative status. In both cases, the response norms are such that there may be a right answer to the question of whether the person is appropriately blamed by the blamer under the circumstances and blamed to the extent and in the way that they are, and why or why not. Moreover, in neither case is the 'answer' of how blameworthy the actor was for doing what was done the beginning or end of the story about what words or actions should ultimately be forthcoming from the blamer or from other actors, legally or non-legally. Finally, and most obviously, within both response-norm concepts, the question will arise as to whether Fate had the capacity to live up to standards of conduct we justifiably expect others to abide by, to what extent he did and did not live up to such standards, and if he did not, why not. This is so even if (as I have argued elsewhere) the standards may vary somewhat in the two cases, and even if results matter a great deal in the patient resentment context and much less so (or not at all) in the detached appraisal version.

For all of the reasons mentioned above, it will not do to distinguish blameworthiness from blame-related responses and suggest that moral luck is a mirage borne of the failure to draw such a distinction (Enoch & Marmor 2007; Zimmerman 1987). Both the detached appraisal conception and the patient-resentment conceptions are conceptions of blameworthiness, both *can, but need not* give rise to justifiable (or unjustifiable) words or actions of a certain sort; both raise questions about truth insofar as they concern the correct applications of a concept used to distinguish when certain propositional attitudes towards others are or are not permissible, not questions about the justifiability all-told of practical actions or utterances. More generally, I am suggesting that we best understand the problems of moral luck by acknowledging the potential viability of alternative conceptions of blameworthiness and blame – each in its own domain – rather than selecting one as correct and the others as defective.[5]

A critic might argue that there is a form of naturalistic fallacy underlying the account I have offered. Even if one accepts my largely informal arguments based on armchair observations that there is a patient-resentment conception of blameworthiness that works as I have described and has its own internal standards, this is really just a descriptive point about conventional mores. Unless one breaks out of the internal standards of the alleged practice of utilising this conception of blameworthiness, it has little relevance to the authentically normative moral luck question: whether the actor whose conduct brought about bad results really is more blameworthy, not whether they are a better fit according to the criteria for one way of using the term 'blameworthy' and thinking about blameworthiness.

Lack of space leads me to gesture at only three of the many important lines of reply to this basic objection. First and most obviously is Strawson's almost quietistic answer that such patterns of human responsiveness as resentment to

[5] One might depict Enoch and Marmor, for example, as selecting some version of a detached appraisal conception as uniquely correct and some form of a patient-resentment conception as defective (Enoch & Marmor 2007), while Scanlon might be depicted as endorsing a variant of a patient-resentment conception while a detached appraisal conception as defective (Scanlon 2010).

being hurt by another are so fundamental to human life that it is not worth asking whether we should abandon them altogether. Second, and more optimistically, a range of scholars – Wallace, Scanlon, and Darwall among others – have indeed offered elaborate first-order normative accounts of the role of blame in human life, and, in all three cases, victim responses and the norms governing them play an explicit role (Darwall 2006; Scanlon 2010; Wallace 1988). Far from selecting an esoteric conception of blameworthiness, I have selected one that appears to lie near the core of several of the most important works of first-order moral theory today. Finally, my own prior work in both private law theory and moral theory suggests that: (i) it is part of how we do and ought to relate to others that when we have been wrongfully injured by another, we at least sometimes attribute those injuries and related setbacks to having been mistreated by them and this attribution has both cognitive and affective content; (ii) some of our duties to others are not merely duties to act in non-injurious ways, but actually duties not to injure others, and the distinction between these kinds of duties – duties not to injure others and duties not to act injuriously toward others – has moral significance (Goldberg & Zipursky 2007; 2020; Ripstein & Zipursky 2002; Zipursky 2007b, 2021). The late John Gardner eloquently developed these themes in the overlap of tort theory and moral and political philosophy (Gardner 2020).

Finally, much of Williams' *Moral Luck* is about neither a putatively detached perspective on the moral status of action nor a second-party, patient-centred perspective, but is instead focused on the first-person point of view, agent regret, agent remorse, and self-reproach. Without being too reductive, however, one might say that moral agents commonly imagine how they might be regarded by those who have been injured, and they are right to do so. To return to our central example, Fate might well feel remorse and engage in self-reproach for having injured Hurt. Fortune would not, for of course he did not injure Hurt. To put it more critically, Fate would appropriately feel self-reproach for having injured Hurt; if Fortune were to do so, that would be wrongheaded and inappropriate. Here, as in the paragraphs above, there is clearly a great deal of work that space precludes addressing: first-person, second-person, and various third-person perspectives will raise a host of difficult issues about which conception of blameworthiness is in play, whether there are multiple conceptions, and, indeed whether the individuation of different conceptions of blameworthiness is the best way to express my main point: that there are not simply different kinds of answers to questions about how blameworthy someone is for what they did, there are different kinds of questions.

## VII. Conclusion

The argument above has been long and, in more than one way, tortuous. Different parts of our legal system respond differently to legally wrongful conduct. While the standards of legal liability in some parts of the law are independent of the results of the impermissible conduct, in other areas – including in the law of torts – the results typically determine whether there is liability at all. If there is a principled and non-consequentialist explanation for such a requirement in tort law, it might shed light on the topic of moral luck made famous by Bernard Williams. This chapter argued that there is such an explanation and that it does shed light on moral luck.

Tort law does not permit a person to hold a negligent actor accountable unless the actor's overly risky conduct ripened into an actual injury to that person. That is because we delimit the legal power to hold another accountable for negligence to those whose rights were invaded by the negligent actor and we do not treat unrealised risks as rights invasions. The basic idea is simple: one cannot hold someone accountable for negligently injuring oneself if one was not injured, even if the defendant was acting negligently.

Nothing in this depiction of tort law was meant to *ground* an argument about moral luck; it was meant as a heuristic device, a means of spawning hypotheses and insights. Blameworthiness in critical morality resembles liability in law: both are what I have called 'response-norm concepts' – concepts that steer norms governing what sorts of responses to others' actions are permissible. Such norms vary not only in whether they pertain to legal or moral responses, but also in whose responses we are considering, what the character of the response is, and whether we are determining its permissibility, fittingness, fairness, mandatoriness or some other normative status. The distinction between tort law and other forms of law reveals that there is more than one normative concept that covers liability, and norms associated with tort law put results in a central place, even if norms associated with other forms of legal liability do not.

The tort example led us to the suggestion that blameworthiness is not a monolith within moral response norm concepts, either. More particularly, even if there is a conception of blameworthiness within critical moral thinking that is importantly detached from consequences – what I have named a 'detached appraisal' conception of blameworthiness – that is not the only one. Another conception of blameworthiness, labelled a 'patient-resentment' conception, requires us to ask whether a person who has suffered an injury would be justified in blaming another for the act of injuring her. Plainly, the answer will turn not only on whether the actor was negligent or intentional in the harmfulness of the action, but also whether the actor actually did injure the person who suffered an injury.

Although Williams' erudition often led him to the classical times and cosmopolitan forays into world literature, he also shared the great philosopher's appreciation of the banal. For him, this apparently included the law of torts. Indeed, Williams contributed the capstone chapter to an important volume on the philosophical foundations of tort law, one published early in the movement over the past 30 years towards philosophical analysis of the common law. In *Afterword: What Has Philosophy to Learn from Torts Law*? he commented that we are able to learn more about a variety of normative concepts by looking at historical and institutional settings where these concepts have been put to work, including the law of torts (Williams 1995). It is in this spirit that I have tried to employ tort theory to generate insight into the conclusion that there is a variety of different ways of reasoning about blameworthiness, and for some of them, the difference between harmlessness and injury is all the difference in the world.

## Bibliography


Coates, DJ & Tognazzini, NA (2012) 7 3 'The Nature and Ethics of Blame' *Philosophy Compass* 197.

Darwall, S (2006) *The Second-Person Standpoint: Morality, Respect, and Accountability* (Cambridge, Massachusetts, Harvard University Press).

Enoch, D & Marmor, A (2007) 'The Case Against Moral Luck' 26 *Law and Philosophy* 405.

Gardner, J (2020) *Torts and Other Wrongs* (Oxford, Oxford University Press).

Goldberg, JCP & Zipursky, BC (2002) 'Unrealized Torts' 88 *Virginia Law Review* 1625.

—— (2007) 'Tort Law and Moral Luck' 92 *Cornell Law Review* 1123.

—— (2020) *Recognizing Wrongs* (Cambridge, Massachusetts, Harvard University Press).

Honoré, T (1988) 'Responsibility and Luck' 104 *Law Quarterly Review* 530.

*Hymowitz v Eli Lilly & Co* (1989) 342 NE2d 1069 (NY).

Keating, G (2023) *Reasonableness and Risk* (Cambridge, Cambridge University Press).

Nagel, T (1979) 'Moral Luck' in T Nagel, *Mortal Questions* (London, Cambridge University Press).

Nelkin, DK (2023) 'Moral Luck' in EN Zalta & U Nodelman (eds), *The Stanford Encyclopedia of Philosophy* (Spring 2023 edn), available at https://plato.stanford.edu/archives/spr2023/entries/moral-luck

Perry, S (2002) 'Responsibility for Outcomes, Risk, and the Law of Torts' in G Postema (ed), *Philosophy and the Law of Torts* (Oxford, Oxford University Press).

Posner, RA (1972) 'A Theory of Negligence' 1 *Journal of Legal Studies* 29.

Ripstein, A & Zipursky BC (2002) 'Corrective Justice in an Age of Mass Torts' in G Postema (ed), *Philosophy and the Law of Torts* (Oxford, Oxford University Press).

Rosenberg, D (2002) 'Mandatory-Litigation Class Action: The Only Option for Mass Tort Cases' 115 *Harvard Law Review* 831.

Scanlon, TM (2010) *Moral Dimensions: Permissibility, Meaning, Blame* (Cambridge, Harvard University Press).

*Sindell v Abbott Labs* (1980) 607 P2d 924 (Cal).

Stevens, R (2007) *Torts and Rights* (Oxford, Oxford University Press).

Strawson, PF (1962) 'Freedom and Resentment' 48 *Proceedings of the British Academy* 1.

Waldron, J (1995) 'Moments of Carelessness and Massive Loss' in D Owen (ed), *Philosophical Foundations of Tort Law* (Oxford, Clarendon Press).

Wallace, RJ (1988) *Responsibility and the Moral Sentiments* (Cambridge, Harvard University Press).

Watson, G (1987) 'Responsibility and the Limits of Evil: Variations on a Strawsonian Theme' in JM Fischer & M Ravizza (eds), *Perspectives on Moral Responsibility* (Ithaca, Cornell University Press).

Weinrib, E (1995) *The Idea of Private Law* (Cambridge, Harvard University Press).
Williams, B (1981) *Moral Luck* (London, Cambridge University Press).
—— (1986) *Ethics and the Limits of Philosophy* (London, Routledge).
—— (1995) 'Afterword: What Has Philosophy to Learn from Tort Law' in D Owen (ed), *Philosophical Foundations of Tort Law* (Oxford, Clarendon Press).
Zimmerman, MJ (1987) 'Luck and Moral Responsibility' 97 *Ethics* 374.
Zipursky, BC (2007a) 'Sleight of Hand' 48 *William & Mary Law Review* 1999.
—— (2007b) 'Two Dimensions of Responsibility in Crime, Tort and Moral Luck' 9 *Theoretical Inquiries in Law* 97.
—— (2021) 'From Law to Moral Philosophy in Theorizing About Negligence' in V Rodriguez-Blanco & G Pavlakos (eds), *Agency, Negligence, and Responsibility* (Oxford, Oxford University Press).

# 6

# Thinking about *Shame and Necessity* in Liberal Constitutional Theory

EMILY KIDD WHITE

## I. Introduction

Bernard Williams had an instinct for incising the mundane, often by rendering *peculiar* (a favourite term) (Williams 1985: Ch 10) a foundational concept within a dominant theory after setting it under the sights of his distinctive analytical philosophical style. Assumptions about human nature, whether featured explicitly in a state-of-nature type argument, or obscurely in the foundations of a theory, function to make certain legal and political arrangements appear justified, natural, and/or necessary (Kidd White 2021; Berry 1986). This chapter calls attention to the philosophy of mind undergirding liberal constitutional theory by reconstructing a series of arguments from Bernard Williams' 1993 book, *Shame and Necessity*, which draws from ancient Greek tragedy to illuminate the strangeness of the conceptions of intention and will at work in modern ethical theory. *Shame and Necessity* juxtaposes the historically contingent and, for Williams, peculiar conception of the will that emerges as a dominant feature in modern ethical theory with a broader and more open ethical psychology evinced though ancient Greek tragedies. This chapter illustrates how this later conception of the will comes to anchor significant strands of liberal constitutional theory, firstly through the apparatus of the social compact, and later as a foundational element within the tradition of normative constitutional theory, a now dominant branch of constitutional theory (Loughlin 2014).

The chapter builds on Williams' philosophical writings by drawing specific attention to the way that a theory of mind constructed at the level of premises that order the status of emotions vis-à-vis other parts of the psyche works to set up a series of conclusions about ethical activity. It argues that the philosophy of mind that undergirds much of liberal constitutional theory is distinctive for its rigidity, hierarchical, and heavily moralised ordering of parts – that is, its strict privileging of the will over emotions and desires. This conceptualisation of the will, which lays its authority in the claim that it is grounded outside of time and place, which generates in turn a constitutional politics that either excludes from view or downranks a series of pressing political questions. This chapter illustrates some troubling implications for the variants of liberal constitutional theory that adopt this peculiar prioritisation of the will, that Bernard Williams had long in his sights, and its claims to be metaphysical and distinctively moral and, as such, uniquely valuable and authoritative.

## II. Ancient Greek Tragedies as Models that Resist the Heavily Moralised Psychology of Modern Moral Philosophy

Part of Williams' enduring interest in looking back at ancient Greek tragedy lay in its ability to critique contemporary ethical thinking by highlighting the turgidity and narrowness of many of its core concepts (Williams 2008). The exercise, as with other instances of critical genealogical work, aims to consider how attention paid to past practices dislodges what appears to be the unshakeable, or unseen, priors embedded in the base assumptions at play in some of our present-day thinking (Srinivasan 2019; Fricker 2024). For Williams, the rich-textured depictions of ethical life in ancient Greek tragedy work well to draw out some of the limitations of modern Western ethical thinking, with its tendency to prize the will and narrow conceptions of intention while minimising roles for luck, ideas of esteem (and the responsibility of connection), self-perception and social position (Williams 2008). For Williams, the plays present a different way of addressing life as an aesthetic whole premised upon a philosophy of action with muddier, and even mundane, or beside-the-action conceptions of intention at work. The plays, for Williams, serve as a resource for a philosophy of mind and action that blows past the naïve emotion-reason divide that has been so pervasive in modern Western moral thinking. For Jonathan Lear, Williams' interest in ancient Greek tragedy stemmed from a rejection of widespread modern philosophical assumptions concerning the mind and its capacities that set reason as a 'higher faculty' capable of recognising moral ends and disciplining other aspects of the mind in light of them (Lear 2004: 517). Such thinking represented an obvious circularity for Williams as 'the only purchase we can get on the idea that the faculty of reason is "higher" is in the terms of the ethical outcome it is designed to support' (Lear 2004: 517). While Williams was committed to a naturalist ethical psychology, he understood that attempts to construct such an account tend to assume the values they aim to justify, and as such, 'collapse into a moralised psychology' (Lear 2004: 516).

The problem is not, as Williams sees it, with the presence of normative or political criteria. Williams' *Ethics and the Limits of Philosophy* is an excoriating book-length rejection of the idea that we might build an ethics outside of history, politics, and place (Williams 1985). On the contrary, Williams is critiquing the idea that one might draw prescriptions (about what to do, and how to live, and how to decide what is valuable or vile, or worth protecting or not) from what is claimed to be an objective philosophy of mind and/or action that prizes rationality above emotions while understanding the former to be wholly distinct from the latter, and distinctively valuable. The problem lies in setting up a philosophical system that reverse-engineers political and ethical conclusions through ground-level claims as though they themselves were beyond the reach of politics. Matthew Queloz frames this well in writing that a 'problematically moralised psychology' lacks a sense of openness by foreclosing 'the very possibility of ineliminable conflict between the psychological and the moral' with 'psychological ideas … distorted to ensure that moral demands can be met' (Queloz 2022: 1609).

One way to read *Shame and Necessity*, then, is to see Williams reaching back to the plays of Sophocles and others for models that resist the heavily moralised psychology he saw as underpinning much of modern moral philosophy (Lear 2004), which set in place the idea of reason as a higher faculty that disciplines other aspects of the psyche, including emotions, desires, and appetites (see Kidd White *forthcoming*). To resist the idea that the will is free, and intention is only valuable, when it acts in accordance with reason untainted by these other elements. We see a variation of this claim working in present day invocations of psychology and neuroscience which rest their authority (and the authority of the ethical and political prescriptions that stem from their accounts) on their purported access to knowledge that is untainted by emotions and desire. Yet, as Thomas Nagel has argued, any claims to ethical knowledge flowing from the disciplines of psychology or neuroscience are themselves indisputably normative (just as any element drawn into a reflective equilibrium, including emotions and moral intuitions) (Nagel 2021). In a 1995 essay entitled, 'Naturalism and Morality', Williams argues that '[a] non-moralised, or less moralised, psychology uses the categories of meaning, reasons and value, but leaves it open, or even problematical, in what way moral reasons and ethical values fit with other motives and desires' (Williams 2008).

The temptation to settle into a heavily moralised psychology is so overwhelming that, for Williams, nothing short of the beguiling texture of the plays can maintain this spirit of openness, and the demanding subtlety, complexity and alertness required of ethical thinking (see Kidd White *forthcoming*). Reading *Shame and Necessity* aided by Lear, we can reconstruct a powerful critique of theoretical approaches that embed a heavily moralised psychology among their foundational claims as a means of side-stepping the pressure and complexity of first-order political and ethical questions.

## III. Resisting the Progressivist Narrative/Resisting Metaphysical Expectations for the Will

In *Shame and Necessity*, Williams draws on passages from ancient Greek tragedy to establish striking juxtapositions with the conceptions of will and intention that play foundational roles in modern moral philosophy, which later embed within certain strains of liberal constitutional theory. The contrast is useful not to glorify a past as Williams takes pains to clarify (2008: 6–7) but to set to light the history of the ideas that lay seamed into present-day understandings. As Williams writes, the comparison is an exercise in historical reconstruction that is fundamentally *philosophical* in nature 'because it has to lay bare certain structures of thought and experience and, above all, ask questions about their value' (2008: 4). Throughout *Shame and Necessity*, Williams argues against the *progressivist* picture of ethical thought that's commonly claimed regarding the move from ancient Greek tragedy through Christianity into Kantian moral theory. The progressivist view has been described by the classicist E.R. Dodds as the ethical development from shame culture to guilt culture that saw ancient Greek ethical ideas being 'replaced by a more complex and refined set of conceptions that define a more mature form of ethical experience' (Williams 2008), including conceptions of autonomy, 'personal responsibility and an internalized conviction of sin' (Knox 1993). Williams sees this as an overly simplistic view, and part of the work of *Shame and Necessity* is to show the fineness and complexity of ethical thinking on display in ancient Greek tragedies. Williams' arguments run along two distinct lines. Firstly, he draws from the plays to show that the ancient Greeks possessed ethical concepts like intention and responsibility that were thought to be missing from their daemonic worldview full of supernatural pressures, and secondly, to show that those ethical concepts were – at times – in better shape than the peculiar versions of them that have come to dominate our ethical thinking, and as argued here, much of our constitutional theorising.

## A. Conceptions of Intention and Responsibility at Work in Ancient Greek Tragedy

Williams challenged the progressivist's claim that the ancient Greeks lacked a conception of the will. His target through much of *Shame and Necessity* is the influential work (Knox 1993) of the classicist Bruno Snell who portrayed the characters of Homer's epics as child-like, unreflective, and wholly lacking in a sense of agency as they find themselves pushed through events and entrapped by fate via external supernatural forces. As Bernard Knox writes, Williams rejected the fallacy that the Homeric mind 'functioned on a more primitive level than ours' by demonstrating how the tragedies were replete with themes regarding agency, responsibility, and intention (Knox 1993). Williams cites, for example, a famous passage from the *Odyssey* depicting the shipwrecked protagonist, Odysseus, stranded on a shore, waging an intense battle with his own thoughts over various schemes of survival. As Williams reminds us, 'every reader of Homer will recall passages in which a hero deliberates and decides on action independently of divine admonition or advice' (Knox 1993). Williams pushes the point deeper finding that even where a god does intervene in events, they do so by exerting pressure on the agency of the character by adding weight to some of the reasons already present in their deliberations. Far from wind-up toys put through paces around a game board, the characters interact with gods that press upon them 'reasons for one or the other of the courses the hero is weighing … and when the agent decides for those reasons and acts on them, he acts on his own reasons' (Knox 1993). Despite the wide purchase of the progressivist's account of this early lack in ethical thought, Williams draws on the plays to show that they contain 'the basic conceptions of action for human life: the capacities to deliberate, to conclude, to act, to exert oneself, to make oneself do things, to endure' (Williams 2008: 40). Pressure, necessity and agency are the components of this form of historical drama and the plays would lack all tragic effect in their absence (Williams 2008: 15). Indeed, the blunt and exquisite pain of ancient Greek tragedy flows from the ability to recognise and be moved by ethical dilemmas that set imperfect but virtue-bearing characters with agency and the responsibilities of role and connection amidst the coarse pressures of necessity and the vulnerabilities of human life. The modern, metaphysical conception of the will is structured to exclude the burden and strain of necessity and herein lies the precise philosophical move that Williams throughout the book is rejecting, which is, the formulation of moral concepts that function to exclude much of the material that seems central to ethical life.

## B. The Will is not a Metaphysical Thing

Williams' first move against the progressivist view, which claimed that the ancient Greeks didn't possess complex understandings of responsibility, agency and intention, was to illustrate these concepts at work in various ancient Greek tragedies. His second more provocative line of argument suggested that ancient Greek ethical thought was, in some ways (certainly not all) better structured, for it 'lacked several things that we do not need, in particular the illusion that the basic powers of the mind are inherently constituted in terms of an ethical order' (2008: 46). While Kantians still find the will they are committed to absent from Plato, they nevertheless find in the *Republic* an ethical psychology that ranks its component parts, and thus, through the progressivist lens see evidence of 'a crucial step in the right direction' (2008: 43). And yet, through his sensitive, superlative read of the plays, Williams helps us to see the narrowness of the singular conception of the will so central to voluntarist action (action that is willed or intended in accordance with reason) that the progressivists champion. The progressivist's *singular* conception of the will functions to elevate its moral status vis-à-vis other aspects of the psyche. For Williams, however, this formulation obscures a series of rich and ethically significant distinctions, which bring into the fold a whole variety of different forms of intention, as well as desire (and the multiplicity of desire), matters concerning roles and relationships, states of mind, and character (Williams 2008: Ch III). Intention is a broad and multifaceted phenomenon, not entirely separable from desires, emotions, and circumstances. Through the plays we can readily grasp that decisions aren't the stand-alone, distinctively ethical component of an action for such an emphasis risks misrepresenting 'the whole range of ascriptions of responsibility both formal and informal' and 'errs in claiming that the notion of the voluntary is supported at some deeper level by basic idea of what it is to be 'really' responsible' (Williams 2008: 67). It is a mistake, Williams argues, 'to think that the idea of the voluntary can itself be refined beyond a certain point' (Williams 2008: 67) (Queloz 2022). Indeed, we 'deceive ourselves if we suppose that public practices of ascribing responsibility can be derived from an antecedent notion of moral responsibility, or that the idea of the voluntary is uniquely important to responsibility' (Williams 2008: 67). Williams continues, it

> is a mistake to suppose that the notion of the voluntary is a profound conception that is threatened only by some opposing and profound theory of the universe (in particular to the effect that determinism is true) … In truth, though it may be extended or contracted in various ways, it can hardly be deepened at all. What threatens it is the attempt to make it profound, and the effect of trying to deepen it is to put it beyond all recognition' (Williams 2008: 68).

The traditional metaphysical problem of the freedom of the will only emerges for those who have 'metaphysical expectations' in the very same way that the 'problem of evil' presents only for those who expect the world to be good (Williams 2008).

One unforgettable laugh in the history of moral philosophy belongs to G.E.M. Anscombe who laughed at promises, and those who understood promises to be at the centre of our moral lives. Anscombe writes that when I say *I promise* – it is akin to my saying I lay myself under an obligation – but the question that must follow will always be – *have I?* (Anscombe 1978). Hume laughed at promises too, and the idea that one could alter the moral universe through an utterance. Williams' laughter here is a quieter one. Commitments undertaken via promises are a part of ethical life – but they are not especially distinctive, or first-order, or trump-card like (Williams 1985).

## C. Resisting a Heavily Moralised Psychology by Attending to the Richness of Emotions

The heavily moralised psychology analysed above works to make modern notions of the will distinctive and metaphysical, when for the ancient Greeks, intention and responsibility were regular features of ethical action, without any special priority. A heavily moralised psychology establishes the will not only at the top of the hierarchy of the various elements of the mind but deigns it the sole bearer of ethical knowledge. This account devalues the body, bifurcates reason from desire, and strips emotion of ethical significance, a position that Williams rejected in a 1973 essay entitled, 'Morality and the Emotions' (Williams 1973). As Iris Murdoch wrote, under such a view, '[w]e no longer see man against a background of values, of realities, which transcend him. We picture man as a brave naked will surrounded by an easily comprehended empirical world' (Murdoch 1961: 18). The rational will separated from emotion and desire from Plato on leaves us with a 'featureless moral self' (Williams 2008: 160; see also Queloz 2022: 1609), a rational will outside of time and place, that is fundamentally alone, and alone in the sense of never having to be confronted with 'real dissimilar others' (Murdoch 1961: 16).

By way of contrast, the plays focus our attention on the complex unity of the person, and the project of a life.[1] The impact of the Homeric poems depend, for example, upon the ethical pressures associated with the complex and divided desires, intentions, and emotions of the characters, depictions which in turn rely upon an ethical psychology that invites a confrontation with the other as a mysterious whole that is bound by time and place and united by a sense of a character (Williams 2008: 49). To underscore this sense of unity, Williams draws on the death of the hero Kebriones in the *Iliad*, whose body lies still and broken in the middle of a raging battle:

> but he lay in the whirling dust,
> mightily in his might, having forgotten all his horsemanship (Williams 2008: 49).

Part of the pain of the poem is the sense of the utter destruction of the whole person who now lies in the whirling dust, and who was more than a featureless rational will whose whole or even principal value couldn't be reduced to that part. The unique skills, aims and character of the deceased underscore the sorrow of the moment, which offers a vivid contrast to a portrayal of moral life limited to one-dimensional portraits of will and intention. This sense of sorrow in the play makes strange and renders pale any view of the character as something less than an embodied self that holds complex plans, ambitions, desires, and ways of seeing the world, and it relies upon a broader and less hierarchical philosophical conceptualisation of the mind and its component parts. Reading *Shame and Necessity*, the recrimination is quiet but clear – the ancient Greek tragedies under Williams' gaze are complex just as ethical life is complex and it is wrong-headed to rely on rigid concepts drawn from a heavily moralised psychology that functions to exclude from consideration so much of the ethical pressure of the plays, which generates from the personal and bound-in-time nature of the insoluble moral dilemmas, and painful pathways at hand.

Williams writes at length in *Shame and Necessity* on Sophocles' great tragedy *Oedipus*. The moral horror of the play, which flows from the protagonist realising he'd committed acts of incest and patricide, is not limited to questions of intention, nor entirely erasable through claim of ignorance. Williams writes,

> Do we understand the terror of that discovery only because we residually share magical beliefs in blood-guilt, or archaic notions of responsibility? Certainly not: we understand

[1] See also Scheffler 1993.

> it because we know in the story of one's life there is an authority exercised by what one has done, and not merely by what one has intentionally done (Williams 2008: 69).

The emotional depth of Williams' engagement with the tragedies, the rich emotional lives of the characters, and the emotional effects of the movements of the plays are elements which reject a heavily moralised psychology that sets the will above and apart from all other aspects of the psyche. Analysing these emotions leads us towards a more muddled and in-between portrait of the psyche, which appears less contorted to set up a strict set of universal ethical conclusions. The emotion-laden ethical concept of regret shores this up powerfully. Regret denotes a complex sensibility capable of picking up far more than the distinction between intentions and effects (Williams 2008: 69). He writes,

> Sometimes regret can focus simply on the outside circumstances that made the action go wrong, and the thought is: I acted and deliberated as well as I could, and it is sad that it turned out that way. But regret cannot always be held at a distance, and then it moves back to the moments of deliberation and action, and you regret acting as you did. This still need not imply that you deliberated carelessly; you may have deliberated as well as you could, but you still deeply regret that that was how the deliberation went, and that this is what you did. This is not just a regret about what happened, such as a spectator might have. It is an agent's regret (Williams 2008: 69).

As regret belongs to an agent, it cannot always be held at a distance. Attending to the ethical experience of regret in tragedy reveals space for the existence of ethical responsibilities beyond intention.[2] As regret is a phenomenon not at all separable from its affective dimensions, it is in many ways beyond the grip of a theoretical account that accepts the metaphysical notion of the will, which sits as the isolated, distinctive centrepiece of the progressivist's account. For Williams, what ancient Greek tragedies demand from our present-day understanding is not that we entertain supernatural ideas 'but that we look for analogies in our experience and our sense of the world to the necessities they express' (Williams 2008: 19). We look for 'structural substitutions', to grasp the ways that we might be responsible for an outcome that we did not intend or which was even outside of our meaningful control. This understanding does not diminish political accountability for structures set in place but, conversely and instead, sets in cold light the ways in which material structures set the conditions and possibilities for ethical activity. We see through this understanding of regret precisely how first-order political questions cannot be excluded from the domain of ethics.

The richness of this idea of regret, for Williams, carried real possibility for ethical life by resisting the sequestering of ethical responsibility from a world replete with the horrors of unjustified suffering, and the contingencies of luck, and material structures that seem to mimic on a personal level this element of *necessity* (Kidd White *forthcoming*). In this way, paying attention to the emotional

[2] See also Goldie 2009.

dimensions of tragedy sets into stark light the stilted nature of many modern ethical concepts that pervade our thinking. These concepts send to the margins, or work to obscure entirely, certain ethical or political dilemmas. For Williams this represents something of a loss in a textured understanding of ethical life and political phenomenon that, as argued below, extends into modern constitutional theory.[3] Philosophical attention to the emotions within tragedy move us back into this in-between muddled – open and flexible – ethical psychology – vis-à-vis this overly moralised, hierarchical, metaphysical portrait of the psyche. With the emotions themselves having the potential to offer a deeper and richer ethical experience of the actions within the play, revealing an ethical psychology that's not quite so contorted to set up a firm set of ethical conclusions. Williams through the book invites us to see how it would be a loss to draw on a series of concepts that were structured to dismiss these elements. None of this to say that our desires and emotions are always valuable. We can be wrong-sighted in our emotions and desires just as we can with our reasons.[4] We simply cannot proceed, however, as though questions within ethical epistemology (as opposed to broader, distinct questions concerning moral scepticism) have been solved,[5] and we cannot imbed a heavily moralised philosophy of mind as a prior into our theoretical accounts to privilege certain conclusions about ethical activity in order to justify or prescribe certain political and legal arrangements.

## IV. The *Peculiar* Will in the Foundations of Liberal Constitutional Theory

This final section of the chapter begins to chart how some of the problematic aspects of present-day understandings of the will – that were Williams' target in *Shame and Necessity* – are reflected in the foundations of liberal constitutional theory, with a focus on one of its dominant variants, normative constitutional theory.[6] Several traditions in liberal constitutional theory rely upon the same heavily moralised psychology which functions to privilege an understanding of the will as a distinctively moral feature of action beginning with voluntarist social compact models of political legitimacy (Locke 2003; Rousseau 2012), followed by an emphasis by some but not all theorists[7] to rely on notions of hypothetical consent, or similar variants of ideal theorising.

This later move relies on a conception of the will that is – via a prior philosophical assumption – set apart from other aspects of the mind. What political

[3] See, generally, van Domselaar 2022.
[4] See, generally, Kidd White 2014; Gardner 2009.
[5] On the status of moral intuitions, see, e.g., Nagel 2024.
[6] On normative constitutional theory, see generally Dyzenhaus 2012.
[7] See, e.g., Decisionism and Relationism in Constitutional Theory in Loughlin 2014.

legitimacy demands on these accounts, then, is the alignment between existing political arrangements and moral principles that have been drawn from the rational aspect of the mind, which is conceptualised as distinct and separable from the mind's other components that are deficient in their ability to access, grasp, or bear them. These voluntarist accounts of political legitimacy build from the progressivist narrative that prizes the exclusion of history and politics, context, and contingency-based-constraints from the domain of morality. Various strains of normative constitutional theory build on these philosophical foundations when they work to construct of an ideal account of constitutionalism that serves moral principles drawn from a faculty unbound by time and place. Where, however, one is suspicious, as Bernard Williams was, of such a hierarchical, bifurcated, and heavily moralised philosophy of mind, and well-versed in a genre such as ancient Greek tragedy that resists such a depiction of the mind through its rich accountings of the dilemmas presented to human lives shaped by station, suffering, longing and loss, then there are clear problems with political theories that purport to draw from apolitical and ahistorical moral principles.

In a 1972 *Spectator* review of John Rawls' *A Theory of Justice*, Williams wrote:

> Rawls's model of the original position is a striking monument to something which contract-theorists and (in *this* respect) utilitarian's have in common, the belief that particular historical situations enter political and social calculation only secondarily, along with particular empirical information about the wants and interests of the persons involved. Thus, Rawls's parties are pictured in total abstraction from history, equipped like their Lockean and Rousseauite predecessors only with the draughty coverings of rationality and (perhaps) morality (Williams 2014: 86).

It is a particularised notion of the will separate from time and place and the contingencies and compromises of political life that makes possible on some (but not all (see, e.g., Simmons 1999)) accounts of political legitimacy the replacement of the requirement of actual consent with hypothetical consent. Liberal theories of political legitimacy that build from notions of hypothetical consent (see, e.g., Rawls 1999) provide a template for normative constitutional theory by setting the aim of theory to produce principles that could be agreed upon by any party properly guided by reason. While these traditions within liberal theorising range, they share at root the prior assumption of an account of human nature characterised by a heavily moralised psychology, which functions to privilege the moral over the political via a philosophy of mind that conceives of the will as distinctive and authoritative. The claim that moral imperatives were separable from other elements of an ethical outlook – so central to modern moral philosophy – is one that Williams explicitly rejected through his writings on thick ethical concepts (Williams 1985).

This conceptualisation of the will at work in normative constitutional theory functions to obscure a series of questions that might otherwise seem pressing for a field intent on thinking carefully about the life of a community under law. A conception of the will that functions principally to frame constitutional theory as outside of politics, or as an antidote to politics, and somehow distinct from the demands of the people. Martin Loughlin writes that normative constitutional theory, 'the prevailing mode of legal thought today', is structured to be disinterested in engaging with the people over which it claims authority for it sets 'the abstract and ideal character of (its) directing idea, whether the ideal constitution or some overarching principle of legality' as its lodestar (Loughlin 2014). Normative constitutional theories fashion themselves 'on the autonomy of legal ordering and in this mode constituent power – the demands of the people – becomes a redundant category' (Loughlin 2014). People, along with their desires, wishes, life-plans, connections and commitments, and politics get washed out of the picture in the first philosophical construction of the matter.

Richard Wollheim writes in a chapter entitled, 'On the Theory of Democracy' in a 1971 book edited by Williams on *British Analytical Philosophy*, that idealist-based solutions to questions about democracy rely on

> a particular assumption about human nature, according to which every rational being, and hence every member of society, possesses two selves or wills; a 'true' or 'real' self or will, and an 'arbitrary' or 'fitful' self or will. Every true self is not merely coherence internally, in all its manifestations are of a piece, but it is also coherent with all other true selves so that their joint activities display a harmony (*volonté Générale* according to Rousseau) (Wollheim 1971: 254).

Wollheim is here resisting '*para-psychological*' (Wollheim 1971: 254) solutions to political questions, that is, the use of *human nature*-like claims to escape from the pressing task of developing a substantive political theory.

Sharon Krause draws on the work of Williams to critique contemporary normative political theory for lacking an account of political agency, citing a long and robust tradition in political theory that's explicitly self-fashioned as a 'normative enterprise', which focuses on the construction of political norms and on what citizens 'ought to do' at the expense of any robust thinking on political action (Krause 2009: 262). Normative constitutional theory is open to the same criticism. A focus on justice or rights abstracted from political action and agency follows from a series of foundational human-nature-like commitments to seeing citizens as rational and autonomous. *Shame and Necessity* raises in sharp and vivid detail

> the many problems with the concept of moral obligation including its categorical claims to trump all other kinds of motivation; its focus on a supposedly autonomous will undermined by particular persons' dispositions, interests, and social roles, in sum, its insulation from their lived experience as members of a community with an outlook that is both partly shared but also meaningfully individual (Williams 2008: xix).

Kraus embraces Williams' sharp renunciation of the – 'the intense moralism' of the field, finding that '(t)he theories of justice that dominate today give strict priority to the moral over the political; (and) in particular they represent "the continuation of a (Kantian) morality as the framework of the political system"' (Krause 2009: 262). Krause finds in Williams:

> a subtle moral psychology of agency (alongside) a complex understanding of how the exercise of agency is always contingent and often internally conflicted. In contrast to the idyll of agency as rational autonomy that is simultaneously present (because

> assumed) and absent (because undertheorized) in liberal theory today, this view elaborates agency in light of the many dimensions of what Williams once called 'the actual' (Krause 2009: 264).

The privileging of the impersonal will establishes a theoretical foundation which reinforces the claim that the most important aspect of human nature is this narrow moral capacity, which can and should be rightly disassociated from other aspects of the person, and the material, political, and historical situations that shape their lives. The theory is structured to cabin off, dismiss even, political demands, which leaves us with a constitutional politics that is impervious to political criticism, and, as such, in many ways prone to elite capture. We can see instances of this in the domain of constitutional rights, which are often interpreted in line with the status quo, and function to exclude interpretations of rights with significant structural or material consequences (Moyn 2018).

This effective cabining of the political and 'the actual' from theorising about constitutional law is similarly reflected in critiques centring the explicit politics of the *legal form*, as they are reflected in liberal constitutional theory. The conceptual apparatus of the *legal form* analysed by Pashukanis privileges abstract and formal legal relations over existing material realities.[8] It is a form of political equality borne out of an equality at law to contract, or to hold a bundle of rights, for example, despite vast existing disparities in negotiating power. The *legal form* is underpinned by the same moralised psychology that Williams is concerned with, the same moralised psychology that serves to privilege the seemingly exceptional faculty of reason, which in turn offers a boundless, unflagging authority to particular, politically motivated, conceptions of consent and the will. Foundational claims about human nature, which include this heavily moralised psychology, function to support exploitative social relations by placing moral faculties outside of circumstances of substantial material inequality. Political histories of subjugation and exploitation are of secondary importance to the constructed equality of the legal form, which rests on an account of human nature that centres man's moral faculties. Social relations of exclusion and exploitation that operate under the veil of formal legal equality should not be obscured by the concepts most central to our understanding of constitutional theory. And yet, normative constitutional theory is functionally disinterested in these social relations, and so too, the specific politics surrounding the inception of any particular constitutional arrangement. As Jedidiah Purdy writes, constitutions mark the cessation of hostilities. They are peace treaties written on the victor's terms, though the violence and political strictures and horizons of the specific historical moment invariably get washed out (Purdy 2017). This 'laundering effort' (Purdy 2017) functions in part through normative constitutional theory for the heavily moralised ethical psychology embedded in its foundations function to make these political features enter the frame only secondarily, if at all.

[8] See, e.g., Knox 2022.

We are left then with a normative picture of constitutional theory that not only sits above the people and their political demands, but also one that claims a certain timelessness. Natasha Wheatley has written powerfully on the importance of analysing 'the more formal tools and techniques that law employs to buck time and insulate itself from history's mutation – what we might call the technologies of its temporal indifference' (Wheatley 2021). *Shame and Necessity* reminds us that we needn't conceptualise the will as a capacity for reason unconstrained by history, nor as one that claims timelessness as a source of its authority. Williams writes that for Kantians or Utilitarians ethical knowledge is beyond history and psychology, with each moral outlook, in different ways, prescribing the withdrawal of 'our ethical interest from both chance and necessity' (Williams 2006: 54). For, when,

> morality itself is disconnected historically and psychologically from the rest of life, as it often is by moral philosophy, and is left as a supposedly self-contained and self-explanatory realm of value, then necessity and chance and the bad news they bring with them are deliberately excluded' (Williams 2006: 54).

The richness of the plays invite us to resist the urge to locate what is valuable in a separate realm, insulated from chance and necessity (Williams 2006: 253; Kidd White 2025).

A constitutional theory that refused this timelessness immediately invites in questions concerning power, vitality, grace, solidarity, suffering, pleasure, care and vulnerability, and as well, questions concerning their just distribution. Setting constitutional theorising in history sets up questions of reparations to emerge as a significant ethical and political concern[9] and crumbles the practice of seeing borders as real boundaries for our ethical and political horizons. Normative constitutional theory relies upon an indefensibly narrow conception of ethical responsibility. Through Williams' discussions of ancient Greek tragedy, however, we might be encouraged to see responsibility in constitutional theory as far broader a phenomenon, as flowing from our actions and stations and the (past and future) harms that are related to them, as tied to our relations, and the quality of our relations, and answerable for the patterns of exploitation and dispossession that communities have profited from.

Drawing out the place of emotions in the presupposed philosophy of mind grounding constitutional theory reveals much about its functions. One consequence of a heavily moralised psychology that downranks emotion, which supports imaginative efforts, empathy and attention (Del Mar 2020; Kidd White 2020), is that it leaves us with a constitutional theory that centres a conception of a will that is fundamentally incurious. The downranking of emotion sets in place a stubborn and imperious resistance to learning about the lives of others under law, leaving us with the conclusions that there are no deep or difficult to access ethically significant differences between persons and group in their experience of a constitutional

[9] See, e.g., Davis 2009.

order (Kidd White 2020). A foundational concept that is structured to be impervious to the impact of constitutional arrangements on other political communities but, also, unconstrained by the ethical imperative to provide restoration for past acts of violence.

## V. A Theory of State, a Theory of Freedom

In a series of passages in *Shame and Necessity*, Williams speaks briefly to the field of legal theory to criticise its sometimes-shared reverence for certain constructions of the will and notions of intention that echo some deeply held commitments within certain dominant strains of modern moral philosophy. In a chapter in *Shame and Necessity*, entitled 'Recognizing Responsibility', Williams writes:

> the question of whether any part of the legal system is in good shape can be discussed only in terms of what we demand of a legal system, and how we conceive the powers of the state. We have conceptions of legal responsibility different from any such conceptions that the Greeks had, but that is because we have a different conception of law – not basically, a different conception of responsibility. It is not that we have managed to substitute for the Greek's ideas a purified notion of something called moral responsibility, and then do the best we can to embody that in the state of the law (Williams 2008: 67).

Drawing from Williams' *Shame and Necessity*, this chapter has generated a critique of normative constitutional theory, which works to establishes an ideal, disentangled from politics, that should be reflected in law. Through Williams we can see how a theoretical account that assumes as a prior a heavily moralised philosophy of mind functions to render unassailable certain conclusions about ethical and political activity. It is this form of theoretical argument, *this supposed reach beyond politics through a philosophy of mind*, that Williams is so vital in ascertaining, and rejecting. It is a call not to embed as a prior a philosophy of mind that generates concepts that allow us to abdicate from the real ethical and political pressures that confront us in all their complexity, which in constitutional theory is nothing less than the challenge of organising life as a community under law. Constitutional theory must begin, then, not with a moral understanding of responsibility and will, abstracted from time and place, but with a political theory of freedom, or emancipation, and the state.[10] Indeed, Williams speaks in just a few lines in *Shame and Necessity* to legal theorists – to explicitly reject the idea that our task – as legal philosophers – is to embody a purified moral ideal as best we can in the law. To use Wollheim's term, we cannot rely, as normative constitutional theory does, *on para-psychological* solutions to political questions. For constitutional theorists, Williams offers a sharp reminder of the stilted and historically contingent conceptions of

[10] See also, Duff & von Hirsch 1997.

will, intention, and responsibility that remain so central to normative constitutional theory today. He shows us how a philosophy of mind, embedded as a prior in a theoretical account, can function principally as a form of retreat from the political. He implores us not to use a heavily moralised philosophy of mind to render a theory impervious to a series of questions that should otherwise be heavy and pressing. A constitutional theory that by aim and design is stationed outside of history functions as cover for an exploitative and fundamentally incurious constitutional politics that has been impervious to demands which flow from needs, relations, and responsibilities, and far too quiet on the subject of political violence, and shamelessly compliant in the face of long-running material structures and social relations that function to support expropriation, exploitation and exclusion.

## Bibliography


Anscombe, GEM (1978) 'Rules, Rights, And Promises' 3 *Midwest Studies in Philosophy* 318.

Berry, CJ (1986) *Human Nature*, Issues in Political Theory (Atlantic Highlands, NJ, Humanities Press).

Davis, PC (2009) 'Responsive Constitutionalism and the Idea of Dignity' 11 *University of Pennsylvania Journal of Constitutional Law* 1373.

Del Mar, M (2020) *Artefacts of Legal Inquiry: The Value of Imagination in Adjudication* (Oxford, Hart Publishing).

van Domselaar, I (2022) 'Law's Regret: On Moral Remainders, (in)Commensurability and a Virtue-Ethical Approach to Legal Decision-Making' 13 2 *Jurisprudence* 220.

Duff, A & von Hirsch, A (1997) 'Responsibility, Retribution and the "Voluntary": A Response to Williams' 56 1 *The Cambridge Law Journal* 103.

Dyzenhaus, D (2012) 'Constitutionalism in an Old Key: Legality and Constituent Power' 1 2 *Global Constitutionalism* 229.

Fricker, M (2024) 'Bernard Williams' Historical Self-Consciousness', in *Harvard University Whitehead Lectures*, available at www.youtube.com/watch?v=bz1Kli6BAS8

Gardner, J (2009) 'The Logic of Excuses and the Rationality of Emotions' 43 *The Journal of Value Inquiry* 315.

Goldie, P (2009) 'Narrative Thinking, Emotion, and Planning' 67 1 *The Journal of Aesthetics and Art Criticism* 97.

Kidd White, E (2014) 'Till Human Voices Wake Us: The Role of Emotions in the Adjudication of Dignity Claims' 3 *Journal of Law, Religion and State* 201.

—— (2020) 'On Emotions and the Politics of Attention in Judicial Reasoning' in A Amaya & M Del Mar (eds), *Virtue, Emotion and Imagination in Law and Legal Reasoning* (Oxford, Hart Publishing).

—— (2021) 'Images of Reach, Range, and Recognition: Thinking about Emotions in the Study of International Law' in S Bandes, J Madeira, K Temple & E Kidd White (eds), *Research Handbook on Law and Emotion* (Cheltenham, Edward Elgar Publishing).

—— (2023) 'Emotions and Precedent' in T Endicott, H Dan Kristjánsson, & S Lewis (eds), *Philosophical Foundations of Precedent* (Oxford, Oxford University Press).

—— *(forthcoming)* 'An International Law of the Emotions' in E Benvenisti & D Kritsiotis (eds), *The Cambridge History of International Law* (Cambridge, Cambridge University Press).
Knox, B (1993) 'The Greek Way: Review Shame and Necessity by Bernard Williams' *The New York Review of Books* (18 November, 1993 issue), available a www.nybooks.com/articles/1993/11/18/the-greek-way
—— (2022) 'Imperialism, Hypocrisy and the Politics of International Law' 3 *TWAIL Review* 25.
Krause, SR (2009) 'Political Agency and the Actual' in D Callcut (ed), *Reading Bernard Williams* (Oxfordshire, Routledge Publishing).
Lear, J (2004) 'Psychoanalysis and the Idea of a Moral Psychology: Memorial to Bernard Williams' Philosophy' 47 5 *Inquiry* 515.
Locke, J (2003) 'Second Treatise of Government' in J Locke (D Woulton, ed), *Political Writings* (Indianapolis, Hackett Publishing).
Loughlin, M (2014) 'The Concept of Constituent Power' 13 2 *European Journal of Political Theory* 218.
Moyn, S (2018) *Not Enough: Human Rights in an Unequal World* (Cambridge, Massachusetts, Harvard University Press).
Murdoch, I (1961) 'Against Dryness: A Polemical Sketch' 16 1 *Encounter* 16.
Nagel, T (2021) 'Types of Intuition' 43 11 *London Review of Books* (3 June), available at www.lrb.co.uk/the-paper/v43/n11/thomas-nagel/types-of-intuition
—— (2024) *Moral Feelings, Moral Reality, and Moral Progress* (Oxford, Oxford University Press).
Purdy, J (2017) 'Laundered Violence: Law and Protest in Durham' *N+1* (23 August), available at www.nplusonemag.com/online-only/online-only/laundered-violence
Queloz, M (2022) 'The Essential Superficiality of the Voluntary and the Moralization of Psychology' 179 5 *Philosophical Studies* 1591.
Rawls, J (1999) *A Theory of Justice* (rev edn) (Cambridge, Harvard University Press).
Rousseau, JJ (2012) *The Basic Political Writings*, 2nd edn (Indianapolis, Hackett Publishing).
Scheffler, S (1993) *Human Morality* (Oxford, Oxford University Press).
Simmons, JA (1999) 'Justification and Legitimacy' 109 4 *Ethics* 739.
Srinivasan, A (2019) 'VII – Genealogy, Epistemology and Worldmaking' 119 2 *Proceedings of the Aristotelian Society* 127.
Wheatley, N (2021) 'Law and the Time of Angels: International Law's Method Wars and the Affective Life of Disciplines' 60 2 *History and Theory* 311.
Williams, B (1973) 'Morality and the Emotions' in B Williams, *Problems of the Self: Philosophical Papers 1956–1972* (Cambridge, Cambridge University Press).
—— (1985) *Ethics and the Limits of Philosophy* (Cambridge, Princeton University Press).
—— (2006) 'The Women of Trachis: Fictions, Pessimism, Ethics' in B Williams (M Burnyeat, ed), *The Sense of the Past: Essays in the History of Philosophy* (Princeton, Princeton University Press).
—— (2008) *Shame and Necessity* (Berkeley, University of California Press).
—— (2014) 'A Theory of Justice by John Rawls' in B Williams, *Essays and Reviews: 1959–2002* (Princeton, Princeton University Press).
Wollheim, R (1966) 'On the Theory of Democracy' in B Williams & A Montefiore (eds), *British Analytical Philosophy* (New York, Humanities Press).

# 7

# Political Realism, Tragedy, and the Violent Foundations of the State

## *Reading* The Man Who Shot Liberty Valance *with Bernard Williams*

DAVID OWEN*

## I. Introduction

Although the theme of realism in ethics and politics may be seen as an abiding concern in Bernard Williams' philosophy (Owen 2018), it is only relatively late in his career that articulating a stance of political realism becomes an explicit focus for him and it cannot be said that it was highly developed prior to his death. In this chapter, I explore the relationship of law and politics in the context of political founding in order to draw attention to dimensions of Williams' political realism that are undeveloped but which can be fleshed out using resources provided by his earlier work. I do so by engaging with the Western as a cinematic genre that, among other things, is concerned with political founding and its implications for the polity, and in its more reflective forms seeks to interrogate the transition to political society in the form of a state and the moral costs of this transition. More specifically, I will attempt to show that John Ford's last film of genius *The Man Who Shot Liberty Valance* can be seen as exploring a range of themes integral to Williams' work and specifically to the tasks of political realism.

## II. Political Realism, Law and the Legitimation Demand

Williams, by now (in)famously, identifies 'the "first" political question in Hobbesian terms as the securing of order, protection, safety, trust, and the conditions of

* An earlier draft of this chapter was presented at the Bernard Williams workshop organised by Veronica Rodriguez-Blanco, Daniel Peixoto Murata, and Julieta A Rabanos. I am grateful to all who were present for their comments. A later draft benefitted from the comments and encouragement of Damian Cueni, Ed Hall, Rob Jubb, Matthieu Queloz, Paul Sagar, Matt Sleat and Rogers Smith.

cooperation' (2005: 3; see also Pettit 2023). It seems for Williams that we enter the domain of politics through the construction of an impartial standpoint, where 'that standpoint must be that of an authority with the power to enforce' (2001: 24). The logic here is that:

> the restriction of our activities by the intentional activities of others … can give rise to a quite specific reaction, resentment; and if resentment is not to express itself in more conflict, non-cooperation, and dissolution of social relations, an authoritative determination is needed of whose activities should have priority (2001: 11).

This argument then leads ineluctably to another, namely, that since the coercively enforced rulings of the authority can themselves give rise to reactions of resentment, the more the institution of authority acquires a monopoly of some means of coercion and hence comes to resemble a state, the more this institution requires a legitimating account that addresses (at least) its citizens in terms that make sense to them (Williams 2001: 12). As Williams remarks:

> For there to be a legitimate government, there must be a legitimation story … Moreover, this story is supposed to legitimate the arrangements to *each* citizen, that is to say, to each person from whom the state expects allegiance (2001: 25).

There may be some people to whom the state does not seek to legitimate itself, but if so neither the state nor its citizens, on Williams' view, stand in a political relationship to those excluded from the legitimation domain (e.g., the Helots in ancient Sparta).

Now we should notice that Williams' account allows for movement from a proto-political condition to a fully political condition, and hence that issues of legitimation do not suddenly burst into being once an effective coercive public authority is achieved. It is true that, at this point, the nature of the legitimation demand takes a determinate form – the relationship of citizens from whom allegiance to laws is demanded to the impartial public authority that issues coercively-backed laws – but questions of legitimacy in less determinate form already arise in the process of constructing an authority of this kind or, and this is the same question differently posed, in choosing whether to join such an institutionally achieved authority from a position that lacks such an effective institution.

This is the terrain which a significant range of great films in the cinematic genre of the Western address – and in doing so raise a range of questions concerning the transition to 'a state' (in Williams' use of this term). One reason that I think this may matter for Williams' political realism can be drawn out by noticing a distinction between two types of generality that arguments concerning the state in modernity can take. The first is a form of generality that applies to the *political form* of the modern state. Thus, for example, in Williams' essay 'From Freedom to Liberty: The Construction of a Political Value' (2001), he offers an argument that, if successful, demonstrates that modern legitimation narratives do not need to address the justification of living under an impartial authority with the power to coercively enforce its rules or the value of liberty as a political value.[1] Rather these can be taken as givens of legitimate political authorities in modernity. The second is a form of generality that pertains to the *common problems of political substance* faced by any actual state. The issue here concerns the need of any actual state for a legitimation narrative that makes sense of the founding (or refounding) of this state, of what makes 'us' as a plurality also make sense as a unity, of how we are to understand our transition to this state, of what it means for us to be ruled like this and what was necessary for this process to occur, and whether the costs are vindicated by the outcome. It is primarily (but not exclusively) this later kind of generality that is exhibited by the kinds of Westerns which are of concern to us here. As Pippin remarks:

> Many great Westerns are indeed about the founding or the early, struggling stages of modern bourgeois, law-abiding, property-owning, market- economy, technologically advanced societies in transition from, mostly, lawlessness (or corrupt and ineffective law) and war that border on classic state-of-nature thought experiments (or mythic pictures of origins) … The question often raised is the question of how legal order (of a particular form, the form of liberal-democratic capitalism) is possible, under what conditions it can be formed and command allegiance, how the bourgeois virtues, especially the domestic virtues, can be said to get a psychological grip in an environment where the heroic and martial virtues are so important. To say that, however relevant to history, the narrative form is not historical or realistic but mythic means seeing such films as attempts to capture the fundamental, common problems in a founding and in the institution of law (sometimes as attempts to understand what the law comes to mean in such situations) or to capture the core drama in a particular form of political life (Pippin 2010: 225–26).

I can bring out one important implication of the contrast between the two types of generality into focus by returning to Williams' essay 'From Freedom to Liberty'.

Part of Williams' purpose in this essay is to offer an account that makes sense of the political value of liberty as a site of political disagreement concerning what counts as a claim in liberty and a cost in liberty. Central to this account is William's rejection of Dworkin's view that 'a claim in liberty must be a claim to a specific kind of right to do the thing in question, such as a right of free speech' and the resulting conclusion that 'there can be no conflicts between liberty, properly understood, and any rightful claim' (Williams 2001: 13).[2] On the contrary, on Williams' construction, it is 'necessary that it should not follow' since the task is to make sense of the role of liberty in political argument and conflict 'and generally of life under a political order' and:

> It is one datum of that experience that people can even recognize a restriction as rightful under some political value such as equality or justice, and nevertheless regard it as a

[1] This is not to say that the state as it currently exists is the best form that such a polity might take – and Williams' incomplete work on realism notably fails to address the international realm sufficiently.

[2] For a lucid and compelling account of the form and stakes of 'the Dworkin-Williams debate' that speaks to this point, see Queloz 2023.

restriction on liberty. The notion of a *cost* in liberty is at least as well entrenched in historical and contemporary experience as that of a rightful claim in liberty (Williams 2001: 13).

Dworkin's account cannot make sense of the reaction of such people (except to see them as confused). Nor, Williams suggests, is the Dworkinian view of those who argue that the restriction is not rightful as 'simply wrong in thinking this' helpful:

> We should take seriously the idea that if, under certain conditions, people think there is a cost in liberty, then there is. Taking that idea seriously, I suggest, is a condition not only of taking seriously the idea of political opposition, but of taking our political opponents themselves seriously (Williams 2001: 14).

However, Williams goes on to argue that there is a class of complainants whose complaints about costs in liberty can be ignored: 'those who complain that their liberty, or indeed their primitive freedom is curtailed by the mere existence of the state'. Williams further claims that 'we need not agree … that the fact that a person is subject to a state is, in itself, a limitation on his primitive freedom' on the grounds that 'the amount of freedom that a person who have without the state is entirely indeterminate or, at any rate, very small' (Williams 2001: 14). This may be true from the perspective of a claim by those Williams presents as the inhabitants of modernity who live under a well-functioning state; however, it is not obviously true of those in the intermediate position of choosing whether to join such an institutionally achieved political authority from a position that lacks such an effective institution. What is at stake here are both the question of a cost in liberty or primitive freedom, and the visions of liberty or freedom that the different sets of political arrangements represent.

This is the scenario that the kind of Westerns that concern us address – in which the actors have a fairly clear and determinate view of what the cost to their liberty or primitive freedom will be and for some, most obviously leading protagonists in these films and those they represent, the cost is not negligible (whether the transitions that Westerns explore are best conceptualised in terms of a cost of liberty or, more radically, a limitation on primitive freedom need not concern us directly).[3] Why does this matter since the issue is, on Williams' account, off the table for us?[4] Because the conflicts in such conditions, the oppositions out of

[3] It might be objected that Westerns of the kind we are concerned with are not addressing losses in primitive freedom but losses of liberty, i.e., that they address the transition from one type of polity to another. I would partly resist this view since liberty as a political value involves reference to a functional legal system characterised by, among other things, enforceable claim rights – and it is just this which we may think is absent from the quasi-'state of nature' conditions that the relevant Westerns address. However, I aim to remain largely neutral on this question here. I am grateful to Rob Jubb for raising this point.

[4] Moreover, in modernity, now that we have reason to reject stories that invoke 'religious or other transcendental justifications, as simply untrue', such a story must make sense of the coercive rule of the state in a way that is broadly truthful. Part of this truthfulness lies in acknowledging that, for us, now and around here, resentment about the loss of liberty that is entailed by living in a state is not politically intelligible because there is no alternative world, within the relevant constraints of

which the transition to a state occurs, shape the self-understanding of the peoplehood of those who live under the modern state. Taking political opposition in such contexts seriously matters because it has implications for how we see ourselves as a people. Thus, Westerns portray what Rogers Smith (2003) calls 'stories of peoplehood' (which is the political substance of any modern state) and are a cultural medium though which we, now and around here, reflect on the issue of 'who we are?' (and do so in a way that is, at least in some respects, similar to the role played by Greek tragic drama in the cultural-political life of ancient Athens) through imaginative retellings of how we became a 'we' in the political sense. They also serve as ways of revealing and exploring different understandings of liberty that are in play in the wider political history and culture of a state by focusing these into character-types whose relations play out in the plots of Westerns concerned with transitions to modern society.

Thus Westerns, or so my claim will go, allow us to draw out a dimension of Williams' political realism that is missing from (or, at best, only sketchily present in) his account of it concerning the relationship between stories of (re)founding and stories of peoplehood that are integral to addressing common problems of political substance confronted by the modern state with respect to its legitimation narrative. However, this is a dimension that I will show is consonant with, and can be developed by reference to, a number of strands in Williams' wider work, including his treatment of tragedy, moral luck, and political ethics, and raises a more general question for liberal society concerning the relationship of truthfulness and legitimation narratives. To explore these issues, we turn to the film *The Man Who Shot Liberty Valance* as an exemplar of this genre in which the issues that concern us are given sharp expression.

## III. The Western as Cinematic Genre

Two forms of the classic Western are salient for our current concerns. The first is the transitional story (often in epic form) that recounts the overcoming of an obstacle or threat to the evolution of liberal political order and commercial society. This overcoming can take the form of the conquest of an external obstacle (nature) or perceived threat (non-European Indigenous peoples) or that of an internal obstacle and threat (a condition of lawlessness), and it's the latter which is our concern. So, for example, *High Noon* highlights both the importance of the heroic and martial virtues in an only partially political condition (that is, one that is neither a pre-political condition nor a fully realised political state) and the

modern political life, in which this loss does not occur: 'The world of the anarchists is too far away – too far away from anything – to ground complaints in liberty at all. Many complaints that fly in the face of modernity equally do not even cross the threshold of offering a serious political consideration' (Williams 2001: 22).

inability of the bourgeois virtues of commercial society to generate or support heroic and martial virtues. The contempt with which Marshall Will Kane (Gary Cooper) throws his badge into the dirt after the shoot-out with the Miller Gang (in which only his wife, acting from love, supports him) as the townsfolk, now safe, venture into the main street gestures both to the dependence of the incomplete commercial republic on an ethical outlook that it cannot understand or emulate, and to how the virtues and vices of such an emerging political order may appear from the standpoint of a martial ethic.

The second is the post-transitional story that addresses the incompatibility of the martial virtues and honour code with a commercial republic. John Wayne's last film *The Shootist* dramatises the way in which the reputation that the legendary sheriff-turned-gunfighter J.B. Brooks (Wayne) acquired for his heroic and martial acts now makes him as target for reasons of commercial celebrity to men who have gunfighting skills, but where these are now divorced from the ethical outlook that gave them their meaning and value. Brooks dies after defeating the three men who explicitly desire his death before being opportunistically shot in the back by the unnoticed bartender of the saloon where the gunfight has occurred. That the hero-worshipping boy Gillom Rogers (Ron Howard) both avenges Brooks by shooting the bartender and then discards the gun (to the approval of the dying Brooks) affirms that the martial virtues no longer have a place in the private realm of the social order of modernity.

What is distinctive about *The Man Who Shot Liberty Valence* in this context is that it combines a post-transitional story with a transitional story in a way that focuses attention on the relationship of the transition to the political society that emerges, on the presence and power of myth in modern legitimation narratives, and on the problem that the bourgeois virtues of modern states confront in acknowledging the unjust violence of their foundations. It thus thematises a point Williams raises when he notes that such transitions are not, in and of themselves, vindicatory (2006: 190).

## IV. Synopsis: *The Man Who Shot Liberty Valence*

Senator Ransom Stoddard (James Stewart) and his wife, Miss Hallie (Vera Miles), arrive in Shinbone by train, unannounced and dressed somberly, where they are greeted by an old friend, Link Appleyard (Andy Devine) who we learn was once, but not for many years, the town Marshall. Shinbone is depicted as bright and clean with a telephone at the station ticket office – the very model of modernity. The newspaper finds out Stoddard is here and demands to know why he has come back ('The press has a right'). While Appleyard and Hallie drive on his buckboard to the ruins of a horse-ranch, Stoddard goes to the newspaper office and explains he is here in a personal capacity 'for a funeral'. It is the funeral of Tom Doniphon

(John Wayne), whom none of the newer people seem to know, but to whose ranch Appleyard and Hallie had gone.

Cut to the coffin where an aging black man, Pompey (Woody Strode), is mourning alone. The newspaper editor, Scott (Carleton Young), insists on the press's right to the story of Stoddard's presence. Given the nodded permission of Hallie, Stoddard agrees to explain. He sees an old stagecoach in the outer room of the undertakers that turns out to be the one he arrived on about 35 years earlier.

## A. Flashback

The stagecoach is held up by Liberty Valance (Lee Marvin) and his gang, Reese and Floyd (Lee Van Cleef and Strother Martin). A young idealistic Stoddard tries to defend one of the female passengers when the bandits grab a brooch from her neck. He is savagely beaten (with Valance's silver-handled whip) and left for dead. The gang forces the coach to proceed on to Shinbone. Doniphon finds Stoddard and brings him into town on a buckboard. He takes him to the Nelson boarding-house/restaurant where he is nursed by Hallie whom Doniphon plans to marry.

Stoddard says he wants to put Valance in jail – he is an 'attorney-at-Law'. Doniphon laughs and says Stoddard needs a gun. 'You know what you are saying to me?' replies Stoddard, 'You are as bad as he [Valance] is! What kind of community is this?'

The Marshall appears – he (as 'the law') is a buffoon. Stoddard is washing dishes, reading his law books which, having been ripped up by Valance, are now taped together. He finds a point of law indicating that the Marshall has jurisdiction over the crime (which happened outside of town). The cowardly Marshall will have none of it. It is determined that Hallie cannot read.

Stoddard is serving tables to pay for his stay at the boarding-house/restaurant; Valance comes in and trips Stoddard who falls on the food he is carrying. Valance tells him to pick it up. Doniphon intervenes – he is the only one who can stand up to Valance and his two henchmen (with the aid of his black handyman Pompey). Stoddard defuses the conflict by picking the steak up himself. Every plate except Stoddard's has steak.

Stoddard starts a law office and a school to teach townsfolk to read. On the blackboard we see 'Education is the basis of law and order'. Flag. Picture of George Washington. Stoddard reads out the newspaper editorial by Dutton Peabody (Edmund O'Neill) in favour of Statehood.

At a town meeting to elect delegates to the Territorial Convention, Peabody (founder and editor of the *Shinbone Star*) and Stoddard are elected after Doniphon turns down nomination (on the grounds he has personal plans – i.e., marriage to Hallie) and the electoral defeat of Valance, now employed as a hired gun by the cattlemen who oppose Statehood (since they wish to preserve the open range). Valance, furious at the delegate vote, challenges Stoddard to a duel.

Stoddard has been secretly practising with a gun. Doniphon finds out and tries to give him a lesson. Stoddard is pretty bad. Showing off, Doniphon hits a paint bucket that spills all over Stoddard. Stoddard is furious and slugs Doniphon. Stoddard leaves and Doniphon, who had repeatedly called him 'pilgrim', now calls him 'gunslinger'. There has been increasing tenderness between Hallie and Stoddard. Doniphon senses that he is losing the woman he wants to marry and for whom he has added a room to his house.

Valance takes revenge on Peabody by half-killing him and wrecking the *Shinbone Star* office. This leads Stoddard to decide to confront Valance despite his moral objection to personal violence and lack of experience with guns.

The standoff between Stoddard and Valence ensues. Valence is killed. Stoddard is injured and Hallie expresses loving concern for him (unknowingly seen by Doniphon). Knowing that he will lose Hallie to Stoddard and because, as we will learn, he has broken his own moral code, Doniphon gets drunk and burns his house down.

As 'The Man Who Shot Liberty Valance', Stoddard becomes a candidate to be the state representative who can guide the transition from Territory to Statehood. Uneasy that he has acquired this standing only by killing Valence against his own moral code, Stoddard leaves the convention hall. Doniphon stops him, explains that it was not Stoddard but he who killed Valence (from the shadows with a rifle) and that Stoddard, as the man that Hallie has chosen, has a responsibility to accept the nomination and give Hallie the life she wants to have. Stoddard returns to the convention hall to acclaim.

## B. The Flashback Returns to the Present

The editor greets the conclusion of Stoddard's narrative by ripping up the pages of notes he has made and burning them in the furnace, commenting in response to Stoddard's query 'You're not going to use the story, Mr Scott?': 'No, sir. [SLAMS FURNACE DOOR.] This is the west, sir. When the legend becomes fact, print the legend'. This view is endorsed by the Mayor (Paul Birch).

The time taken by Stoddard's recounting means that he and Hallie must now get the train back to Washington – and hence miss the burial they came to attend though he has, in effect, given a funeral oration. He notices that a cactus rose has been placed on Tom's coffin. On the train, Stoddard asks Hallie how she would feel if he gave up his political career and they returned to Shinbone. She indicates this has been an unspoken wish of hers for some time. He asks her who put the cactus rose on Tom's coffin. She tells him she did. The conductor comes to explain the special arrangements made for Stoddard who responds that he will write to railroad to thank them. The conductor concludes the dialogue of the film with the line 'You think nothing of it. [PATS STODDARD's SHOULDER.] Nothing's too good for the man who shot Liberty Valance'.

## V. What is Shown: The Tragic Hero and the Modern State

*The Man Who Shot Liberty Valance* pictures the transition from an incompletely political condition to a fully realised political state across three main registers: the political, the personal, and the public. The first is engaged through the characters of Stoddard, Doniphon and Valance, although it also invokes wider collectives (the cattlemen versus the townsfolk). The second is explored through the changing relationships of Hallie, Stoddard and Doniphon. The third is addressed through the contrast between Peabody and his modern successor Scott as editors of *The Shinbone Star*. The relationship between the political and personal registers is symbolised in the film's invocations of the opposition wilderness/garden and the figure of the cactus rose (in its contrast with a 'real' rose).

The political story recounted by Stoddard in the long flashback section of the film concerns the transition from the partially political condition of being a 'Territory' to the fully political condition of being a 'State'. It is a feature of Territories of the United States that they have a non-voting delegate in the House of Representatives. This delegate may participate in discussions of issues but doesn't have any say in whether a bill passes or not. Territories are not represented in the US Senate. Generally speaking, the requirements for statehood are:

1. Creation of a constitution with a republican form of government.
2. Population of sufficient size to be able to financially support the operations of a state government and to provide support for the operation of the federal government.

That the Territory in which Shinbone resides meets these requirements sets the context in which the drama unfolds and in which the political and personal are become insuperably entangled.

Pre-transition Shinbone is not then a pre-political 'state of nature' (although it exhibits some features of such a condition), it is a town with a sheriff and there are, as Stoddard points out to the inept Marshall, laws. But it is also not a fully realised political condition in Williams' sense. Hobbes' dictum that covenants without swords are but words and Locke's reflections on the 'inconveniences' of the state of nature would both appear to have salience for the people of the town. Its incomplete political character is, indeed, sharply drawn out by the contrast between Stoddard, on the one hand, and Doniphon and Valance, on the other, in terms of their understandings of freedom. For the newly arriving Easterner Stoddard, freedom is conceived in terms of liberty, that is, that the possession of legally enforceable claim rights which protect the citizen from public and private domination. By contrast, Valance and Doniphon both operate with a contrasting understanding of freedom that is made explicit in their invocation of the oxymoron 'Western law' as denoting nothing other than the individual's ability to exercise private power (note that the extent of this ability may be augmented by their capacity to draw on the abilities of cooperating others – Valance's two 'Myrmidons' and, in Doniphon's case, Pompey). You possess a 'right' only insofar as you, as a private individual (or group), have the power to make good your claim to it.

Although a central strand of the film concerns Stoddard's education in the limits of the moral idealism that he initially represents, there is an important sense in which his commitment to a liberal-republican view of liberty (grounded in natural rights, enacted through the rule of law, and exercised in political participation) remains constant even as he comes to a realistic outlook that sees that the establishment of such an order of liberty may necessitate violence. More immediately relevant for our concerns are the reactions of Valance and Doniphon to the understanding of liberty that Stoddard prefigures (and on which the Territorial Convention will vote). Both see this transition as involving a cost to freedom (and, if best conceived as 'primitive freedom' then, contra Williams, this proposed limitation of their freedom is not, from their standpoint, 'entirely indeterminate' nor is their existing freedom 'very small'). The contrast between their reactions, in Williams' language, is that Doniphon comes to see the restriction on his freedom as justified by other values (such as equality), whereas Valance does not. These distinct reactions, in part, express the fact that Doniphon's understanding of his freedom is bound up with an ethical outlook in which self-reliance is combined with chivalry, whereas Valance's understanding of his freedom is unconstrained by considerations of honour or ethics more generally.

The contrast between the two reactions can be understood in terms of Williams' model of internal reasons where having a reason to ø entails that there is some path from one's original motivational set S, where 'S can contain such things a dispositions of evaluation, patterns of emotional reaction, personal loyalties, and various projects … embodying commitments of the agent' (Williams 1981: 81), via practical deliberation to the conclusion that he has reason to ø. It is an important part of this picture that through the process of practical deliberation and the imaginative routes that it can engage, 'an agent can come to see that he has reason to do something which he did not see he had reason to do at all' (Williams 1981: 80). Thus, in the case of Doniphon, there is an intelligible imaginative route in terms of which Doniphon can bring his practical deliberations to a conclusion that endorses supporting the transition to Statehood despite this not being something that he started out by seeing himself as having a reason to do (and the film effectively presents us with this route). That he believes in self-reliance does not debar him from this conclusion because he is also brought to recognise (not least, and perhaps specifically, by the combination of courage and martial incompetence exhibited by Stoddard and also by Peabody) that the fact that other men need protection from people like Valance need not signify their lack of moral value, their being worthy of protection that cannot be generally available without Statehood.

Doniphon may be further helped in reaching this conclusion by two further facts: first, that he does not see such a political transition as impinging on his own plans and, second, that Hallie, whom he loves, values the form of society that Stoddard represents, while Doniphon himself is largely indifferent to it. By contrast, it is hard to envisage any intelligible imaginative route by which Valance could bring himself to affirm the transition to political society. Indeed, it is hard to see how Valance could be brought into the domain of morality in which considerations beyond his own immediate desires get a grip on him since he represents a figure closer to the psychopath than the amoralist and if he is a psychopath 'the idea of arguing him into morality is surely idiotic' (Williams 1993a [1972]: 10).

Both Doniphon's protective concerns and his relative indifference are already apparent when the town hold a meeting to elect the delegates to the Territorial Convention. The former is manifest in Doniphon's refusal to let Valance cower the assembled townsfolk into electing him as a delegate (to serve the anti-Statehood interests of the cattle barons who also clearly discern the cost in freedom that Statehood would impose on them[5]) and the latter by his refusal of nomination because he has personal plans (i.e., marriage to Hallie now the additional room to his house has been completed).[6] It is only, however, when Hallie sends Pompey to him with what amounts to a desperate plea to save Stoddard from Valence that Doniphon comes to realise both that Hallie's feelings for Stoddard run deeper than he had realised (this will be confirmed to him by her reaction to Stoddard following his survival of the gunfight) and to confront the fact that killing Valance in the only way practically available to him – with a rifle from the shadows – will require him to breach the fundamental tenet of his moral code, to dishonour himself (or become polluted as the Greeks would say). Confronted with this tragic dilemma, Doniphon chooses 'cold blooded murder' (as he will later describe it) out of his love for Hallie and concern for her well-being. Doniphon's recognition that he has lost his honour in committing this act of murder and in doing so also ceased to be worthy of 'his girl' – and this explains why he does not struggle to regain her affections – is expressed in an act of drinking to excess and attempting to burn his house down indifferent to his own survival (his life being saved by Pompey). That he starts the fire in the new room added for his planned life with Hallie starkly registers the drive to self-destruction to which his shame impels him. Doniphon's actions are not explicable within the terms of the picture of human morality

[5] As Rogers Smith has stressed to me, the cattle barons were settler colonialists who wanted enforcement of a regime of property rights, just ones that privileged their dispossession of tribal lands and their preferred uses of it, over different commercial uses and owners representing a different vision of the settler colonial state.

[6] The cattle ranchers are largely background figures in this film, but the treatment of their clear understanding of the cost in freedom of the transition to a fully political society to them, and their opposition to it, is an implied topic in at least two kinds of Westerns. Those dealing directly with the conflict between cattle ranchers' desire to sustain the open range and homesteaders' and farmers' attempt to establish private property rights over land (*Shane*, *Heaven's Gate*) and what may be called 'empire ranch' stories where the power of a de facto lord is threatened by the coming of an impartial and enforceable legal order and/or the dissolution of the next generation (*Giant*, *The Big Country*, *Chisum*).

characteristic of modern moral philosophy, but they are perfectly intelligible in terms of the ethical language of Greek tragedy that Williams brilliantly elucidates in *Shame and Necessity* (1993b) with regard to the case of Ajax. Like Ajax, Doniphon's shame expresses his internalisation of the gaze of an imagined other, one whose reactions he would respect. As Williams comments:

> The internalised other is indeed abstracted and generalised and idealised, but he is potentially somebody rather than nobody, and somebody other than me. He can provide the focus of real social expectations, of how I shall live if I act in one way rather than another, of how my actions and reactions will alter my relations to the world around me. (1993b: 84)

Ajax kills himself because he 'has no way of living that anyone he respects would respect' (Williams 1993b: 85). Doniphon survives, through the agency of care personified by Pompey, and perhaps because his choices were motivated by love.

We do not see Doniphon again until he comes to reveal the truth of Valance's shooting to Stoddard in order to make him stand for the position of Representative of the Territory. This is a complex act of obligating Stoddard in which Doniphon appears to express passing regret at saving Stoddard before affirming that he can bear the burden of having killed Valance in a way that Stoddard clearly cannot ('Cold-blooded murder. But I can live with it. Hallie's happy.') and avowing that he no longer has a claim on Hallie, assigning responsibility for her well-being to Stoddard ('She's your girl now'). Giving Hallie 'something to read and write about' by accepting the nomination (and marrying her) is the debt that Stoddard owes Doniphon for saving his life and bearing the moral cost of the killing as well as for surrendering his claim to Hallie – and Stoddard's return to the Convention Hall to accept nomination is his acknowledgment of this debt.

The return of Stoddard and Hallie to Shinbone for Doniphon's funeral will make clear the costs of this personal and political story are tragic for all three characters. Doniphon is unknown to the Mayor and newspaper staff, the costs of his funeral are being covered by the County presumably because he died without resources, and Pompey reveals that Doniphon has not worn a gun for many years (the implication is since Statehood was achieved). He lost everything that he most valued about himself as well as the woman he loved and appears to have withdrawn from public life. Stoddard is the 'beneficiary' of political luck who is trapped in a reputation he could not disavow without betraying Doniphon and exposing him to charges of 'cold-blooded murder' (when he was alive), who knowingly confronts the coarsening performative demands of politics on his character, and who lives with the underlying worry that he is not worthy of Hallie and that she has never stopped loving Doniphon (not that she did not also love him, but that Doniphon remained first in her heart). Hallie is caught in a childless marriage in which she has felt unable to express her deepest desires (such as her desire to leave Washington and return to Shinbone) and is brought to recognise that her love for Doniphon – and the wilderness he represented symbolised in the cactus rose – was deeper and more truthful to her authentic self than she knew.

Doniphon's death provides Stoddard with the opportunity finally to discharge the debt he owes Doniphon by revealing him as the tragic hero of the transition to Statehood and thereby also to escape the fate in which he, Stoddard, has been trapped. It has been noted that Stoddard's recounting may not be entirely reliable (Pippin 2010: 78–79), but it is important to notice that the purpose of the account is to centre the tragic heroism of Doniphon. Stoddard is offering a *funeral oration* and he is doing so in a way that recalls and subverts the role of that mode of oratory in classical Athens in which it was inextricably tied to the *epainos* – praise of the city – as opposed to simply lamentation for the dead (Loreaux 2006). It is as if Stoddard's words are precisely aimed at a re-founding of the city, one that disavows his own mythological role in its founding and re-assigns civic glory to Doniphon where it belongs.

However, Stoddard's attempt to make public the role of Doniphon is denied by the newspaper editor – 'This is the west, sir. When the legend becomes fact, print the legend.' – and this political judgment is endorsed by the mayor. This has fateful implications for Stoddard who thereby remains bound to, and haunted by, a reputation that he knows he does not deserve – and having been denied this form of political suicide, he is prompted to propose another to Hallie, that of retirement from political life. But it is important to ask why the newspaper editor and the mayor both come to this judgment, and what the implied comparison of the modern editor, Scott, with the paper's founding editor, Peabody, is doing in the film.

A plausible answer to the first of these questions is that Scott and the mayor recognise the power of founding myths and, more specifically, how the identity of the community that they represent has been shaped by this myth. Here the fact that Stoddard has been such a key figure in the foundation and post-foundational formation of the political community (this is the point of the recital of his many high offices by Scott in the opening scenes of the film when they first meet) means that the revelation of the true story would be a serious threat to the coherence and stability of this community. However, at stake is also a specific legitimating feature of this myth, namely, that the triumph over Stoddard over Valence is the vindication of the view of liberty and community that Stoddard represents (one of a legally ordered political community in which the state has a monopoly of the legitimate use of violence) over the (effectively) lawless condition of primitive freedom exemplified by Valance. The story recounted by Stoddard threatens this vindicatory myth by revealing that the triumph of the modern liberal state was not of its own doing[7] but relied on the intervention of a type of ethical character that is not compatible with it. This revelation thereby raises the question of the costs of the transition to the modern liberal state in a way that forces the acknowledgement that this transition was not without moral cost, the loss of forms of excellence

[7] As Williams wryly notes: 'The circumstances in which liberal thought is possible have been created in part by actions that violate liberal ideals and human rights, as was recognised by Hegel and Marx, and, in a less encouraging spirit, by Nietzsche' (2005: 25). I am grateful to Ed Hall for reminding me of this remark.

and value from the world. Whereas the end of the type represented by Liberty Valence can, taken by itself, be a subject of unconditional affirmation, the end of the type exemplified by Tom Doniphon cannot – and the fact that the loss of the former entails the loss of the latter makes the question of the costs of transition more complex and ambivalent. The implied contrast between Peabody and Scott also speaks to this complexity with the former's courageous commitment to truth-telling even at significant personal risk being compared to the latter's unwillingness to reveal the truth behind the killing of Liberty Valence, thereby registering that the kind of heroic stance represented by Peabody is, like its martial variant in Doniphon, something that is lost in the transition to the commercial republic. We may also note that the film registers the complexity of the issue of loss at a communal level by the contrast in depiction between the brightly lit ordered sanitised cleanliness of modern Shinbone and the dim and shadowed boisterous but unsafe social liveliness of its earlier incarnation.

## VI. What is Being Done: Ford and Williams on Legitimation Narratives

In *The Man Who Shot Liberty Valance*, John Ford thus engages a range of themes that are present in Williams' philosophy – moral luck, tragic dilemmas, legitimacy, truthfulness, and myth, and does so in a way that is consonant with Williams' accounts of internal reasons, shame, and the limits of reason in recruiting individuals into ethical life. In this section I want to turn to what I take Ford to be doing in his telling of this story to an audience for whom the modern liberal state is the only political option available and how this relates to Williams' political realism. I will be concerned with articulating affinities between other outlooks, with answers that Williams offers to questions posed by Ford, and with challenges that Ford poses to Williams.

In the first instance, Ford is acknowledging (as Williams also does[8]) the power of mythic narratives in political life and the particular importance of mythic narratives of political foundation in American political life, but he is also raising the issue of the kind of mythic narratives that we tell ourselves. More specifically, he is posing a question about the role that Westerns (including his own huge body of previous work) as a form of mythic narration play in American political life. The heroic story of Ransom Stoddard (who takes up the gun out of necessity and then puts it away) and his triumph over Liberty Valance that is known to the people of Shinbone and has become integral to their self-understanding is representative of one kind of mythic narrative presented by the Western as a genre. It is a triumph of good over evil without remainder that vindicates a politically moralised vision of America as

[8] See Williams 2002: 265.

the exemplary modern liberal state. Ford's subversive retelling of this narrative as a tragic drama performs several roles that are salient to Williams' political realism.

First, it asks the audience to consider whether they can trust the legitimation narratives that are expressed in the founding myths of American political life and the moralised narrative forms that they exhibit in, for example, much of the Western genre. Ford's deliberate use of stylistic elements of film noir in the shooting of the film signal to the audience that issues of political trust and ethical confidence are in play here, and hence raises the question of what ideological role these founding myths may serve as well as the more general question of whether these legitimation narratives would survive a truthful history of the state.[9]

Second, it aims to draw the audience into reflection on what is lost with the formation of the modern liberal state and why it may be important to recognise the moral costs as well as gains of the transition, while also acknowledging that there is no realistic option for us but to inhabit the post-transnational state and that nostalgia for, or the desire to revive, a heroic martial ethic have no place in the modern liberal state. It thus sets out two desiderata that a realistic legitimation narrative needs to acknowledge if it is to vindicate an answer to the question 'who are we?' that makes political sense to its audience as subjects of a modern liberal legal order.

Both of these first two features of what the film is doing speak to an issue that is fundamental to Williams' realism, namely, the view that the political moralism of contemporary liberal political thought cannot provide a truthful account of the emergence of the modern liberal state that is, at the same time, vindicatory. This is exemplified by the decision of the newspaper editor and the mayor' s to repress publication of the history that Stoddard has recounted. But also there are further implications represented in the figure of Stoddard who can be seen to exemplify the position of someone who begins as a political moralist and, having been educated to the limitations of that view, becomes haunted by their inability to acknowledge the unjust violence at the foundation to the legal order and the forms of excellence and value that are lost in the transition to the commercial republic. If Stoddard is an exemplar of something like a truthful liberal, this suggests that within a culture of political moralism, such a position comes with significant costs. Ford's film is critical in the sense that it suggests that what we may think of as a political moralist view of liberalism (represented by Scott and the Mayor) leaves us unable to reconcile truthful history and legitimacy, and it thereby raises the question of whether we have reason to affirm liberal society.

It is addressing this issue that leads Williams to Judith Shklar's proposal of the liberalism of fear (Williams 2005: 52–61): 'a lot can be said in favour of liberal society in terms of its helping people to avoid what every human being everywhere has

[9] John Ford's other important late film *Cheyenne Autumn* may be understood as directed against the blindness – cultivated in part by Westerns such as those previously made by Ford – of Americans to the foundational and continuing injustice committed against Indigenous Indian tribes.

reason to avoid' (2002: 264) – and specifically to his views concerning the relationship of liberalism and truthful history.

Williams' notes that liberal society has two kinds of relationship to truthful history. The first is that it 'helps to make truthful history possible' (2002: 265) not least by removing illiberal constraints on speech and social interaction that allow plural accounts to encounter and potentially challenge each other. However, Williams immediately also remarks: 'Liberal society, we need to say, *can* do these things. Commercial society in itself does not guarantee them' (2002: 265). Ford's film illustrates this very point. The second, and more pertinent to our concerns, is that liberal society 'quite specifically needs truthful history':

> This claim may seem a joke, granted the raft of myth that has sustained liberal societies in the past and still helps to do so. But it is truthful inquiry that has taken those myths to pieces, and we do not have to see this as merely a terminal scene of dialectical destruction. Liberalism may have destroyed in some part its distinctive supporting stories about itself – certainly its spirit of critique has soaked them in suspicion – but the resources of the liberalism of fear, which work everywhere, may keep it afloat. A truthful history will remind us of those resources, and of what it costs in terms of quite basic loss if a mythical order takes over (Williams 2002: 265).[10]

A liberalism of fear, in other words, is not threatened by a truthful history of the transition to a fully political society because it can acknowledge the losses and moral remainders of this transition in a way that political moralist versions of liberalism cannot. Turning back to Ford's film, we can say that if the liberalism of the modern state is to be vindicated in ways compatible with its commitment to truthfulness, that vindication will need to start from a focus on the social ills from which the modern state will protect us (represented by Liberty Valance, both in his own person and as an instrument of the cattle barons) and acknowledge that certain forms of excellence and value that are integral to the transition are also necessary sacrifices of it.

Third, Ford's film tries to cultivate in its audience an ethical and political outlook that is best described as a tragic vision in which our actions (however moral or well-intentioned) expose us to moral and political luck that can fundamentally shape how well, or ill, our individual and collective lives go. One of the reasons that Ford's film is so powerful is that the story it tells is immediately intelligible to us and makes visible how little of the course of our lives turns out to be under our control, yet it also illustrates how resistant the morality of modern liberal society is to acknowledging the ethical language of tragedy and the costs (exemplified by Stoddard and Hallie) of this resistance.

Ford's film here speaks to Williams' critique of the morality system and specifically his efforts to show how, despite our distance from the Greeks, there are

[10] This is an issue that has considerable contemporary resonance in the context of Brexit, Trump, Modi and the virulent return of nationalist-populist forms of far-right politics that live off myths.

elements of their outlook that make better sense of our ethical lives than 'morality' does. Williams highlights a point that Ford's film shows us:

> If these similarities [concerning the concepts that we use in interpreting our own and other people's feelings and actions] between our own ways of thought and those of the ancient Greeks are, in some cases, unobvious, this is not because they arise from a structure hidden in the unconscious, but because they are, for cultural and historical reasons, unacknowledged. It is an effect of our ethical situation, and of our relations to the ancient Greeks, that we should be blind to some of the ways in which we resemble them (1993b: 2–3).

This is important because it raises the further question of the relationship of the liberalism of fear, and political realism more generally, to the ethical culture of modern bourgeois liberal society. Thus a question that Ford's film poses to its audience is whether affirming political realism, of embracing the kind of truthful history that the liberalism of fear offers in which the myth of Stoddard as 'The Man Who Shot Liberty Valence' is dispelled, can be accomplished without a wider transformation of ethical culture that finds a way of acknowledging our exposure to moral and political luck, to tragic conflicts and moral remainders.

Is the project of political realism viable without such an ethical shift – or, to put the question another way, can it get a psychological grip on the subjects of modern liberal society in terms that they are willing to affirm without their recognition of the ethical terrain that Williams' work, both generally and particularly in *Shame and Necessity*, aims to articulate? This is a challenge that we can see Ford's film as posing to Williams. Williams articulated his political realism as if it stood apart from his wider critical reflections on the morality system, but *The Man Who Shot Liberty Valance* raises the question of whether political realism as a public outlook is viable independently of the wider re-orientation of our ethical thought to which Williams was committed.

## VII. Conclusion

It is one measure of the richness of Ford's *The Man Who Shot Liberty Valance* that it can engage on equal terms with one of the major philosophers of the late twentieth century. In this chapter I have sought to show that Ford's film can be illuminatingly read in terms of Williams' central philosophical concerns in ethics and politics, and that doing so highlights understandable limitations in the account of political realism that Williams was able to articulate prior to his death. I have also argued that the limitations highlighted by Ford's film can be addressed in terms of resources from Williams' early work on ethics. However, more fundamentally, I have proposed that *The Man Who Shot Liberty Valance* raises a significant challenge to Williams' articulation of political realism as an outlook that is independent of the citizens' ethical orientations by showing that the political relationship of truthfulness and myth in liberal politics is not independent of the ethical outlook of the citizens of the state. Stoddard's attempt at re-founding the city through his funeral oration fails – and this failure is a challenge to which Williams' political realism must respond.

## Bibliography

Loreaux, N (2006) *The Invention of Athens: The Funeral Oration in the Classical City*, 2nd edn (Boston, Mass, Zone Books [MIT]).

Owen, D (2018) 'Realism in Ethics and Politics' in M Sleat (ed), *Politics Recovered* (New York, Columbia University Press).

Pettit, P (2023) *The State* (Princeton, Princeton University Press).

Pippin, R (2010) *Hollywood Westerns and American Myth* (New Haven, Yale University Press).

Queloz, M (2023) 'The Dworkin–Williams Debate: Liberty, Conceptual Integrity, and Tragic Conflict in Politics' 109 *Philosophy and Phenomenological Research* 1.

Smith, R (2003) *Stories of Peoplehood* (Cambridge, Cambridge University Press).

Williams, B (1981) 'Internal and External Reasons' in B Williams, *Moral Luck* (Cambridge, Cambridge University Press).

—— (1993a [1972]) *Morality* (Cambridge, Cambridge University Press).

—— (1993b) *Shame and Necessity* (Berkeley, University of California Press).

—— (2001) 'From Freedom to Liberty: The Construction of a Political Value' 30 *Philosophy and Public Affairs* 3.

—— (2002) *Truth and Truthfulness* (Princeton, Princeton University Press).

—— (2005) *In the Beginning was the Deed* (Princeton, Princeton University Press).

—— (2006) *Philosophy as a Humanistic Discipline* (Princeton, Princeton University Press).

# PART II

# Williams on the Methodology of Philosophy and Jurisprudence

# 8

# Creon's Revenge: Lawfulness and the Genealogy of Law

STEPHEN BERO*

## I. Introduction

> Let every American … swear by the blood of the Revolution, never to violate in the least particular, the laws of the country; and never to tolerate their violation by others … [T]o the support of the Constitution and Laws, let every American pledge his life, his property, and his sacred honor; – let every man remember that to violate the law, is to trample on the blood of his father, and to tear the [charter[1]] of his own, and his children's liberty. Let reverence for the laws, be breathed by every American mother, to the lisping babe, that prattles on her lap … And, in short, let it become the political religion of the nation; and let the old and the young, the rich and the poor, the grave and the gay, of all sexes and tongues, and colors and conditions, sacrifice unceasingly upon its altars.

So said Abraham Lincoln in 1838, in one of the early addresses that established his reputation as a public figure (Lincoln 1984: 10). Because of his rhetorical gifts, because he was responding in this speech to a spate of murderous, often racist mob violence, and because we now read the speech in light of Lincoln's subsequent accomplishments, we can experience this passage as inspiring and elevating. Yet there is also something discordant in hearing one of the preeminent icons and defenders of American liberal democracy advocate such an intense – even abject – reverence for law. The references to religion, altars, and ritual sacrifice sound in a devotional idiom; the emphasis on blood and honour verges on what we now

* Many thanks for helpful discussion and feedback to the editors of this volume and to the participants in the April 2023 workshop at the University of Surrey where this work was first presented. I owe a special debt to Daniel Peixoto Murata, my former PhD student, whose thought and work (e.g., 2022) have been a crucial inspiration and influence with respect to the themes treated here.

[1] An alternative reading of this word, which is not fully legible in the surviving source, is 'character' (Lincoln 1984: 10).

consider a nationalistic or even authoritarian one. There is more than an echo in this passage of Sophocles's Creon, proclaiming that

> if someone goes too far and breaks the law / Or tries to tell his masters what to do, / He will have nothing but contempt from me. / But when a city takes a leader, you must obey, / Whether his commands are trivial, or right, or wrong (2001: 29, ll. 663–67).

The fact that Lincoln's call for devotion to law can strike us as unsettling in this way represents an important kind of progress; our commitment to liberal values and our confidence in the robustness of our legal institutions are reflected in the fact that we do not ordinarily feel the need to fortify them in such drastic terms.[2] But at the same time, this confidence conceals an important blind spot in liberal legal thought, which is uncomfortable with the kind of reverence for law that Lincoln urges, yet struggles in its own terms to provide an adequate account of the attitude toward law that a legal regime can be expected to elicit from its subjects.

One of H.L.A. Hart's significant contributions in *The Concept of Law* was to establish that we cannot properly distinguish a regime of law from a regime of orders backed by threats without attributing at least to certain participants in the legal system a characteristic attitude toward the law, which he called the 'internal point of view' (2012: 89). Hart tells us that a community takes up the internal point of view towards a body of rules when it 'accepts and uses them as guides to conduct' (2012: 89), but his further comments on this topic are limited and often negative in character (e.g., the acceptance need *not* be based on moral endorsement; 2012: 203, 257).[3] The thinness of his characterisation of the internal point of view reinforces and reflects a general sense among Hart's followers and fellow travellers that there is little that legal theory as such can or indeed should say about Lincoln's and Creon's exhortations, because the questions they raise are matters of political morality rather than jurisprudence.

I wish to suggest that this is an unnecessarily narrow view of legal theory,[4] and that the notion of reverence or devotion or commitment to law – what I will refer to as the quality or disposition of *lawfulness* – has an important role to play in our understanding of what law is and how it exercises its distinctive authority. In one specific sense, I will be proposing that Creon was right, at least as regards what is essentially involved in the project of establishing and maintaining a system of law.

The argument will proceed genealogically – or rather, by comparing two different philosophical genealogies.[5] The first is Philip Pettit's in 'Social Norms and the

[2] Of course, this can change, and perhaps is changing. When this confidence is deeply shaken, it is no surprise to see American commentators returning to Lincoln's address to regain their footing. See, e.g., Sunderland 2024 and Stephens 2021.

[3] For especially illuminating commentary on Hart's internal point of view, which is the subject of a large literature, see Kaplan 2017, 2023; Shapiro 2006.

[4] I am certainly not the first to make a similar suggestion; for a version of this point grounded in a different set of concerns, see section II of Christopher Tollefsen's contribution to this volume in chapter 9.

[5] Philosophical genealogy differs from other methods of philosophical inquiry in its emphasis on the significance of the relation between a target concept or phenomenon (e.g., lawfulness) and the

Internal Point of View: An Elaboration of Hart's Genealogy of Law' (2019), which extends Hart's own story of the emergence of law backwards in time by providing a genealogical account of the 'primary rules' of conduct that precede the appearance of law. (I have chosen Pettit's account simply because it is the richest and most fully worked out genealogy of its kind that I am aware of.) The second is Bernard Williams' genealogical account in *Truth and Truthfulness* (2002) of certain virtues and values associated with our concern for the truth. Pettit's genealogy and Williams' are substantively and methodologically akin in several respects, but one striking difference is that Williams considers it important to his story that his characters come to attribute *intrinsic* value to various practices and dispositions; whereas Pettit, consistent with the Hartian tradition in which he is working, studiously avoids any reference to changes in valuations.

Among the advantages that Pettit claims for his genealogy is that it 'supports a rich psychological model of what it means for people to take an internal point of view, as [Hart] calls it, on the rules that they follow' (2019: 232). I will contend, however, that Pettit's genealogy and the model of the internal point of view that it supports are, notwithstanding their ingenuity and insight, importantly incomplete; what is needed to complete his story is something like the change in valuations that figures in Williams' genealogy, in which group members develop a special or intrinsic attachment or regard for the primary rules.

Completing the story in this way has important implications for our understanding of the character of legal systems. Hart taught us that law can be understood as a system for organising, interpreting, and changing primary rules of conduct. But if people have a special or intrinsic attachment or regard for the primary rules that precede the emergence of law, then the law cannot establish or maintain itself without overcoming or displacing that attachment by somehow cultivating a competing attachment or regard for the law itself.[6] We can read Creon as a despot or megalomaniac, and perhaps he is, but by trying to instil the quality of lawfulness in his compatriots, he – like Lincoln – also sought to establish one of the essential elements of a legal order.

process of development of the practice(s) with which the concept or phenomenon is closely associated (see Pettit 2019: 231, and n 7 below). It differs from straight history in that (a) by starting from an abstracted and hypothetical initial situation, it seeks to ground the target phenomenon in relatively universal human characteristics and circumstances; and (b) by foregrounding the role of purposes and functions in the development of the relevant practices, it seeks to shed light on the target phenomenon's rational character (or its lack thereof) (on the latter point, see Williams 2002: 33–34). At the same time, the aim is to be broadly consistent with actual history, and history can inform and flesh out the genealogical inquiry – as discussed further in section V below (see also Williams 2002: 39). Thanks to the editors for urging clarification here.

[6] John Deigh has similarly argued that legal systems must cultivate what he calls an 'allegiance' or 'emotional bond' to the law (1999: 287–88, 295); his account, which draws on theories of childhood moral development rather than philosophical genealogy (1999: 295–97; *cf.* 2016: 59), is distinct but complementary to the one offered here. Another complementary discussion is provided by Daniel Peixoto Murata, who draws on various aspects of Williams' work, including particularly his reasons-internalism, to develop a more general account of the way in which 'the law characteristically demands respect' (2022: 164, and generally Ch 6).

## II. Pettit on the Genealogy of Primary Rules

Lying at the centre of *The Concept of Law* (Hart 2012) is a briefly sketched genealogy or 'fable' of the emergence of law.[7] Hart argues in his fifth chapter that while it is easy to imagine communities existing without law – indeed, such communities have existed – as they grow larger or more complex they will face challenges that will lead them spontaneously to develop what we would call a legal system.

To illustrate this, Hart starts with an imagined community that is governed only by basic, informal standards of behaviour – including restrictions on violence, deception, and theft – which he refers to as 'primary rules' of conduct (2012: 91). A regime of primary rules alone, he points out, suffers from some crucial limitations – specifically: (i) the lack of a method to settle doubts about the content of the rules; (ii) the absence of a way to change the rules to adapt to new circumstances; and (iii) a lack of procedures to settle disputes about the rules and their application (2012: 92–94).

'The remedy', Hart suggests, 'for each of these three main defects in this simplest form of social structure consists in supplementing the *primary* rules of obligation with *secondary* rules which are rules of a different kind' (2012: 94). These secondary rules comprise: (i) rules of recognition to facilitate the identification of the primary rules (for instance, by writing them down in an authoritative text); (ii) rules of change to allow the introduction of new primary rules and elimination of old ones; and (iii) rules of adjudication to govern the resolution of disputes about the application of the primary rules (e.g., whether a rule has been violated in a particular case). The introduction of these elements, Hart suggests, marks the transition from a system of primary rules to a system of law (2012: 98).

Note that Hart does not seek in this story to explain the emergence of the internal point of view or to elucidate its character – he instead assumes that the members of a group governed by primary rules will generally take the internal point of view towards those rules (this is part of what it is for them to be the primary rules of the group; 2012: 117), and further assumes that there will be at least a tendency to extend the same point of view to the secondary rules as they are introduced (2012: 90, 98).

[7] It is described by John Gardner as a 'fable' in 'Why Law Might Emerge: Hart's Problematic Fable' (2013), and by Pettit as a 'philosophical genealogy of the concept of law' (2019: 230). The genealogical method has subsequently been widely used by legal theorists working under Hart's influence, as illuminatingly analysed by Murata (2022: Ch 2). Hart's story of law's emergence is a 'philosophical genealogy' in the sense that it uses an abstract but plausible hypothetical history to illustrate how and why a set of practices that we would recognise as a system of law could emerge among participants who lack any concept of law at the outset, and suggests that our own concept of law picks out practices that have similar salient features and play a similar role in the organisation of our social life (see Pettit 2019: 231; Williams 2002: 33–35; and n 5 above). Pettit and Williams agree that useful philosophical genealogies possess these features; Williams also attributes to them a further feature that Pettit does not, namely that genealogies may go beyond purely functional accounts by explaining the role that function plays in the emergence of practices or dispositions whose significance and role cannot be fully explained in functional terms (Williams 2002: 35). The significance of this will be developed below.

Pettit undertakes to expand Hart's story in two ways. First, he extends it backwards in time to provide a genealogical account of how the sort of primary rules with which Hart's story begins could spontaneously emerge amongst people who at first recognise no such rules (2019: 231). Second, he offers an account of how the emergence of such primary rules would involve and depend upon the parallel emergence of 'an intuitively internal point of view on the emergent rules' (2012: 233).[8]

Pettit's story begins with an imagined group of people each of whom is generally concerned with their own well-being, instrumentally rational, and 'dependent for their well-being on others reliably eschewing violence and deception and the like' (2019: 235). Assuming some plausible conditions, he contends that we can reconstruct why, 'for purely self-interested reasons, each member of the society should display certain patterns of cooperative behaviour in dealing with others' (2019: 235).

As an example, Pettit considers the norm of truthfulness in communication (2019: 235–37). Each person, he reasons, will want to be able to rely on others' reports regarding information to which she does not have direct access, as well as to have others rely on her reports, in order to secure the benefits of cooperation. Thus truth telling as a general pattern of behaviour will be favoured, because each person is better off to the extent that everyone is both reliably truthful and trusts everyone else to be truthful.

Of course, there will be a countervailing temptation to defect and freeride, because truth telling is collectively beneficial but at times individually burdensome – each person will face instances in which they would like to have some information to themselves, or to have others believe false information (Pettit 2019: 236). But in Pettit's view this sort of defection will be heavily deterred by the threat of reputational effects: Because truthfulness in cooperation partners is so important, each person will keep track of the reliability of others (including by communicating with others about the reliability of third parties) and will herself be concerned to maintain a general reputation as a reliable truth-teller. Pettit thus expects gossip and a resulting 'economy of esteem' to have a decisive influence in weakening the temptation to defect (2019: 237–38). He concludes: 'The concern for how we are likely to be seen by others in general – the concern with our good name – should serve to keep most of us onside in most relevant cases' (2019: 239). And just as in the case of truthfulness, the same reasoning will apply to other collectively beneficial patterns of behaviour, including non-violence, promise-keeping, respect for property, and so on.

The only further condition that is needed, Pettit argues, to have a genuine *social* norm – that is, a *rule*, rather than a merely statistical or descriptive norm – is that the situation just described be common knowledge amongst the group's members.

[8] The genealogy that Pettit develops is highly intricate and resourceful, and draws on Pettit's significant body of related work on the emergence of ethical concepts and practices (especially his 2018 publication). Here I will have to make do with an extremely condensed summary.

Then it will be the case not only that most people conform to the norm most of the time and that this conformity is supported by expected reputational effects, but also that everyone knows this to be the case, and so can see conformity as expressive of a generally acknowledged standard of behaviour, and can understand their own and other's conduct under the description of conformity to (or deviation from) a rule (2019: 241–42).

Pettit observes that this might be thought to be the point at which Hart's internal point of view first emerges, for it is now possible for the group members to have an attitude toward the norm as such, and moreover conformity with the norm can now be understood to have a special relationship with group membership:

> The reputational incentive on which you act will be that if you do not conform with the universal pattern involved, then you will not be one of the gang; your social identity and allegiance will be in doubt. You will not be in tune with how things, as we others may say, are done around here. This suggests that, recognising the incentive on offer, you will not view the norm from an outsider or outlier perspective; you will display the sort of profile that Hart associates with the internal point of view (Pettit 2019: 243).

Pettit entertains this notion, but does not fully endorse it. He notes that compliance with social norms on the basis of this kind of reputational incentive is consistent with an entirely detached and strategic attitude toward those norms (2019: 243). Indeed, someone might view the norms and the reputational incentives to comply with them cynically or even contemptuously, and see maintaining a reputation for compliance merely as the best means to other ends (taking, as it were, the external point of view, from within the system).[9] As Pettit puts it, the reputational concern that supports compliance with the norm still has a purely 'causal-instrumental character' – what is feared is a 'downstream, causal effect' of violating the norm, whereas the violation itself may be viewed neutrally, or even positively, by a person who is for one reason or another alienated from the norm. And this would seem to threaten a collapse back into the very sanction-centred mindset ('orders backed by threats') with which Hart sought to contrast the internal point of view.[10]

For this reason, Pettit is inclined to say that the full-blown internal point of view does not emerge until a crucial further step is taken, which he calls *internalisation*:

> In order for the norm to be internalised, the members of the relevant group must generally prefer that X-ing be the established pattern – rather than any feasible, salient alternative, if indeed there is one – and must, in consequence, be disposed to think ill of someone who fails to abide by it and well of someone who lives up to it (2019: 245).

As Pettit points out, it is possible for a social norm to be recognised and to prevail within a group even while all members of that group would prefer a different norm. In such a case, the members will share an understanding of the content of the norm and of the negative reputational effects of defection, and will strive to conform with the norm out of regard for those reputational effects, but will each

[9] On this possibility and its significance, see generally Shapiro 2000.

[10] Pettit also reads Hart as likely to agree with this line of reasoning (2019: 257; *cf.* Hart 2012: 91–92).

prefer that a different norm were in place instead (for instance, because group members are mistaken about each other's preferences regarding the norm; 2019: 244–45). In such a case, the norm is generally recognised and complied with, but the group members remain in an important sense alienated from the norm; they have not *internalised* it, in Pettit's specific sense.[11]

But, as Pettit goes on to argue, this is not likely to be the case with the primary rules of conduct regarding truthfulness, non-violence, and the like, because it is better for each member of the group if these norms prevail, rather than any more permissive norm. In particular, any norm that would allow one person to freeride is ruled out as simply 'infeasible; being a pattern that no one else could be expected to support, it hardly counts as an alternative at all' (2019: 246). In other words, such a pattern could never be generally accepted as a rule by the group. 'The upshot', Pettit concludes, is that the primary rules 'are not only likely to be perceived as social demands … but also to be internalised spontaneously by those who live under them' (2019: 246).

Moreover, this internalisation marks a significant development beyond a sanction-centred mentality: 'the internalisation of the norm certainly marks the advent of an internal point of view. It puts into play a new respect in which the viewpoint of members contrasts with the detached perspective of outsiders or outliers' (Pettit 2019: 246). It does this by giving someone who has internalised the norm a new kind of reason for conforming – one that is no longer purely strategic or 'causal-instrumental' in character – because 'by conforming you contribute a necessary element to the universal pattern of truth telling or non-violence, where that is a pattern that you prefer to obtain, given that you cannot feasibly hope to freeride' (Pettit 2019: 246). This reason, Pettit observes, is still an instrumental reason, because complying with the norm is a means to the further end of achieving a general pattern of compliance; but it is no longer a *causal*-instrumental reason, because the general pattern is not a downstream result of your compliance, but rather in part *constituted* by your compliance. The reason in question is thus 'constitutive-instrumental'. This, Pettit contends, takes us for the first time clearly and decisively beyond the detached or estranged point of view of an outsider, and puts us squarely within the internal point of view.

Internalisation is not the final step in Pettit's genealogy of the primary rules or in his elaboration of the internal point of view. He goes on to contend that once the group members have internalised the primary rules, they will come collectively to *ratify* those rules – by which he means that they will as a matter of common awareness join in tacitly endorsing and committing themselves to the rules, endorsement and commitment being understood in the game theoretic (rather than moral)

[11] The alienation at issue here can admit of degrees – a group member may be contemptuous of the prevailing norm and prefer that there were no norm at all, but nevertheless comply for reputational reasons; or they may find that there is much to be said for the prevailing norm and be glad that the norm is in place (as opposed to no norm at all), but consider that there is another possible norm that would be even better. In either case, this group member would fall short of *internalising* the prevailing norm, in the strong sense that Pettit describes. Thanks again here to the editors for discussion.

sense that members will effectively stake their reputation on their support for and compliance with the rules, and thereby implicitly invite one another to rely on this in various ways (2019: 247–53).

These additional developments, Pettit argues, further enrich the internal point of view, by maximising 'the contrast between our attitude towards the norms and the attitudes of an outsider or outlier' (2019: 255). But I will set these further developments to one side, and focus on the decisive step of 'internalisation', which in Pettit's telling represents the first full emergence of the internal point of view.

## III. Williams on the Genealogy of Truthfulness

*Truth and Truthfulness* offers a genealogical account of certain virtues and values associated with our concern for the truth, including the norm of truthfulness or sincerity in assertion (Williams 2002). Very much like Pettit, Williams starts with an imagined group of people living in an abstracted 'State of Nature' in which there are advantages to be gained for all group members by sharing information with one another (2002: 38, 41–43, 57). These circumstances will give rise, he reasons, to a 'division of epistemic labour' in which those who are in a position to do so will acquire information that is useful to the group and report that information for use by other members (2002: 44).

A person may of course perform her role in the division of epistemic labour more or less well from the point of view of the group's shared interest, and people may accordingly be 'discouraged or encouraged, sanctioned, shamed, or rewarded with respect to this' (Williams 2002: 44). Williams identifies two relevant dimensions of epistemic performance, concerning acquisition and transmission of correct information, on the one hand, and honest reporting without deception or concealment, on the other. These 'two basic *virtues of truth*' he labels 'Accuracy' and 'Sincerity', respectively (2002: 44). Because behaviour that manifests these virtues is valuable to the group, everyone has an incentive to use the social sanctions mentioned above to promote this behaviour and the associated virtues, and to sanction failures and misbehaviour. As Williams summarises, this State of Nature story illustrates why the two 'virtues, and the fact that people possess those virtues, have a value. They are useful, indeed essential, to such objectives as the pooling of information, and those objectives are important to almost every human purpose' (2002: 57).

As is evident from these passages, Williams, in contrast to Pettit, focuses on behavioural dispositions and associated qualities of character – 'virtues' – rather than social norms. But in other respects the first part of Williams' genealogy is very similar to Pettit's. A crucial shared feature is that up to this point in Williams' story 'the values of Accuracy and Sincerity alike are *instrumental*: they are entirely explained in terms of other goods, and in particular the value of getting what one wants, avoiding danger, mastering the environment, and so on' (2002: 58). As we have seen, in Pettit's account, prior to the 'internalisation' of the primary rules of conduct (which, in his telling, marks the full arrival of the internal point of view) the group members' conformity with the rules, even if voluntary and based on reputational rather than material sanctions, continues to have a purely 'causal-instrumental character' (2019: 244).

At the next step, however, the accounts diverge sharply. Williams is more impressed than Pettit by the temptation to freeride, and by the fact that in real life people do sometimes freeride: 'Despite the fact that there are norms which lay it down that assertions are supposed to be true, many assertions are not true, often because they are not sincere' (Williams 2002: 85). He observes that even if the members of the group collectively have reason to prefer that a general norm of truthfulness prevails, there remains 'a gap in the motivations to truthfulness' for each individual: 'the collective value of Sincerity (and in *that* sense, its value to each person) does not translate into a reason that each person has for possessing that quality himself' (2002: 39, 58). (We will further explore this point of disagreement in the next section.)

Thus, while strategic reasoning supports a preference for the truthfulness norm over other possible norms, such reasoning alone is not sufficient in Williams' view to give individuals a reason to comply with the norm in difficult cases – as confirmed by the simple fact that people sometimes lie. But at the same time, it does not seem that our practices of sharing information simply devolve into a cynical exercise in strategic reasoning – we do sometimes tell the truth even in difficult cases, and we sometimes trust others to do the same. How is this possible? As Williams puts it, granted that strategic reasoning alone cannot secure reliable compliance with the truthfulness norm, 'it is a good question, how the assertion system replicates itself' at all (2002: 85).

Williams' response to this problem is grounded in the observation that actual people are not solely strategic reasoners, and more generally are 'not devices which have dispositions merely in the sense that reliable predictions can be made about their behaviour'; rather, they are 'human beings' who have, and are understood by one another to have, a range of motivations, as well as 'a sense of what it most important to them' (2002: 89).[12] If strategic reasoning is not enough, Williams proposes, we should explore some of these other aspects of human character and motivation as possible resources for understanding how 'the dispositions of trustworthiness are secured' (2002: 90). He continues:

> One important way of securing them [i.e., the dispositions of trustworthiness] is that the parties come to think that trustworthy behaviour, such as keeping one's word, has an *intrinsic value*, that it is a good thing (many other things being equal) to act as a trustworthy person acts, just because that is the kind of action that it is (2002: 90).

So one important part of the explanation of how general (yet less than perfect) compliance with the norm of truthfulness is possible is that people come to value

[12] This central theme of Williams' work is more fully explored by Murata (2022: especially Chs 3 and 6).

compliance with the norm, and the dispositions that support such compliance, directly, as valuable in themselves, without reference to other ends or values.

Williams' account of how such a change in valuations may come about is, perhaps necessarily, somewhat gestural, with many details left to be filled in by actual history and psychology. But in general this kind of thing happens, he suggests, when valuing something intrinsically is necessary ('or nearly necessary') in order to secure other important goods, and when the thing to be valued is sufficiently related to other valued things (without being simply reducible to or derivative of them) that 'the agent has some materials in terms of which he can understand this value in relation to other values that he holds' (2002: 92). If these two conditions are satisfied, Williams claims, 'then we shall have *constructed* an intrinsic good' (2002: 92).

Whether Williams' fairly loose sketch of this process is accurate or sufficiently developed is not as important for present purposes as his suggestions that, first, *some* such process could be invoked to explain how people might develop an attachment to or regard for something that cannot be fully explained in terms of their previously held values; and second, appeal to such a process can play an important role in filling the explanatory gap between strategic reasoning and individuals' general dispositions to comply with the norm of truthfulness (as also, we might add, with the other primary rules of conduct that are the subject of Pettit's genealogy).

## IV. 'Internalisation' and the Internal Point of View

Williams concludes that purely strategic reasoning leaves 'a gap in the motivations to truthfulness' because 'the collective value of Sincerity … does not translate into a reason that each person has for possessing that quality himself' (2002: 39, 58). If this is correct, a version of the same problem would seem to apply to the various primary rules (regarding truthfulness as well as violence, theft, promise-breaking, etc.) that are the subject of Pettit's genealogy: The collective value of general compliance with a norm will not translate into a reason that each person has for complying with the norm herself. Pettit is of course aware of this problem, and we have already outlined his response to it. But as I will argue, his response, despite its subtlety and ingenuity, falls short. An important further consequence of this is that Pettit's account ultimately lacks the resources to support the kind of 'rich psychological model of what it means for people to take an internal point of view' that he aims to provide (2019: 232).

As we have seen, Pettit's response to the problem pressed by Williams comes in two parts: First, he argues that each individual has good reason to prefer that a norm of truthfulness prevails (as also norms of non-violence, etc.), given that the alternative in which others comply while she herself freerides is unacceptable to others and thus infeasible as a social norm. (This is why, in Pettit's account, individuals will 'internalise' the norm.) Second, he suggests that, in light of this preference, each person will have not only a causal-instrumental reason – grounded in their other ends – to comply with the norm, but also a constitutive-instrumental reason, because their own compliance is partly constitutive of the state of affairs that they prefer, in which the norm of truthfulness (etc.) prevails.

Like Pettit's account in general, these points are sophisticated and appealing, and seem to capture some significant truths about our complex practical situation as social creatures. As a response to Williams' problem, however, they ultimately amount to a non sequitur, because Pettit's discussion does not address the practical question that confronts an agent choosing whether to comply with a norm or to violate it. Instead, Pettit constructs the relevant choice as the choice of which norm, among socially feasible alternatives, should prevail. But when an individual is choosing whether to comply with a norm in a particular situation what they face is of course not a choice between norms but a choice between actions. There is no inconsistency in preferring a pattern of compliance with the norm of truthfulness over compliance with any other feasible social norm (i.e., 'internalising' the norm of truthfulness, in Pettit's sense), while also preferring to violate the norm in a particular case (e.g., when confident that the violation will not be discovered, or that the rewards of defection will outweigh any negative reputational effects).

Pettit's discussion appears to exclude the latter possibility by eliding the difference between preferences or choices between different norms, and preferences or choices between different courses of action. Earlier he was quoted saying that

> People may each wish they could themselves breach those norms [i.e., the primary rules] while others conform, but that alternative is not only infeasible; being a pattern that no one else could be expected to support, it hardly counts as an alternative at all' (2019: 246).

This is correct as regards the feasibility of different candidate social norms: the pattern in which everyone else complies while I breach is not feasible as a social norm, because no one other than me would accept it. But later on the same page Pettit asserts that once the norm is preferred in this way, and thus in his sense 'internalised', then

> you will … be responsive to the consideration that by conforming you contribute a necessary element to the universal pattern of truth telling or non-violence, where that is a pattern that you prefer to obtain, *given that you cannot feasibly hope to freeride*' (2019: 46 – emphasis added).

But the latter is not given – people often do hope to freeride, and sometimes they succeed. What is not feasible is that the *norm* according to which only you get to freeride should become a generally accepted social norm; but to repeat, freeriding as an action (rather than a norm) sometimes *is* feasible, and indeed sometimes occurs.

Pettit's appeal to the existence of a 'constitutive-instrumental' reason to comply with the norm is similarly inapposite in this context. The thought seems to be that when you prefer a pattern of compliance with a given norm over compliance with other possible norms, you thereby also acquire a reason that weighs in favour of *your* complying with the norm, and this reason can compete with any reason you may have to violate the norm. But it is not clear how a reason with these characteristics could arise in this way. The fact that you prefer general compliance with a norm of truthfulness to any feasible alternative norm simply has no bearing on whether you may nonetheless prefer to violate the norm when it appears to be to your advantage. In other words, your preference for a pattern of compliance with the norm *as against patterns of compliance with other socially acceptable norms* says nothing about your preference regarding your own compliance with the norm *as against your violating the norm*.

The upshot of this is that the 'internalisation' of a norm, in Pettit's sense, cannot narrow the 'motivational gap' that Williams identifies between the norms that strategic reasoning identifies as collectively beneficial and individuals' reasons to comply with those norms.[13] Moreover, this reveals why such 'internalisation' also cannot represent the full emergence of the Hartian internal point of view. This is because, as we have just seen, 'internalising' a norm in Pettit's sense is compatible with an entirely sanction-centred mindset regarding compliance with the norm. It is perfectly consistent, for instance, to 'internalise' the norm of truthfulness – in the sense that you prefer a general pattern of compliance with this norm over general compliance with any socially feasible alternative norm – while nonetheless being willing to comply with the norm *only* to the extent that the negative effects – reputational or otherwise – of violating the norm outweigh the advantages of doing so. But to regard the norm in this way would be to see it in purely instrumental terms, and is compatible with otherwise being entirely alienated from or even contemptuous of the norm; in other words, it is compatible with the very kind of sanction-centred mindset with which Hart sought to contrast the internal point of view. This belies Pettit's claim that his account supports 'a rich psychological model of what it means for people to take an internal point of view' (2019: 232).[14]

Another set of considerations provides a different kind of support for the same conclusion. The 'internalisation' that is assigned a crucial role in Pettit's account is itself premised upon cognitively complex strategic considerations and involves

[13] Perhaps Pettit could instead seek to narrow the gap by pointing to the reputational effects that play a significant role in the earlier stages of his account (2019: 237–39). But, first, this would raise some difficult and disputable questions about how powerful and reliable we should expect reputational effects to be in a 'state of nature'; Williams could plausibly deny that they would be sufficiently efficacious to close the gap. And second, as Pettit would concede (2019: 243), this move would leave individuals with exclusively 'causal-instrumental' reasons to comply with the primary rules. For this reason, it would not shield his model of the internal point of view from the further difficulty explored below.

[14] The subsequent step in Pettit's account of ratification – mentioned above at the end of section II – introduces further complexities, but does not, I think, answer the fundamental concern. Throughout Pettit's discussion there seems to be some slippage between the narrow stipulative definitions given to key terms of art – including 'internalisation,' 'ratification,' and 'commitment' – and the richer evaluative connotations carried by those words in their ordinary senses.

attitudes with highly specific contents; in particular, a preference 'that X-ing be the established pattern – rather than any feasible, salient alternative, if indeed there is one' (2019: 245). Those who 'internalise' the primary rules must thus have at least an implicit facility with the notions of social feasibility and salience, as well as the ability to apply them in considering the primary rules and relevant alternative norms, and the ability to imagine what patterns of general compliance with the relevant norms would look like, so as to evaluate them and reach a specific judgment about the relative desirability of patterns of compliance with the primary rules.

All of this seems a poor match with the familiar phenomenology of primary-rule acceptance as we actually experience it. It is doubtful whether our commitments to the norms of promise-keeping or non-violence, for instance, derive any significant support from the idea – if indeed such an idea should occur to us outside the seminar room – that a pattern of general promise-keeping or non-violence is preferable to patterns of compliance with alternative possible norms. (It is a complex question, for instance, which norms have the right kind of salience to be candidates, how complex those norms can be, who the relevant others are and what they might be willing to accept, etc.) Ordinary commitment to the primary rules seems to have a simpler and more direct character than this.

A similar discrepancy is apparent if we consider the process by which commitment to the primary norms is ordinarily acquired. Pettit's genealogy describes how relatively mature, rational agents could come to 'internalise' primary rules through a process of deriving and accepting these rules on the basis of strategic considerations. But it seems that the process he describes must be a far cry from the process by which *we* acquire an attachment to those norms, because for us this takes place through a process of socialisation that begins when we are very young – any rationalisation comes only much later, if at all.

Of course, philosophical genealogy as a method relies upon hypothetical rather than actual history, and moreover need not be committed to the idea that the rational connections it postulates correspond directly to stages in the psychological development of individuals. It is thus no objection merely to say that Pettit's genealogy does not closely match the process of internalisation that we actually undergo. The concern, however, is not merely that the story is simplified or abstracted or idealised, but rather that it describes the wrong *kind* of process to meaningfully model the sort of socialisation on which internalisation of the relevant norms depends, and for this reason it misrepresents the fundamental character of the attitude toward the primary rules that is essentially involved in the establishment and persistence of such rules. This suggests again that Pettit's proposed 'rich psychological model of what it means for people to take up the internal point of view' is inapt as a model of the internal point of view as we actually exhibit it.

Williams's genealogy of truthfulness may be in various ways incomplete or suffer from other drawbacks, but his approach does at least point the way towards a possible answer to the challenges that we have identified for Pettit's account. Indeed, if we can postulate a process by which members of a group may come to attribute some kind of special or intrinsic value or significance to the primary rules, then these difficulties would seem to be easily resolved. The change in valuation could take the form of a simple conviction that it is good or obligatory to conform with the primary rules and evil or forbidden to violate them (as in Williams' suggestion that 'the parties come to think that trustworthy behaviour, such as keeping one's word, has an *intrinsic value*, that it is a good thing … to act as a trustworthy person acts, just because that is the kind of action it is'; 2002: 90).[15] Alternatively, the change might involve the development of more elaborate conceptions of the sort familiar from history and anthropology, such as that the ancestors' long-established practices have acquired an authority that must be respected, or that the gods disapprove of and will punish violations of their injunctions. Yet another possibility is that this change in valuation could be connected to more basic processes of psychological and emotional development, such as the formation of a Freudian superego.[16] There is vastly more that could be said about the variety of different ways in which this could come about and the significance of the differences between them.[17] But the point, for present purposes, is simply that the characters in the story develop *some* sort of special, stable attachment to or regard for the primary rules, which goes beyond what can be derived from purely strategic considerations combined with the relevant natural facts.

Such a change in valuation would directly address Williams' 'motivational gap' by giving the individuals in whom it occurs a reason not just to prefer general compliance with the rules, but to comply themselves. Moreover, this new reason to comply would not be merely strategic or instrumental but intrinsic – compliance would be seen as an end in itself – and would therefore take us beyond the sanction-centred mindset that Hart was so concerned to distinguish from the internal point of view. And direct commitment to or regard for the primary rules themselves would be both more consistent with the everyday phenomenology of primary rule acceptance, and easier to understand as the outcome of a process of internalisation that takes place through socialisation from a young age.

## V. Lawfulness and the Emergence of Law

Completing the genealogy of primary rules in this way turns out to have important implications for our understanding of how legal systems emerge and

[15] It is worth noting that Williams would of course resist the conflation of intrinsic value with moral value; this leaves room within a Williamsian genealogy to accommodate Hart's view that the internal point of view need not involve moral endorsement (2012: 203, 257).

[16] See Deigh 2016: 59; for an extended development of the Freudian framework in relation to law specifically, see West 1986.

[17] For instance, the process by which this comes about may tend either to vindicate and reinforce, or to cast suspicion upon and undermine, the resulting valuation. On the difference between vindicatory and non-vindicatory genealogies, see Williams 2002: 35–38. See Tollefsen's contribution for a lucid vindicatory genealogy of lawfulness in chapter 9 of this volume.

maintain themselves. Hart held that law arises to cure the defects inherent in a pure system of primary rules, and that it does this by claiming jurisdiction to formulate, change, and interpret the primary rules. But if group members have a special attachment or regard for the pre-existing primary rules, then the interventions and innovations of an incipient legal system cannot help but generate resistance and conflict. In contrast to the dry and seemingly bloodless stories that Hart and Pettit tell about the origins of law,[18] we should expect law's emergence out of a system of primary rules to be *troubled*, a site of struggle and contestation. And law could not survive this struggle, or long persist, without somehow cultivating an attachment or regard for the law that competes with the existing regard for the primary rules – that is, without cultivating a disposition of *lawfulness*.

Law's struggle to establish and sustain itself will thus, if successful, leave a profound mark on the attitudes of legal subjects, and it is an important benefit of a genealogical inquiry that it can shed light on this process in a way that more abstract, ahistorical investigations do not. Indeed, a fully realised genealogical inquiry of this kind could fruitfully combine, in the way modelled by Williams in *Truth and Truthfulness*, fictional and historical elements – for law's struggle to establish and sustain itself is not merely a hypothetical conjecture, but an ongoing series of historical episodes, some of which are accessible to us.

To explore in a satisfying way the range of historical evidence that bears on this thesis would be a massive undertaking. Instead, by way of suggestion rather than demonstration, let me briefly offer three diverse examples of the law's struggle with its subjects' attachments to pre-existing norms. In each case there is a primary rule of conduct, embodied in a traditional or informal practice of norm compliance or enforcement, that comes into conflict with an incipient or established legal order, provoking a response intended to encourage a disposition of lawfulness.

First, return to Lincoln. Here is his description of one of the episodes to which his 1838 address was a response:

> In the Mississippi case, they first commenced by hanging the regular gamblers: a set of men, certainly not following for a livelihood, a very useful, or very honest occupation; but one which, so far from being forbidden by the laws, was actually licensed by an act of the Legislature, passed but a single year before (1984: 7).

So here a group of vigilantes exercised lethal force to demonstrate their commitment to an informal norm that was not only unrecognised but indeed directly challenged by the law. Understandably distressed by this and several similar cases, in the passage quoted at the opening of this chapter Lincoln rallies his listeners to a very uncompromising ideal of lawfulness.

[18] Regarding the transition from a pre-legal social order to a Hartian legal system, Pettit remarks simply that while his genealogical story 'focuses only on primary rules, the account it offers of the internal viewpoint … extends, with suitable amendments, to the secondary rules on which Hart concentrates' (2018: 232). Others have told similarly bloodless stories – e.g., Scott Shapiro (2011). For general discussion, see Murata (2022: Ch 2).

Lincoln thus sought to fortify the legal culture of a community in which the law's ability to assert itself in the face of commitment to extra-legal primary rules seemed to be eroding. An example of a different kind appears in the anthropologist Christopher Boehm's work on the first establishment of a modern legal order among 19th century Serbian tribes.[19] At the time, a dozen or so tribes had been working together only sporadically to resist conquest by the Ottomans. The *vladika*, a kind of warrior-bishop, was elected by the tribes to coordinate their joint military activities. Several vladikas sought to consolidate authority and establish a more centralised, law-governed state, but these efforts were resisted by the fiercely independent tribes, who were accustomed to a traditional style of social organisation – in essence, a pre-legal regime of primary rules. Boehm writes:

> Eventually, and particularly after 1830, the tribesmen themselves became divided about what kind of political order they wanted. Some agreed with the claims of their final vladika that he should have the power to tax and to punish 'murderers' – men who enacted the politically disruptive blood revenge killings that by tribal tradition were honorable, right, and morally necessary (1999: 100).

Here, just as in Lincoln's case, there is a primary rule – regarding revenge killing – to which group members are vehemently committed. But this practice is 'disruptive', and by the mid-19th century some are starting to feel that it has outlived its usefulness. Recall that in Hart's view, the lack of a ready means to change or remove primary rules that have become obsolescent is precisely the kind of defect that the introduction of a system of law is meant to solve. But here the law's innovations, however well-intentioned, are met with passionate resistance, grounded in attachment to a primary rule that is regarded as 'honorable, right, and morally necessary'.

In 1849, as Boehm relates, the last vladika was succeeded by his nephew Danilo Petrović, a 'ruthless, domination-prone individual' who chose to serve as a secular leader rather than as bishop, in order to marry. Shortly after succeeding to this role, he

> had broken the backbone of a still highly recalcitrant tribal system. He accomplished this feat by getting several loyal tribes to serve as his army, and by putting down a tax rebellion in the large and intransigent Kuči tribe. More than two hundred human heads were cut in a single day, and from that time forward the dozen or so tribes of Old Montenegro accepted centralized authority (1999: 101).

This episode well illustrates that positive exhortation is not the only way to cultivate lawfulness. Earlier we saw Williams imagining that 'the parties come to think that trustworthy behaviour, such as keeping one's word, has an *intrinsic value*, that it is a good thing … to act as a trustworthy person acts' (2002: 90). This is not quite what happened among the Serbian tribes with respect to the new legal order, at

[19] Thanks here to Ira Lindsay for pointing me to Boehm's *Hierarchy in the Forest* (1999).

least not directly. Two hundred beheadings is a grand gesture, intended to foster fear and awe (rather than positive attachment) as the basis for a special regard for the law. But nonetheless, by making this kind of impression, Danilo Petrović, no less than Lincoln though by horrifically different means, sought to cultivate in his would-be subjects a disposition of lawfulness.[20]

Finally, return to Creon. Sophocles was writing in an Athens that had a sophisticated legal system of which the Athenians were understandably proud, but in which memories of the transition from a regime of traditional or primary rules were still relatively fresh.[21] The convulsions that attended this transition are vividly reflected in *Antigone*, which is often read as a dramatisation of the conflicts between obligations to family and to the state, between natural law and positive law, between youth and age, between the sexes, etc. Of course it is all of these; but it is also a dramatisation of nascent law's struggle to assert itself and to discipline or displace its subjects' attachment to pre-existing primary rules.[22] In this case, the struggle focuses on a traditional injunction that the dead must be buried, and Creon's contrary decree that the traitor Polyneices's body was to be left exposed.

Throughout the play, Creon argues vigorously that traditional standards of right and wrong must yield to the law:

> So, if someone goes too far and breaks the law / … / He will have nothing but contempt from me. / But when a city takes a leader, you must obey, / Whether his commands are trivial, or right, or wrong (Sophocles 2001: 29, ll. 663–67).

Antigone's diametrically opposed view is that the unchangeable, unwritten laws of the gods – the pre-existing primary rules – have a force that can never be superseded by human law: 'And I never thought your announcements / Could give you – a mere human being – / Power to trample the gods' unfailing [*asphalēs:* immovable], / Unwritten laws. These laws weren't made now / Or yesterday. They live for all time' (Sophocles 2001: 19, ll. 450–54]). In the end, of course, Creon relents (though all too late), yielding to the enduring sway of the established primary rules: 'I'm afraid it is best to obey the laws, / Just as tradition has them, all one's life' (2001: 48, ll. 1113–14).

But in this resolution Sophocles was likely indulging a reactionary fantasy. In Athens at the time it was in fact as Creon had sought to decree: contrary to the traditional injunction, it was by law forbidden to bury a traitor in Attic

[20] I do not mean to claim this gesture was the only reason for Petrović's success, nor to settle the question of what role there may be for fear and awe in the best general genealogical account of lawfulness. But this sort of example, like the example of Creon, suggests how a genealogical inquiry into law and lawfulness might fall short of vindicating our disposition to obey the law (see also n 17 above).

[21] This is also apparent, for instance, in discussions across the Ancient Greek world about the statuses of written and unwritten 'law' (*nomos*; see Thomas 1995, 2006). The reduction of rules to writing being, as Hart noted, a significant early step in the establishment of a legal system (2012: 94).

[22] Another notable dramatisation of this struggle, well deserving of a separate treatment, is Aeschylus's Eumenides (thanks to Daniel Peixoto Murata for discussion).

soil.[23] The stability of this legal regime reflected the ascendance of lawfulness over traditional attachments to pre-existing primary rules, even as the persistent yearning for a restoration of the status of those earlier attachments, represented with apparent sympathy by Sophocles in Antigone's principled resistance to Creon's high-handedness, illustrates that this ascendance could not have been achieved without struggle.

## Bibliography

Boehm, C (1999) *Hierarchy in the Forest: The Evolution of Egalitarian Behavior* (Cambridge, Massachusetts, Harvard University Press).
Deigh, J (1999) 'Emotions and the Authority of Law: Variations on Themes in Bentham and Austin' in S Bandes (ed), *The Passions of Law* (New York, New York University Press).
—— (2016) 'The Emotional Significance of Punishment' 8 *Emotion Review* 56.
Gardner, J (2013) 'Why Law Might Emerge: Hart's Problematic Fable' in L Duarte d'Almeida, J Edwards & A Dolcetti (eds), *Reading HLA Hart's The Concept of Law* (Oxford, Hart Publishing).
Hart, HLA (2012) *The Concept of Law*, 3rd edn (Oxford, Oxford University Press).
Kaplan, J (2017) 'Attitude and the Normativity of Law' 35 *Law and Philosophy* 469.
—— (2023) 'The Internal Point of View' 42 *Law and Philosophy* 211.
Lincoln, A (1984) 'The Perpetuation of Our Political Institutions (Address Before the Young Men's Lyceum of Springfield), January 27, 1838' 6 *Journal of the Abraham Lincoln Association* 6, available at http://hdl.handle.net/2027/spo.2629860.0006.103.
Murata, DP (2022) *Reason, Respect, and the Law: Bernard Williams and Legal Normativity* (PhD thesis, University of Surrey).
Nussbaum, M (1986) *The Fragility of Goodness: Luck and Ethics in Greek Tragedy and Philosophy* (Cambridge, Cambridge University Press).
Pettit, P (2018) *The Birth of Ethics: Reconstructing the Role and Nature of Morality* (Oxford, Oxford University Press).
—— (2019) 'Social Norms and the Internal Point of View: An Elaboration of Hart's Genealogy of Law' 39 *Oxford Journal of Legal Studies* 229.
Shapiro, S (2000) 'The Bad Man and the Internal Point of View' in SJ Burton (ed), *The Path of the Law and its Influence: The Legacy of Oliver Wendell Holmes, Jr.* (Cambridge, Cambridge University Press).
—— (2006) 'What Is the Internal Point of View?' 75 *Fordham Law Review* 1157.
—— (2011) *Legality* (Cambridge, Massachusetts, Harvard University Press).
Sophocles (2001) *Antigone*, Paul Woodruff (trans) (Indianapolis, Indiana, Hackett).
Stephens, B (2021) 'Lincoln Knew in 1838 What 2021 Would Bring' *New York Times* (19 January) A23, available at www.nytimes.com/2021/01/18/opinion/trump-lincoln-mobs-democracy.html.

[23] See Nussbaum 1986: 437–38, n 14. Nussbaum cites as evidence for this law a passage in Thucydides (I.138) in which the relatives of Themistocles, who had been found to have collaborated with the Persians, are said to have defied Athenian law by secretly burying him in Attica. This report thus reflects conflict around the same legal rule regarding burial that animates *Antigone*.

Sunderland, LV (2024) 'Abraham Lincoln's Lyceum Address Highlights Why the Rule of Law Matters' *Chicago Tribune* (9 February), available at www.chicagotribune.com/2024/02/09/opinion-abraham-lincoln-lyceum-address-rule-of-law.
Thomas, R (1995) 'Written in Stone? Liberty, Equality, Orality and the Codification of Law' 40 *Bulletin of the Institute of Classical Studies* 59.
—— (2006) 'Writing, Law, and Written Law' in M Gagarin and D Cohen (eds), *The Cambridge Companion to Ancient Greek Law* (Cambridge, Cambridge University Press).
West, R (1986) 'Law, Rights, and Other Totemic Illusions: Legal Liberalism and Freud's Theory of the Rule of Law' 134 *University of Pennsylvania Law Review* 817.
Williams, B (2002) *Truth and Truthfulness* (Princeton, Princeton University Press).

# 9

# Law and Lawfulness: Genealogy, Jurisprudence and the Thought of Bernard Williams

CHRISTOPHER TOLLEFSEN

## I. Introduction

In this chapter, I investigate the prospects for an intellectually interesting and fruitful way to think about law modelled after Bernard Williams' treatment of truth and truthfulness in the book by that title (Williams 2002). Williams there attempts a genealogical account of how we may be understood to have 'constructed' the intrinsic value of trustworthiness – virtue as regards truth – in a way that is naturalist but not reductive, explanatory yet stable in the face of reflection. Through a combination of fiction and history, Williams aspires to provide something that is of the foremost importance in his thought more generally, namely, self-understanding that is sensitive to the role of historical contingency in the story of how we came to be who we are (see Williams 2006). Ultimately, Williams aims to show that his account of the virtues of truth reveals how those virtues respond to genuine human needs *without* the intervening governance of a 'Moral Law', an institution for which Williams' scepticism is well-known.

Could one likewise show that law also emerges from basic human purposes and needs and could one show how lawfulness – virtue as regards respect for law – might come to be treated as intrinsically good in Williams' sense? To show this would resolve a problem about the nature of law that I describe in the next section.

## II. Truth and Truthfulness, Law and Lawfulness

The set-up in *Truth and Truthfulness* begins with the identification of two contemporary attitudes toward truth and truthfulness. One is what Williams calls an 'intense commitment to truthfulness' (Williams 2002: 1); the other is an 'equally pervasive suspicion about truth itself' (2002: 1), suspicion voiced by what Williams calls 'the deniers' (2002: 5). Williams identifies a deep problem with the position of the deniers. The problem is one of academic authority. According to the deniers, 'everything, including argument and truthfulness, is force, persuasion, and manipulation (really)' (2002: 9). Yet the 'authority of academics must be rooted in their truthfulness', which Williams understands as a combination of two virtues, Accuracy and Sincerity (2002: 11). By virtue of the first, academics take care in pursuit of truth; by virtue of the second, 'they do not lie' (2002: 11).

Yet how can truthfulness matter, or even be possible, if everything is merely force, persuasion, and manipulation? And if there is no truthfulness, then there is no authority in the claims made by academics, no normativity in taking what they say as true or even as to be seriously entertained as true. As Williams puts it, 'if no authority, then only power' (2002: 8).

At risk of belabouring what may seem obvious, let me here identify some parallels between the situation as regards truth and truthfulness as described by Williams, and the situation as regards law – and also, as I'll show, lawfulness – in contemporary analytic jurisprudence.

Consider the question of the normativity of law. Law makes claims on us, and is thought to possess an authority that generates an obligation to obey; law is likewise thought to lack legitimacy when it cannot offer appropriate justifications for its claims, particularly when in the enforcement of those claims it exercises coercion upon its subjects. Recognition that the law presents itself to those subject to it as normative was central to Hart's criticisms of his positivist predecessors. Objecting to an account of legal rules as mere predictions that punishment would occur following breach, Hart noted that 'the judge, in punishing, takes the rule as his *guide* and the breach of the rule as his *reason* and *justification* for punishing the offender' (Hart 1961: 10). What may be taken only as signs from the external point of view are, from the internal view of the participant in law, signals, indications of how those who accept the rules are to regulate their behaviour. Hart identified, that is to say, the ways in which his positivist predecessors had neglected the normativity of law.

Yet Hart himself also aspired to a conception of the nature of law according to which there is, in his words, 'no necessary connection' between law and morality, no grounding of law's normativity in morality or perhaps anything more than simply the social fact that a rule of recognition is accepted by those who, having accepted it for whatever reasons they have, now treat those rules identified by the rule of recognition as legally valid as giving them reasons for action (Hart 1983: 57, n 25). As Nigel Simmonds summarises,

> Judges and citizens may attach prescriptive force to the law for various reasons. Legal theorists can understand the law's normative character simply by appreciating the possibility of such diverse attitudes, and seeing how the action-guiding character of law may be related to them. As citizens upon whom the law places demands, we need to consider the moral and prudential reasons for compliance or for non-compliance with the law; but as theorists seeking to comprehend the law as a distinctive type of social institution, we can set these questions on one side (Simmonds 2007: 123).

Simmonds expresses his own dissatisfaction with Hart's theory in a way that resonates with Williams' criticisms of the deniers: Hart's view amounts to banishing from the theory of the nature of law concern for law's authority. 'Validity' of a law is a function of its relation to the rule of recognition, but the rule of recognition itself is not something that can be assessed as valid or not on Hart's account. One might ask moral questions about that rule – is it good or right that this rule is accepted – but then in an important sense one is no longer asking a question about law *as law*.[1]

But then law, considered as ultimately in itself no more than an interesting kind of social fact, seems to have no authority to itself just as such. There might be good reasons to be lawful; or, on the other hand, law might be 'too iniquitous to be applied or obeyed' (Hart 1961: 203). But neither condition has any bearing on the fact of its being law. So it is a kind of category mistake to say that there is something authoritative to law as law: social facts just as such have no authority.

The denial of authority to law as law is tantamount also to a denial of what I am here calling 'lawfulness', for that virtue involves not just obedience to the law, but respect for its authority. For my purposes, that respect has two central loci: first, on the side of those subject to the law, considering whether or not to obey. 'Respect' for the law frames the question of obedience not primarily in terms of, for example, prudential concerns, but in terms of a recognition of obedience as responsive to the law's genuine authority. Second, respect resides in those who make and adjudicate the law. For, from their internal point of view on the law that they make or apply, such figures must treat the law as something worth making or applying, and indeed worth making or applying as law. And so treating the law with respect requires them to make or apply law in a way that acknowledges and is guided by those features of law that make it worth making or applying.[2]

However, the disposition of lawfulness so described can hardly be virtuous if there is or can be no authority in the law as law to respect. So the problem that Williams faces in *Truth and Truthfulness* is relevantly similar to that which is faced by someone who, like Simmonds, Robert Alexy, or John Finnis (among others) acknowledges the 'dual existence' of law – law as social fact, and law as ideal standard – when faced with those who acknowledge only the social facticity of law in their account of what law is.[3]

## III. Genealogy and Naturalism

A difficulty of method is also common to Williams' treatment of truth and truthfulness and contemporary thought about law, a difficulty raised by the question: how

[1] The tensions surrounding this point in Hart's thought are helpfully explored in Dyzenhaus 2022.

[2] For a defence of the idea that law is worth making, and hence of the value of legislation, see Webber et al 2018; and before that, Waldron 1999.

[3] In addition to Simmonds (2007), see, e.g., the exchange between Robert Alexy (2013) and John Finnis (2013).

is normativity possible in a naturalised and de-mythologised world? Naturalism seems at home in the positivist denial that there is anything authoritative about law as such, and might suggest the necessity of conceptual analysis as the only available tool for the study of law. That investigation, aimed as it would be at 'our' concept of law, might be little more than glorified ethnography.[4]

Most dramatically, naturalist commitments might lead to a form of scientific reductionism that allowed no room for normativity at all, save as a folk concept in need of elimination.[5] The prospects for a study of the nature of law and lawfulness from within such a framework are not promising.

Williams faces the same set of questions in *Truth and Truthfulness*. Here is Williams' characterisation of naturalism:

> Naturalism is a general outlook which, in relation to human beings, is traditionally, if very vaguely, expressed in the idea that they are 'part of nature' – in particular, that they are so in respects, such as their ethical life, in which this is not obviously true (Williams 2002: 22).

But, Williams continues, questions about naturalism are 'questions not about reduction, but about explanation', where the *explanans* includes nothing other than 'the rest of nature' (Williams 2002: 23). What we are concerned with, he says, is the emergence of the capacity of human beings to live in some form of ethical system, that is, the capacity to live under 'rules and values and to shape [our] behaviour in some degree to social expectations, in ways that are not under surveillance and not directly controlled by threats and rewards' (Williams 2002: 24). This raises a problem, for our psychology is shaped by culture, and our culture is a culture in which we live under an ethical system. So there might seem to be no explanatory, non-reductive path from where we are in culture to the capacities that make possible our location in culture, since that location is partly responsible for the current shape of our capacities.

It is here that for Williams, genealogy offers a way forward. We need to connect the psychology of humans living under an ethical system with other aspects of nature – but which aspects? Williams is suspicious of sociobiology, which takes the psychologies of the rest of the natural world as the starting point and sees 'the ethical' as merely another instantiation of what we see across other species' life forms. He is likewise sceptical of approaches that radically disjoin human psychology from the rest of nature. Williams argues instead that the needed connection is to other aspects of human psychology, for if we grant the *ex-ante* 'naturalness' of that psychology, then connecting our life under ethical culture to the rest of our psychology is appropriately naturalist.

This is what genealogy does. In particular, we suppose a State of Nature (an admittedly fictional construct) in which humans are possessed of capacities recognisable as natural but not – yet – capacities shaped by an ethical culture. Having

[4] As is suggested by Brian Leiter in *Naturalizing Jurisprudence* (2009).
[5] A programme found in its paradigmatic form in Churchland 1979.

described the parameters of that psychology, we can then show how, given a set of basic needs, humans could develop the concept or concepts under study, in Williams' case, those of truth and truthfulness. Genealogy based on a State of Nature escapes the explanatory difficulty mentioned above:

> we are asking about human ethical life in relation to the rest of human nature. If we can make sense of this undertaking, of explaining the ethical in terms of an account of human beings which is to the greatest possible extent *prior to the ideas of the ethical*, then there is a project of ethical naturalism which is intelligible, non-vacuous, and not committed to a general physicalistic reductionism that is (to put it mildly) dubious (Williams 2002: 26–27 – my emphasis).[6]

While some genealogies are primarily or even entirely historical, the fictional State of Nature story makes naturalist explanation possible for Williams. Williams sees in state of nature accounts generally an attempt to answer a particular sort of 'why' question: why do we have a concept – justice, knowledge, promise, truthfulness – by giving a particular kind of answer: out of the state of nature, that concept, and the role it plays in our practical or intellectual life, arose as a functional response to this or that need.

Two constraints on this kind of story are important, one for maintaining Williams' commitment to naturalism, and one for arriving at a concept that does the necessary work in the economy of our practical lives. First, the story cannot simply involve a direct recognition of a reason and then intentional action for the sake of that reason. Rather, the story must build from simple elements – motivations or needs that people will have anyway, even in the absence of the emerging functional concept – while maintaining a 'rational' relationship between the derived and the more primitive motivations. And it must be the case that the functional is derived from what is not functional or, as Williams says, is 'functional only at a lower level'. Given certain needs, the emergence of a concept as functional in relation to those needs is explained by the presence of the needs and certain other facts, but not by the collective recognition of the *explanandum* as a reason for action.

Second, the genealogical approach must also satisfy an explanatory need, and one that appears to be in competition with the functional account. Does genealogy offer more than just a colourful story? It does, according to Williams, because a straightforwardly functional account of a concept like justice or truthfulness is false. Such concepts are not understood internally in functional terms, that is, they are not understood by participants in the justice or truth space of reasons as functional. Indeed, to be so understood would diminish the capacity of the concept to stay within the space of reasons:

> It is just not true that the dispositions of truthfulness that we have … can be adequately explained in functional terms … their value always and necessarily goes beyond their

[6] Williams' inspiration for this form of genealogy is Humean rather than Nietzschean.

> function. Nevertheless, at a more abstract level, function plays a role in explaining them. These dispositions have taken different forms in different historical circumstances, and in grouping them and explaining them as examples of the same kind of disposition, we are relying on a functional interpretation, that every society needs there to be dispositions of this general kind and also needs them not to have a purely functional value (Williams 2002: 35).

The goal here is to give an account that can explain how a property, concept, or reason that arises because of a functional need for it, then also, in service of that same functional need, can come to be seen by the parties who share that property, concept, or reason as having intrinsic value. If one can tell such a story plausibly, then one will have '*constructed* an intrinsic good' (Williams 2002: 92). Were such a programme carried out in the philosophy of law, its aims and constraints would be substantially similar to those described by Williams, yet its success would go some way towards bridging the gap between law as social fact, and law as a normative concept.[7]

## IV. Truth and Truthfulness

The state of nature is a linguistic community in which people communicate to one another; Williams says that from the beginning its members have an awareness of the idea of a 'purely positional advantage': some persons are better situated with regard to certain information than others, and so pooling of information is needed, a division of epistemic labour. But such persons are capable, from their own standpoints, of asking 'such questions as whether to express a belief on a particular occasion or how much effort it is worth spending to get the answer to a particular question'. And this in turn gives rise to the idea that it is desirable to inculcate in members of the community two dispositions, one that applies to the acquiring of correct beliefs in the first place – accuracy – and one that applies to the spontaneous communication of what someone believes – sincerity.

It is important to the story that these dispositions are needs for the community, and indeed their being so can sometimes cut across what might be desirable from the standpoint of the agent: both taking less care in obtaining correct beliefs, and keeping to oneself some belief – 'as when a hunter has found a prey which he would rather keep for himself and his immediate family' – can be desirable from the agent's standpoint (Williams 2002: 44).

Williams is at pains to deny that he is describing an entirely instrumental view of truth. Indeed, he thinks that 'no society can get by … with a purely instrumental conception of the values of truth' (2002: 59). For, as just noted, the 'collective value' of, e.g., Sincerity for the community 'does not translate itself into a reason that each

[7] Hart's own account of the development of law is genealogical, as discussed by Pettit (2019). Yet, Hart's resting place at the conclusion of his genealogy does not, as I have noted, adequately address the question of law's normativity or authority.

person has for possessing that quality itself' (2002: 58). There is, as he notes later, a familiar problem:

> as soon as a *question* comes up, whether an individual or group should on a given occasion continue to work the system … – whether, for instance, they should tell a lie – the sense we have recovered so far in which truth is a value gets us nowhere (2002: 84–85).

The problem of this question is not simply that people may default on the expectation of Sincerity, but that if it is known that this is a live possibility, then the possibility of trust in communication is undermined, and trust, and hence trustworthiness, are essential for the maintenance of a community. So there must be some way of valuing Sincerity that brings the possessor of that disposition beyond the willingness to default whenever it is to her personal advantage: that way of *valuing* Sincerity is to treat it as having intrinsic value.

Williams argues that what is needed is not simply the pretence that trustworthiness, or its communicative dimension, Sincerity, is intrinsically valuable, for that view is not stable under reflection. Sincerity must be able to be treated as an intrinsic good and that would not be possible for one who believed that the treatment was based on a pretence. Rather, Williams talks about the 'construction' of an intrinsic value. What is needed is that

> the agent has some materials in terms of which he can understand [a] value in relation to other values that he holds, and this implies, in turn, that the intrinsic good … or rather the agent's relation to it, has an inner structure in terms of which it can be related to other goods' (2002: 92).

An agent who can consider some value in this way is not pretending; but if the 'conditions are satisfied, then we shall have *constructed* an intrinsic good' (2002: 92).

There are two central parts of this task of construction. The first is identifying what a virtue such as Sincerity needs to be in order to serve the purposes for which it is needed. The second is being able to identify what other values 'surround' the value in question, whether that value be trustworthiness, or its communicative aspect, Sincerity. This is in part the work of genealogy, but for Williams it is also importantly a part of the work of history, for a value such as Sincerity will have a history, and it is in that history that we find how (and in what form) Sincerity becomes related to other values such as autonomy and honour in such a way that it can come to be stably considered intrinsically valuable.

Williams' reflections on Sincerity are of interest but not necessary here to pursue in depth. He argues that trustworthiness in speech cannot be – not if it is to serve the needs for which it exists – mere refraining (or even always refraining) from lying. Hearers must be able to rely upon speakers more than is guaranteed by simple avoidance of false assertion, the 'fetishisation' of which Williams scorns. But there is no universal template either: the ways in which insincerity is made a matter of dishonour, for example, will be different from society to society. Or, more accurately, the ways in which honour and dishonour are disarticulated from the nature of a hierarchical society and reconstrued in a society that eventually is one that we would recognise as 'liberal', in which the manipulation and domination effected by various forms of insincerity offends our sense of equality, are a matter of history, history that could be made available to those who wished to understand how *we* have constructed Sincerity as an intrinsic value. Williams' history goes further to identify how the virtue of sincerity becomes a demand for authenticity; that history, of which I will say little, is, however, notable for being local to Western modernity.

## V. Legitimacy and Law

I turn now to a reconstruction of a possible Williamsian account of law and lawfulness. That account must be situated in the context of a further theme in Williams' late work, his political realism. For in between what Williams identifies as the beginning of politics, or the political, and a properly *liberal* politics, is a need for the complementary notions of law and lawfulness. In the posthumously published collection *In the Beginning Was the Deed*, Williams expresses his opposition to 'political moralism' (PM), roughly, any position that begins with moral principles that are then to be applied in the political context (politics as 'applied morality') (Williams 2005: 1–3). Williams contrasts PM with an approach that begins from the 'first political question', which concerns the 'securing of order, protection, safety, trust, and the conditions of cooperation' (2005: 3). Solving this question – i.e., meeting this demand – is both the beginning of politics, and a necessary condition for legitimacy within the political. What is required beyond the establishment of order, protection, etc., is that the solution be 'acceptable' to those to whom it is proposed.

If we imagine that the situation of those to whom a solution is proposed is very bad – those to whom it is proposed are in a war of all against all, for example, in which life is nasty, brutish, and short – then even a highly coercive solution such as Hobbes's might seem acceptable, and thus meet what Williams calls the Basic Legitimation Demand (BLD). This demand is not pre-political, but arises with the coming into being of the political, that is, the attempt to render coercion authoritative by establishing 'order, protection, safety, trust, and the conditions of cooperation'.

Suppose that there is a group within the power of those proposing the solution who are simply not offered the benefits of order and protection but are instead slaves. Such persons have no reason to accept the proposed solution, but then, neither is it really *offered* to them; in an important sense, the question of legitimacy does not even arise in relation to them. They do not exist in a *political* relation with those using coercive power over them. Other failures of justification are imaginable, however, that are within the domain of the political, for with regard to some people all the time, and some or all people some of the time, the state may exercise its power over citizens in ways that are not acceptable, that cannot be justified to those citizens, even as the state claims legitimacy. Then the BLD has not been met, for the 'idea of meeting the BLD implies a sense in which the state has to offer a justification of its power *to each subject*' (Williams 2005: 4).[8]

The BLD is, when met historically, not usually met in conditions that we would recognise as liberal. This distinguishes Williams' approach, to his mind, from a political moralism approach: there is no template for legitimacy in the meeting of moral demands that are prior to the political demand to solve the first political question in a way that is acceptable to the citizens, and how that question is addressed will be local in both time and place. Historical circumstances well short of those portrayed by Hobbes might yet require a high degree of restrictive coercion in the establishment of order without being found unacceptable by those to whom the solution is offered. Yet there is also always the concern that the solution will become again the problem, that the particular form of bringing order and security will become intolerably coercive and cease to be acceptable. Williams summarises:

> It may be asked whether the BLD is itself a moral principle. If it is, it does not represent a morality which is prior to politics. It is a claim that is inherent in there being such a thing as politics: in particular, because it is inherent in there being a first political question. The situation of one lot of people terrorizing another lot of people is not per se a political situation: it is, rather, the situation which the existence of the political is in the first place supposed to alleviate (replace). If the power of one lot of people over another is to represent a solution to the first political question, and not itself be part of the problem, *something* has to be said to explain (to the less empowered, to concerned bystanders, to children being educated in this structure, etc.) what the difference is between the solution and the problem, and that cannot simply be an account of successful domination. It has to be something in the mode of justifying explanation or legitimation: hence the BLD (Williams 2005: 5).

Now central to Williams' view about the BLD is the claim, as I have mentioned, that what it means to meet the demand can and does change; that is, the nature of justifying to those subject to the power of those claiming authority can, and does, change through time. Why might it do so?

Williams surely wants to say that part of the answer to this question will depend upon the contingent circumstances of those demanding, and those offering justifications. Williams is ultimately concerned with the nature of *liberal* justifications, which involve more demanding standards than are found elsewhere in history: a concern that human rights are being respected, that rationalizations 'of disadvantage in terms of race and gender are invalid', and that 'hierarchical structures which generate disadvantage are not self-legitimating' (Williams 2005: 7). But these sorts of justifications are surely well down the line from one lot of people's taking control as a solution to the first political question. So a reasonable question to ask is: what happens in between and why? And the answer that I want to suggest is that precisely what happens in between is the construction of the

[8] The idea here is similar to that in Dyzenhaus 2022, that each subject of the law must be able to answer the question, 'But, how can that be law for me?'

complementary notions of law and lawfulness, notions that, like truth and truthfulness in Williams' other account, arise in service of a functional need but cannot serve that need by being understood only functionally by those using the concepts from the inside.

What is the functional need in question? The BLD arises because there is a demand first that the political question be answered: a way must be proposed, or more likely seized upon, by some to provide and secure order, protection, safety, trust, and the conditions of cooperation. There is no political reality for Williams absent the effort to settle the question of the provision of these. But built into the list is a problem: a solution to the first political question that relies on little more than personal force or command is almost from the very beginning incapable of securing at least one of the items on Williams' list, namely, trust: for a solution that relies on personal force and command can in obvious and dangerous ways be arbitrary and capricious; of course, to the extent that it is, it undermines its ability to provide the conditions of cooperation, and this in turn has effects on the securing of order, protection, and safety and the stability of the proposed solution to the political question.

What can be offered in mitigation? Precisely that the authoritative and coercive coordination and protection of those to whom the justification is being made will be provided in the form of impersonal rules, made and administered by those who are themselves subject to the rules, and in accordance with procedures governed by those rules. Thus 'law' is here seen as a solution to a problem of legitimation that arises because of the inadequacy of the first possible solution – one lot's having power over another lot – as a stable justification to the 'second' of the two lots.

What must be built into this offer for it to be successful, i.e., for it to constitute a successful justification to those who will be governed by and under law? An offer that simply proposed rules as a 'neutral tool' of social coercion and direction, a tool that could be used at will by the lot in power to effectively maintain and wield power over the other lot again offers too little to solve the problem. Such rules might be, *inter alia*, retroactive, or impossible to follow, or unclear, or incoherent or … There is a need for something more or the difficulty that Williams sees – the solution's becoming once again the problem – will recur.

So the idea of law, understood as a system of impersonal rules as a solution to the instability of the political offer of governance and as an answer to the need for trust, cannot really be disentangled from the ideal of Rule of Law, understood in the way laid out by Fuller (following Aquinas), but soon extending to include, as John Finnis suggests, some form of constitutional government, separation of powers, and so on.[9] The emergence of these features will no doubt be gradual (and likely, as Stephen Bero argues in chapter eight of this volume, to be a stage of conflict): law and the Rule of Law did not spring forth fully formed from the functional need for

[9] See Fuller 1964; Finnis 1980, 2011.

a stable answer to the BLD. That emergence is a matter of history, contingent to be sure and with abundant backsliding, but with its own internal rationale that the genealogical method helps us to articulate.

In any event, we can see that the idea that law as a solution to the problem comes already with the ideal of the Rule of Law built into it embeds within the idea of law an idea of its possessing a normative dimension, for this normative dimension is needed if law is to succeed in playing its functional role, a functional role that is described by Finnis as that of ensuring 'the positive good of a certain quality of association and interaction between ruler and ruled' (Finnis 1980, 2011: 272). That 'quality' points in the direction of equality and reciprocity between ruler and ruled and, again in Finnis's words, to the need to 'secure to the subjects of authority the dignity of self-direction and freedom from certain forms of manipulation' (1980, 2011: 273).

Now the understanding of law I am articulating here might actually seem at odds with Williams' approach to truth–truthfulness, as can be seen in an objection that Williams raises to his own account. Williams' focus is on the value of truth*fulness*; but

> People have spoken about the value of *truth*; is this what they had in mind? Are we right to consider only certain attitudes toward the truth, people's dispositions to discover and express it? My answer is yes – it is right only to consider human attitudes ... It may be that there have been metaphysical outlooks which have associated truth and goodness in ways that represented these things as altogether prior to human interest in them (Williams 2002: 61–62).

But Williams is as always sceptical of such forms of transcendence. The appropriate form of inquiry is 'into human concerns with the truth'.

But is it not the case that I have reified 'the law' and the 'rule of law' into something altogether prior to the human interest in law? I do not think so: interest in law arises out of a recognisably *human* concern to escape the forms of domination made possible by the rule of persons over others and a functional need that whatever meets that description – of aiding in that escape – must be capable of the form of respect I have called lawfulness: respect for the solution as having authority, as something that is neither a mere instrument of power, nor a mere artifact fabricated to serve some instrumental need. Law as having the kind of intrinsic value such as to demand respect, and lawfulness as a multifaceted virtue of the law-respecting, both among the ruled and the ruling and contributing to a form of reciprocity between them, can be said to be 'constructed' in Williams' sense.[10] But this does not entirely resolve the problem of the status of 'human concerns', and I will return to this issue at the end of the chapter.

Describing the Rule of Law as I have done is thus already to take a position on the disputed question of whether the rule of law is merely a neutral

[10] Indeed, the case is stronger for law; Williams asserts that the concept of truth is timeless, but that does not seem to me a plausible position to take on the concept of 'law'.

tool equally available for the use of bad as of good rulers.[11] But the position I've described so far does appear to be compatible with Williams' understanding of the construction of intrinsic values. Law, as including the rule of law, and lawfulness, as including respect for law, must arise together if they are to solve the functional problem that demands their existence. This co-emergence is in fact made possible by an asymmetry between law and truth, for while there is no history to the concept of truth, there is a history to the concept of law. Thus, while truth precedes truthfulness, law in any recognisable sense cannot significantly precede lawfulness. So not just lawfulness but also law must co-emerge as a solution to the instability of a world in which the solution to the BLD may shortly again become the problem.

But is the Rule of Law enough? It is not *for us*, and here Williams would, presumably, want to tell a story that increasingly moved into real history about the emergence of law as the primary way in which to ensure respect for human rights, as well as the denial of rationalisations in terms of race and gender and the non-self-legitimating quality of hierarchical structures that generate disadvantage. This, for Williams, is part of the history of the emergence of liberalism, and it requires more historical knowledge than I possess to tell it. However, I here venture two brief thoughts about such a history.

The first is a suspicion that such a historical narrative should not be too modern-centric: the idea that law protects human rights seems present in, e.g., the work of Thomas Aquinas even if not articulated in modern nomenclature, and many of the central concepts in a modern understanding of law, as, for example, that law protects human dignity, seem barely intelligible outside the pre-modern Christian and Jewish frameworks in which they emerged.[12] I'll return to this point below.

The second is that such a narrative would also have to identify a point, perhaps complex and multidimensional, in modernity in which *scepticism* of the claims of authority generally, and hence legal authority, became part of Western culture in a way that potentially threatens the stability of law as a solution to the problem posed by Williams. Concern for such a history is not, as should be clear, detached from the concerns in *Truth and Truthfulness* with which I began the discussion: loss of confidence in the possibility of truth, and suspicion that all is just power threaten more than just the authority of academics, and the Rortian 'irony' that Williams is opposed to seems equally to play some role in contemporary attitudes towards law and politics.

But let us put such concerns aside for the moment. In closing, I wish to identify two strengths of the Williamsian account, before moving the discussion in a somewhat un-Williamsian direction.

The first strength: Is it possible to provide an account of law – of what it is and why we have it – that does not advert to the nature of the *human needs* that

[11] The debate is outlined, and a position similar to that presented here is articulated, in George 1999.
[12] See, e.g., the discussion in Finnis 1998, especially chs V–VIII.

guide the creation and ultimately adherence to law? I doubt it. The Williamsian approach encourages us to focus in on those needs in the context in which they arise, the inevitable context of the exercise of power by some over others as a necessity for bringing about order, security, and the conditions of cooperation. Within that context, a stable solution must be one that also brings about trust, that can be respected by those ruled as well as those ruling, and the idea of law can emerge as that solution, just as, a bit further down the road, the idea of liberal democracy and democratic citizenship can also emerge. In this way we get to something, I think, like the position articulated in the opening sentence of John Finnis's *Natural Law and Natural Rights*: 'There are human goods that can be secured only through the institutions of human law and requirements of practical reasonableness that only those institutions can satisfy' (Finnis 1980, 2011: 3). I see it as a strength of a Williamsian naturalistic genealogical method that it converges to a certain extent with such a claim, something no mere conceptual analysis of 'law' can accomplish any more than can some form of reductive naturalism.

It is also a strength that Williams evidences a respect for the actual history of 'can emerge': law and lawfulness are not inevitabilities, and there are cultures in which they did not emerge or have not yet emerged in their focal sense, or in which they are in danger of being lost. The self-understanding of a people for whom law and lawfulness, and eventually the idea of democratic citizenship, will be different from that of other peoples.

But why not say, as Williams in certain respects wants to resist saying, that the emergence of these ideas is an accomplishment, and indeed, an accomplishment precisely because they are a response to *successful practical reasoning*, reasoning that encompasses not just the apprehension of basic human needs but also of what is necessary and hence obligatory for persons in meeting those needs, both in view of their own flourishing and that of others? Williams does not deny that from our own perspective, the Rule of Law and liberalism are accomplishments; but in an important passage in 'Philosophy as a Humanistic Discipline', Williams seems to cast doubt on the claim that such accomplishments can be framed as part of a vindicatory narrative.

When we consider concepts central to our own moral and political self-understanding, such as those of equality and equal rights, Williams writes, we can 'deploy arguments which claim to justify our ideas against … others', or we can look at the historical story of how those ideas came to prevail among us. But when we consider the relation between the argument and the historical story,

> we realize that the story is the history of those forms of argument themselves: the forms of argument, call them liberal forms of argument, are a central part of the outlook that we accept. If we consider how those forms of argument came to prevail, we can indeed see them as having won, but not necessarily as having won an argument (Williams 2006: 190).

For there to have been an argument, there would have needed to be some common conception of what the argument was about, and not just at some high level of generality such as 'the way to live or the way to order society'. Liberal ideas of equality would need to be shown to accomplish something that the adherents to the *ancient régime* were also seeking; but those liberal ideas were in fact part of the change, not a solution to a pre-existing shared aim.

But at least from the advent of the political, as Williams understands it, there *does* seem to have been a common aim, that of legitimacy, and the growth of law and lawfulness, I have argued, is necessary if the first political problem is to be solved and remain solved. Relative to all those for whom there is a political problem, then, law and lawfulness are vindicated, and their defenders have won an argument.

Nor does it matter that the argument took a long time. In 'Realism and Moralism', Williams writes that political moralism

> has no answer in its own terms to the question of why what it takes to be the true moral solution to the questions of politics, liberalism, should for the first time (roughly) become evident in European culture from the late seventeenth century onward, and why these truths have been concealed from other peoples (Williams 2006: 9).

But the sense of recent and inexplicable novelty is mitigated if we look not to the completion of the argument (indeed, why think the argument is over) but to its sources: practical, in the perceived need for legitimacy, and theoretical, in the work of those figures and traditions such as Plato and Aristotle, and the Abrahamic religions, whose ideas recognisably inform the shape of liberalism as it exists now. To adopt the title of David Dyzenhaus's recent book (2022; and see its source in King 1968), the arc of legality is *long*.

So law, lawfulness, and, I believe, something like liberalism can be assessed by way of a vindicatory narrative in which they appear to have won an argument. But what about those who exercised coercive power with no thought of legitimacy? Surely no argument was won against *them*; rather, Williams might say, we can only point to pre-political social groupings and anti-liberal tyrannies and note the historical transition from the raw imposition of power to a claim to exercise coercive power by right (at least, when that transition took place).

Indeed, to tell *this* story as one of vindication smacks of appeal to 'external reasons'. As Williams lays out in his famous 'Internal and External Reasons' essay, something is an internal reason only if it is related to an agent's 'subjective motivational set' (1979: 102). Internal reasons are thus available to play an explanatory role in accounting for some action. An external reason by contrast need stand in no such relation to an agent's subjective motivational set, and thus seems incapable of playing any such explanatory role.

Accordingly, Williams characterises appeal to such external reasons as mere bluff. And he would surely have similar suspicions were the transition to the political from the pre-political said to be in accordance with reasons that were no part of the subjective motivational set of those who, as we are assuming, were simply exercising power in the space of the pre-political, except that in this case, it is surely pointless bluff since we are not even in an argument with those who so exercised power.

Here, though, we might draw upon John McDowell's response to Williams on this topic (McDowell 1995). The transition from raw exercise of coercive power to an initial attempt at legitimacy need not be seen as the winning of an argument, as successful practical *reasoning*, in order to be seen as a practical *recognition* of something that was already true. Williams writes that 'one thing can be taken as an axiom, that might does not imply right, that … the power of coercion offered simply as the power of coercion cannot justify its own use' (Williams 2006: 5). True, I think. But whence does the thought emerge that the use of coercion should be justified except from some form of recognition of the person as a being morally beyond straightforward coercion, a recognition that is perhaps new in a way that *what is recognised* is not? If so, the moral quality of personhood – let us call it the dignity of the person – was a kind of external reason waiting for recognition, and the transition to the political, an accomplishment of practical awareness, albeit one not accomplished by argument.

## Bibliography

Alexy, R (2013) 'Some Reflections on the Ideal Dimension of Law and on the Legal Philosophy of John Finnis' 58 *American Journal of Jurisprudence* 97.

Churchland, P (1979) *Scientific Realism and the Plasticity of Mind* (New York, Cambridge University Press).

Dyzenhaus, D (2022) *The Long Arc of Legality: Hobbes, Kelsen, Hart* (Cambridge, Cambridge University Press).

Finnis, J (1980; 2nd edn 2011) *Natural Law and Natural Rights* (Oxford, Clarendon Press).

—— (1998) *Aquinas: Moral, Political, and Legal Theory* (Oxford, Oxford University Press).

—— (2013) 'Law as Fact and as Reason for Action: A Response to Robert Alexy on Law's "Ideal Dimension"' 58 *American Journal of Jurisprudence* 85.

Fuller, L (1964) *The Morality of Law* (New Haven, Yale University Press).

George, RP (1999) 'Free Choice, Practical Reason, and Fitness for the Rule of Law' in RP George, *In Defense of Natural Law* (Oxford, Oxford University Press).

Hart, HLA (1961) *The Concept of Law* (Oxford, Clarendon Press).

—— (1983) 'Positivism and the Separation of Law and Morals' in HLA Hart, *Essays In Jurisprudence and Philosophy* (Oxford, Clarendon Press).

King, ML, Jr (1968) 'Remaining Awake Through a Great Revolution' Speech given at the National Cathedral (31st March 1968).

Leiter, B (2009) *Naturalizing Jurisprudence* (Oxford, Oxford University Press).

McDowell, J (1995) 'Might There Be External Reasons?' in JEJ Altham & R Harrison (eds), *World, Mind and Ethics: Essays on the Ethical Philosophy of Bernard Williams* (Cambridge, Cambridge University Press).

Pettit, P (2019) 'Social Norms and the Internal Point of View: An Elaboration of Hart's Genealogy of Law' 39 *Oxford Journal of Legal Studies* 229.

Simmonds, NE (2007) *Law as a Moral Ideal* (Oxford, Oxford University Press).

Waldron, J (1999) *The Dignity of Legislation* (Cambridge, Cambridge University Press).

Webber *et al* (2018) *Legislated Rights: Securing Human Rights Through Legislation* (Cambridge, Cambridge University Press).
Williams, B (1979) 'Internal and External Reasons' in B Williams, *Moral Luck* (Cambridge, Cambridge University Press).
—— (2002) Truth and Truthfulness: An Essay in Genealogy (Princeton, Princeton University Press).
—— (2005) 'Realism and Moralism in Political Theory' in B Williams (G Hawthorn, ed), *In the Beginning Was the Deed* (Princeton, Princeton University Press).
—— (2006) 'Philosophy as a Humanistic Discipline' in B Williams (AW Moore, ed), *Philosophy as a Humanistic Discipline* (Princeton, Princeton University Press).

# 10

# The Idea of Humanistic Middle-Range Theory

DAMIAN CUENI*

## I. Introduction

In his Annual Lecture of the Royal Institute of Philosophy in the year 2000 on 'Philosophy as a Humanistic Discipline', which subsequently lent its name to a posthumously published edited collection, Bernard Williams prominently called for philosophy to be understood and practised as a 'humanistic discipline' (Williams 2006a: 180). But while especially Williams' later work was clearly meant to exemplify such an approach,[1] it is far from clear *what* it ended up exemplifying. In this chapter, I shed light on this question through an analogy between theories of the middle range in sociology and Williams' work on a range of topics such as truthfulness, blame, voluntariness, and liberty. This will highlight the *humanistic middle-range* character of significant parts of Williams' work that has so far largely been missed and suggest new ways of thinking about how 'a space is to be found between facts and norms' – a phrase that Williams (2005c: 10) adopted from Jürgen Habermas (1996) – that can then also be generalised to legal scholarship.

My chapter makes three contributions: first, I develop the relevant sense of *humanism* by contrasting it with two other '-isms' that preoccupied Williams throughout his work, scientism and moralism. I will show that both scientism and moralism are connected to an ideal of *purity from contingency* and suggest that Williams himself, in calling for philosophy as a *humanistic* discipline, meant to embrace the *impurity* of a more integrative approach. Second, I explicate the sense

* This chapter was first written during my time as a postdoctoral fellow at the Bonavero Institute of Human Rights and Lincoln College, University of Oxford. I thank all the participants of the conference on this volume at the University of Surrey for their helpful feedback as well as Matthieu Queloz, David Owen, and the editors for written comments on an earlier draft. My research for this chapter was supported by grants no 191264 and no 206544 of the Swiss National Science Foundation.

[1] See in particular the reference to 'a case on which I am presently working, the virtues associated with truthfulness' in (Williams 2006a, 192). This ultimately became Williams' final major work (Williams 2002).

in which Williams was a humanistic *middle-range theorist* along five dimensions. To do so, I take Williams' invitation to look for 'models or ideals or analogies' that help us think 'about the ways in which philosophy should be done' (Williams 2006a: 180) to heart and draw a surprisingly illuminating analogy between his philosophical work and 'theories of the middle range' in sociology, especially in the work of Robert K. Merton.[2] Third, what emerges from my account is the precise sense in which Williams was a *humanistic middle-range theorist* that can then also be generalised to legal scholarship. I provide a general methodological framework for humanistic middle-range theories, and thus for practising both philosophy and law *as a humanistic discipline.*

Given my aim to develop the idea of humanistic middle-range theory in philosophy and legal scholarship, my chapter is written in Williams' spirit of engaging with the history of philosophy – in this case with Williams' own philosophy – to contribute to contemporary philosophical and legal debates. Section II explains what intellectual currents Williams was responding to in calling for philosophy as a *humanistic* discipline and what this implies for how we are to understand this idea. Section III suggests that Williams' understanding of philosophy as a humanistic *discipline* can be further elucidated by drawing an analogy to theories of the middle range in sociology and presents an account of such theories that can serve as a basis for the analogy. Section IV draws on that account to explain the sense in which Williams' work on topics like truthfulness, blame, and voluntariness can be understood as a *humanistic middle-range theory.* Finally, section V uses Williams' account of liberty as a political value to sketch a humanistic middle-range theory of the doctrinal distinction between 'infringing' and 'violating' basic rights and thus illustrates how we can extend the idea of humanistic middle-range theory from philosophy to legal scholarship.

## II. Philosophy as a Humanistic Discipline?

Williams himself never offered a complete account of what he meant by his call to practise 'philosophy as a humanistic discipline'. I will thus begin by offering my own negative and a positive characterisation.

Starting with the negative characterisation, Williams' call to practise philosophy as a humanistic discipline can be understood as a response to two intellectual distortions that preoccupied him throughout his work: scientism and moralism. Whereas scientism concerns our empirical picture of the

[2] While this analogy is primarily of independent interest, Williams was also an enthusiastic reader of Merton's work, which provides an additional reason for pursuing it in the context of this chapter. I thank Patricia Williams for making me aware of Williams' keen interest in Merton's work in our personal conversations.

world and aims to rid that picture of the impurities of more local descriptions, moralism concerns our normative outlook towards the world and aims to rid that outlook of any empirical influences. Both are intellectual distortions that attempt to escape what Richard Moran (2016) has called the inescapable 'impurity' of any inquiry that engages with the contingencies of human sense-making and acting. In considering these two intellectual distortions together, we can thus also come to understand that what animated Williams' 'humanism' was a search for something that lies beyond the purity demanded by scientism and moralism.

The problem of scientistic distortion is central to Williams' lecture on philosophy as a humanistic discipline. With the term *scientism*, Williams refers to an outlook that 'tends to assimilate philosophy to the aims, or at least the manners, of the [natural] sciences' (2006a: 182). What preoccupied him the most was the idea that philosophy should aspire to emulate the natural sciences in describing the world 'as it is in itself, independent of perspective' and thus remain pure from the contingencies of more local ways of sense-making (2006a: 184). Williams did not agree with those who deny that such independent descriptions are possible at all. For him, there *is* a fundamental contrast between philosophy and the natural sciences, because the aim to describe the world in a way that is 'to the largest possible extent independent of the local perspectives or idiosyncrasies of enquirers' (2006a: 184) is at least *intelligible* in the natural sciences in a way that it is not in philosophy (and indeed in the whole humanities and social sciences). But against those that conclude from this contrast that more absolute descriptions are 'intrinsically superior to more local conceptions' (2006a: 187), Williams defended the value of engaging with the more local conceptions as part of the philosophical enterprise. Williams' rejection of scientism is thus the first reason that led him to look towards the humanistic disciplines, and particularly history and the interpretive social sciences.

In contrast to scientism, the problem of moralistic distortion receives no mention in Williams' lecture on philosophy as a humanistic discipline.[3] But it is clear from his other philosophical writings, especially his most famous book *Ethics and the Limits of Philosophy* (2011: 218), that Williams' second main reason for practising philosophy as a humanistic discipline was to get away from *moralism*, which is a particular style of ethical thought that distorts our practical thinking across the board. While scientism models itself on the aims of the natural sciences, moralism wishes to remain pure from *any* empirical commitments. It draws a stark dichotomy between empirical and normative considerations, and also between *pure* moral and *impure* non-moral normative considerations that may be shaped by historical, social, and psychological contingencies. Apart from the fact that these dichotomies are inadequate to account for the

[3] But see Williams 2006b: 155 for an argument that connects political philosophy to the idea of philosophy as a humanistic discipline.

thick normative terms in which we often make sense of the world, moralism sometimes goes so far as to maintain that empirical and non-moral normative considerations may not even inform practical theorising, but merely serve as an input within a moral calculus or formula that is determined through a process of pure abstraction (2011: 58). The closest disciplinary analogue here is mathematics: the normative considerations that seem pertinent to us in everyday life are subjected to an ideal of systematicity that at the limit means that everything can ultimately be derived from one pure moral consideration. While this aspect is often missed in responses to Williams' various critiques of 'moralism',[4] the aspirations of philosophy in a moralistic style are thus intimately connected to an ideal of ethical *theory*.

Having considered these intellectual distortions generated by scientism and moralism, we are better able to understand the sense in which philosophy as a humanistic discipline is a search for a model of practising philosophy that *lies in between facts and norms*. Whereas scientism aims for a purely descriptive inquiry that is insensitive to more local perspectives, moralism aims for a purely normative inquiry that is insensitive to empirical commitments. Both scientism and moralism thus wish to practise philosophy in a way that lives up to an ideal of *purity from contingency*. To paraphrase Jean-Paul Sartre (1946), moralism is a scientism and vice versa, because both are rooted in the same demand for purity. But if moralism is a scientism and scientism is a moralism, *what is humanism?* Understanding Williams' reasons for rejecting the demand for purity also helps us to develop a positive characterisation of 'philosophy as a humanistic discipline' as a *solution* to the intellectual problems raised by scientism and moralism. This solution draws an analogy between philosophy and the 'humanistic disciplines' instead of the natural sciences and involves a very different ideal of philosophical theory that contrasts with the search for purity.

We can transition to this positive characterisation of philosophy as a humanistic discipline by noting that Williams explicitly starts his lecture by stating that his animating question is: 'what models or ideals or analogies should we look to in thinking about the ways in which philosophy should be done?' But while he subsequently focused on developing the connections between philosophy and history (Williams 2006a: 180),[5] I will argue that the kind of 'theory' that he ended up doing in most of his work is best illuminated by an analogy to 'theories of the middle range' in sociology.[6] This analogy helps us to understand that, although Williams always emphasised the limits of *moral* theory, he himself presented

[4] See especially the various reactions to the posthumously published 'Realism and Moralism in Political Theory' (Williams 2005c), where the relevant sense of 'moralism' cannot be properly understood without reference to Williams' critique of moral *theory* in Williams 2011. See also Owen 2018 on the connection between Williams' political realism and his critique of what he called 'the morality system'.

[5] See especially Williams 2014b.

[6] It should be stated at the outset, however, that any positive analogy also presupposes negative analogies, in the terminology of Hesse 1966. My claim is not that Williams' philosophical work should be understood as a kind of sociology.

*explanatory theories with a distinctive normative upshot* in his philosophical work on notions like truthfulness, blame, and voluntariness. In what follows, I will suggest that these contributions are best understood as an exercise in 'humanistic middle-range theory'.[7]

## III. Theories of the Middle Range in Sociology

To develop the idea of humanistic middle-range theory, I will now provide the basis for an analogy to theories of the middle range in sociology.[8] In the words of Robert K. Merton – who introduced the term 'theories of the middle range' in the first edition of *Social Theory and Social Structure* (1949: 5) and then significantly expanded his account in the third edition – such theories 'lie between the minor but necessary working hypotheses that evolve in abundance during day-to-day research and the all-inclusive systematic efforts to develop a unified theory' (Merton 1968: 39). But as Peter Hedström and Lars Udehn note in the most extensive discussion of such theories in sociology, much like Williams, Merton never so much defined the idea of 'theories of the middle range' as he exemplified it in his work (Hedström & Udehn 2011: 25). I will therefore draw on Hedström and Udehn's discussion of the idea of middle-range theory in Merton's work to identify the features of such theories that can then serve as the basis for an analogy.

The most obvious basis for an analogy between Williams' and Merton's middle-range theories is that Merton himself also primarily characterised the idea of middle-range theory in a negative way, namely in contrast to 'minor but necessary working hypotheses' and 'the all-inclusive systematic efforts to develop a unified theory'. Consider first the contrast between theories of the middle range and 'unified' or 'grand' (Merton 1968: 48) theories: examples of the latter that Merton explicitly discussed include Parson's theory of social systems (1968: 68), Marxist social theory (1968: 43), German idealism (1968: 45), the work of the founding fathers of sociology Comte and Spencer (1968: 46), and the historical grand narratives of Sorokin and Toynbee (1957: 107). Insofar as there is a common thread in this contrast between theories of the middle range and grand theories, it seems to be the idea of an *esprit de système*[9] that pervades

[7] What follows elucidates just one way of practising philosophy as a humanistic discipline, and I do not suggest that it captures everything Williams himself meant by this term. For a related discussion that focuses much more on the link to history than I do here, see Queloz 2021a. See also Sagar (2016; 2018: 217–19, 238–40) for an account that is more focused on political theory.

[8] For an argument that sociology itself should be understood as a humanistic discipline, see Berger 1963.

[9] While this is the term used by Merton, see Merton 1968: 46, his use is arguably closer to what d'Alembert's *Discours préliminaire* (1751) called the *esprit systématique* in his rejection of the *esprit de système*.

all 'total systems of sociological theory' (Merton 1968: 45–48).[10] But if Merton rejected total system-building, what did he then propose instead in striving for a middle-range *theory*?

To arrive at a positive understanding of what is meant by theories of the middle range that can then serve as a basis for a more sustained analogy, we can draw on Hedström and Udehn's analytical notions of middle-range generality and middle-range isolation. First, *generality* concerns variation along a dimension of the *explanandum* (Hedström & Udehn 2011: 28). A more general theory explains a wider range of phenomena, whereas a less general theory explains only specific phenomena. This notion of generality allows us to sharpen the contrast between theories of the middle range and grand theories while also clarifying the contrast with 'minor working hypotheses' that we have so far left unexplained. Grand theories in Merton's sense purport to explain all social phenomena, whereas minor working hypotheses only purport to explain specific phenomena or occurrences. For example, whereas a quasi-Hegelian account of the inevitable progression towards more truthfulness in human affairs would be a grand theory, a folk psychological explanation that purports to explain why somebody acted truthfully in a particular instance is a minor working hypothesis in Merton's sense.[11] Of any explanatory theory, we can always ask: what is the generality of the explanandum? The first dimension along which theories can lie in the middle range is thus *the middle-range generality of the explanandum.*

The second analytical notion proposed by Hedström and Udehn to offer a more positive characterisation of theories of the middle range concerns variation along a dimension of the explanans. Drawing on work by Uskali Mäki (1992) on the methodology of economics, they introduce the idea of *isolation* as

> a certain kind of abstraction, which consists in focusing attention on certain explanatory factors at the expense of others. For example, if the set of possible explanatory factors consists of [a,b,c,d] and we focus exclusively on [a,b] we have performed an isolation (Hedström & Udehn 2011: 28).

It is not difficult to see that many economic forms of explanation, especially in rational choice theory, are characterised by a very high degree of isolation. To render the sense of degree more precise, Mäki (1992) also introduced further terminology to distinguish between the excluded set [c,d], which he refers to as the *excluded field*, and the included set [a,b], which he refers to as the *isolated field*. Of any explanatory theory, we can always ask: what is the size of the isolated field in relation to the excluded field, and thus the degree of isolation in the explanans? The second dimension along which theories can lie in the middle range is therefore *the middle-range isolation of the explanans.*

[10] Interestingly for present purposes, Merton also argued that this urge to develop a system found its roots in a 'misplaced comparison with the physical sciences' (see 1968: 48).

[11] Compare Dennett 1989 on how the 'intentional stance' allows us to construct such hypotheses in our everyday interactions.

Hedström and Udehn then use these notions to derive a graphical illustration of the sense in which a sociological theory can be said to be a theory of the *middle range* along the two axes of generality and isolation.[12]

**Fig 10.1** Generality, isolation, and the defining characteristics of middle-range theories

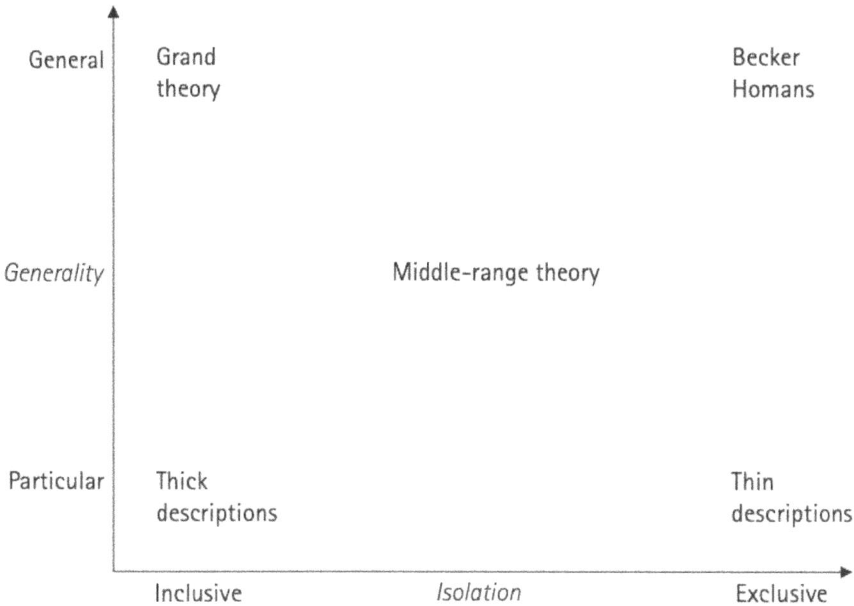


In this Figure, the horizontal axis refers to the degree of isolation and the vertical axis charts the degree of generality. Middle-range theories live up to their name by lying *in the middle range* of both axes. Starting with the degree of generality on the vertical axis, grand theories and rational choice explanations purport to explain virtually all social phenomena and are thus at the top end; whereas at the bottom end are explanations of particular phenomena or events such as the ethnographic descriptions of local practices that Clifford Geertz (2017: Ch 1) called 'thick descriptions' as well as thinner descriptions like a mere chronicle of the 2008 financial crisis. To distinguish between these 'theories' at the top and the bottom end of the vertical axis, we must then bring in the horizontal axis, which charts the degree of isolation. Whereas a grand theory purports to explain all social phenomena by taking into account all explanatory factors and is thus all the way on the top-left, rational choice theories such as the ones proposed by Gary S. Becker (1976, 2009) explicitly *isolate* certain factors at the expense of others and are thus on the top-right.[13] Similarly, more inclusive thick descriptions are on the

[12] See Fig 2.1 in Hedström and Udehn 2011: 29, which is reproduced as Fig 10.1 above.

[13] As grand theories like Marx's historical materialism make clear, a low degree of isolation is compatible with a very narrow initial set of possible explanatory factors. In fact, a grand theory probably

bottom-left, whereas mere chronicles, which privilege the events in the chronicle over more structural factors,[14] are on the bottom-right. Through the notions of generality and isolation, we thus have a graphical illustration of theories in the *middle range.*[15]

But before we proceed to illustrating how Williams' work can similarly be understood as an exercise in *humanistic middle-range theory*, I want to highlight two other features of middle-range theories in Merton's sense that will provide a further basic for my analogy. First, it is central to Merton's particular development of theories of the middle range that they make the link between the micro and the macro level an explicit part of the theory and thus take a *middle-range perspective*. As Hedström & Udehn (2011: 32–37) explain, this distinguishes Merton's form of 'structural individualism' (Udehn 2002: 318–19) from the more common associations of his work with functionalism (Merton 1968: Ch III) and structuralism (Stinchcombe 1986). Second, Merton's emphasis on the link between the micro and the macro level, together with an emphasis on what John Elster (1989, 1999) has called mechanism-based explanations, gives rise to something that may justifiably be described as a *middle-range general orientation* (Hedström & Udehn 2011: 32).[16] This emphasis on the link between the micro and the macro level as well as the idea of a more general orientation will also be important in understanding Williams' work by way of an analogy to theories of the middle range.

## IV. Williams as a Humanistic Middle-Range Theorist

In this section, I will develop the analogy between theories of the middle range in sociology and Williams' philosophical work on truthfulness, blame, and voluntariness by identifying a positive analogy to each of the four factors – (1) *middle-range generality* of the explanandum, (2) *middle-range isolation* of the explanans, (3) *middle-range perspective* in emphasising the link between the micro and the macro level, (4) and *middle-range general orientation* – that I have identified. This will allow me to conclude this section with a discussion of the main negative analogy that Williams had both explanatory *and* normative aims. The final sense in which Williams is a humanistic middle-range theorist is due to the fact that he offers theories that present us with a (5) *middle-range normativity*. These five factors

could not be offered without narrowing the set of possible explanatory factors in such a way. But what analytically distinguishes highly inclusive grand theories from highly exclusive theories such as rational choice theories is that the latter acknowledge that they isolate certain explanatory factors from a much larger set of possible factors.

[14] On this idea, see also Williams 2002: Ch 10.

[15] Those interested in what a theory of the middle range in sociology amounts to should look at the discussion in Hedström & Udehn 2011: 37–40 of Merton's work on self-fulfilling prophecies and the Matthew effect.

[16] See also Merton 1963: xxiv.

explicate the sense in which Williams is a *humanistic middle-range theorist* – and thus embraces the *impurity* of philosophy – that can also be generalised to legal scholarship.

The *first feature* of a humanistic middle-range theory is the *middle-range generality* of the explanandum.[17] Williams highlights this feature when he counters the objection that one can only practise philosophy as a humanistic discipline by 'being an amateur of altogether too much' (Williams 2006a: 197) by insisting that we need not abandon the intellectual division of labour but instead reconsider it. Rather than ask 'what can philosophy tell us about everything?' – which is the style of philosophical grand theory[18] – we can ask 'what can philosophy as a humanistic discipline tell us about X?', where this X is an idea or social phenomenon in the middle-range of generality. Thus, Williams suggests that we might make philosophical progress by focusing on 'one given ethical idea … and the various considerations that might help one to understand it' (Williams 2006a: 198). This is of course precisely what he did in his account of the virtues of truthfulness (Williams 2002). It is also, more surprisingly, what he did in offering constructive philosophical accounts of blame (Williams 1995) and voluntariness (Williams 1993: 67–68). I will therefore build on these examples to develop the sense in which Williams was a humanistic middle-range theorist.

Yet if humanistic middle-range theories are to exhibit *middle-range* generality, Williams' emphasis on *one* ethical idea requires further clarification. It may seem to suggest that these are not theories of the middle range at all, but highly specific theories in the style 'applied ethics'. But Williams' accounts of truthfulness, blame, and voluntariness are primarily explanatory – they aim to tell us *why* we have these ideas in the first place, not *what follows from them* in particular situations[19] – and he was first and foremost interested in how a general prototype of these ideas relates to their specific elaborations in any actual historical periods and cultures.[20] This is most obvious in *Truth and Truthfulness* (Williams 2002), where the general prototypes of accuracy and sincerity are initially depicted as being of purely instrumental value for the effective pooling of information about one's immediate environment. Williams leaves no doubt that this account could not possibly work in any actual society, and the theory is thus fictional up until this point, even though it is based on a general concern that we actually have. What he then tries to show is how accuracy and sincerity could come to be understood as *virtues* that are of intrinsic value, and how they moved beyond their purely functional rationale in the effective pooling of information about one's immediate

[17] See also the explicit use of the phrase 'middle level of generality' in Williams' introduction to the French edition of *Ethics and the Limits of Philosophy* (Williams 2021: 274), which was first published in French but now made available in the original English.

[18] The paradigmatic example here is Aristotle's *Metaphysics*, where he argues that philosophy is the first and most fundamental science because it studies being under its most general aspect *qua* being.

[19] For the underlying distinction between reasons for concept use and reasons for concept application, see Queloz & Cueni 2021.

[20] This is most explicit in his work on liberty, see Williams 2001.

environment. By way of a journey that takes us from Thucydides to Rousseau and Diderot, we finally come to understand how the virtues of truthfulness took the shape that they have for us now and around here.

Though it is less obvious, the same middle-range generality also underlies Williams' work on voluntariness in *Shame and Necessity*. Far from being a specific study of how the Ancient Greeks understood the idea of the voluntary, which is how the book at first glance might be understood, Williams argues that other scholars have only felt compelled to assert that the Ancient Greeks lacked the idea of the voluntary because these scholars identified it with a more specific idea. This more specific idea is *our contemporary notion* of voluntariness, which understands the voluntary as an idea that is meant to justify ascriptions of moral responsibility rather than merely as making reference to 'an intentional aspect of an action done in a normal state of mind'. Williams then goes on to suggest that our modern efforts of 'trying to deepen' the voluntary, while they to some extent serve the purposes of justice, are also the source of many ethical and metaphysical problems that threaten to put the idea of the voluntary 'beyond all recognition' for us (Williams 1993: 66–68).[21] The very point of the mid-level generality in *Shame and Necessity* is thus to help *us* recover a notion of the voluntary that we can actually recognise in a world that has been shaken by metaphysical doubts about determinism and free will. This brings us to the next factor that relates to the distinct middle-range sense in which Williams isolated the explanans that is meant to answer the question of why we would come to cultivate these notions in the first place.

The *second feature* of a humanistic middle-range theory is that it relies on an explanans that lies in the *middle-range of isolation*. Much of Matthieu Queloz's work over recent years, and also some of our co-authored work (see Queloz & Cueni 2021), is best read as outlining the sense in which Williams should be understood as a humanistic middle-range theorist along the isolation dimension of the explanans. In his book *The Practical Origins of Ideas* (Queloz 2021a), Queloz highlights the particular manner of isolation that we find in certain of Williams' humanistic middle-range theories that he refers to as 'pragmatic genealogies'. To simplify for present purposes, pragmatic genealogies start out from a basic model that builds on a functional abstraction from highly general human concerns – e.g. the need to effectively pool information about one's immediate environment in the case of truthfulness – and then gradually include more local factors within the isolated field to tailor the explanation to our present-day situation.

I will first focus on the degree of isolation in the *functional abstraction*: Williams' key idea here is to exclude most explanatory factors from the isolated field in order to focus on the most general human concerns that a concept, virtue, or practice serves. In the case of the virtues of truthfulness, this general concern is the need to effectively pool information. But whereas the need to effectively pool information is a human

[21] For a general discussion of this idea of 'deepening' the voluntary, see Queloz 2022.

universal, the *general* concerns that a concept serves – and thus the factors that Williams includes in the isolated field – do not need to be completely universal. In the case of his account of our concept of liberty, for example, Williams relies on *both* the universal concern of individual human agents for doing what they want unimpeded by humanly imposed coercion *and* the more local concern of being able to legitimately object to the actions even of a perfectly just state (Williams 2005b). In other words, while Williams' humanistic middle-range theories are based on functional *abstraction*, functional abstractions may be *informed* by more historical considerations and thus exhibit a middle-range isolation.

This idea of providing a model that is based on functional abstraction, even historically informed functional abstraction that decreases the degree of isolation, is still different from then *adding real history* to the isolated field. This strategy was also used by Williams to great effect, which can again best be illustrated with the case of truthfulness. If we start out from a functional model based on the general human concern to effectively pool information, from the perspective of the explanans, the question is then what we need to *add* to the isolated field to get to our explanandum, namely to how we understand the virtues of truthfulness now and around here. One answer offered by Williams for the virtue of sincerity is the distinctively Romantic concern with personal authenticity, and thus with *expressing one's true self*, that was elaborated differently by Rousseau and Diderot (Williams 2002: Ch 8). As Queloz (2021a) explains in great detail, Williams often offered dynamic models that vary the degree of isolation even within a single humanistic middle-range theory by sequentially adding more local historical factors and thus enlarging the isolated set. The way in which Williams did this was by first deriving a functional prototype of the relevant notion before then involving himself in real history to account for how the notion actually developed. Williams' more constructive accounts of notions like truthfulness and liberty are thus best understood as based on a form of *functional abstraction* where historical considerations may both *inform* the functional abstraction and then *add* to it.

The *third feature* of a humanistic middle-range theory is that it is articulated from a *middle-range perspective* that takes the perspective of the individual participants of a social practice into account. Whereas in Merton's case the link between the micro and the macro level was emphasised for the purely explanatory purposes of the detached social scientist, in Williams' case the main challenge is to *make sense* of a given practice *from the perspective of the individuals within this practice*. This characteristic middle-range perspective that emphasises the link between the micro and the macro level can best be illustrated with the examples of truthfulness and blame. From a philosophical perspective that draws on broadly functional explanations, one key problem in both the case of truth-telling (i.e. what Williams calls the virtue of sincerity) and blame is how the functional considerations at the macro level relate to the perspective of individual agents at the micro level. With sincerity, the problem is how to get from the *general* concern for a well-functioning system of testimony based on the value of true information to the claim that *an individual agent* should tell the truth in a particular situation, instead of free-riding based on the contributions by other agents (Williams 2002). But the importance of emphasising the link between the micro and macro level is most obvious in the case of blame. There the problem is how to get from the instrumental value of the general practice of blame to the individual judgment that someone is *blameworthy* in a concrete situation, which requires more than a mere insight into the instrumental value of the practice as such (Williams 1995). In both cases, Williams highlights the self-effacing nature of the functional rationale so that our practices, to function properly, must come to be understood in more than purely functional terms from the perspective of individual participants.[22]

The *fourth feature* of Williams' humanistic middle-range theories is that they depend on a general humanistic outlook that we may refer to as a *middle-range general orientation*.[23] This general humanistic outlook primarily concerns the sense in which *humanistic* middle-range theories may not just explain but also *vindicate* our practices that is not part of the more specific theories themselves. For example, *Truth and Truthfulness* lacks an account of why its naturalistic,[24] functional explanations that are rooted in general human concerns provide us with genuine reasons for cultivating the virtues of accuracy and sincerity.[25] Depending on someone's pre-commitments,[26] the idea that our practices of truth-telling could be vindicated by considering their instrumental value may seem absurd; and matters are even worse when that same someone is told that our concern with individual liberty can, at least to some extent, be vindicated by considerations that are specific to the circumstances of modern and pluralistic societies (Williams 2005b). There is thus a need for a defence of the more general philosophical outlook that explains how such functional considerations and local concerns can vindicate a practice for us now and around here. Matthieu Queloz and I have elsewhere tried to offer such a defence under the label of 'Left Wittgensteinianism' (Queloz & Cueni 2021), and I will not reproduce that argument here. But it is important to highlight that the vindicatory claims of humanistic middle-range theories depend on a much more general philosophical outlook that further characterises the humanism that contrasts with both scientism and moralism and their search for purity from contingency.[27]

The *fifth feature* of Williams' humanistic middle-range theories is their *middle-range normativity*. The main *negative analogy* between *humanistic* middle-range

[22] See generally Queloz 2018 and 2021b.

[23] Compare also Williams 2002: 17–19, 22–23 and 2000: 149–50 on Williams' naturalism and how it relates to issues of reduction and explanation.

[24] In the sense outlined in Williams 2000.

[25] For a reaction that is baffled about Williams' view on this particular point, see Finnis 2011.

[26] See also the discussion of the ascetic ideal in Queloz & Cueni 2019 and especially the conclusion of that article, where we draw the connection between a general outlook based on certain pre-commitments and the idea of *naturalism without subversion*.

[27] On this general philosophical outlook in Williams' work, see especially also Fricker 2024 and Fricker 2025.

theories and theories of the middle-range in sociology relates to the sense of philosophical, as opposed to sociological, explanation at issue. Williams always emphasised that he was still doing philosophy when practising 'philosophy as a humanistic discipline' (Williams 2006b: 165–66). Humanistic middle-range theories may draw on other humanistic disciplines, namely history and the interpretive social sciences. But the underlying aim is to answer a distinctively philosophical question: to explain our *concern with truth*, for example (Williams 2002: 7). The starting point is always a philosophical puzzlement about *why* we have a concept, virtue, or practice in the first place; and what we seek from a philosophical explanation is not merely an explanatory account, but a genuine *reason* for going on as we do. This means that certain kinds of explanation that will qualify as a theory of the middle range in the sociological sense will provide the wrong kind of explanation for this philosophical purpose because they provide the wrong kind of reason. By contrast, some more philosophical, sometimes even fictional explanations will make the cut because they help us to resolve the philosophical puzzlement that originally sparked the inquiry.[28]

But speaking of *middle-range normativity* also makes clear that the sense of normativity at issue is distinct from how that term is typically used in contemporary moral and political theory. As Jorah Dannenberg has recently argued, 'current usages of the term [normativity] are inextricably bound up with a recognizably moralistic style of thought' that Williams opposed. This style of thought searches for 'some transcendental foundation for our moral and political convictions' that contrast with something that is 'merely social, psychological, and historically conditioned' (Dannenberg 2023: 1, 11). As I already explained above when describing the general outlook of humanistic middle-range theories, we should reject this moralistic contrast between transcendental foundations and mere contingency,[29] and thus also any sense of the term 'normativity' that is inextricably connected to it. But instead of getting rid of the term 'normativity' altogether, we must rather recognise the *middle-range normativity* of functional accounts of a virtue like tolerance that draw on new social needs under conditions of pluralism (Williams 2005d). Such accounts provide *us* with genuine reasons, and they are thus genuinely normative (Queloz & Cueni 2021: 763–64).

Based on these *five analogies* between theories of the middle range in sociology and Williams' philosophical work, we can conclude this section by observing that Williams' accounts of truthfulness, blame, and voluntariness are humanistic middle-range theories in the following sense: they (1) provide a philosophical explanation of a set of phenomena in the middle range of generality, (2) based on a combination of general and local concerns as well as real history in the middle-range of isolation, (3) are articulated from a middle-range perspective that always takes the perspective of the individual participants of

[28] For the fictional nature of pragmatic genealogies, see Queloz 2021a.

[29] See also Queloz 2024 for a critique of the underlying moralistic dualisms between morality and prudence as well as between principle and interest.

any given social practice into account, and (4) depend on a more general philosophical outlook that contrasts with the search for purity from contingency in both scientism and moralism. This final point gives rise to a fifth feature of *humanistic* middle-range theories, namely that they (5) exhibit a distinctive middle-range normativity.

## V. Humanistic Middle-Range Theories in Legal Scholarship?

My account of Williams as a humanistic middle-range theorist raises the question whether and how we should also practise *law as a humanistic discipline*. The framework for humanistic middle-range theories just offered need not be limited to Williams' philosophical concerns but may also form the basis of a legal methodology that integrates insights from other disciplines but remains guided by legal questions and aims to be doctrinally relevant. Legal scholarship bears many similarities to philosophy, not least in the fact that both disciplines are partly concerned with answering questions about why we go on as we do. Legal scholars are also sometimes puzzled about why we have a doctrinal distinction or procedural practice in the first place. I thus finish this chapter by sketching a humanistic middle-range theory of the doctrinal distinction between 'infringing' and 'violating' a basic right that illustrates that *the idea of humanistic middle-range theory* can be generalised from philosophy to legal scholarship.

To start with the negative characterisation of 'humanistic', both intellectual distortions that preoccupied Williams throughout his work – scientism and moralism – have close analogues in legal scholarship. On the one hand, while the aspiration to model legal scholarship on the natural sciences seems rather far-fetched, we can certainly, especially in the United States (US), see an aspiration to model legal scholarship on those social sciences that most closely try to approximate the natural scientific ideal, namely quantitative social science and rational choice economics.[30] On the other hand, the idea that legal scholarship should be modelled on the aims of highly abstract moral theory is also never far from the legal scholar's imagination, although most legal scholars of course try to account for the fact that law is ultimately a local practice.[31] In the remainder of this chapter, I do not wish to deepen this diagnosis beyond this admittedly stylised sketch, but rather suggest the potential remedy in the idea of humanistic middle-range theories *in legal scholarship*.[32] Humanistic middle-range theories

[30] See, e.g., Posner 1983.

[31] Compare the way in which Williams (2014a: 257) describes Dworkin's aspirations: 'Dworkin looks to a timeless moral framework in matters of justice, and … one of his major preoccupations is to explain how judgments which have to be determined by the traditions of a given body of law can nevertheless be regulated, as he supposes they should be, by the timeless moral framework.'

[32] I am not the first person to suggest that we should draw on Merton's idea of theories in the middle range to elucidate theory-building in legal scholarship, see Lepsius 2014.

offer a distinctive answer to the question of 'why the law works or why it does not' (Lepsius 2014: 699) that can be characterised using the five features that I have identified.

To provide a basis for illustrating this claim, I will show how a humanistic middle-range theory may help us think about whether we should have a certain concept within our doctrinal arsenal.[33] The two-step framework of 'scope' and 'justification' that is used in those jurisdictions that recognise basic rights that can routinely be limited – and especially the corresponding doctrinal distinction between 'infringing' and 'violating' a basic right – has puzzled many legal commentators. The way in which this doctrinal distinction is used in legal practice does not fit a philosophical understanding of 'rights', not even if that understanding includes a distinction between 'infringing' and 'violating' a right, which is controversial (Feinberg 1978; Thomson 1976). This has led some to deny the normative significance of the doctrinal notion of a basic rights infringement (Letsas 2013, 2018), whereas others instead suggest that doctrine should adopt a more rigorous philosophical understanding of what constitutes a genuine basic right (Tasioulas 2010, 2019). The situation is thus not unlike the philosophical puzzlement that frames Williams' discussion in *Truth and Truthfulness*, which initially contrasts the truth-deniers and the truth-enthusiasts (Williams 2002: Ch 1). There is a general uneasiness about the doctrinal distinction between 'infringing' and 'violating' a basic right that basic rights theory wishes to resolve by either abandoning the distinction as utterly pointless (akin to the truth-deniers) or by rendering it more philosophically rigorous (akin to the truth-enthusiasts). By contrast, I will now sketch how we might make sense of this doctrinal distinction through a humanistic middle-range theory.

A humanistic middle-range account of liberty as a political value must start out from an explanans in the middle-range of isolation that incorporates the *local need* for a greater presumption in favour of the individual point of view in the circumstances of modern and pluralistic societies.[34] In his account of liberty, Williams highlights that the notion of liberty *as a political value* should not be identified with a *rightful claim* to liberty. This is in large part due to the specific circumstances of modern and pluralistic societies: such societies require a concept of liberty as a political value that allows individual subjects to object to even rightful decisions by their public institutions that do not *violate* any rights, and also allows citizens to reach across the aisle and *take up the evaluative perspective* of their political opponents that use different conceptions of political values like equality in forming opinions about what is rightful (Williams 2001, 2005a, 2005b).

These local concerns regarding what liberty needs to be for us now and around here are then also reflected in the doctrinal notion of a basic rights

[33] In what follows, I am drawing on my previous work on the relationship between costs in political value and basic rights in Cueni 2024 and Cueni 2025.

[34] See Williams 2005b. On the idea of such local needs, see generally Queloz & Cueni 2021 as well as Queloz 2021a.

infringement, which *mediates* between political and legal discourse by allowing our *legal institutions* to express special acknowledgment and respect for *particularly grievous* costs in liberty. To have a legal concept that discharges this expressive function is important, among other things, to secure the continuing allegiance of those individuals who end up on the losing side of legal decisions that do not violate any rights but nevertheless give rise to a loss in liberty that legal institutions of modern and pluralistic societies should acknowledge and respect. Because it allows legal institutions to express such a special form of respect, the doctrinal notion of a basic rights infringement has distinctive expressive advantages in circumstances where individual liberty must routinely be justifiably restricted, and it should thus not come as a surprise that many liberal democratic orders have come to cultivate it.[35]

But if the doctrinal notion of a basic rights infringement finds its distinctive normative significance in the characteristically modern need to acknowledge and respect particularly grievous costs in liberty, then a theory with middle-range generality may also help us to understand those modern and pluralistic societies that ostensibly seem to lack the doctrinal distinction between 'infringing' and 'violating' a basic right.[36] For example, US constitutional law does not seem to distinguish between 'infringing' and 'violating' a basic right in the same way that the jurisdictions that have explicitly adopted a proportionality framework for thinking about restrictions of basic rights do.[37] But if the doctrinal notion of a basic rights infringement is pointful for 'us' now and around here in a sense that includes not just the citizens of those jurisdictions that actually use the distinction, but also the more inclusive sense of 'us' that characterises citizens of modern and pluralistic societies,[38] then the distinction would likely also be pointful for them, where 'them' are the citizens of the modern-day US.[39] In fact, it might be argued that the US already acknowledges the underlying evaluative distinctions,[40] even though it does not express them in its legal framework for thinking about restrictions of basic rights. Not unlike in the philosophical cases of truthfulness and voluntariness, a central upshot of a theory with middle-range generality may then also be that it leads us to probe how the need for a greater presumption in favour of the individual point of view expresses itself differently in the various legal doctrines and procedures of actual jurisdictions.

While the middle-range perspective and general orientation of humanistic middle-range theories do not require a separate discussion for this doctrinal

[35] In fact, it would have been very odd if so many jurisdictions around the globe had come to draw a doctrinal distinction that, upon closer inspection, turned out to be utterly pointless. See also Matthieu Queloz's chapter 13 in this volume, which offers a discussion of Williams' views on philosophy's relationship to common sense and ordinary legal experience.

[36] See Williams 2006a: 196 on the relevant sense of 'us'.

[37] Compare Greene 2018.

[38] On why even this more inclusive sense is still a contrastive sense of 'us', see Queloz & Cueni 2021.

[39] For suggestions in that direction, see Greene 2018 and 2021.

[40] See also Yowell 2014.

illustration, their distinctive middle-range normativity merits further elaboration in relation to legal scholarship. In offering my account of the doctrinal distinction between 'infringing' and 'violating' a basic right, I have not suggested decisive reasons for why *any* particular jurisdiction – both past *and* present, liberal democratic or not – *must* use this distinction. Rather, my account of the *practical point* of the doctrinal notion of a basic rights infringement has offered a *pro tanto* reason for using the distinction that is rooted in the need to acknowledge and respect losses in liberty in the circumstances of modern and pluralistic societies.[41] How does such a humanistic middle-range theory compare to other accounts of a notion's practical point in the legal literature?[42] Nick Barber has drawn a helpful distinction between sociological accounts of 'practical point' that imply causal explanations and moral accounts of 'practical point' that imply an overall moral assessment.[43] But a humanistic middle-range account of a notion's practical point implies neither: it purports to be explanatory, but not necessarily in a causal sense;[44] and it includes a normative assessment, but not in the overall moral sense (which is anyway a mode of evaluation that Williams would have rejected as an outgrowth of the moralism described above). The idea of humanistic middle-range theory thus highlights that we can also offer more piecemeal *vindications* of our present ways of going on that help us to think about whether certain concepts, virtues, and practices do or do not *earn their keep* in both philosophy and law.

## VI. Conclusion

In this chapter, I have taken my cue from Williams' lecture on 'Philosophy as a Humanistic Discipline' to explore the question of what models or analogies we should look for in practising philosophy and legal scholarship. As many of the contributions in this volume attest, there is now an increased interest in how Williams' philosophical work relates to the law. But if my own experience is any guide, the reception of Williams' work in legal scholarship is currently hampered by the fact that much of it focuses on Williams' avowed 'political realism' (Williams 2005c: 3), which implicates legal scholarship in debates about how exactly this realism should be understood, and how it differs from other forms of normative political theory.[45] For the prospects of a Williamsian approach in legal scholarship, this focus on the abstract issue of political realism

[41] See also Khaitan & Steel (2022: 339–40) on what they call a 'pro tanto theory'.
[42] See also the discussion of 'point-based explanations' in Queloz & Cueni 2021.
[43] Barber 2020: 68–69.
[44] Compare Queloz 2021a: 14–16.
[45] For an overview of this large body of literature, see Rossi & Sleat 2014 as well as Maynard & Worsnip 2018. In addition, this statement is also based on personal conversations with my colleagues at the University of Oxford between 2020 and 2023.

is regrettable, because it leads to insufficient attention being paid to the concrete methodological approach that Williams urged us to practise.[46] In this chapter, I have attempted to rectify this neglect by outlining this approach in great detail and putting it in terms of a general methodological framework. I have also deliberately tried to coin a new term for it, namely *humanistic middle-range theory*. But little turns on the precise label, or indeed on whether we are comfortable calling it a middle-range *theory* or would rather prefer to call it a middle-range *approach*.[47] All that matters is that philosophers and legal scholars continue to practise this methodological approach in elucidating concrete ideas and social phenomena in a Williamsian spirit.

## Bibliography

Barber, NW (2020) 'Law and the Point of the State' in E Fisher, J King and AL Young (eds), *The Foundations and Future of Public Law: Essays in Honour of Paul Craig* (Oxford, Oxford University Press).

Becker, GS (1976) *The Economic Approach to Human Behavior* (Chicago, University of Chicago Press).

—— (2009) *Human Capital: A Theoretical and Empirical Analysis, with Special Reference to Education* (Chicago, University of Chicago Press).

Berger, PL (1963) *Invitation to Sociology: A Humanistic Perspective* (New York, Anchor Books).

Cueni, D (2024) 'Constructing Liberty and Equality – Political, Not Juridical' 15 3 *Jurisprudence* 341.

—— (2025) 'Basic Rights and Costs in Political Value: The *Expressive Point of the Two-Step Framework' 23 1 International* Journal of Constitutional Law 87.

d'Alembert, JLR (1751) *Discours préliminaire de* l'Encyclopédie.

Dannenberg, J (2023) 'Bernard Williams, Realistic Liberalism, and the Politics of Normativity' 32 2 *European Journal of Philosophy* 489.

Dennett, D (1989) *The Intentional Stance* (Cambridge, Massachusetts, MIT Press).

Elster, J (1989) *Nuts and Bolts for the Social Sciences* (Cambridge, Cambridge University Press).

—— (1999) *Alchemies of the Mind: Rationality and the Emotions* (Cambridge, Cambridge University Press).

Feinberg, J (1978) 'Voluntary Euthanasia and the Inalienable Right to Life' 7 *Philosophy & Public Affairs* 93.

[46] For a similar diagnosis in philosophy, see now also Maynard 2021 and especially Dannenberg 2023. That Williams did not want to settle the realism and moralism debate in the abstract can also be seen from his close engagement with the concrete views of Ronald Dworkin that was based on a joint seminar at the University of Oxford. These writings, especially Williams 2005a and 2005b, probably best illustrate the *constructive* form of realism that Williams can bring to philosophical and legal debates. On the particular methodological approach that is evident in these writings, see also Cueni 2024.

[47] Here the label 'theory' is partly preferred for the simple reason that it allows me to use the corresponding noun in calling Williams a 'humanistic middle-range theorist'.

Finnis, J (2011) 'Bernard Williams on Truth's Values' in J Finnis (ed), *Reason in Action: Collected Essays* (Oxford, Oxford University Press).
Fricker, M (2024) 'A Project of "Impure" Enquiry – Williams' Historical Self-Consciousness' 32 2 *European Journal of Philosophy* 301.
—— (2025) 'Williams' 'Philosophical Anthropology': A Humean and Nietzschean Synergy' *European Journal of Philosophy* (online first).
Geertz, C (2017) *The Interpretation of Cultures* (New York, Basic Books).
Greene, J (2018) 'Foreword: Rights as Trumps?' 132 *Harvard Law Review* 28.
—— (2021) *How Rights Went Wrong: Why Our Obsession with Rights Is Tearing America Apart* (Boston and New York, Houghton Mifflin Harcourt).
Habermas, J (1996) *Between Facts and Norms: Contributions to a Discourse Theory of Law and Democracy* (Cambridge, Massachusetts, MIT Press).
Hedström, P & Udehn, L (2011) 'Analytical Sociology and Theories of the Middle Range' in P Hedström & P Bearman (eds), *The Oxford Handbook of Analytical Sociology* (Oxford, Oxford University Press).
Hesse, MB (1966) *Models and Analogies in Science* (Notre Dame, University of Notre Dame Press).
Khaitan, T & Steel, S (2022) 'Theorizing Areas of Law: A Taxonomy of Special Jurisprudence' 28 *Legal Theory* 325.
Lepsius, O (2014) 'The Quest for Middle-Range Theories in German Public Law' 12 *International Journal of Constitutional Law* 692.
Letsas, G (2013) 'The Scope and Balancing of Rights: Diagnostic or Constitutive?' in E Brems & G Janneke (eds), *Shaping Rights: The Role of the European Court of Human Rights in Determining the Scope of Human Rights* (Cambridge, Cambridge University Press).
—— (2018) 'Proportionality as Fittingness: The Moral Dimension of Proportionality' 71 *Current Legal Problems* 53.
Mäki, U (1992) 'On the Method of Isolation in Economics' 26 *Poznan Studies in the Philosophy of the Sciences and the Humanities* 317.
Maynard, JL (2021) 'Political Realism as Methods not Metaethics' *Ethical Theory and Moral Practice* 1–15, available at https://doi.org/10.1007/s10677-021-10183-7.
Maynard, JL & Worsnip, A (2018) 'Is There a Distinctively Political Normativity?' 128 *Ethics* 756.
Merton, RC (1963) 'Introduction' in AH Barton (ed), *Social Organizations Under Stress* (Washington, DC, National Academy of Sciences – National Research Council).
Merton, RK (1949) *Social Theory and Social Structure* (Glencoe, Ill, Free Press).
—— (1957) 'The Role-Set: Problems in Sociological Theory' 8 *The British Journal of Sociology* 106.
—— (1968) *Social Theory and Social Structure*, enlarged edition (New York, Free Press).
Moran, R (2016) '2015 Mark Sacks Lecture: Williams, History, and "the Impurity of Philosophy"' 24 *European Journal of Philosophy* 315.
Owen, D (2018) 'Realism in Ethics and Politics: Bernard Williams, Political Theory and the Critique of Morality' in M Sleat (ed), *Politics Recovered: Realist Thought in Theory and Practice* (New York, Columbia University Press).
Posner, RA (1983) *The Economics of Justice* (Cambridge, Massachusetts, Harvard University Press).
Queloz, M (2018) 'Williams's Pragmatic Genealogy and Self-Effacing Functionality' 18 *Philosophers' Imprint* 1.

—— (2021a) *The Practical Origins of Ideas: Genealogy as Conceptual Reverse-Engineering* (Oxford, Oxford University Press).
—— (2021b) 'The Self-Effacing Functionality of Blame' 178 *Philosophical Studies* 1361.
—— (2022) 'The Essential Superficiality of the Voluntary and the Moralization of Psychology' 179 *Philosophical Studies* 1591.
—— (2024) 'Moralism as a Dualism in Ethics and Politics' 1 2 *Political Philosophy* 432.
Queloz, M & Cueni, D (2019) 'Nietzsche as a Critic of Genealogical Debunking: Making Room for Naturalism Without Subversion' 102 3 *The Monist: An International Journal of General Philosophical Inquiry* 277.
—— (2021) 'Left Wittgensteinianism' 29 *European Journal of Philosophy* 758.
Rossi, E & Sleat, M (2014) 'Realism in Normative Political Theory' 9 *Philosophy Compass* 689.
Sagar, P (2016) 'From Scepticism to Liberalism? Bernard Williams, the Foundations of Liberalism and Political Realism' 64 *Political Studies* 368.
—— (2018) *The Opinion of Mankind: Sociability and the Theory of the State from Hobbes to Smith* (Princeton, Princeton University Press).
Sartre, J-P (1946) *L'existentialisme est un humanisme* (Paris, Les Editions Nagel).
Stinchcombe, AL (1986) 'Merton's Theory of Social Structure' in AL Stinchcombe (ed), *Stratification and Organization: Selected Papers* (Cambridge, Cambridge University Press).
Tasioulas, J (2010) 'Taking Rights out of Human Rights' 120 *Ethics* 647.
—— (2019) 'Saving Human Rights from Human Rights Law' 52 *Vanderbilt Journal of Transnational Law* 1167.
Thomson, JJ (1976) 'Self-Defense and Rights' in JJ Thomson (ed), *Rights, Restitution, and Risk* (Cambridge, Massachusetts, Harvard University Press).
Udehn, L (2002) *Methodological Individualism: Background, History and Meaning* (London and New York, Routledge).
Williams, B (1993) *Shame and Necessity* (Berkeley, University of California Press).
—— (1995) 'How Free Does the Will Need to Be?' in B Williams, *Making Sense of Humanity* (Cambridge, Cambridge University Press).
—— (2000) 'Naturalism and Genealogy' in E Harcourt (ed), *Morality, Reflection, and Ideology* (Oxford, Oxford University Press).
—— (2001) 'Liberalism and Loss' in M Lilla, R Dworkin & R Silvers (eds), *The Legacy of Isaiah Berlin* (New York, New York Review of Books).
—— (2002) *Truth and Truthfulness: An Essay in Genealogy* (Princeton, Princeton University Press).
—— (2005a) 'Conflicts of Liberty and Equality' in G Hawthorne (ed), *In the Beginning Was the Deed: Realism and Moralism in Political Argument* (Princeton and Oxford, Princeton University Press).
—— (2005b) 'From Freedom to Liberty: The Construction of a Political Value' in G Hawthorne (ed), *In the Beginning Was the Deed: Realism and Moralism in Political Argument* (Princeton and Oxford, Princeton University Press).
—— (2005c) 'Realism and Moralism in Political Theory' in G Hawthorne (ed), *In the Beginning Was the Deed: Realism and Moralism in Political Argument* (Princeton and Oxford, Princeton University Press).
—— (2005d) 'Toleration, a Political or Moral Question?' in G Hawthorne (ed), *In the Beginning Was the Deed: Realism and Moralism in Political Argument* (Princeton and Oxford, Princeton University Press).

—— (2006a) 'Philosophy as a Humanistic Discipline' in AW Moore (ed), *Philosophy as a Humanistic Discipline* (Princeton and Oxford, Princeton University Press).
—— (2006b) 'Political Philosophy and the Analytical Tradition' in AW Moore (ed), *Philosophy as a Humanistic Discipline* (Princeton and Oxford, Princeton University Press).
—— (2011) *Ethics and the Limits of Philosophy* (Abingdon, Routledge).
—— (2014a) 'A Matter of Principle, by Ronald Dworkin' in M Woods (ed), *Essays and Reviews 1959–2002* (Princeton, Princeton University Press).
—— (2014b) 'Why Philosophy Needs History' in M Woods (ed), *Essays and Reviews 1959–2002* (Princeton, Princeton University Press).
—— (2021) 'Ethics, a Matter of Style? Introduction to the French Edition' 9 *Philosophical Inquiries* 269.
Yowell, P (2014) 'Proportionality in United States Constitutional Law' in L Lazarus, C McCrudden and N Bowles (eds), *Reasoning Rights. Comparative Judicial Engagements* (London, Hart Publishing).

# 11

# Why Can't Law be More Like Morality?

CHRISTOPHER KUTZ

## I. Introduction: Chaos on the Tracks

Bernard Williams, perhaps wisely, mostly avoided any discussion of contemporary legal decision-making in his work. One of the few examples with which I am familiar is in *Shame and Necessity* (Williams 1993a: 60 ff and notes), in which in the course of examining the classical Greek conceptions of causal responsibility, Williams adverts to a range of modern cases, discovered, it appears, in Hart and Honoré's *Causation in the Law* (1985).[1] Strikingly, Williams even appears to endorse for its subtlety the opinion by Benjamin Cardozo in the famous case of *Palsgraf v Long Island*.[2] The facts (as Cardozo understood them) of the case are worth reciting: a Mrs Palsgraf was at one end of a train platform, waiting for a train, and apparently standing next to a heavy metal scale. Two men at the other end of the platform were rushing to board the train before hers, and an overzealous railroad employee attempted to help them board by giving them a push. Alas, the push caused one of them to drop a package containing some fireworks, which exploded; the explosion then either caused the scale to topple onto Mrs Palsgraf, or frightened others on the platform enough that they jostled it over onto her.

Everyone agreed (at least among the judges) that the railroad employee's push caused the explosion, which caused the toppling, which caused the injury to poor Mrs Palsgfraf. The question for the lawyers was whether this causal relation was enough to ground a claim of financial responsibility by the railroad for the harm. In the terms of Anglo-American law, this is the question of whether a cause is 'proximate', which is to say, whether it was closely enough related to the injury to be deemed the basis for a claim for recompense.[3] The railroad's lawyers argued that, however mistaken

[1] Williams' other brief discussion of law occurs in his introduction to the Censorship report he chaired in 1979, reprinted in *In the Beginning was the Deed* (2005).

[2] *Palsgraf v Long Island* 248 NY 339, 162 NE 99 (1928). For a rich discussion of the case, see Zipursky 2012.

[3] The Greek case that led Williams to *Palsgraf* bore some similarities: it concerned a javelin thrower practising his throw, whose javelin accidentally struck a boy running across the practice field. Both the throwing and the running were clearly each causes and necessary conditions of the injury, but left open the question whether the throwing-cause could ground a claim for expiation.

the employee was with respect to the passengers he helped, causing an explosion that might cause an injury to someone at the other end of the platform was too unlikely to be foreseen, and could not be a reasonable basis for a claim to damages. Cardozo bought the argument, essentially on the grounds that all our actions radiate outwards in infinite and unpredictable ways, and that unless our responsibility is cabined by specific ties to foreseeable harms and victims, we will never have freedom enough to act. With this view, Cardozo was able to persuade three of his colleagues on New York's highest court; and with his reputation as one of America's most powerful legal thinkers, his opinion was enshrined in every treatise and textbook to this day.

Now, Mrs Palsgraf's lawyers argued differently. For them, it was enough that a railroad employee acted carelessly in pushing the passenger. It was enough to know that his act was careless, as all agreed; it was irrelevant that the specific form that risk would take or victim it would find was unforeseeable. A railroad company faces no unfair expectation or burden in trying to keep its employees from acting carelessly in general. From a social point of view, the aim should be to have more careful railroad workers, hence fewer accidents, whatever the particulars of the accidents they cause. This view, expressed by dissenting Judge William Andrews, lost the day but effectively states the current legal rule in the majority of jurisdictions in the United States (US). As long as you can show that someone's negligence was a direct cause of an injury – for instance a car accident involving a pedestrian child causes a mother who sees it to suffer emotional trauma – you can recover.[4]

Williams' interest in *Palsgraf*, and tort law more broadly, had nothing to do with an interest in the foreseeability rule, nor does his endorsement of Cardozo's opinion reflect a particular view about the limits of responsibility. Rather, what caught his eye was Cardozo's enunciation of a broader principle:

> A cause, but not the proximate cause. What we … mean by the word 'proximate' is that because of convenience, of public policy, of a rough sense of justice, the law arbitrarily declines to trace a series of events beyond a certain point. This is not logic. It is practical politics (239 NYS 252).

We would label Cardozo's statement today an emblem of Legal Realism: a declaration that legal decision-making in its particulars is guided by a vague and broad set of material interests and a congeries of values, rather than dictated by a set of abstract rules. In the even more famous formulation of Oliver Wendell Holmes, Jr, 'The life of the law has not been logic; it has been experience' (1881: 1). Such could be the motto, of course, of Williams' view of what he called 'the morality system': the framework of normative expectations and obligations built around the quintessentially modern conception of an impersonal will aiming to act rightly in relation to abstract rational principle (Williams 1993a: 6).

My aim in this chapter is to discuss how Williams' thoughts about morality, and specifically the error he saw in trying to buttress moral claims with sophisticated

[4] *Dillon v Legg* 68 Cal 2d 728, 441 P2d 912, 69 Cal Rptr 72 (1968).

theories, might give us some insight about how we should understand law. This may seem peculiar, both because, as I mentioned above, Williams evinces almost no actual interest in legal decision-making, and because Williams' scepticism about morality would be yet more acid to be poured on law's legitimacy. Nonetheless, I want to suggest that a dose of Williams' scepticism about morality may be just what we need to feel better about the law.

## II. Law's Uneasy Relation to Morality

The great chestnut of traditional legal philosophy is law's relation to morality. Morality, understood in its critical sense, is meant to stand eternal, a set of abstract principles and standards which provide a special kind of ultimate normative justification for action, both by individuals and groups. Law, by contrast, changes with the whim of the ruler. Parliament, or a head of state, can create or snuff out a legal obligation with a new statute or order; but no comparable moral figure can create or snuff out a moral obligation. If I have a moral duty to be kind to my elderly relatives, that is simply a fact about my relation to morality. At best I can seek advice from moral experts about whether I am meeting those obligations. But not even the Pope or chief Rabbi can relieve me of the obligation itself.

Given this stark difference, one might think there is little meat in the chestnut. Law is law, morality another thing, even if law sometimes aspires to mimic morality in its form or content. Such is the view of the positivist tradition in legal thought, whose most straightforward, if crudest, version was expressed two centuries ago by John Austin, in the idea that a law is nothing less and nothing more than a command backed by a threat, issued by someone who has the power of realising that threat and who has succeeded in creating a habit of obedience around him (Austin 1832). Contemporary positivists have complicated the picture by noting that many laws retain their authority without either a credible threat behind them, or without issuance by an identifiable figure commanding obedience (Hart 1961, Raz 1970). But the general picture of an opposition between law, as grounded in contingent and local social and political acts, and morality as grounded in absolute or at least highly general truths, is a centrepiece of the whole positivist tradition.

Since law and morality do seem to differ in this way, a naïve reader – or even a jaded teacher of legal theory – might wonder why there has been such a fuss for a millennium about law's relation to morality. The reason lies in the crucial notion of a legal obligation. As the positivists themselves noticed (Hart 1961: Ch 2), commands issued simply on the basis of social or political hierarchy don't seem to create actual obligations, any more than, in Hart's famous phrase, a 'gunman' demanding your wallet creates an obligation for you to turn it over. At best he makes you an offer you can't refuse – perhaps because of separate moral obligations you already hold to those who will miss you if you try to defy the robber. Lawyers, and robbers, can tell you that you have an obligation to obey a legal command, but telling doesn't make it so. If we actually do have legal obligations, it seems, it's a mistake to think that law is their source, rather than a triggering condition. It's no different than when I promise to meet you for lunch tomorrow. My words, 'I promise to meet you', trigger and fill out the content of my obligation, but the actual source of that obligation isn't the words, it's the background principle that if I use those customary words, I have a moral duty to do what they mean (Enoch 2011).

We can go in one of two directions at this point. One direction is to hold that law uses the language of obligation to bully and harass, but that it doesn't actually create them, unless there is no background moral principle it can ground itself on. Since many laws, apart from the core of criminal law and perhaps a bit of accident and contract law, don't seem to have much to do with morality, it follows that they don't actually create obligations. (Or, in Hart's awkward formulation, they create 'legal' obligations which, whatever they are, are not 'moral' obligations.) Hart thought that a view like this could be clarifying in times when law's bullying might need to be resisted, as when a fascist government emerges and starts shouting orders (Hart 1958). Clear-eyed citizens should realise that law is a form of rhetoric, and perhaps (as Holmes advised) a guide to predicting how state power will fall, but it does not actually enjoin us to obey.

Whatever the advantages of a hard-nosed positivist view in a fascist regime – advantages we may well be pressed to accept when police start issuing orders to denounce our non-citizen neighbours, for instance – one can see that it presents a problem for a legal system that aspires to justice. For if specific legal obligations are at best only accidentally attached to morality, so too is the entire legal order. And this might seem to present a first-order crisis of legitimacy. Why should a subject accept a legal decision contrary to their interests, whether about taxes or reproductive rights or hazardous waste disposal, if they cannot see how to seat that decision in a moral framework? Better to have anarchy.

A path out of this legitimation crisis is to accept its premise, that legal rights without moral rights are empty. Therefore, moral rights must be called from the vasty deep. This call has been made over the last half century by Ronald Dworkin, and more recently by his former students, Mark Greenberg and Scott Hershovitz, who hold (with some intramural disagreements) that law's requirements are just special kinds of moral requirements.[5] On their view, when we create or transform our relations to one another through law, say by incurring a debt or issuing a command, we create moral obligations for one another, to pay our debt or obey the command. This is because (on their view) the ultimate justification of any legal claim sounds ultimately in morality, albeit often mediated in institutional circumstances, such as the fact that the command followed from an act of collective deliberation and equal decision-making in a representative democratic process,

[5] See, especially, Dworkin's last summary of his views in Dworkin 2013; Greenberg 2014; Hershovitz 2023.

or the debt followed from a prescribed system of making mutual promises to one another. The fact that we followed the legal forms in issuing the command or promise makes them instances of law without undercutting their claim to being at the same time instances of specific moral obligation. The problem is solved: legal obligations are real obligations, and necessarily so, because they are simply ways of moving the basic moral furniture around. While the theorists I have mentioned think that their view makes sense of the way American law in particular is practised and discussed by appellate courts, with veiled and sometimes unveiled references to moral considerations, its principal support is not judicial rhetoric but moral necessity.[6] Unless we accept their account of law's relation to morality, we must find ourselves deeply alienated from the most basic facts about our social and political lives.

I have of course elided many complications and dialectical turns in my description of the debate, but the general lines of it are accurate: either law merely purports to provide the force of moral argument, or it actually does (at least when it is successful). But notice that both sides of the debate share a common rhetorical question, expressed in my title: why can't law be more like morality? The positivists meet the question with resignation, the non-positivists with insistence. But perhaps both, like Professor Higgins, ought instead to wonder whether perhaps morality is not all it's cracked up to be either.

## III. (Not Viewing) the Law from Nowhere

Enter Bernard Arthur Owens Williams. Williams claimed for himself the difficult stance of scepticism about not just the excess of academic theorising but even the basic ideas of what he took to be a common late-Modern moral culture, built around the image of a freely choosing rational will seeking to align its actions with principle. Such a view, he thought, echoing the Nietzsche of *Genealogy of Morals*, 'mistook the lightning for the flash': it imagines that there is a doer, stripped of commitments and identities, able to survey the possibilities thrown up by the world and then to act, rather than the messy, embedded and always partly unfree creatures that we are (Williams 1993b). The problem with the Modern view of morality, especially as adumbrated by philosophers, is threefold in Williams' view. First, it pretends that the stance of moral decision-making and judgment is both alienated from our central commitments and detached from history, rather than a view 'from here, now'. Second, it reduces the wide variety of moral judgments that we make in real life, such as 'he's a real bastard, avoid him', or 'don't kowtow to that jerk, that's shameful', to a radically etiolated set of concepts that ask merely whether the action we intended was right or wrong, in keeping or in conflict with our moral obligations. Third, and worst, the etiolated set of concepts collapse under reflective

[6] Brian Leiter's review of Hershovitz's book (Leiter 2024) is acute on this.

deliberation, Williams says. If we ask by what necessity we should meet our obligations, or why we should do right, we are led to confront either (in Williams' view) the absence of an account of human nature that could show us that such acts are repugnant to that nature, or the absence of an account of practical rationality that could show that acting wrongly violates some fundamental precept. (The promises of both Aristotle and Kant cannot be kept.)

I don't mean here to contest or defend Williams' scepticism about moral knowledge, though I share his doubt that abstract moral theory is a better foundation for moral action or criticism than a more historicised, pluralistic, and fact specific sensibility. Rather, I want to highlight a mostly unnoticed constructive possibility in his work. Let us focus on what I called Williams' second criticism of the Morality system, that it reduces a rich, socially embedded moral vocabulary to a spare one. This is Williams' famous contrast between 'thick' ethical terms, by which he seems mainly to refer to strongly approbative or derogatory adjectives or adjectival uses of nouns, such as 'asshole' or 'valiant', and the 'thin' terms of moral theory, such as Kant's terminology of maxims willable as universal law (Williams 1984: Ch 8). He notes that thick concepts have a clear historicity and hence an obvious sell-by date; his central example is an adjective like 'chaste', which once had strong action-guiding force, but which now, if applied, would seem at best quaint and more likely creepy. 'Badass', by contrast, is an approbation now and newly in force, and sought after as a badge of pride, though likely also quickly decaying.

The evident value of such thick concepts is that you don't need a course in moral theory to know when and how to apply them. Their circulation in common discourse, combined with facts in the world made salient by that discourse, give us a clear sense of how and when to apply them – who is genuinely badass, who an asshole. This combination of what Williams calls 'world-guidedness' – the factual specificity that creates necessary conditions for their correct application – and the broader shared cultural and moral values give them an anchor in argument and action. Whereas the question whether one should primarily respect others as ends in themselves or treat them as inputs to a social welfare function quickly outstrips our ability to resolve an argument, we really can converge on judgements about bravery, badassery, and treachery, and we have no trouble dismissing questions about whether we 'really' should be brave and avoid treachery as either idle scepticism or remarks from someone who simply doesn't speak our common language.

But Williams thinks that identifying thick ethical concepts is of limited solace, because he also thinks – in some of the most puzzling pages he wrote – that although they are much handier, because world-guided – than purely theoretical constructs, they are prone to dissolve under a certain kind of rational deliberation. One form of this reflection comes from theory itself: if we ask, 'well, really, why should I avoid treachery', we have to ascend to the levels of theory anyway, and then we find ourselves as stuck as if we had begun with the abstract questions of right in the first place. The second form of reflection comes from noticing (if we do) that other cultures, perhaps at other times, seem to deploy these thick concepts very differently, or to deploy very different concepts. These reflections lead me to think that there is no more to my thick concepts than the contingent fact that I happen to have them. Once we have ascended to reflect, either in relation to theory or in trans-cultural tourism, reflection 'destroys knowledge', our knowledge that such an act was shameful or cowardly and therefore not to be done. At one point Williams suggests that only 'traditional societies' can have ethical knowledge – a status barred to those of us resident in anthropologically 'hot', transformative societies aware of our place in a diverse community of other peoples.

Hart, in a critical review of Williams, noted that he seems to want to have his thick concepts both ways: as both a viable alternative to the kind of disembodied moralism he despises, and as a tragic example of the Existentialist problem of our freedom to reflect (Hart 1986). But in fact, as Hart notes, Williams says at the same time that even in a modern society it is at least possible that we can continue to rely on claims like 'he's a bastard, don't trust him':

> The objective grounding would not bring it about that judgments using those concepts were true or could be known: this was so already. But it would enable us to recognize that certain of them were the best or most appropriate thick concepts to use … There is some [ethical knowledge] and in the past there has been more (Williams 1986: 155).

While it's far from clear, given the contrast Williams had heretofore sketched of the true-or-false conception of the non-normative aspects of the universe, how such ethical claims can enjoy a similar status, it seems that Williams' ambivalence about the inter-subjective grounding of normative judgements may be, not an inconsistency, but his actual position, and a well-founded one at that.[7]

Cheryl Misak, in an insightful recent article, notes that Williams is very much a product of the Cambridge tradition of philosophical pragmatism, in his rejection of a conception of a universe we can conceive separately from our practices of inquiry and argument (Misak 2021). Williams makes use of this tradition to dismiss the flippant relativism about fact and value of Richard Rorty, on the grounds that part of our practice of scientific inquiry includes vindicating a desire to explain why a world independent of our thought can explain the contents of our thoughts, as Rorty's 'truth is just a compliment we pay to ideas we like' attitude cannot. Even if the idea of a causally explanatory independent world prior to our thoughts is inevitably internal to our thoughts, its function in our practices of argument and inquiry is sufficient to give us confidence in the claims made (mostly) by science. Williams, Misak notes, is right to see moral argument as different from scientific argument, and not susceptible to the same kind of arguments about convergence and causal explanation. But he fails, at a crucial point, to recognise that pragmatists about science can also be pragmatists about ethics, without succumbing to relativism. If we recognise that we have a distinctive practice of ethical argument, one sensitive to the need that our ethical concepts be both world-guided and action-guiding (that is to say, normative), we can vindicate specific ethical claims

[7] Samuel Scheffler (1987/2002), too, notes the instability in Williams' view of thick concepts.

by seeing how they survive through the fiercest first-order argumentative tests to which we can put them.[8] It can still be true that they will fail as Williams insists, if we pose second-order questions about their congruence with claims of rational necessity. That kind of reflection could undermine our capacity to function with these concepts. But first-order inquiry and argumentation can still be reflective enough to satisfy members of a hot, alert culture. Williams could, Misak suggests, have his ethical cake and eat it too.

I now want to suggest that Williams' oblique reference to law, and to Cardozo's insight that a crucial legal term like 'proximate cause' is guided by a mix of facts and values, points to a way out of the positivist/anti-positivist dilemma. Both sides accept that the only real obligations are moral obligations, and that law's obligations, if stripped of moral foundations, are just piles of words and hortatory rhetoric. But once we have deflated the claims of morality a bit, we can see that the piles of words and hortatory rhetoric can amount to something significant.

Law, after all, is anything but an abstract set of propositions. It is a set of nouns ('precedent', 'canon', 'statute'), adjectives ('proximate', 'reasonable', 'wilful'), and verbs ('carry', 'interfere', 'perform') whose meaning comes from use by subjects, their more reflective lawyer-advisors, and their (in principle) even more reflective adjudicators. These concepts are as thick as they come, guided by patterns and facts, transformed by arguments. The normativity inheres holistically in the practice of argument. A Williams-ey view of law can reflect the crisis of legitimation when we push too hard on the concepts – when we ask, as in the American constitutional case law, what this thing called 'substantive due process' really can be, for instance, or when we query whether our habitual use of 'reasonable' reflects class or gender stereotypes. But the solution to the doubts raised by such questions need not be despair, a conclusion that legal decisions just are moral decisions, and that in cases of moral dispute, we should turn away from courts and towards representative moral decision-makers.[9]

Of course a responsible polity may go that route, and decide that some cases are too ungoverned by law, or that a line of legal decision-making has so lost its mooring or become so straightforwardly a vehicle of policy preferences by the adjudicators that it should be turned back to legislators to determine which moral values ought to apply. But we need not take that attitude wholesale. Instead, we can see the bulk of our concepts as persisting even under the cynical acid of jurisprudential reflection. At the same time, this is not a call for a purely inward-looking conception of legal practice. We can treat the work of the lawyer-philosophers as helping to organise those debates, tidying our store of concepts, just as we can treat the work of the lawyer-sociologists and economists as helping to keep the world-guidedness of those concepts on track. We emerge, as Williams does, with

[8] Ronald Dworkin's (1996) view of moral argument, expressed in 'Objectivity and Truth: You'd better believe it', seems to be a view of this ilk.

[9] This was the view held by the Critical Legal Studies movement of the '70s and '80s, lately resuscitated by Ryan Doerfler and Samuel Moyn. See Moyn (2024).

a glimmer of hope for the enterprise of law. But a glimmer is better than a false idol. Perhaps neither law nor morality was what we thought, but are none the worse for it.

## Bibliography

Austin, J (1832) *The Province of Jurisprudence Determined* (London, John Murray).
*Dillon v Legg* 68 Cal 2d 728, 441 P2d 912, 69 Cal Rptr 72 (1968)
Dworkin, R (1996) 'Objectivity and Truth: You'd Better Believe it' 25 2 *Philosophy and Public Affairs* 87.
—— (2013) *Justice for Hedgehogs* (Cambridge, Massachusetts, Harvard University Press).
Enoch, D (2011) 'Authority and Reason-Giving' 89 2 *Philosophy and Phenomenological Research* 296.
Greenberg, M (2014) 'The Moral Impact Theory of Law' 123 *Yale Law Journal* 1288.
Hart, HLA (1958) 'Legal and Moral Obligation' in A Melden (ed), *Essays in Moral Philosophy* (Seattle, University of Washington Press).
—— (1986) 'Who Can Tell Right from Wrong? Review of *Ethics and the Limits of Philosophy* by Bernard Williams' *New York Review of Books* (17 July 1986 issue).
—— (1961) *The Concept of Law* (Oxford, Oxford University Press).
Hart, HLA & Honoré T (1985) *Causation in the Law*, 2nd edn (Oxford, Oxford University Press).
Hershovitz, S (2023) *Law is a Moral Practice* (Cambridge, Massachusetts, Harvard University Press).
Holmes, OW (1881) *The Common Law* (Boston, Little, Brown, and Company).
Leiter, B (2024) 'Law is a Moral Practice – Review' *Notre Dame Philosophical Reviews* (2 April 2), available at https://ndpr.nd.edu/reviews/law-is-a-moral-practice/
Misak, C (2021) 'Williams, Pragmatism and the Law' 27 *Res Publica* 155.
Moyn, S (2024) 'Reconstructing Critical Legal Studies' 134 *Yale Law* Journal 29.
Raz, J (1970) *The Concept of a Legal System* (Oxford, Clarendon Press).
Scheffler, S (2002) 'Morality through Thick and Thin: A Critical Notice of Ethics and the Limits of Philosophy' (originally appearing in *The Philosophical Review* in 1987, republished in S Scheffler, *Boundaries and Allegiances* (Oxford, Oxford University Press)).
Williams, B (1986) *Ethics and the Limits of Philosophy* (Cambridge, Massachusetts, Harvard University Press).
—— (1993a) *Shame and Necessity* (Berkeley, University of California Press).
—— (1993b) 'Nietzsche's Minimalist Moral Psychology' 1 *European Journal of Philosophy* 4.
—— (2005) *In the Beginning Was the Deed: Realism and Moralism in Political Argument* (Princeton and Oxford, Princeton University Press).
Zipursky, B (2012) 'Palsgraf, Punitive Damages, and Preemption' 125 *Harvard Law Review* 1757.

# 12

# An Unusual but Successful Philosophical Marriage in Bernard Williams: Nietzsche and Wittgenstein

RONALDO PORTO MACEDO JR

## I. Introduction: Many Influences, Controversial and Diversified

Williams was indeed a very erudite man. This statement is trivial. It is common sense that he was a sage and cultivated man. He was highly proficient in many areas of philosophy, including Greek philosophy, moral philosophy, Descartes, Nietzsche, Wittgenstein, and analytic philosophy. This fact is not entirely unusual, especially among historians of philosophy. However, it is rare among original philosophers such as Williams. This rarity is likely due to the tradition and well-known fact that analytic and continental philosophies have experienced an (unfortunate) divide during the last century and the beginning of the 21st century. For this reason, finding an author so profoundly influenced by both Nietzsche and Wittgenstein in contemporary scholarship is quite unusual. Besides, it is relevant to remember that these authors are always subject to controversial philosophical interpretations.

Bernard Williams acknowledges the importance of both Nietzsche and Wittgenstein very early during his formation years. In an interview in 1983, he said:

> Although I hardly ever refer to Nietzsche in my writings, he has had a growing influence on what I think. The great thing about Nietzsche is that he is one of those thinkers whom you have to use and not copy. It is not a question of his having doctrines which you might adopt. It is not like that. It is something about the tone of voice, or rather some of the tones of voice, for he had many tones of voices and some I do not like at all. I don't like the high poetic tone of voice of Zarathustra. I like the dry, aphoristic tone of voice; what he says in that tone seems to be quite extraordinary. It is in many ways revelatory philosophy (Williams 1983: 42).

His words already reveal something important about how the Nietzschean influence is present in his works, not as a system of ideas to be blindly followed but as a philosophical style of doing philosophy.

In the same interview, he expressed how he got acquainted with Wittgenstein.

> I graduated in 1951 – I was interested in the philosophy of that time. It was just when Wittgenstein's posthumous work was being published. His *Philosophical Investigations* came out in 1950, I think. And a lot of this sort of Wittgensteinian literature had been circulated before that – things that had not been published, but copies of which were in circulation informally, including the *Blue Book* and the *Brown Book*, as they were called. Well, like everybody else, I was interested in that philosophy; I was turned on and excited about it. … Oxford philosophy in the fifties was very clever, very sophisticated, and great fun to do because it was a shared skill and there were a lot of clever people around. In a way, that gave one a lot of insight. But the philosophical tone had to be kept down, muted English, dry, and that was a loss. That is why, in a way, I was drawn to the Wittgensteinian thing to some extent. Wittgenstein put much greater weight on the imaginative and the unpredictable aspects of philosophy (Williams 1983: 41).

Interpreting Wittgenstein and Nietzsche is a challenging task. Complexities, originality, and a non-traditional style of writing mark their thinking. Besides, there is much controversy among scholars about how to understand their ideas best.

The interpretation of Wittgenstein is one of the most disputed ones in philosophical academia. Some scholars interpret his later ideas (from the *Philosophical Investigations* (2009)) as supporting some kind of relativism, while others read in his texts a refutation of it. Besides, some readers interpret his ideas as a special kind of conventionalism, while others believe he is presenting a refutation of conventionalism. One influential work among those who side with a relativistic and sceptical reading is Saul Kripke (1982). Despite not being Wittgenstein scholars, Jean-François Lyotard (1984) and Richard Rorty (2010) also adopted some relativistic and conventionalist views in their interpretation of *Philosophical Investigations*. Another group of scholars, composed of Peter Hacker (2001), Gordon Baker (2008, with Hacker), Jacques Bouveresse (1973) and Marie McGinn (2013) among others, challenge the sceptical interpretation.

This chapter supports the idea that although many different philosophical backgrounds can be found in Williams' ideas, one can find a significant influence of the late Wittgenstein's approach to the philosophy behind his major books. *Many* philosophers influenced Williams in his studies of Wittgenstein: David Pears, Gilbert Ryle, Elizabeth Anscombe and Stanley Cavell (Queloz & Krishnan 2023: 04; Williams 1983). Williams incorporates many features of Wittgenstein's ideas, particularly his critique of objectivity, certainty, and the acknowledgement that language functions in different language games that keep a connection to reality through their embeddedness in different *forms of life*. He takes from the Austrian thinker the view that reality should be understood through the lenses of perspectivism, without relativism (if we have a traditional understanding of relativism). He calls this approach *relativism of distance*.

However, Williams adds an important new conceptual apparatus to his analysis. He borrows many philosophical concerns from Nietzsche's *toolbox*, building a richer approach useful for moral analysis. This addition allows him to move forward towards deciphering the local moral grammar embedded in different forms of life, deeply affected not only by human biological nature but also by psychology and history.

The best way to address how Nietzsche and Wittgenstein influenced Williams' ideas and how he combined them (producing a successful marriage) is to indicate the familiar themes and debates that serve as common ground among him, Nietzsche and Wittgenstein. The chapter first explores some of the fundamental contributions made by Bernard Williams to moral philosophy and how they offered new lenses for reappraising moral philosophy. The chapter will point out some general affinities between Wittgenstein's critique of relativism and its influence on Williams. Later, it analyses how the genealogical method inspired by Nietzsche's ideas allowed him to build a refined description of how different forms of life are constituted by history, psychology and human biology. Finally, the chapter will explain how this unusual *philosophical marriage* is possible and coherent and illuminates the interpretation of Williams' approach to ethics.

## II. The Fundamental Insight in Reappraising Modern Moral Philosophy: Nietzsche and Anscombe

Many commentators point out that Bernard Williams has continued and developed a philosophical path reopened by G.E.M. Anscombe's claim in the famous article 'Modern Moral Philosophy' that 'it is not profitable for us at present to do moral philosophy … until we have an adequate philosophy of psychology, in which we are conspicuously lacking' (1997: 26; see Clark 2001: 115 and Jenkins 2006: 2). Williams' and Anscombe's claim for the inclusion of a realistic psychology into moral analysis. According to Williams, a *realistic psychology* involves 'a perspective, and to some extent a tradition … in which what seems to demand more moral material makes sense in terms of what demands less' (Williams 1995b: 68).

Moreover, Williams also states a clear connection between genealogy and the interests of ethical naturalism, grounded on biology, ethology and the analysis of human nature. Mark Jenkins correctly points out that a '*realistic* psychology appears to line up pretty well with what Williams identifies elsewhere as "an appropriately suspicious rule of method," a rule that he believes probably comes as close as is possible to giving a general condition for naturalism' (Jenkins 2006: 162). This could be condensed in the slogan: 'Never explain the ethical in terms of something special to ethics if you can explain it in terms that apply to the non-ethical as well' (Williams 1995c: 204).

This aspect of this work is noticeable in some of his most famous writings. In *A Critique of Utilitarianism*, for example, Williams questions consequentialism's reliance on 'the notion of negative responsibility: that if I am ever responsible for anything, then I must be just as responsible for things that I allow or fail to prevent, as I am for things that I myself … bring about' (Williams 1973a: 95). The artificiality of blind faith in impartiality, derived from endorsing negative responsibility as a philosophical doctrine, contradicts certain features of human psychology. It sounds like taking God's point of view in a kind of *Immitatio Christi* behaviour that is entirely unnatural (Williams 2006: 145).

A second example of how a realistic psychology is a precondition of philosophical progress in ethics is evident in his belief that moral conflicts are neither systematically avoidable nor all soluble without remainder in the form of regret (Jenkins 2006: 179 and Williams 1973b, 1981a). Williams' acknowledgement of the philosophical requirement of realistic moral psychology is also influenced and inspired by Nietzsche's preference for explaining moral phenomena in terms of basic instincts instead of based on the wills of rationalised theories (Williams 1995b: 68). In this respect, Anscombe and Nietzsche share the same concern about modern moral philosophy (Nietzsche 1998: I, §13).

Furthermore, the third most salient mark of Nietzsche's influence on Williams' ideas is manifest in the idea that philosophy in general (and most obviously moral philosophy) is only possible or accurate as the historical sense it incorporates and expresses. Thus, 'a sense of history is not achievable through a mere factuality. It is by means of some kind of genealogy in its Nietzschean guise that mixes history, phenomenology, realistic psychology and conceptual interpretation' (Williams 1995b: 75, n 12). In other words, genealogy is a precious method for incorporating history, psychology, impulses and *forms of life* into philosophical analysis (Clark 2001: 105, 119).

History is an essential dimension of the genealogical approach. Williams' contributions to philosophy are also related to his works on the history of philosophy. This point is crucial in his appraisal of ethical theory. His book *Shame and Necessity* (1993) exemplifies this commitment to the importance of history for philosophy. He points out that

> those who see discontinuities between Greek and current conceptions of responsibility, agency, and emotion must be blind to the fact that the ancient conceptions have been not so much replaced as covered up, in most cases, by an insidious Kantian wallpaper of duty and obligation (Jenkins 2006: 3).

Besides, according to Williams, 'if we can understand the ethical concepts of the Greeks, we shall recognize them in ourselves' (Williams 1993: 10).

*Truth and Truthfulness* follows the same track, arguing that sometimes even an 'imaginary past' or 'hypothetical history reconstruction' of the past could be a valid method to illuminate our understanding of the present. The strategy he adopts in this book is to use a Nietzschean-inspired idea of vindicatory genealogy to deal with the following question: 'Can the notions of truth and truthfulness be intellectually stabilized in such a way that what we understand about truth and our chances of arriving at it can be made to fit with our need for truthfulness' (Williams 2002: 3). Some of his most influential and insightful contributions to ethical theory, such as his critique of *morality*, adopt a similar approach.

Williams differentiates his own employment of the genealogical method in *Truth and Truthfulness: An Essay in Genealogy* from Nietzsche's in *On the Genealogy of Morality*. The very subtitle *An Essay in Genealogy* relates to Nietzsche's focus on this historical method (Nietzsche 1998: Preface, §§5–6; Williams 2002). However, Williams' conception of genealogy, although considerably indebted to Nietzsche's own, differs in two important ways.[1] The first relates to the character of Williams' genealogical picture as avowedly fictional. The second is linked to the non-full endorsement of the character of Nietzsche's picture, especially the Nietzschean story about the slave revolt and the subsequent revaluation of values and whether it represents fact, fiction or some composite of the two. However, on this matter, as stressed by Jenkins (2006: 163), neither Nietzsche nor Hegel serves as Williams' archetype, whether for genealogy, realistic psychology or ethical naturalism. Thucydides is his more direct model.

Williams' praise of Thucydides is twofold: On one hand, he admires his tragic sensibility. On the other hand, his certain impartiality, since, for Williams, 'the psychology he deploys in his explanations is not in the service of his ethical beliefs' (Williams 1993: 161). In this sense, his attitude is more in line with Williams' genealogical project than the over-ethicised moral psychologies of Plato and Aristotle, which he uses as contrasts. For Williams,

> [a] non-moralized, or less-moralized, psychology uses the categories of meaning, reasons, and value, but leaves it open, or even problematical, in what way moral reasons and ethical values fit with other motives and desires, how far they express those other motives, and how far they are in conflict with them (Williams 1995c: 202).

History provides few examples of psychology so practised and so few examples of successful naturalism. Besides Thucydides, Williams singles out Sophocles and Freud as other rare examples of realist psychologists and successful naturalists who are helpful for sound genealogy and explaining his views on shame and necessity. As Williams puts it:

> [Moral philosophy] tries to withdraw our ethical interest from both chance and necessity, except inasmuch as necessity sets the parameters of effective action. … When, in addition, morality itself is disconnected historically and psychologically from the rest of life, as it often is by moral philosophy … then necessity and chance and the bad news they bring with them are deliberately excluded (Williams 1996: 48).

[1] For differences, see Leiter 2022. For affinities, see Owen 2001 and Glock 2006.

## III. Some Philosophical Achievements or Contributions – The Critique of *Morality*

Williams' critique of *morality* is one of his most important philosophical achievements. Like Anscombe before him, he argues that the analysts' accurate and careful focus on such words as 'ought', 'right', and 'good' has come, in moral theory, to give those words (when used in their alleged 'special moral sense') an air of authority which they could only earn against a moral and Christian world-view that is nowadays largely missing. For this reason, modern moral theory, similar to Nietzsche's idea that morality can 'work' without religious belief, is an illusion that shows a lack of historical sense. However, 'God is dead', and this changes the context in which traditional morality could make a better-fitted sense (Anscombe 1958: 30; Queloz & Cueni 2019; Williams 1985: 38).

Describing these features of modern morality criticised by Nietzsche about its historicity and deep roots in religious beliefs is complex and connects many values and philosophical, psychological, and historical assumptions. Most of his work is devoted to carefully describing them and their interconnections. Williams' most straightforward, and perhaps the definitive, summary of what the 'morality system' comes to can be found in the last chapter of *Ethics and the Limits of Philosophy* (1985).

In this book, Williams points out that many modern moral problems would only make sense if understood internally in a system he technically describes as *morality* (1985). For him, ethics is not a synonym of *morality*, rather, morality is a particular conception of ethical life that excludes the possibility of authentic ethical conflicts. Contrary to the *morality* system aspirations, however, rational arguments do not always eliminate ethical conflicts. He argues, '[i]t is surely falsifying of moral thought to represent its logic as demanding that in a conflict … one of the conflicting oughts must be totally rejected on the grounds that it did not actually apply' (1973a: 183–84; also 1972). The *morality* system historically produces this view of moral problems, and two of the most important philosophical constructors are Utilitarianism and Kantianism.

For Williams, utilitarianism, consequentialism, and deontological Kantianism, though opposite on normative grounds, are good examples of the system of *morality* (Williams 1981d: 4–5). He believes that any systematic account of morals that fails to acknowledge the significant role emotions (and realist psychology) play in our ideas of good lives and right actions, and the a-historical assumptions embedded in it, inevitably falsifies that account.

*Morality* is rooted in what he calls 'the absolute conception of the world', an epistemological perspective in philosophy, science and ethics that leads to a mistaken picture of our understanding in these fields. The absolute conception is based on what he sometimes calls the *absolute conception of reality*. It holds that 'science has some chance of being more or less what it seems, a systematized theoretical account of how the world really is, while ethical thought has no chance of being everything it seems' (Williams 1985: 135). The *absolute conception* involves robust realism ('knowledge of a reality that exists independently of that knowledge') or the 'knowledge of what is there *anyway*' (Williams 1978: 64). It is a conception 'to the maximum degree independent of our perspective and its peculiarities' (Williams 1985: 139).

Williams first developed the *absolute conception of the world* by explicating Descartes' views on the nature of knowledge and the possibility of certainty (Williams 1983: 344). Here, the influence of the later Wittgensteinian critique of mentalism is quite evident. The Williamsian critique of Descartes parallels the *Philosophical Investigations*' critique of the many significant failures of the *Tractatus* (see Hacker 2021: 279–83 and Kenny 1973). The later Wittgenstein's critique of the orthodox mentalism (and cartesian absolute conception of the world) also influenced Williams' view on relativism and foundationalism. Relativism is the counterpart of the absolute conception of the world difficulties in dealing with ethics.

In sum, the relationship between the concept of morality in Williams' theory and the absolute conception of the world is characterised by a fundamental critique of universal moral laws. While an absolute conception of the world seeks to establish objective and unchanging epistemic principles, when transplanted to morals it leads to a defence of immutable ethical principles. Williams advocates for a more nuanced understanding of morals that is rooted in personal identity, emotional experiences, and the particular contexts of moral life. This perspective highlights the limitations of absolute moral frameworks (which he describes as morality) in accounting for the richness and complexity of human moral experience.

## IV. Williams as a Left Wittgensteinian

In 'Pluralism, Community and Left Wittgensteinianism', Williams notices that 'despite the efforts of some of his followers, the tendency of Wittgenstein's influence has been distinctly conservative' (2005b: 29). He strongly criticises it (even though there is some controversy concerning his first essays on the subject; see Mulhall: 2015; Queloz: 2021). For him, there is an orthodox and very influential reading of Wittgenstein and the *Philosophical Investigations*, which he rejects due to its holism and its over-emphasis in roots and in an organic view of society (Williams 2005b: 34–35). This interpretation sometimes converges into a conventionalist understanding of the conditions of meaning a mere shared practice, which Williams also rejects. He argues that:

> for those who dislike biological analogies, much the same point may be put in terms of consensus. In this picture of things, to understand anything is to share in understanding, and nothing sustains understanding or knowledge except a shared social practice (Williams 2005b: 34–35).

A corollary of this interpretation is also linked to a non-acceptable kind of relativism (traditional or vulgar) with which many scholars mistakenly associate Wittgenstein. According to it, ethical concepts can only be evaluated from a perspective based on preferences. Thus, vulgar relativism leads to the belief that incommensurability is unavoidable and the impossibility of philosophical scrutiny on them (Williams 2005b: 35). However, this view impoverishes the ethical analysis that could be extracted from Wittgenstein's texts. This situation also leads to a contradiction, where the very idea of philosophical criticism loses grip and determinacy. In Williams' words:

> It is at this point that a certain paradox in the view begins to emerge. If all social phenomena equally are just whatever they are, merely part of this interwoven net of practices, then all of them equally will be opaque to philosophical criticism. But the Wittgensteinian philosopher is himself criticizing something, if only the practices of ethical theorists and other philosophers who misunderstand the proper nature of our thought (2005b: 35).[2]

This is a puzzling conclusion. According to it, making a philosophical critique would be nonsense and at odds with Wittgenstein's philosophical practice. Notwithstanding, this conclusion serves the purpose of 'social philosophers of a conservative tendency who have taken up Wittgensteinian ideas in order to justify their conservatism' (Williams 2005b: 35). However, here comes the paradox: 'For they will wish to criticize not just the misconceptions of philosophy, but the aspirations of radicals, and there is a paradox in their doing so on the basis of such a philosophy' (Williams 2005b: 36). Besides, 'according to this philosophy itself, all that philosophy can do is to remind us how our ethical ideas are rooted in our ethical practice' (2005b: 36).

This conclusion is wrong since 'part of our ethical practice consists precisely in this, that people have found in it resources with which to criticize their society. Practice is not just the practice of practice, so to speak, but also the practice of criticism' (Williams 2005b: 36).[3] Thus, we cannot explain our ethics in terms of foundationalist descriptions of shared conventional practices. In other words, if we reject orthodox foundationalism, we must acknowledge that a central feature of our history and self-understanding is the consciousness that our ethical concepts and thoughts have a history and are embedded in a form of life that differs from other ancient societies. Besides, our modern society is conscious of that fact.

Again, the central failure of conservative anti-foundationalists is not rooted in Wittgenstein's ideas but in many Wittgensteinians' flawed and reductionist interpretations of him. The expressions 'we' and 'our' basically represent not us as against others but an 'us' that embraces anybody with whom we could intelligibly hold a conversation. The conservatives misrepresent the nature of these concepts.

[2] See also Queloz & Krishnan 2023 & Ackeren & Qualoz 2025.
[3] Ronald Dworkin has also emphasised this point (2011, and 1996: 87–139).

For Williams,

> we cannot simply take this idea over into ethical and social thought, if 'our' way of life is to be that you and I live and find particular meaning in *our* lives; since that form of life is precisely not the form of life of other human beings who have lived within some ethical system or other (Williams 2005b: 36).

For this reason, '[i]t is, for one thing, the life of a distinctively modern society, and that is very different from other lives that have been lived, and no doubt from other lives that will be lived in the future' (Williams 2005b: 36). In other words, the kind of life 'we' live differs and marks the way 'we' understand ourselves and other ethical systems.

There is a double dimension of this understanding of the internal perspective (the '*we* perspective') for our understanding of ethical concepts. One is internal, typically adopted by anthropologists, and another is external and comparative. In this sense, it extrapolates the internal dimension. Moreover, it is the case that our own ethical ideas come from very various sources. This leads to the conclusion that '*our* perspective' is always somehow historical and contextualised without being relativistic in its traditional sense (Williams 2005b: 36).

Williams' conclusions acknowledge that neither traditional relativism nor foundationalism are the unavoidable alternatives when facing ethical values. Thus, in one specific sense, foundationalism is also necessary for social critique. For the *Williamsian interpretation of Wittgenstein*, 'what we are left with, if we reject foundationalism, is not an inactive or functionalist conservatism that has to take existing ethical ideas as they stand'. His conclusion goes in the opposite direction:

> On the contrary, once the resultant picture of ethical thought without foundationalism is made historically and socially realistic, in particular, by registering in it the categories of modernity, it provides a possibility of deploying some parts of it against others and of reinterpreting what is ethically significant, so as to give a critique of existing institutions, conceptions, prejudices, and powers (Williams 2005b: 37).

This means that the correct understanding of the historicity of 'our' modern anti-foundationalism requires *us* to compare and contrast concepts, prejudices, institutions and powers in order to allow the critique of what is valuable in ethics.

Williams finds in Wittgenstein's ideas a new philosophical stance that rejects both relativism and cartesian orthodoxy, the simplistic dualism between foundationalism and non-foundationalism. This is precisely what he describes as *Left Wittgensteinianism*. He endorses this philosophical stance and combines it with Nietzsche's genealogical approach, fostering an unexpected marriage between these thinkers.

For Williams, the causes of the misinterpreting of Wittgenstein are related to the philosophical opportunity to combine his ideas with a Nietzschean approach. The misreading of Wittgenstein (even some versions of Left Wittgensteinianism) resides in the fact that his philosophy primarily focused on abstract language problems and not on more historically situated problems concerning contemporary morals. Thus, most of Wittgenstein's followers refused to think in concrete terms about the extent of 'we'. However, there are differences here that matter.

On political and ethical matters of pluralism and community, it is crucial to understand the specific nature of the 'we' and be suspicious of the abstract, non-situated perspective (what Thomas Nagel calls a view from nowhere in 1989). For this reason,

> once a realistic view of communities is applied, and the categories that we need to understand anyone who is intelligible at all are distinguished from those of more local significance, we can follow Wittgenstein to the extent of not looking for a new foundationalism, but still leave room for a critique of what some of 'us' do in terms of our understanding of a wider 'we' (Williams 2005b: 37).

Williams points to the limitations of Wittgenstein's toolbox to deal with the questions that involve who is to count as 'we'. This is where Nietzsche's psychological, naturalistic and historical approach, especially some kind of genealogical-inspired analysis, comes into play. In other words, Williams accepts the basic Wittgensteinian ideas for rejecting foundationalism but also recognises that there is possibility for criticism of what some of us do in terms of a wider 'we'. How is that possible? Before addressing this question, it is helpful to deepen the analysis of the Wittgensteinian presence in Williams' conception of relativism.

In another essay called 'Wittgenstein and Idealism' (1981c; see Williams 1981a),[4] Williams stresses that

> I take it that Wittgenstein was not very interested … in language in the narrow sense, and that he characteristically uses the term 'language' in a very extensive way, to embrace world-view rather than to stand in narrow and explanatory contradistinction to it. Hence his notoriously generous use of the expression 'language-game'; hence also, in the converse direction as it were, the tendency to use *form of life* to refer to some quite modest linguistic practice (Williams 1981c and 1981a).

Again, Wittgenstein's presentation of his own ideas leads interpreters to take his philosophical concerns as limited to describing the language in a very narrow and technical sense. However, this approach is misleading and excessively narrow. Williams points this out by comparing it with excerpts in which Wittgenstein's words suggest a broader meaning for some of his key categories (Williams 1981c: 155; see Wittgenstein 1972: 256, 96; Wittgenstein 2007: 388, 378, 380, 387; and Wittgenstein 2009).

However, a non-reductionist reading supports the idea that different world pictures are not inaccessible to one another. For Williams, this is the third alternative between relativism and non-relativism:

> Those who had one picture might come to see the point (in terms of interests, etc.) of another picture, and also perhaps come to understand why those who had it, did

[4] Mulhal (2015: 331) accused Williams of unjustly attacking Peter Winch (1958) and Peter Hacker's first edition of *Insight and Illusion* (1972), later revised (3rd edn 1986) in this 1981 text. However, this does not change my main argument. See also Queloz 2021.

> so. In that light, they could reflect also on their own world-picture, and understand, perhaps, something of why they had it (Williams 1981c: 15556; see Wittgenstein 1972: 94–95, 298, 559, 609, 610, 612; Wittgenstein 1978: 7; Wittgenstein 2005: 55 and Wittgenstein 2009: 50).

None of this yet implies anything about the evaluative comparability of different world pictures.

Certainly, some unclear points in Wittgenstein's ideas affected some disputed interpretations of his work. One of the most salient aspects of these contested interpretations is linked to understanding the association of *Philosophical Investigations* to some kind of relativism. It is revealing that Williams himself was often accused of defending unclear ideas about his own 'relativism of distance' since it is deeply indebted to Wittgenstein's insights that were also criticised for the same reason.

Understanding Williams' account of Wittgenstein may help us to dissolve some of these ambiguities (Williams 1981c: 159). He raises the question of whether 'Wittgenstein is really thinking at all in terms of actual groups of human beings whose activities we might want to understand and explain'. Williams answers it straightforwardly: 'I think the answer to that is basically "no"; we are not concerned so much with the epistemology of differing world-views, still less with the methodology of the social sciences, as with ways of exploring our world-view' (1981c: 159). Instead, he believes, 'we are concerned with the imagination … to make a different practice a more familiar idea to us, and hence to make us more conscious of the practice we have' (1981c: 159).

This point is crucial since, for Williams, Wittgenstein was neither interested in checking whether the alternatives are not the sort of socially actual alternatives, relativistically inaccessible or not, nor whether they are offered as possible objects of any kind of explanation. In other words,

> The imagined alternatives are not alternatives *to* us; they are alternatives *for* us, markers of how far we might go and still remain, within our world – a world leaving which would not mean that we saw something different, but just that we ceased to see (Williams 1981c: 160).

Williams stresses in many passages that it is misleading to imagine that the 'we' of Wittgenstein's remarks often look like the 'we' of our group as contrasted with other human groups. For him,

> Such a 'we' is not his prime concern, and even if one grants such views as the 'justified assertion' doctrine, the determination of meaning by social practice and so on, all of that leaves it open, how much humanity *shares* in the way of rational practice. Nor is it just a question of a final relativization of 'we' to humanity. We cannot exclude the possibility of other language-using creatures whose picture of the world might be accessible to us (Williams 1981c: 160).

In other words, the statement that there is no possible communication among people living in non-radically different forms of life is false.

Of course, there might be limits to the possibility of understanding among beings situated in different contexts. However, for Williams and for the Williamsian Wittgenstein, '[i] t must … be an empirical question what degree of conceptual isolation is represented by what groups in the universe – groups *with* which we would be in the universe' (1981c: 160). For this reason, '[i]f they are groups with which "we" are in the universe, and "we" can understand that fact (namely, that they are groups with a language, etc.), then they also *belong* to "we"' (1981c: 161). But of course, there are limits, since 'if a lion could speak, we could not understand it' (Wittgenstein 2009: 22). In this case, lions and humans would be living in entirely different forms of lives.

The possibility of comparing *us* (the 'we') with others and understanding how some hinge concepts (Moyal-Sharrock & Sandis 2022) depend on different contexts and forms of life transformed by history. Understanding other values and societies from a perspectivist view is possible if we also understand the background assumptions shared by other communities. This would not mechanically lead to a vulgar (conventionalist) relativism, where no comparison is possible, but rather to the possibility of some knowledge based on constructive perspectivism without (naïve) relativism. Alternatively, in Williamsian words, adopting some relativism of distance.

The major arguments presented by Bernard Williams on relativism can be found in two articles: 'The Need to Be Sceptical' and 'The Truth in Relativism' (2016b and 1981e), and his most important book, *Ethics and the Limits of Philosophy* (1985). In 'The Need to Be Sceptical' (2016b: 311–18), Williams points out that the system of morality contains a severe limitation for a sound understanding of the current language of morals. As mentioned, this kind of moral philosophy was fully developed in theories that assume some variant of *impartial observer* (as suggested by Adam Smith) or a detached conception of rationality such as that found in Kantian or Benthamite traditions (2016b: 314). This conception shows the philosophical need to explain how the 'we' functions. He says:

> The difficulty is to know, in the ethical case, who 'we' are, whose practices and form of life are in question. When Wittgenstein spoke of mathematics resting, in the end, not on any absolute foundations, but only on how 'we' go on, the 'we' would seem naturally to embrace all those who share an understanding of mathematics (Williams 2016b: 314).

However, here is the difficulty of this analysis since *thick* ethical concepts (Williams 1985: 130) 'are not typically shared by everyone, and the concepts belonging to other cultures that we (that is to say, we here) may come to understand, we by no means necessarily share with them' (Williams 2016b: 314).

Here, the contrast between classical universalism (Kantian or Utilitarian version) and classical relativism (conventionalist) is at stake, and Williams is looking for the possibility of overcoming them. He continues: 'If the "we" to which the Wittgensteinian account speaks includes all humanity, then it still needs to explain how it is that some of us structure our ethical life with concepts that are unknown, strange or even repellent to others' (2016b: 314). He explicitly claims against both universalism and the correspondent conception of moral objectivity. Besides

> If, on the other hand, the 'we' that is relevant is that of a real community, a set of people whose ethical language and practices have a genuine social identity, then this philosophy still has to tell us how we can pick up and understand the ethical concepts of others (as to some extent we clearly can) and yet reject those concepts. Equally, it has to tell us how we can come to embrace new ethical concepts (Williams 2016b:315).

Here, Williams criticises conventionalist relativism.

This is the stage in which moral relativism is located. Generally speaking, relativism is understood as the doctrine that knowledge, truth, and morality exist in relation to culture, society, or historical context, and are not absolute. However, the uses of the concept of relativism in Williams is not always easy to grasp and demands some qualifications. He preliminary distinguishes what he calls *vulgar relativism*, which is the target of his criticism, from the *relativism of distance*, that he endorses.

Vulgar relativism is criticised in *Morality* (1972). It is a philosophical position that can be captured in two statements thought to be obviously inconsistent. The first is 'that *right* means (can only be coherently understood as meaning) *right for a given society*; The second is that (therefore) it is wrong for people in one society to condemn, interfere with, etc., the values of another society' (Williams 1972: 20). The statement that it is universally *wrong* seems contradictory with the very idea of relativism present in the first statement. As Jenkins correctly points out, describing ethical differences among cultures through ethical relativism does not provide a valid basis for promoting ethical relativism as a universal principle of tolerance (Jenkins 2006: 142).

Furthermore, relativism can result from some kind of disagreement. Therefore, '[i]f we reflect on disagreements of a certain kind and come to the conclusion that they cannot be objectively settled, we may react by adopting some form of relativism' (Williams 1985: 136). Relativism is not peculiar to ethics since it can also be found in many areas of philosophy of science. Thus, '[i] ts aim is to take views, outlooks, or beliefs that apparently conflict and treat them in such a way that they do not conflict: each of them turns out to be acceptable in its own place. The problem is to find a way of doing this, in particular by finding for each belief or outlook something that will be its own place' (Williams 1985: 136).

Besides, relativism has an aim. It is not a mere descriptive tool. Thus, relativism aims to explain away a conflict, and this involves two tasks. It has to say why there is no conflict and also why it looked as if there were one (the disguise) (Williams 1985: 136). Williams criticises standard versions of relativism for being implausible.

Relational relativism is *a more fruitful kind of relativism*, which introduces a compatible structure and then has to say what disguised it (Macedo Jr 2020: 97–98). In this approach,

> we should ask what happens if we start by conceding that two beliefs or outlooks do indeed conflict and are genuinely exclusive. The problem will then be to find a sense in which each may still be acceptable in its place (Williams 1985: 157).

Williams tackles this challenge in the following way. For him, one idea that requires us to think more broadly about relativism is *incommensurability*. Different scientific theories will not straightforwardly contradict one another. However, they do exclude one another. You cannot work within both of them (1985: 158).

However, this situation raises an important question about the relationship among different cultures that needs to be answered. How is relativism possible if two cultures, outlooks, or ways of life exclude one another? Not instantly, he would reply, since 'someone who has certain dispositions and expectations as a member of one culture will often be unwilling, when confronted with an alternative way of life, to do what is done in the other culture' (Williams 1985: 158). Again, it is relevant to remember that for Williams, the relationships between these cultures and outlooks are very much like Wittgenstein's thread metaphor (Wittgenstein 2009: para 67).

For this reason, 'the dispositions and reactions that are exercised within one culture are not merely diverted or shown to be inappropriate by the fact that its members are presented with the behaviour of another culture' (Williams 1985: 158). Treating these matters as if they always involved two clearly self-contained cultures is artificial. Moreover, the relationships among

> cultures, subcultures, fragments of cultures, constantly meet one another and exchange and modify practices and attitudes. Social practices could never come forward with a certificate saying that they belonged to a genuinely different culture, so that they were guaranteed immunity to alien judgments and reactions' (Williams 1985: 158).

These traditional forms of relativism should be abandoned.

Nevertheless, this still does not make all kinds of relativism implausible. The role played by reflection is a central feature in understanding how relativism can be plausible. For Williams,

> the fact that people can and must react when they are confronted with another culture and do so by *applying their existing notions* – also by *reflecting on them* – seems to show that the ethical thought of a given culture can always stretch beyond its boundaries. It is important that this is a point about the content or aspirations of ethical thought, not about its objectivity (Williams 1985: 159).

*Objectivity is not a requirement for moral thought* (in general), even though it might be considered a central feature of the system of *morality*. However, even if objectivity does not imply a relativistic attitude, it is not irrelevant or unresponsive to it. Thus, for Williams, it is a grave mistake to think that believing in a relativistic view requires you to be equally well disposed to everyone else's ethical beliefs (1985: 160).

The point in Williams' relativism is that we must not simply draw a line between ourselves and others. Instead, we should, in a Wittgensteinian way, recognise that others are at varying distances from us. In other words, 'we must also see that our reactions and relations to other groups are themselves part of our ethical life, and we should understand these reactions more realistically in terms of the practices and sentiments that help to shape our life' (1985: 160). Therefore, some disagreements and divergences matter more than others and 'above all, it matters whether the contrast of our outlook with another is one that makes a difference, whether a question has to be resolved about what life is going to be lived by one group or the other' (Williams 1985: 160).

Wittgenstein's thread metaphor is at play once again (2009: 67). According to it, the insulation of different sets of practices and beliefs is not absolute. The standards function as a thread made of many different fibres, intertwined and setting family resemblances patterns. These different relationships among these practices should be analysed as *family resemblances* rather than distinguished by a rigid divide. This is why he introduces the distinction between *real* and *notional confrontations* (Williams 1985: 160).

Williams calls this kind of relativism the *relativism of distance* (1985: 162). There is room for it in a *reflective ethical outlook*. This kind of relativism is connected to ethical outlooks rather than particular practices, and it is to large-scale systems or bodies of beliefs and attitudes that have to be applied. The relativistic suspension of ethical judgment attached to this kind of relativism requires conceiving the society in question as a whole.

Furthermore, Williams points out that thoughts about the past and the future raise different problems because we are caused by one and cause the other. Moreover, the past and our understanding of it are especially related to the *reflectiveness* that starts these problems. The growth of reflective consciousness has not always been positive. The phenomenon of self-consciousness, together with the institutions and processes that support it, constitutes one reason why past forms of life are not a real option for the present.

Finally, it is essential to settle the role of reflection itself and its relation to ethical knowledge. Williams says that, in a way, reflection might destroy knowledge because thick ethical concepts that were used in a less reflective state might be driven from use by reflection, while the more abstract and general ethical thoughts that would probably take their place would not satisfy the conditions of propositional knowledge. For Williams, 'it is an important feature of modern science that it contributes to explaining how creatures with our origins and characteristics can understand a world with properties that this same science ascribes to the world' (1985: 139–40).

Nevertheless, this important explanatory feature Williams finds conspicuously absent in ethics (1985: 138). In such cases,

> it is the explanation of the perspectival perceptions that enables us, when we come to reflect on them, to place them in relation to the perceptions of other people and other creatures. … The question is whether we can find an ethical analogy to that. Here, we

> have to go outside local judgments to a reflective or second-order account of them, and here, the analogy gives out (Williams 1985: 150).

Thus, although there may be human convergence upon the belief that torturing cats for fun is wrong, in Williams' view, such convergence will not be explained by 'how things (anyway) are' (1985: 139). This is not a matter of plain fact (to use Dworkin's concept – 1986: 06–14). Williams writes, '[m]y aim in introducing the notion of the absolute conception was precisely to get around the point that one cannot describe the world' (1985: 142)

> without describing it. … The idea was that when we reflect on our conceptualization of the world, we might be able to recognize from inside it that some of our concepts and ways of representing the world are more dependent than others on our own perspective, our peculiar and local ways of apprehending things. In contrast, we might be able to identify some concepts and styles of representation which are minimally dependent on our own (Williams 2006: 482).

However, this prospect leaves Williams far from sanguine:

> The project of giving to ethical life an objective and determinate grounding in considerations about human nature is not, in my view, very likely to succeed. But it is at any rate a comprehensible project, and I believe it represents the only intelligible form of ethical objectivity at the reflective level (1985: 153).

As far as determining that nature goes, he believes the most natural and promising field for this kind of inquiry involves the virtues. Such talk of virtues leads naturally to talk of Aristotle's theory of virtues and Anscombe's presence in his thinking.

## V. Conclusions

Williams was clearly inspired by Nietzschean and Wittgensteinian ideas and their philosophical methodologies, even if tracking such influences is not always easy. One can find some of these marks in Williams' Left-Wittgensteinian approach to relativism, the partial localism of language games, and their relevance in different *forms of life*. Wittgenstein's influence is also present in Williams' critique of vulgar relativism and the understanding of the concept of objectivity and certainty. Williams' relativism of distance owes a lot to Wittgenstein's perspectivism without relativism, even though the comparison may sound puzzling at first sight. Perspectivism means that the only possible approach to reality and morals depends on some context formed by a language game and embedded in a settled form of life. He was also significantly influenced by Wittgenstein's conception of philosophical practice (Glock 1996: 294; Queloz & Krishnan 2023: 3).

Wittgenstein's very abstract use of the concept of form of life, with many dimensions and elements (natural, psychological and historical), has never been addressed deeply or in more contextualised ways. His immediate philosophical concerns were more focused on the elements of the grammar of different language games than on the accurate description of the elements themselves. Nevertheless, his general description of the possibility of perspectivism without relativism is crucial for understanding Williamsian relativism of distance.

Williams' debts to Nietzsche are neither easier to track nor less controversial (Clark 2001: 100; Leiter 2022: 31). The Nietzschean-like genealogy applied by Williams serves his purpose of incorporating history and psychology into the very abstract concept of form of life. Williams' vindicatory genealogy, sometimes fictional, sometimes entirely historical, serves his intentions to *remember* (or put a *reminder*) that our own 'we' is not the only one, universal, a-historical, or a-contextual or transcendental. Combined with historical comparisons (such as with the Greeks, Thucydides, Neanderthal men, or the medieval Samurais), fictional genealogies serve the same comparative purpose. It offers new perspectives to address reality and normativity.

Williamsian creative use of Wittgensteinian and Nietzschean traditions is not of a blind follower. Moreover, in so doing, he shows more fidelity to both Wittgenstein's and Nietzsche's philosophical practices and essential insights. The marriage he makes possible between these two apparently unreconcilable or unmarriageable traditions is proof of his genius as a contemporary philosopher.

## Bibliography

Altham, JEJ & Ross, H (eds) (1995) *World, Mind, and Ethics: Essays on the Ethical Philosophy of Bernard Williams*, with 'Replies' by Bernard Williams (Cambridge, Cambridge University Press).

Anscombe, GEM (1958) 'Modern Moral Philosophy' *Philosophy* 33, no 124.

—— (1997) 'Modern Moral Philosophy' in R Crisp & M Slote (eds), *Virtue Ethics* (Oxford, Oxford University Press).

Baker, GP & Hacker, PMS (2008) *Wittgenstein: Understanding and Meaning: Volume 1 of an Analytical Commentary on the Philosophical Investigations, Part I: Essays*, 2nd edn (London, Wiley-Blackwell).

Bouveresse, J (1973) *Wittgenstein: La rime et la raison. Science, éthique et esthétique* (Paris, Éditions de Minuit).

Clark, M (2001) 'On the Rejection of Morality: Bernard Williams's Debt to Nietzsche' in R Schacht (ed), *Nietzsche's Postmoralism* (Cambridge, Cambridge University Press).

Dworkin, R (1986) *Law's Empire* (Cambridge, Harvard University Press).

—— (1996) 'Objectivity and Truth: You'd Better Believe It' 25 2 *Philosophy and Public Affairs* 87.

—— (2011) *Justice for Hedgehogs* (Cambridge, Massachusetts, Harvard University Press).

Glock, H (1996) *A Wittgenstein Dictionary* (Oxford, Blackwell).

—— (2006) 'Wittgenstein and History' in A Pichler & S Saatela (eds), *Wittgenstein: The Philosopher and His Works* (Frankfurt, Ontos).

Hacker, PMS (2001) 'On Misunderstanding Wittgenstein: Kripke's Private-Language Argument' in PMS Hacker (ed), *Wittgenstein: Connections and Controversies* (Oxford, Oxford University Press).

—— (2021) *Insight and Illusion: Themes in the Philosophy of Wittgenstein*, 3rd edn (London, Anthem Press) [1st edn (1972)].
Jenkins, M (2006) *Bernard Williams* (London, Routledge).
Kenny, A (1973) *Cartesian Privacy in The Anatomy of the Soul: Historical Essays in the Philosophy of Mind* (London, Basil Blackwell).
Kripke, S (1982) *Wittgenstein on Rules and Private Language: An Elementary Exposition* (Cambridge, Massachusetts, Harvard University Press).
Leiter, B (2022) 'Bernard Williams's Debt to Nietzsche: Real or Illusory' in A Szigeti & M Talbert (eds), *Morality and Agency: Themes from Bernard Williams* (Oxford, Oxford University Press).
Lyotard, JF (1984) *The Postmodern Condition: A Report on Knowledge*, translated by G Bennington and B Massumi (Minneapolis, University of Minnesota Press).
Macedo Jr, RP (2020) 'Is Bernard Williams' Distance Relativism Really Defeated by Heidi Hurd's Attack on Perspectivalism?' 14 *Problema. Anuario de Filosofía y Teoría del Derecho* 79.
McGinn, M (2013) *The Routledge Guidebook to Wittgenstein's Philosophical Investigations* (London, Routledge).
Moyal-Sharrock, D & Sandis, C (eds) (2022) *Philosophical Perspectives on Moral Certainty.* (London, Routledge).
Mulhall, S (2015) '"Hopelessly Strange": Bernard Williams's Portrait of Wittgenstein as a Transcendental Idealist' in S Gardner & M Grist (eds), *The Transcendental Turn* (Oxford, Oxford University Press).
Nagel, T (1989) *The View from Nowhere* (Oxford, Oxford University Press).
Nietzsche, F (1998) *On the Genealogy of Morality*, translated by M Clark and AJ Swensen (Indianapolis and Cambridge, Hackett).
Owen, D (2001) 'Wittgenstein and Genealogy' 2 (2) *Nordic Journal of Philosophy* 5.
Queloz, M (2021) 'Left Wittgensteinianism' 29 4 *European Journal of Philosophy* 758.
Queloz, M & Cueni, D (2019) 'Nietzsche as a Critic of Genealogical Debunking: Making Room for Naturalism without Subversion' 102 3 *The Monist* 277.
Queloz, M & Krishnan, N (2023) 'Williams's Debt to Wittgenstein' in MV Ackeren & M Queloz (eds), *Making Sense of the Past: Bernard Williams and the History of Philosophy* (Oxford, Oxford University Press), available at http://dx.doi.org/10.2139/ssrn.4541123
Rorty, R (2010) 'Wittgenstein and the Linguistic Turn' in A Ahmed (ed), *Wittgenstein's Philosophical Investigations: A Critical Guide* (Cambridge, Cambridge University Press).
Williams, B (1972). *Morality: An Introduction to Ethics* (Cambridge, Cambridge University Press).
—— (1973a) *Problems of the Self* (Cambridge, Cambridge University Press).
—— (1973b) 'Ethical Consistency' in B Williams, *Problems of the Self* (Cambridge, Cambridge University Press).
—— (1978) *Descartes – The Project of Pure Inquiry* (London, Pelican Books).
—— (1981a) *Moral Luck* (Cambridge, Cambridge University Press).
—— (1981b) 'The Truth in Relativism' in B Williams, *Moral Luck* (Cambridge, Cambridge University Press).
—— (1981c) 'Wittgenstein and Idealism' in B Williams, *Moral Luck* (Cambridge, Cambridge University Press).
—— (1981d) 'Persons, Character and Morality' in B Williams, *Moral Luck* (Cambridge, Cambridge University Press).

—— (1981e) 'The Truth in Relativism' in B Williams, *Moral Luck* (Cambridge, Cambridge University Press).
—— (1983) 'The Uses of Philosophy: An Interview with Bernard Williams'. Interview by Donald McDonald. The Center Magazine, Issue November/December 40–49.
—— (1985) *Ethics and the Limits of Philosophy* (Cambridge, Massachusetts, Harvard University Press).
—— (1993) *Shame and Necessity* (Berkeley, University of California Press).
—— (1995a) *Making Sense of Humanity* (Cambridge, Cambridge University Press).
—— (1995b) 'Nietzsche's Minimalist Moral Philosophy' in B Williams, *Making Sense of Humanity* (Cambridge, Cambridge University Press).
—— (1995c) 'Replies' in JEJ Altham & H Ross (eds), *World, Mind, and Ethics: Essays on the Ethical Philosophy of Bernard Williams*, with 'Replies' by Bernard Williams (Cambridge, Cambridge University Press).
—— (1996) 'The Women of Trachis: Fictions, Pessimism, Ethics' in RB Louden & P Schollmeier (eds), *The Greeks and Us: Essays in Honor of Arthur W. H. Adkins* (Chicago, University of Chicago Press).
—— (2002) *Truth and Truthfulness: An Essay in Genealogy* (Princeton, Princeton University Press).
—— (2005a) *In the Beginning Was the Deed: Realism and Moralism in Political Argument* (G Hawthorn, ed) (Princeton, Princeton University Press).
—— (2005b) 'Pluralism, Community and Left Wittgensteinianism' in B Williams, *In the Beginning Was the Deed: Realism and Moralism in Political Argument* (G Hawthorn, ed) (Princeton, Princeton University Press).
—— (2006) *Philosophy as a Humanistic Discipline* (AW Moore, ed) (Princeton, Princeton University Press).
—— (2016a) *Essays and Reviews: 1959-2002* (Princeton, Princeton University Press).
—— (2016b) 'The Need to Be Sceptical' in B Williams, *Essays and Reviews: 1959-2002* (Princeton, Princeton University Press).
Winch, P (1958) *The Idea of a Social Science and its Relation to Philosophy* (London, Routledge).
Wittgenstein, L (1972) *On Certainty* (New York, Harper).
—— (1978) *Philosophical Remarks* (London, Wiley-Blackwell).
—— (2005) *Philosophical Grammar* (Berkeley, University of California Press).
—— (2007) *Zettel* (London, Blackwell).
—— (2009) *Philosophical Investigations* (PMS Hacker & J Schulte, eds) 4th edn (London, Wiley-Blackwell).

# 13

# Law as a Test of Conceptual Strength

MATTHIEU QUELOZ*

## I. Introduction

There is a long tradition in jurisprudence of inquiring into what the law can learn from philosophy. In 'What Has Philosophy to Learn from Tort Law?', Bernard Williams reverses this traditional direction of inquiry (Williams 1995e).[1] He asks what philosophy can learn from the law – and especially from tort law. Why tort law in particular? Not merely because the essay forms the afterword to a collection entitled *The Philosophical Foundations of Tort Law* (a title which connects law and philosophy in the traditional direction); but also because tort law, which addresses civil wrongs that do not arise out of contract, is among the most down-to-earth branches of the law, doing the necessary work of remedying the damages inflicted by one person on another, and allocating the costs associated with those damages. As one legal scholar observes: 'Tort law is in many ways the simplest area of law … it stands to the legal philosopher as the ball of wax does to the epistemologist or the metaphysician' (Zipursky 2005: 135).

The mundane indispensability of tort law is relevant for Williams, because what philosophy stands to learn from tort law, he contends, is 'the difference between practical reality and philosophical frivolity' (1995e: 487). In highlighting the value of tort law in marking the difference between practical reality and philosophical frivolity, Williams self-consciously echoes J.L. Austin. Yet while Austin regarded tort law as just another repository of time-tested concepts, on a par with common sense as represented by a dictionary, Williams argues that 'the use of certain ideas in the law does more to show that those ideas have strength than is done by the mere fact that they are part of the currency of common sense' (1995e: 488). Concepts like *cause*, *consequence*, *intention*, *voluntariness*, *fault*, *carelessness*, or *negligence* figure both in common sense and in tort law. Williams' contention

* I am grateful to Damian Cueni, Emmanuel Voyiakis, Veronica Rodriguez-Blanco, Daniel Peixoto Murata, Christopher Tollefsen, David Owen, Ulrike Heuer, Gerald Lang, Iris van Domselaar, Ronaldo Porto Macedo Jr, Julieta Rabanos, Emily Kidd White, Benjamin Zipursky, Miodrag Jovanović, Bojan Spaić, and Stephen Bero for feedback on an earlier draft of this chapter.

[1] As observed also by Feldman (1997: 168).

is that their performance in court can tell us more about whether these concepts have strength than their performance out of court.

But what does it mean to show that ideas or concepts 'have strength'? How does conceptual strength relate to the distinction between practical reality and philosophical frivolity? And what special features of the law are supposed to make it a better test of conceptual strength than common sense?

In this chapter, I reconstruct and develop Williams' answers to these questions. I show why Williams believes that the concepts forming the currency of common sense need to be tested against practical reality as embodied notably by legal practice, and I identify seven features of tort law that make it particularly suitable to act as such a test. I then distinguish three respects in which concepts can show strength, and unpack Williams' metaphor of *microwave-resistant concepts*: concepts capable of holding, structuring, and presenting material for intense critical scrutiny without succumbing to it themselves. Finally, I show how philosophy can learn to identify systematically weak concepts, and the limits of otherwise valuable concepts, by considering which concepts *fail* the test. Here, Williams' foray into jurisprudence, though seemingly marginal to his oeuvre, proves surprisingly programmatic, as it traces a pathway from the law to some of his signature theses.

## II. The Need to Test Common Sense: Williams v Austin

In stressing the contrast between philosophical frivolity and practical reality, Williams situates himself in the vicinity of J.L. Austin, a figure he gave a wide berth to when they were contemporaries in Oxford.[2] According to Austin, philosophy was apt to degenerate into frivolity if it lost touch with practical reality. Disenchanted with past philosophers' metaphysical flights of fancy, Austin was especially critical of their willingness to coin new jargon. He thought that leaving ordinary language behind put philosophers at risk of becoming unmoored from common sense, blurring its distinctions, and losing touch with quotidian concerns.

Making philosophy accountable to common sense was therefore meant to be a safeguard against frivolity. The studiedly mundane examples, the rhetoric of plain-speaking, the seemingly trivial questions – these may have seemed frivolous to outsiders, but they were part of a self-conscious effort to remain moored in common sense, so as to replace light-headed speculation with serious work.

[2] Williams remarked: 'I was always rather careful of Austin. I kept at a certain distance from him … He seemed to me a bit like the British Treasury, busily engaged in deflating the economy when everybody is already out of work' (1983: 41). Williams recorded some of his reactions to Austin and his methodology in Williams (1995d: 220, n 1; 2007: 145–46; 2014b). Austin, for his part, seems to have 'singled [Williams] out for praise among the young Oxford philosophers' (Cavell 2010: 149), but 'was pained to find … that he could not attract the interest of Bernard Williams' (Rowe 2023: 587).

As the title of Nikhil Krishnan's (2023) history of that period puts it, adherence to common sense made ordinary language philosophy feel like 'a terribly serious adventure'.

Accordingly, Austin was, 'if not quite a *defender* of common sense', then certainly 'unwilling to give it up at the first whiff' (Krishnan 2023: 86) of suspicion born of airy philosophising. That is not to say that Austin considered common sense to be beyond reproach: he acknowledged that 'superstition and error and fantasy of all kinds do become incorporated in ordinary language' (1961: 133). But while Austin granted that 'we may wish to tidy the situation up a bit', he still urged philosophers 'always to bear in mind … that the distinctions embodied in our vast and, for the most part, relatively ancient stock of ordinary words are neither few nor always very obvious, and almost never just arbitrary' (1962: 63). The fine-grained discriminations enshrined in ordinary language were likely to prove subtler and sounder than anything philosophers could dream up.[3] As he put it in a famous passage:

> our common stock of words embodies all the distinctions men have found worth drawing, and the connexions they have found worth marking, in the lifetimes of many generations: these surely are likely to be more numerous, more sound, since they have stood up to the long test of the survival of the fittest, and more subtle, at least in all ordinary and reasonably practical matters, than any that you or I are likely to think up in our arm-chairs of an afternoon (Austin 1961: 130).

It is most likely this passage that Williams has in mind when he attributes to Austin a 'quasi-evolutionary' reason for supposing that common sense provides us with distinctions more adequate than those of philosophy. As Williams reads Austin, the thought was that common sense 'had been, at least with regard to central human concerns, under heavy selective pressure for a very long time', and that, as a result, 'the distinctions that had survived and flourished in it were likely to answer fairly reliably to human needs' (Williams 1995e: 487).

Confusingly, Williams immediately proceeds to distance himself from Austin by adding: 'This was not a very good answer' (1995e: 487). But why is it not a very good answer? And what is Williams rejecting here? Not, it turns out, the quasi-evolutionary picture on which heavy selective pressure with regard to central human concerns makes it probable that the resulting concepts would answer fairly reliably to human needs. That picture, as we shall see, is one that Williams relies on in his own argument.

What Williams takes issue with, rather, is the idea that the concepts crystallised *in common sense* can confidently be expected to answer to our needs. For the question that Austin offers an answer *to*, Williams tells us several lines earlier, is the following: 'What is it that supposedly provides us with distinctions more adequate than those offered by philosophy?' (1995e: 487). Austin's answer is: 'common

[3] Austin thereby revived the views of an earlier Oxford philosopher, John Cook Wilson, who remarked: 'The authority of language is too often forgotten in philosophy, with serious results. Distinctions made or applied in ordinary language are more likely to be right than wrong' (1926: 874).

sense'. By Williams' lights, however, Austin is insufficiently sceptical of common sense. Williams insists that we should not imagine common sense to be 'consistent', 'free of ideology', and 'self-validating' (1995e: 487, n 1). This is why he does not share Austin's confidence in common sense. Let me try to fill in each point in turn.

First, Williams does not expect common sense to be consistent. His picture is a more Nietzschean one, on which what we call 'common sense' is a product of the vicissitudes of history, a jumble of concepts and distinctions likely to have been extended, transformed, appropriated, repurposed, and rendered otiose many times over by competing factions and opposing forces. Consequently, once we see common sense as the local outgrowth of historical forces, it is only to be expected that 'some widely accepted parts of it may stand condemned in the light of perfectly plausible extrapolations of other parts' (Williams 2005b: 37). Common sense is likely ridden with inconsistencies and tensions.[4]

Second, Williams does not expect common sense to be free of ideological distortions. Far from being 'the inherited wisdom of ordinary practical people in comparison with which the philosophers and their theories were mere johnnies-come-lately' (1995d: 218), common sense is already teeming with misconceptions and prejudices. Instead of expecting common sense to be in immaculate health as long as it remains untouched by the pretences of philosophical theorising, Williams is more sympathetic to Bertrand Russell's remark that common sense presents us with the fossilised 'metaphysics of the stone age' (1995d: 218) – a remark whose reference to metaphysics also reminds us to ask how much of common sense would have been there to be inherited in the first place if our ancestors had been as scrupulous about coining new concepts as Austin suggests we should be. 'In language, as in politics', Williams notes, 'the conservative runs into the fact that the old is only what used to be new' (2014b: 44).

On Williams' picture, however, it is not only, or even mainly, philosophical theorising that introduced misconceptions into common sense. He urges us to take seriously 'the idea not only that we are deceived, but that we are deceived by forces worth worrying about, such as our own fears and resentments, our misunderstanding of social representations, and the effects of tradition' (1995d: 219). Williams repeatedly points to the oppressive sexual morality enshrined in common sense as an example.[5] If he criticises philosophical theories such as Kantianism and Utilitarianism, it is not because he takes them to be the root causes of more widely held misconceptions, but because they themselves *express* these misconceptions.[6] The hope is that the demolition of the theories may help to liberate common sense from the misconceptions of which these theories are

[4] See Queloz & Cueni 2021 for further discussion of this point.

[5] See Williams 1995c: 159; 1995e: 493, n 10.

[6] Of Kant's moral philosophy, for example, Williams writes that it 'certainly does not overlook everyday human experience; rather, it radically distorts it, not just by taking part, and a rather local part, of moral experience as its essence but by doing so in the spirit of making final and vindicatory sense of it, so turning us away from other kinds of sense we need to make of many other things that are more recalcitrant' (2003: 39).

elaborations. As Williams puts it: 'ethical theory is not itself the basic condition with which we should be concerned, but a symptom, the expression of that condition in the tissue of a certain type of philosophy' (2021: 275). The misconceptions laid up in common sense are not so much *caused by* as *expressed in* philosophical theorising (Williams 1995d: 219). Following Nietzsche, Williams thus looks for the all too human motives that implicitly find expression in supposedly universal philosophical theorising: the fear of being vulnerable to luck, the longing for ultimate justice, the desire for good news, or the wish to escape painful conflicts of values.[7]

The third point, which falls out of the preceding two, is that common sense is not self-validating. It stands in need of validation by something other than itself. We need to *test* the concepts that form the currency of common sense. Austin's confidence in common sense still brings him too close to an uncritical celebration of the folk-ways. Williams, by contrast, is 'suspicious of the folk-ways' (2014a: 315).[8]

As a result, Williams pushes Austin's conviction that philosophical frivolity should be checked by practical reality further than Austin himself does. Williams interprets 'practical reality' as something *extraconceptual*, by which even the concepts of common sense might be criticised. Instead of uncritically tying philosophy to the apron strings of common sense, philosophy should be accountable to something beyond common sense, which the concepts accumulated in common sense may or may not be well suited to make sense of: in the first instance, to *ethical experience* in all its untidy, emotional complexity. Williams maintains that philosophy should start 'from the ways in which we experience our ethical life' (1985: 103). That does not make ethical experience the incontrovertible be-all and end-all of philosophical reflection – even when philosophy takes its bearings and authority from ethical experience rather than from a tidy theory, it should retain 'the Socratic aim of improving that experience' by liberating the reflective individual 'from distortions or misunderstandings in his or her own experience' (Williams 1995d: 218). Yet philosophy should at least start by comparing its concepts not just against a 'linguistic phenomenology', as Austin put it, but against a 'phenomenology of the ethical life' (Williams 1985: 103).

Where its concepts bear on political action, moreover, philosophy will also need to draw on 'a more realistic view of the powers, opportunities, and limitations of political actors' (Williams 2005c: 12), so as to understand how politics distinctively combines principles and interests, high-minded ideals and a preoccupation with political survival. Writing about efforts to engineer the concept of *person* into a precise sortal notion that would draw a sharp line between abortion and infanticide, for example, Williams condemns 'the sheer frivolity of such proposals' – not because they deviate from common sense, however; rather, their frivolity 'lies

[7] See Williams 1985: 43, 64, 217; 1995b: 73–75; 1995d: 216; 1999: 150; 2002: 83; 2006d: 49. I elaborate on this point in Queloz 2024.

[8] This is why Williams insists on the need for a 'Left' Wittgensteinianism that can make sense of radical critique (2005b: 37; 2014a: 315; 2021: 278–79). On Williams' debt to Wittgenstein, see Queloz & Krishnan 2025. On his Left Wittgensteinianism, see Queloz & Cueni 2021.

in their refusal to engage with the only two things that matter: the politics of trying to make rules for such situations, and the experience of people engaged in them' (Williams 1995d: 221, n 10).[9]

Williams' contention that philosophy might learn from the law can then be heard as adding the thought that practical reality is embodied not merely by ethical experience and the realities of politics out of court, but also by legal practice. The legal process can thus be part of the extraconceptual practical reality against which Williams proposes to test the concepts of common sense.

## III. Williams' Quasi-Evolutionary Picture

Why would the law be an ideal testing ground for certain concepts of common sense? After all, the law has its own specialised conceptual repertoire, which lawyers take years to master. But Williams points out that there is nonetheless 'an extent to which the law is uncontroversially using the materials of common sense', for instance when it uses materials 'offered in evidence by citizens' (1995e: 493–94). Moreover, tort law in particular has many 'commonsensical aspects' (Goldberg & Zipursky 2020: 1). It uses various concepts – Williams mentions fault, intention, carelessness, proximate cause and consequence (Williams 1995e: 490) – that are at least 'recognizable to common sense' (1995e: 489). And for Williams, the fact that the law uses concepts and distinctions recognisable to common sense constitutes a reason to think 'that those concepts and distinctions provide a sound and reliable way of thinking about the relevant areas of experience' (1995e: 488).

But why would the fact that the law uses concepts recognisable to common sense yield reasons that are sufficiently *independent* from common sense to act as a test for it? Williams' answer is: because the quasi-evolutionary dynamics which Austin correctly identified as informative are a great deal stronger in the law, and in tort law especially, than they are in everyday discourse. The use of common sense concepts in the legal arena, particularly in tort law, puts a great deal more selective pressure on those concepts than their ordinary use does.

But what features of tort law create this added selective pressure? Williams only gestures towards a couple of them, but the following seven features of Anglo-American tort law would plausibly figure in a more detailed rational reconstruction of his line of argument:

(1) Compared to the day-to-day use we make of concepts like cause, consequence, intention, voluntariness, fault, carelessness, or negligence out of court, the stakes tend to be higher when these concepts are used in court: it is normally

[9] On Williams' privileging of ethical experience over common sense, see Krishna 2014. In his debate with Ronald Dworkin, Williams also treats the fact that certain political notions are 'entrenched in historical and contemporary experience' (2005a: 84) as significant for deciding which concepts to rely on in political thought; see Cueni 2024; Peixoto Murata *forthcoming*; and Queloz 2023 for further discussion.

only if a lot turns on the outcome that a case reaches the courts; moreover, a resolution reached in court may carry implications for other parties that a settlement out of court would not have carried.

(2) The use of these concepts in court is more frequently and more unwaveringly adversarial.

(3) The arguments tend to be more thorough and sustained, as different sides of a case are systematically presented, as forcefully as possible and for as long as it takes, by people trained to do so.

(4) Any assertions made tend to be subjected to more careful scrutiny, as their evidential basis, their presuppositions, and their implications are examined by people who have strong incentives to question them.

(5) In tort law – in contrast to other branches of the law, such as criminal law – the cases before the court tend to be especially *hard* cases, which ended up in court precisely because they were hard to decide or involved claims that were evidentially hard to prove, since easy or obvious cases are more likely to be settled out of court.

(6) Despite the cases being hard, some of the questions that common sense would be happy to leave open or indeterminate in ordinary situations out of court *must* receive clear-cut answers by the end of the proceedings. Judges may skirt around some contested theoretical issues and try to predetermine or constrain as few other cases as possible,[10] but they cannot fudge or leave open the issues on which the case turns. Whereas we often productively postpone decisions in ordinary group deliberations or in politics, the court has to have an answer. *Someone* has to bear the cost of the loss or damage at issue. That can be both the plaintiff and the defendant in some well-defined proportion, but in the end, there needs to be a clear allocation of costs.

(7) Anglo-American tort law is predominantly common law, so the scrutiny of concepts does not take place only in the context of particular cases, but across time, too, thereby giving greater purchase to the idea that certain concepts have survived scrutiny in a quasi-evolutionary sense.[11]

Many of these features are, of course, present also in other branches of the law. But not all of them. The observation that the cases before the court tend to be especially hard cases, for example, is true of tort law; but in other branches of the law, such as criminal law, it is rather the *clearest* cases that are *easiest* to back with evidence which are most likely to end up in court.[12] As a result, tort law is a particularly suitable testing ground for certain concepts of common sense, since it tends to combine hard questions about

[10] See Sunstein (1996, 2001) on judicial minimalism as well as Queloz & Cueni (2021) on an analogous phenomenon in ordinary practical deliberation.

[11] My thanks to Emmanuel Voyiakis for bringing this aspect to my attention.

[12] Williams briefly discusses this and other contrasts between tort law and criminal law, including the observation that while 'in an absolutely ideal world all and only guilty criminals would be prosecuted … there could be no world in which it was only successful plaintiffs whose cases were heard' (1995e: 491). He also notes that 'the setting of the requirements on intention is typically different in tort law from what it is in the criminal law' (2006a: 98).

mundane situations with a pressure to arrive at clear-cut answers that is usually lacking in everyday applications of common sense.

If one is going to look for quasi-evolutionary pressures in the law as Williams does here, tort law is indeed the obvious place to look. Unlike constitutional law, administrative law, or international law, tort law does not structure the relationships between abstractly elaborate legal frameworks that vary wildly over time and from one jurisdiction to the next. As a part of private law, tort law regulates the relationships between private individuals, and is more particularly rooted in the practical problems that ensue when one person or group commits a civil wrong against another: problems to do with remedying loss or injury, and determining who is liable for what and on what grounds (e.g. negligence, wilful misconduct, or strict liability). 'Tort law engages with two of the most fundamental questions of morality and social life', Arthur Ripstein observes: 'how people are permitted to treat each other, and whose problem it is when things go wrong' (2022). These questions continually arise in every human society, and everywhere, they have to receive an answer. The form of law that addresses these questions thereby answers to comparatively basic, constant, and widely shared human needs that are not so sensitive to variations in the constitutional or international legal framework. This may be part of the explanation of why tort law has proved comparatively stable since the *lex Aquilia* of Roman law,[13] and why it tends to retain many similarities across jurisdictions.[14]

This, then, is Williams' quasi-evolutionary picture of tort law – what he labels 'the Picture'. Such a picture will only be as determinate as our theoretical background understanding of the various functions it discharges and the practical exigencies it answers to – in short, of 'what tort law is up to' (1995e: 492):

> If philosophy can be instructed by the law in the terms offered by the Picture – that is to say, through seeing what distinctions and considerations prove robust in circumstances in which we have to have an answer – it will need an understanding of what the forces are that operate on the law and are expressed in it … Philosophy, then, will not only have to attend to the principles and goals of tort law; it will also have to understand at a theoretical level why it has those principles and goals (Williams 1995e: 492).

Understanding that the law of torts functions notably as a system of cost allocation and compensation, for instance, gives us some sense of the pressures acting on it, and of how else the functions it performs could in principle also be discharged (e.g. through no-fault insurance systems).[15] But we gain an even richer sense of the relevant

[13] See Stein 1999 and Ibbetson 2003 for retrospective comparisons.

[14] Though there have also been significant developments: the advent of compulsory insurance schemes has reduced tort litigation by a great margin, and New Zealand, which has effectively abolished tort litigation in respect of personal injuries by replacing individual tort liability for personal injury with a public insurance scheme, exemplifies a different and effective way of doing things. For a discussion of the New Zealand system which draws on Williams, see Voyiakis 2021.

[15] For recent examples of such theoretical accounts of the functions of tort law, see Goldberg & Zipursky 2020 and Ripstein 2016, and see Peel & Goudkamp 2014: Ch 1, §1 and Ripstein 2022 for overviews of the various tort theories on offer. For a Williams-inspired critique of Goldberg and Zipursky's theory, see Rodriguez-Blanco 2022. See also Cueni 2020 for an approach to international law that develops this strand in Williams' methodology.

dynamics if we see, in addition, the respects in which the law of torts is at the same time required to function as a system of appeasement, deterrence, and occasionally even retribution (by awarding what is known in the United Kingdom as 'exemplary damages' and in the United States as 'punitive damages'). Once we have some sense of these various functions that tort law performs, we can make better sense of some of its distinctive features: why it has to force the particular issues it does, why it lacks the array of procedural protections for the defendant at work in criminal law (e.g. there is no privilege not to testify), and why the standard of proof in tort law is lower than in criminal law (O.J. Simpson was acquitted in his criminal trial, but the tort of wrongful death was held to be proven in his civil trial).

Notice how Williams' quasi-evolutionary picture of tort law differs from superficially similar pictures of the law sketched by the likes of Oliver Wendell Holmes or John Dewey, who also discerned quasi-evolutionary dynamics in the law.[16] Holmes and Dewey were interested in how the legal principles and statutes crystallised in common law represented the accumulated deposit of generations of legal experience. The fact that these legal principles had survived and been refined by this process imbued them with a certain degree of authority. Williams, by contrast, is interested not in the survival of legal principles, but in the survival of the concepts forming the currency of common sense. His point is that the ordinary concepts we use anyway elsewhere instructively come under special selective pressure once they enter the legal arena. The fact that tort law uses certain concepts and distinctions can do more to show that 'those ideas have strength' than the mere fact that common sense uses them.

Of course, Austin himself adverts to the law, and even to tort law in particular, as something that philosophy should look to: 'the common law, and in particular the law of tort', he writes, 'is the richest storehouse' (1961: 135–36). Yet Austin sees the law in the first instance as a valuable 'source-book' (1961: 135) of distinctions and cases. Alongside psychology, anthropology, ethology, and, above all, a good dictionary, the law is a 'resource' (1961: 135) that his philosophical method invites us to draw on in collecting cases and distinctions so as to arrive at a maximally fine-grained picture of common sense.[17]

For Williams, however, the role of the law is not to refine our picture of common sense, but to put its conceptual currency to the test. As he sees it, Austin 'collects linguistic distinctions like types of beetles' (2006c: 160–61), and views the law of torts as an opportunity to expand his collection. Williams, by contrast, is interested not in discovering new types of beetles, but in seeing which among the garden variety beetles are capable of surviving in the legal environment.

This difference between Austin and Williams comes out in their contrasting reactions to the fact that tort law must have a determinate answer. Austin, like Williams, remarks upon the law's 'overriding requirement that a decision be reached, and a relatively black and white decision' (1961: 136). Yet Austin

[16] See Menand 2001 and Misak 2013; and see Queloz (2017, 2018, 2021), Misak (2021), and Cueni (2020) for a discussion of Williams' relation to American pragmatism.

[17] On Austin's method, see Urmson 1965 and, for a recent revaluation, Birken-Bertsch 2014.

views this difference between legal practice and everyday use primarily as a reason for caution: he warns that this pressure to reach a determinate answer may lead lawyers to stretch and bend terms beyond their ordinary meaning. On Williams' view, however, it is precisely this pressure, at work in the law but not in ordinary usage, that promises to make the law into an independent test for common sense. If concepts can cope with this pressure that they do not encounter in ordinary usage, that might provide independent reasons to think that these concepts have strength. But what does it mean to show that ideas or concepts *have strength*?

## IV. Microwave-Resistant Concepts

A guiding image that Williams offers to clarify what he has in mind when speaking of concepts that display conceptual strength is the metaphor of *microwave-resistant concepts*: concepts capable of holding, structuring, and presenting material for intense critical scrutiny without falling prey to it themselves. Such concepts function like containers in the microwave in enabling the forces acting on them to transform and reconfigure what they contain while themselves remaining unaltered:

> a certain store of shared interpretations and concepts survive scrutiny, every day, under legal process and provide the structure of the law's operations. They are like containers that can withstand the microwave. On any given occasion it is the stuff they contain that is the center of interest, and the legal process is directed to seeing how that stuff will turn out; but it is significant … that there are some familiar materials that serve to hold and present this stuff, and have a structure that enables them, day in and day out, to withstand radiation at courtroom intensity (Williams 1995e: 494).

The idea is that the law can act as a test of strength for the concepts of common sense by revealing how they behave under extraordinary pressure, when the stakes are high, the confrontation particularly adversarial, and a determinate answer has to be given to questions on which the case turns.

In such a context, for a concept to prove its strength is for it to prove that it can provide a shared framework for the operations of the law without falling prey to the intense scrutiny and the cut and thrust of legal argument. While much is contested in the courtroom, the concept manages not to become itself contested. Rather, it acts as part of the conceptual common ground that is required for the contestation to become intelligible *as* a contestation of a definite issue at all.

But what exactly does it mean for a concept not to become contested in this connection? Wherein does the absence of contestation manifest itself? Williams offers the following clarificatory example:

> Consider the matter of intent … It may indeed be controversial in a particular connection whether it matters or not that the agent intended the outcome; and it may, further,

> be controversial what would count as showing that he did intend the outcome (or at any rate should be treated as someone who intended the outcome). But behind all this there will be a steady stream of assumptions about situations in which it is absolutely clear that he did intend the outcome, and that it is relevant that he intended the outcome (1995e: 493).

This passage indicates three respects in which a concept may or may not be contested. One is with regard to its *applicability* to a particular case: did the agent in question intend the outcome in question here? In more general terms: is concept F really applicable to x? The second is with regard to *what counts as showing that* it is applicable: what counts as showing that someone intended an outcome? More generally, what are the criteria governing the applicability of concept F to x? This criterial issue differs from the first issue of applicability, since there may be complete agreement on what would count as showing that the concept applies, and nonetheless be disagreement over whether it applies (because the two parties give different descriptions of what actually happened, for instance). Thirdly, the very *relevance* of a concept to a given question may be contested: it may be claimed that the question of whether the agent intended the outcome or not is neither here nor there; it then becomes contested whether x's being F even matters to the question at hand. A concept's *strength* shows itself in its tendency not to become contested in any of these three respects.

Williams speaks interchangeably of the *robustness* of concepts (1995e: 493). The modal connotations of the term 'robustness' are apposite here: a strong or robust concept does its work, without itself being called into question, across a variety of different cases. Such a concept thereby comes to form part of the comparatively stable background against which legal argument rages. Strong or robust concepts form the shared framework within which legal disputes can play out, day after day, over less strong or robust concepts – concepts whose applicability, criteria of application, or relevance people are precisely not willing to take for granted.[18] What tort law as a test of conceptual strength indicates is the degree of a concept's robustness under legal pressure.

A strong or robust concept *can* become the focus of attack – its applicability may be questioned (is x really F?), its criteria of application may be questioned (what counts as showing that x is F?), or its relevance may be questioned (does x's being F matter here?). But the concept's strength will lie in the fact that these attacks remain exceptions, occurring against the background of a steady stream of cases in which it is absolutely clear for all sides *that* x is F, *what counts as showing* that x is F, and that its being F is *relevant*. Insofar as tort law accumulates a record of cases demonstrating the presence of this tendency in commonsensical concepts, it offers independent reasons to regard these concepts as sound and reliable ways of thinking about the relevant areas of experience.

[18] On the need for the law to offer some formal framework in which to conceptualise reality in terms that most people do not have to question most of the time, see also Stinchcombe 2001. Thanks to Damian Cueni for the pointer.

Of course, these reasons might still be outweighed by other kinds of reasons counting against regarding the concepts as sound or reliable. Moreover, it follows from the quasi-evolutionary rationale underlying these attributions of conceptual strength that conceptual strength must be a context-sensitive phenomenon: concepts that answer fairly reliably to human needs in some circumstances might cease to do so if circumstances change.

Accordingly, Williams' inference from legal to everyday contexts is defeasible: if a concept proves robust in court, it is merely *probable*, but not necessary that it will prove robust out of court. The conditions and constraints under which commonsensical concepts are deployed in courts are in many respects specific to courts – as Williams himself acknowledges elsewhere, 'decisions within a given legal system … are bound by … constraints, such as *stare decisis*' (2005a: 87). Indeed, the common law's respect for precedent might be thought of as the opposite of a quasi-evolutionary pressure.[19] One thus needs to take seriously the possibility that a commonsensical concept's strength in the courtroom is an artefact of the conditions and constraints specific to the courtroom. Further argument is required to show that even once these conditions and constraints fall away, a concept's strength will not fall with them.

In view of these qualifications suggesting that the law cannot be a definitive test of conceptual strength, it might seem more apt to speak of the law as an *indicator* of conceptual strength. But how good an indicator it is, and what better indicators there might be, depends not merely on how plausible the generalisation from the legal to the extra-legal context is, but also on one's more general commitments, in particular regarding one's conception of conceptual authority. If one believes that the soundest and most reliable concepts are to be identified on the basis of timeless rational foundations of one sort or another – Platonic Forms, the Mind of God, natural law, the dictates of universal reason, or the eternal structure of normative reality, for example – then the evidence of conceptual strength provided by the legal record will count for little. If, however, one believes that human affairs are themselves the last court of appeal when it comes to the authority of concepts, the specially demanding conditions of the law may seem like the closest thing to a test of conceptual strength we are going to get.

Williams, for his part, rejects models of conceptual authority which cast us as 'unencumbered intelligences selecting in principle among all possible outlooks' (2006b: 193). He tends to foreground the question of what concepts do for us in the crucible of human experience – more precisely, of the particular form that our experience takes as a result of the historical, cultural, and institutional peculiarities of our situation. We should consider, as he puts it, whether concepts 'indeed help us to live' (Williams 2000: 161). If tort law can show us that some concepts of common sense help us to arrive at determinate answers even in hard cases with high stakes, that certainly counts for something.

[19] My thanks to Christopher Tollefsen and Damian Cueni for suggesting this point to me.

## V. Learning from Failures to Pass the Test

Philosophy can, finally, also learn from the ways in which concepts may *fail* the test of conceptual strength that the law subjects them to: 'it is not just the success of our concepts under the extreme conditions of the law that has something to tell philosophy', Williams remarks, 'but also their occasional failure to survive that exposure' (1995e: 496–97).

I propose to distinguish two types of cases in which the lack of conceptual strength revealed by the stresses of the legal process can inform philosophy: the simpler case in which a concept constantly breeds controversy; and the more complex case in which a concept turns out to do a great deal of valuable work, but ceases to work once a certain kind of pressure is put on it.

First, some concepts may simply turn out to be altogether unable to sustain a steady stream of cases in which their applicability, criteria of application, and relevance are taken for granted. As Williams notes, 'some concepts constantly cause trouble in the law and provide a focus for reinterpretation and controversy' (1995e: 494) – the much-debated concept of negligence offers an example.[20]

These are significant data for philosophy. But they do not yet settle the question of whether the fault lies with the concepts themselves or with those who expect too much of them. It may be that some of the concepts laid up in common sense simply are not fit to do anything like the work that the law requires of them, and that we had better look for stronger concepts to replace them with. Then the role of tort law in relation to philosophy will be that of a stress test that starkly reveals the weak links in our conceptual apparatus.

But just because tort law is, *ex hypothesi*, a domain subjecting concepts to strong selective pressure, it would come as a surprise if many concepts of common sense at once constantly found their way into it and invariably failed to do any work in it. The likelier scenario, on this quasi-evolutionary picture, is that concepts prove perfectly capable of doing *some* valuable work in the law, but start to break down once additional demands are placed on them. The mistake, however, may then lie with those who place these additional demands on the concepts, and not with the concepts themselves.

This second type of case may be what Williams has in mind when he writes that the way concepts suffer under the law can show philosophers something about the nature of these concepts, and thereby give them occasion to *come to the rescue* of those concepts (1995e: 494). What a concept's performance under the legal process can reveal is that the concept only breaks down if a certain kind of pressure is put on it, and otherwise does important work for us.

For Williams, the paradigm case here is the concept of the *voluntary*, which is also central to his critique of the morality system in *Ethics and the Limits of*

[20] A recent collection exploring the challenges that negligence poses for conceptions of responsibility is Rodriguez-Blanco & Pavlakos 2023.

*Philosophy* (1985) and to his plaidoyer for Presocratic conceptions of agency in *Shame and Necessity* (1993).[21] Both philosophy and the theory of law, Williams believes, strive to find a way to ground all proper acknowledgements of responsibility in a suitably theorised conception of the voluntary. But the practice of law, and of tort law in particular, can remind us that 'there is an authority exercised by what one has done, and not merely by what one has intentionally done' (1993: 69). Philosophers' longstanding focus on understanding the will of the agent as the true carrier of responsibility can blind them to aspects of responsibility that are less closely tied to the will. Williams labours to bring out these various aspects across a number of his essays. In 'How Free Does the Will Need to Be?', for example, he argues that one can acknowledge responsibility for actions even when one thinks that one could *not* have done otherwise. He takes this to show that 'acknowledgement of responsibility has less to do with the concerns of blame … than is made out' (1995a: 19). In 'Moral Luck', Williams describes agents who seem to appropriately feel regret for things they have unintentionally done, and takes this to count against the morality system that struggles to recognise the ethical significance of such 'agent-regret' (1981: 27). Yet just because the morality system is focused on blame and has no room for the significance of agent-regret, Williams' arguments have been heavily contested, and have done little to sway those who are firmly committed to the morality system.

Tort law, by contrast, offers philosophy a much less contestable reminder of the fact that responsibility extends beyond what we intentionally do. As Williams puts it, a 'truth' that 'emerges unequivocally from the law of torts' is that 'responsibility in the sense of a duty to compensate inevitably runs beyond responsibility for the outcome in the sense of an intention or even a desire to bring it about' (1995e: 495). One can be liable for things one did not mean to bring about, or even tried to keep from happening.

Indeed, as hinted by Williams' suggestion that responsibility in this sense *inevitably* runs beyond what is intended, the law of torts could not effectively discharge its functions within society if it limited responsibility to intentional torts. To provide relief to those who suffer loss or damage through acts that are negligent or reckless, or to regulate ultrahazardous activities, tort law needs to recognise responsibility for acts that do not rise to the level of an intentional tort. The law here offers a vivid illustration of the fact that we not only can, but *need to* acknowledge responsibility for at least some things we have unintentionally done.

Legal theorists are less likely to deny this than moral philosophers, Williams acknowledges, but even legal theorists are still prone to ask whether there must be at least 'a grain of (something like) the voluntary on which to grow the elaborate crystal of liability' (1995e: 495). Moreover, he notes that the felt need for a

[21] For discussions of the importance of the concept of the voluntary to Williams' critique of the morality system, see Krishnan & Queloz 2023; Louden 2007; Moore 2003 & 2006; and Queloz 2022b.

concept of the voluntary providing a metaphysical foundation for responsibility can also manifest itself *negatively*, in calls to decouple the law from its reliance on the notion of the voluntary because no conception of the voluntary that could satisfy that need is forthcoming.

Yet here, too, legal practice is instructive, because it shows that the concept of the voluntary only causes trouble once one tries to metaphysically 'deepen' it, and actually does valuable work in its 'superficial' form. A 'superficial' conception of voluntariness is satisfied already if what was done was an intentional aspect of an action performed in a normal state of mind. That conception is 'superficial', I have suggested elsewhere (Queloz 2022a), in being uninterested in the detailed causal underpinnings of the action – we do not have to peer deep into the agent's physiology or causal history to determine whether the concept *voluntary* applies, but can rely on the most easily observable and most immediate causes of the action, such as whether the agent *intended* to do what he did, and whether his state of mind was deliberatively normal in the undemanding sense that he was not sleepwalking, intoxicated, or in the grip of passion, and would thus have been able to shape the action to his more settled concerns.[22]

Such a superficial conception of voluntariness notably serves our concerns for fairness and self-determination by focusing attributions of responsibility or liability on those aspects of actions that we comparatively have most control over.[23] This serves our concern for fairness by reducing the impact of sheer luck on what one ends up being held accountable for. And it serves our concern for self-determination by making it easier for individuals to predict and influence the course of their lives with regard to whether they stay on the right side of the law. Cases of strict liability, where agents are held to account regardless of their mental state, are not as much of a counterexample to this as first appears. By transparently declaring in advance what kinds of wrongs or damages people will be held strictly liable for, the legal system expresses respect for the individual as a choosing being 'at one remove' (Williams 1993: 65):[24] the state gives most agents a fair opportunity to voluntarily decide whether to embark on the kinds of enterprises that entrain strict liability to begin with (whether to acquire certain animals or engage in abnormally dangerous activities, for example).

Another lesson Williams explicitly sees as emerging from the law of torts is that 'grave problems arise for the notion of the voluntary when we seek to deepen it' (1995e: 494) – when we cease to regard the applicability of the concept of voluntariness as decidable by determining what the agent intended and what state of mind he was in, and try to ground attributions of responsibility on acts that in no way reflect the influence of anything beyond the control of the agent. The idea of

[22] See Queloz 2025 for a detailed theorisation of the notions of conceptual depth and conceptual superficiality.

[23] As I argue, drawing on Williams and Hart, in Queloz 2022a.

[24] Williams employs the phrase in talking about strict liability in criminal law, but the point carries over to tort law.

the voluntary is an 'essentially superficial notion': it 'works on condition that one does not try to deepen it' (1995e: 494). 'This truth', Williams insists further, 'can be recovered from studying the law in practice', because the

> pressures that the law applies can in this case help philosophy to see what common sense morality and philosophy's own arguments on these subjects can help it to overlook, that the concept of the voluntary adds up to not much more than we are offered by its surface criteria, by which a voluntary act is, roughly, an intentional aspect of an act done in a normal state of mind (1995e: 494).

Legal practice provides a powerful reminder of the merits of more superficial concepts.

## VI. Conclusion

If Williams seeks an independent test of conceptual strength in the law of torts, then, it is because he is more sceptical of common sense than Austin was, and believes that we need to test the concepts forming the currency of common sense against practical reality. I have identified seven features of tort law that make it particularly apt to act as such a test, and argued that concepts show strength through their tendency not to become contested with regard to their applicability, the criteria governing their application, and the relevance of their applicability. This has also allowed us to elucidate Williams' notion of microwave-resistant concepts, which are capable of holding, structuring, and presenting material for intense critical scrutiny without themselves becoming contested. And it has enabled us to illustrate how philosophy can identify systematically weak concepts as well as the limits of otherwise valuable concepts by considering which concepts fail the test.

Williams' foray into jurisprudence thus proves surprisingly programmatic in relation to his own work in philosophy. Not only can we make sense of the claim that philosophy can learn something from tort law. What can be learned from it turns out to include some of his signature theses about the essential superficiality of voluntariness and the authority of what one has done. This raises the biographical question of how much Williams himself learned from the law. But it also speaks to the deep underlying coherence of an oeuvre whose illuminating interconnections we are only just beginning to draw out into the open.

## Bibliography

Austin, JL (1961) 'A Plea for Excuses' in JO Urmson & GJ Warnock (eds), *Philosophical Papers* (Oxford, Clarendon Press).
Austin, JL (1962) *Sense and Sensibilia* (GJ Warnock, ed) (Oxford, Oxford University Press).

Birken-Bertsch, H (2014) 'Austin's Method' in B Garvey (ed), *J. L. Austin on Language* (London, Palgrave).
Cavell, S (2010) *Little Did I Know: Excerpts from Memory* (Stanford, Stanford University Press).
Cueni, D (2020) *Public Law Analogies in International Legal Theory* (doctoral thesis, Rechtswissenschaftliches Institut, University of Zurich).
—— (2024) 'Constructing Liberty and Equality: Political, Not Juridical' 15 3 *Jurisprudence* 341.
Cueni, D & Queloz, M (2021) 'Whence the Demand for Ethical Theory?' 58 2 *American Philosophical Quarterly* 135.
Feldman, HL (1997) 'Blending Fields: Tort Law, Philosophy, and Legal Theory' 49 1 *South Carolina Law Review* 167.
Goldberg, JCP & Zipursky, BC (2020) *Recognizing Wrongs* (Cambridge, Massachusetts, Belknap Press).
Ibbetson, D (2003) 'How the Romans Did for Us: Ancient Roots of the Tort of Negligence' 26 *University of New South Wales Law Journal* 475.
Krishna, N (2014) *The Morality of Common Sense: Problems from Sidgwick* (doctoral thesis, University of Oxford).
Krishnan, N (2023) *A Terribly Serious Adventure: Philosophy at Oxford 1900–60* (London, Profile Books).
Krishnan, N & Queloz, M (2023) 'The Shaken Realist: Bernard Williams, the War, and Philosophy as Cultural Critique' 31 1 *European Journal of Philosophy* 226.
Louden, RB (2007), 'The Critique of the Morality System' in A Thomas (ed), *Bernard Williams* (Cambridge, Cambridge University Press).
Menand, L (2001) *The Metaphysical Club* (New York, Farrar, Straus and Giroux).
Misak, C (2013) *The American Pragmatists* (Oxford, Oxford University Press).
—— (2021) 'Williams, Pragmatism, and the Law' 27 *Res Publica* 155.
Moore, AW (2003) 'Williams on Ethics, Knowledge and Reflection' 78 *Philosophy* 337.
—— (2006) 'Bernard Williams: Ethics and the Limits of Philosophy' in J Shand (ed), *Central Works of Philosophy Volume 5: The Twentieth Century: Quine and After* (Chesham, Acumen).
Murata, DP *forthcoming*, 'Practical Reasoning as Interpretation: Williamsian Remarks on Dworkin's Methodology' in D Peixoto Murata, JA Rabanos & V Rodriguez-Blanco (eds), *Bernard Williams: From Responsibility to Law and Jurisprudence* (Oxford, Hart).
Peel, E & Goudkamp, J (2014) *Winfield and Jolowicz on Tort* (London, Sweet and Maxwell).
Queloz, M (2017) 'Does Philosophy Have a Vindicatory History? Bernard Williams on the History of Philosophy' *Studia Philosophica* 76.
—— (2018) 'Williams's Pragmatic Genealogy and Self-Effacing Functionality' 18 17 *Philosophers' Imprint* 1.
—— (2021) *The Practical Origins of Ideas: Genealogy as Conceptual Reverse-Engineering* (Oxford, Oxford University Press).
—— (2022a) 'The Essential Superficiality of the Voluntary and the Moralization of Psychology' 179 *Philosophical Studies* 1591.
—— (2022b) 'A Shelter from Luck: The Morality System Reconstructed' in A Szigeti & M Talbert (eds), *Morality and Agency: Themes from Bernard Williams* (New York, Oxford University Press).
—— (2023) 'The Dworkin–Williams Debate: Liberty, Conceptual Integrity, and Tragic Conflict in Politics' 109 1 *Philosophy and Phenomenological Research* 3.

—— (2024) 'Internalism from the Ethnographic Stance: From Self-Indulgence to Self-Expression and Corroborative Sense-Making' *The Philosophical Quarterly* 2024, available at https://doi.org/10.1093/pq/pqae051
—— (2025) *The Ethics of Conceptualization: Tailoring Thought and Language to Need* (Oxford, Oxford University Press).
Queloz, M & Cueni, D (2021) 'Left Wittgensteinianism' 29 4 *European Journal of Philosophy* 758.
Queloz, M & Krishnan, N (2025) 'Williams's Debt to Wittgenstein' in M van Ackeren & M Queloz (eds), *Bernard Williams on Philosophy and History* (Oxford, Oxford University Press).
Ripstein, A (2016) *Private Wrongs* (Cambridge, Massachusetts, Harvard University Press).
—— (2022) 'Theories of the Common Law of Torts' in EN Zalta (ed), *The Stanford Encyclopedia of Philosophy*, available at https://plato.stanford.edu/entries/tort-theories/
Rodriguez-Blanco, V (2022) 'The Law of Negligence, Blameworthy Action and the Relationality Thesis: A Dilemma for Goldberg and Zipursky's Civil Recourse Theory of Tort Law' 41 *Law and Philosophy* 63.
Rodriguez-Blanco, V & Pavlakos, V (eds) (2023) *Agency, Negligence and Responsibility* (Cambridge, Cambridge University Press).
Rowe, MW (2023) *J. L. Austin: Philosopher and D-Day Intelligence Officer* (Oxford, Oxford University Press).
Stein, P (1999) *Roman Law in European History* (Cambridge, Cambridge University Press).
Stinchcombe, AL (2001) *When Formality Works: Authority and Abstraction in Law and Organizations* (Chicago, University of Chicago Press).
Sunstein, CR (1996) *Legal Reasoning and Political Conflict* (New York, Oxford University Press).
—— (2001) *One Case at a Time: Judicial Minimalism on the Supreme Court* (Cambridge, Massachusetts, Harvard University Press).
Urmson, JO (1965) 'J. L. Austin' 62 *The Journal of Philosophy* 499.
Voyiakis, E (2021) 'Moral Luck, Responsibility, and Systems of Tort Liability' 27 *Res Publica* 271.
Williams, B (1981) 'Moral Luck' in B Williams, *Moral Luck* (Cambridge, Cambridge University Press).
—— (1983) 'The Uses of Philosophy: An Interview with Bernard Williams'. Interview by Donald McDonald. *The Center Magazine*, Issue November/December, 40–49.
—— (1985) *Ethics and the Limits of Philosophy* (London, Routledge).
—— (1993) *Shame and Necessity* (Berkeley, University of California Press).
—— (1995a) 'How Free Does the Will Need to Be?' in B Williams, *Making Sense of Humanity and Other Philosophical Papers 1982–1993* (Cambridge, Cambridge University Press).
—— (1995b) *Making Sense of Humanity and Other Philosophical Papers 1982–1993* (Cambridge, Cambridge University Press).
—— (1995c) 'The Point of View of the Universe: Sidgwick and the Ambitions of Ethics' in B Williams, *Making Sense of Humanity and Other Philosophical Papers 1982–1993* (Cambridge, Cambridge University Press).
—— (1995d) 'Replies' in JEJ Altham & R Harrison (eds), *World, Mind, and Ethics: Essays on the Ethical Philosophy of Bernard Williams* (Cambridge, Cambridge University Press).
—— (1995e) 'What Has Philosophy to Learn from Tort Law?' in D Owen (ed), *The Philosophical Foundations of Tort Law* (Oxford, Oxford University Press).

——(1999) 'Bernard Williams' in A Pyle (ed), *Key Philosophers in Conversation: The Cogito Interviews* (London, Routledge).
——(2000) 'Naturalism and Genealogy' in E Harcourt (ed), *Morality, Reflection, and Ideology* (Oxford, Oxford University Press).
——(2002) *Truth and Truthfulness: An Essay in Genealogy* (Princeton, Princeton University Press).
——(2003) 'Fictions, Philosophy, and Truth' *Profession* 37.
——(2005a) 'From Freedom to Liberty: The Construction of a Political Value' in G Hawthorne (ed), *In the Beginning Was the Deed: Realism and Moralism in Political Argument* (Princeton, Princeton University Press).
——(2005b) 'Pluralism, Community and Left Wittgensteinianism' in G Hawthorne (ed), *In the Beginning Was the Deed: Realism and Moralism in Political Argument* (Princeton, Princeton University Press).
——(2005c) 'Realism and Moralism in Political Theory' in G Hawthorne (ed), *In the Beginning Was the Deed: Realism and Moralism in Political Argument* (Princeton, Princeton University Press).
——(2006a) 'The Actus Reus of Dr. Caligari' in AW Moore (ed), *Philosophy as a Humanistic Discipline* (Princeton, Princeton University Press).
——(2006b) 'Philosophy as a Humanistic Discipline' in AW Moore (ed), *Philosophy as a Humanistic Discipline* (Princeton, Princeton University Press).
——(2006c) 'Political Philosophy and the Analytical Tradition' in AW Moore (ed), *Philosophy as a Humanistic Discipline* (Princeton, Princeton University Press).
——(2006d) *The Sense of the Past: Essays in the History of Philosophy* (M Burnyeat, ed) (Princeton, Princeton University Press).
——(2007) 'Truth and Truthfulness' in J Baggini & J Stangroom (eds), *What More Philosophers Think* (London, Continuum).
——(2014a) 'The Need to Be Sceptical' in M Wood (ed), *Essays and Reviews 1959-2002* (Princeton, Princeton University Press).
——(2014b) 'Sense and Sensibilia and Philosophical Papers, by J. L. Austin' in M Wood (ed), *Essays and Reviews 1959-2002* (Princeton, Princeton University Press).
——(2021) 'Ethics, A Matter of Style? Introduction to the French Edition' 9 2 *Philosophical Inquiries* 269.
Wilson, JC (1926) *Statement and Inference* (ASL Farquharson, ed) (Oxford, Clarendon Press).
Zipursky, BC (2005) 'Philosophy of Tort Law' in MP Golding & WA Edmundson (eds), *The Blackwell Guide to the Philosophy of Law and Legal Theory* (Oxford, Blackwell).

# 14

# Practical Reasoning as Interpretation: Williamsian Remarks on Dworkin's Methodology

DANIEL PEIXOTO MURATA*

## I. Introduction

Consider the following scenarios. As I am leaving the theatre, I am convinced that I have seen you entering. Later that week I mention that to you, and you assure me that you were working at the office the day I thought I saw you at the theatre. Faced with your statement, I can either reason my way to the conclusion that I was mistaken or that you were lying to me. That is, when it comes to my system of beliefs, when facing a conflict between two or more beliefs, I must reason in a way that renders my whole system coherent. In the theatre case, I do this by either concluding that I was mistaken (and therefore my reason to believe that you were at the theatre is no reason at all) or by concluding that you were lying to me (and therefore my reason to believe is still valid, that is, still retains its character as a reason). We engage in this sort of theoretical reasoning about the states of things in the world all the time: we check our sources, revise our beliefs, further our inquiries and ask questions to experts. In situations of conflicts of belief, according to Bernard Williams, we have the following: 'if a pair of beliefs conflict, then (a) they are consistent and (b) there is a true factual belief which, if added to the original pair, will produce a set that is inconsistent' (1973: 167). We reason our way out of the conflict by adding new information that could make both statements true, or that could make at least one of them false. In our case, that could be done if you

* I would like to thank Veronica Rodriguez-Blanco, Stephen Bero, Hrafn Asgeirsson and Ronaldo Macedo for their comments on earlier versions of this chapter. I discussed earlier versions of the chapter at the Cambridge Legal Theory Discussion Group and at the Workshop 'Bernard Williams: From Responsibility to Law and Jurisprudence'. I am thankful to the comments of the audiences of both events. This chapter was possible thanks to the support of Fundação de Amparo à Pesquisa do Estado de São Paulo (The São Paulo Research Foundation – FAPESP), proc. n. 2022/11660-0.

were to provide evidence that you were working the day I thought I saw you at the theatre.

Now the second scenario. As I completed my PhD programme abroad, I was faced with a number of options of what to do next. The most prominent two were the following. I could either stay abroad, thus increasing my chances of pursuing a successful academic career, or I could go back home, thus being able to spend much needed time with my family. Following the first path would allow me to fulfil my professional aspirations at the cost of harming my personal relationships. Following the second path would do the opposite. After much deliberation, I decide to go back home. This decision is not one that I took lightly, and I do feel, from time to time, a sense of regret. It is not that I would have chosen differently if I were to go back in time, but that independently of the decision taken, there would be something to lose. In a sense, what I really wanted was to have both ways, but that was simply not possible given the facts of the case.

The two scenarios illustrate, respectively, theoretical and practical reasoning. There is much to unpack in those scenarios – and I will do that in what follows – but what I want to call attention to at this early stage is that many moral theorists, Richard Hare, for instance, have tried to explain *moral* reasoning (roughly, reason about what I ought to do. Many theorists do not distinguish clearly between moral and practical reasoning) in terms of *theoretical* reasoning.[1] According to Hare, when a given case presses a conflict between two moral principles I endorse, what I ought to do is analogous to the theatre case. I need to look for a way of accommodating both principles given the facts of the case and I can do that either by modifying principles or finding something in the facts that allows me to keep both (Williams 1973: 176–77).

A more recent version of the same argument, the one I want to focus on and which is very influential in legal philosophy, is advanced by Ronald Dworkin (1986, 2006, 2011). Dworkin is explicit in claiming that – for him – moral reasoning is interpretive reasoning.[2] See what he says, for instance, right at the beginning of *Justice for Hedgehogs* (2011) (throughout this chapter, I will focus on Dworkin's argument as presented in this book):

> Our moral judgments are *interpretations* of basic moral concepts, and we test those interpretations by placing them in a *larger framework of value to see whether they fit* with and are supported by what we take to be the best conceptions of other concepts. We generalize, that is, the interpretive approach I described. We must take that approach to all our moral and political concepts. *Morality as a whole, and not just political morality, is an interpretive enterprise* (Dworkin 2011: 12 – my emphases).

Some pages later, Dworkin claims that: '*we should treat moral reasoning as a form of interpretive reasoning* and that we can achieve moral responsibility only by

[1] See Williams' reconstruction of Hare's argument in 'Ethical Consistency' (1973: 176–77).

[2] Dworkin affirms that much several times throughout *Justice for Hedgehogs* (2011: 12, 38–39, 118–20, 127, 157–58).

aiming at the most comprehensive account we can achieve of a larger system of value in which our moral opinions figure' (2011: 38–39 – my emphasis). As I will try to elucidate, Dworkinian interpretation is similar to what I have been calling theoretical reasoning.[3]

Here lies the contribution of this chapter. A proper understanding of the way we engage with reasons, an understanding that is closer to what Williams has said about practical reason and conflicts, shows that a model like Dworkin's (or, at least, like Dworkin's in *Justice for Hedgehogs*) misrepresents the way we agents are. I will probe Dworkin's argument through Williamsian insights that I will try to present and to a limited extent refine. In the next section I will lay out in reasonable detail Dworkin's argument that moral reasoning is interpretation. After that, I will proceed to the criticisms, drawing mostly from what Williams has said in 'Ethical Consistency' (1973), *Moral Luck* (1981a) and *In the Beginning was the Deed* (2005a). A final section will discuss some Dworkinian replies and the possibility of convergence between the authors, a convergence that is indeed suggested by Dworkin in some earlier writings and that would, ultimately, benefit Williams' original arguments as well. Although much of this chapter is offered in the spirit of a cartography of the differences between the two authors, its more important function is to be a reminder of the importance of taking seriously the point of view of a concrete practical agent when doing philosophy.[4]

## II. Ronald Dworkin on Interpretation and Morality

What does Dworkin mean when he claims that moral reasoning is interpretation? Dworkin's views on interpretation received their most influential form in his work *Law's Empire*, from 1986, but have been refined over the years until the publication of *Justice for Hedgehogs*, in 2011. As mentioned in the Introduction, *Justice for Hedgehogs* will be the main target of this chapter.

To understand what Dworkin means by interpretation and why interpretation is so important to him, we should notice first that he distinguishes two activities

[3] Dworkin actually uses the more technical terms interpretive and interpretivism. Since nothing follows, for the purposes of this chapter, of the use of those terms, I will use the more conventional term interpretative.

[4] I am not the first person to claim that Dworkin somehow confuses theoretical and practical reasoning. See Veronica Rodriguez-Blanco (2016). Rodriguez-Blanco relies on Aristotle and Anscombe to show how 'judges need to engage with the activity of deciding what is of value and why we should value it to produce decisions and actions. Other legal participants do not either impose value, purpose or meaning, but rather engage with the structure of the practice and its good-making characteristics' (2016: 456). For a use of Williams' work on 'Ethical Consistency' to make jurisprudential claims, see Iris van Domselaar (2022). Domselaar's article 'elaborates on the relevance of Williams's concept of a moral remainder in the theory and practice of legal decision-making in a liberal legal order' (2022: 221). Domselaar's emphasis is on how virtue theory can help us with legal decision-making.

that form an 'embracing dualism of understanding' (Dworkin 2011: 123). Those are science and interpretation. The distinguishing mark of science, says Dworkin, is that in it we can have what he calls *bare truths* (2011: 153–54). Something is barely true if a change to this thing would not change the world in any other way. Dworkin's example is that of a pen on his table. Let us say that the pen is blue. It is possible that in an alternative world that pen is black. The change in colour, says Dworkin, would not necessarily bring with it any other changes between the two worlds. That is what he means with the idea that something can be *barely true*. It being true does not depend on anything else (2011: 113–14). Bare truths are, then, truths you can point out in the world, and they are the main concern of scientific endeavour.[5]

We do not only engage with bare truths, however. For many things we demand reasons and explanations that cannot be reduced to the scientific model. For instance, we do not want to merely know that 'it is wrong to lie' or that 'charity is praiseworthy', we want to know the reasons why those statements are true, if they are (Dworkin 2011: 114–15). In law, morality, politics, aesthetics and so on we deal with the *normative*. When dealing with the normative we need to make a case, to justify the claims we are making in terms of reasons (2011: 116). For Dworkin, we do that by *interpreting* things. For him, the main difference between scientific investigation and interpretation is that 'interpretation is purposive, not just in the vocabulary of its claims but in the standards of its success' (2011: 152).Let us unpack Dworkin's view through the use of an example. After a series of controversial decisions from the Supreme Court regarding privacy and reproductive rights, Johnny and Dio are two friends discussing the ethics of abortion. Johnny, more liberal-minded, argues that freedom and privacy require a more permissive legislation. Dio is more conservative, and argues the other way around, that real freedom is not about reproductive rights and that privacy does not cover what one does that affects innocent third parties (to his mind, the foetus). Unless Johnny and Dio are out of their minds, they know what they are disagreeing about and that their disagreement has the same object (i.e., what freedom or privacy is and requires). The disagreement between the two friends is of a different nature from the disagreement between two people that are talking about a 'bank', but in which one person has in mind Santander and the other has in mind the bank of a river. This later disagreement, says Dworkin, is spurious. But how can we make sense of Johnny and Dio's disagreement?

According to Dworkin, through a theory of interpretation. Dworkin offers a general theory of interpretation in *Justice for Hedgehogs* that is supposed to cover what we do when we interpret law, literature, moral values, and the rest. He calls this the 'value theory' of interpretation. If I may be excused a rather lengthy (and edited) quotation that summarises the main tenets of his theory:

> *Interpretation is a social phenomenon.* We can interpret as we do only because there are practices or traditions of interpretation we can join …

[5] There are many things that one can raise against this depiction of what would be barely true, but those will not be of relevance for my purposes in this chapter.

> *These social practices are truth-seeking.* In each case, when we offer an interpretation of something, we state and are understood to be stating what we take to be the truth of some matter. We do not treat these interpretive practices as pointless exercises: we assume that something of value is and ought to be served by forming, presenting, and defending opinions …
>
> … *A particular interpretation succeeds – it achieves the truth about some object's meaning – when it best realizes, for that object, the purposes properly assigned to the interpretive practice properly identified as pertinent.* Interpretation can therefore be understood, analytically, to involve three stages. We interpret social practices, first, when we individuate those practices: when we take ourselves to be engaged in legal rather than literary interpretation. We interpret, second, when we attribute some package of purposes to the genre or subgenre we identify as pertinent, and, third, when we try to identify the best realization of that package of purposes on some particular occasion (Dworkin 2011: 130–31 – my emphases).

Let us pause to consider what he is saying. The first point Dworkin calls attention to is the fact that interpretation is something social. By that he means that one cannot interpret *ex nihilo*: as an interpreter, I must join some socially shared practice of interpretation. Johnny and Dio are doing so when they debate the value of privacy, but if I were to look at the tea leaves at the bottom of my cup, this would only be an interpretation if there were a practice of interpreting tea leaves that I could join. Otherwise, my act would not be intelligible as interpretation.

The second and third points emphasised in the quotation are the most relevant for my purposes. For Dworkin, when we present interpretations of things (be they values, poems or statutes), we aim at presenting the truth about those things. Interpretation is not just a matter of personal taste or agenda. Johnny and Dio do not merely think that they are stating their tastes about privacy; each of them believes that they are tracking the truth of the matter. Finally, we know that an interpretation is successful when it presents the interpreted object in its 'best light' (to use Dworkin's favoured term in *Law's Empire*), taking into account the values and purposes we attribute to that object. Now, interpretations can be better or worse for Dworkin depending on how they present the interpreted object according to the values we attribute to it. However, those same values are themselves interpretive and depend on an exercise of interpretation to have meaning. This means that, as Dworkin puts right at the beginning of *Justice for Hedgehogs*, regarding political values:

> [A] defense of some particular conception of a political value like equality or liberty must draw on values beyond itself: it would be flaccidly circular to appeal to liberty to defend a conception of liberty. So political concepts must be integrated with one another. We cannot defend a conception of any of them without showing how our conception fits with and into appealing conceptions of the others (2011: 7).

Later in the book Dworkin presents the same point in a slightly more detailed way: 'If you organized all your moral convictions into an ideally effective filter encapsulating your will, they would form a large interconnected and interdependent system of principles and ideas' (2011: 117). Johnny and Dio would, according to Dworkin, present their case for their understanding of privacy by drawing from their understandings of other values, such as the already mentioned freedom, equality, autonomy, and so on. At the end of the day, the interpretation that presented the values in the most coherent way with other values would be the true(est) one. Dworkin claims that we proceed in this same way in the diverse domains of value. 'What is the law?' is an interpretive question, and much of his work was devoted to this. In *Law's Empire*, Dworkin advances three different interpretations of law – conventionalism, pragmatism, and integrity – and argues for the latter one (1986). More importantly for us in this chapter, in *Justice for Hedgehogs* Dworkin understands that answering the question 'what shall I do?' is an interpretive effort in the same way: 'We suppose that even the most abstract moral concepts – the concept of what is good and of what we ought to do – are interpretive' (2011: 180).[6]

## III. Interpretation and Practical Deliberation

Let us revisit the scenarios from the Introduction. What Dworkin would say about them? The theatre scenario is likely to be considered a case of scientific inquiry, trying to find out what were the bare truths of the matter, and in earlier writing Dworkin presents this is a probably clearer way with the idea of an *empirical disagreement*. Empirical disagreements are about given states of things in the world, for example, in the law we can have an empirical disagreement about the number of witnesses to a contract: the plaintiff claims that only two (out of the three needed) witnesses were present whereas the defendant claims the opposite (Dworkin 1986: 3–6). Empirical disagreements are solved by finding out what was really the case. In our theatre case, if a trusty co-worker of yours told me that they were with you all day, then I would know that my first impression (that you were at the theatre) was wrong. All my beliefs are rendered consistent once again. It seems that what Dworkin takes to be scientific inquiry and/or theoretical disagreement would squarely be classed as theoretical reasoning in the classical scheme.

Things are not that simple with the second scenario. There are actually three issues in it that must be distinguished from the start. When facing the prospects after the completion of the PhD, I might deliberate and conclude that both courses of action – staying abroad or going home – are well supported by reasons and that those reasons underdetermine what I shall do. The reasons 'run out', so to say. As Joseph Raz pointed out, in a case like this, the decision I end up picking up would

[6] Throughout our discussion, when referring to practical deliberation, I will prefer to frame it in terms of what shall I do, instead of what I ought to do. The reason for this choice is that by framing the practical question as what shall I do, we avoid further complications about the concepts of ought and obligation. I am thankful to Veronica Rodriguez-Blanco for suggesting this.

be influenced by other things, notably my character (Raz 1999a). A different issue, or maybe the same issue in different clothes, regards incommensurability.[7] This is the idea that the reasons in favour and against certain courses of action are not liable to comparison. Raz thus explains this issue: 'the possibility that the value of two items, or that the goodness of two options, is incommensurate, in that neither of them is better than the other nor are they of equal value' (Raz 1999b: 46). A third issue relates to the notions of regret, or more specifically what Williams calls 'agent-regret'. It may be the case that after deliberation, I do know what I shall do, but that comes at a cost that I regret. Doing what I now think I need to do will cause a sense of loss, that I am sacrificing something valuable to pursue something else I understand as (equally or more) important (Williams 2001). What I will have to say in this chapter will not turn on the specifics of those three situations, but we need to bear in mind that they are not the same. What really matters is that all those situations illustrate paradigmatic aspects of our practical reasoning.

When agents deliberate about what they shall do, their deliberative starting point is whom they are, that is, what Williams has called their 'subjective motivational sets' (1981c). Such sets are made up by the desires, dispositions, values, attachments, ground projects, and so on. For instance, elements as my professional project and my family values are going to figure in my deliberation about what path to follow after the PhD. I do not think that Dworkin would have issues with *this* initial claim, however, he would insist that there is a right way to deliberate, namely, interpretation. Dworkin would invite me to, first, identify what are the relevant values or goods involved, and then to interpret them 'constructively', as he would say in *Law's Empire* (1986: 45–86). 'Caring about one's family' and 'professional success' are two possible candidates. Dworkin would tell me that I must interpret those values in a way that ultimately makes them mutually reinforcing and in doing so I would find out what is the right answer for the dilemma at hand. The form of a Dworkinian answer would be the following: 'given the best interpretation of values A and B, there is a right answer to the case at hand, namely, one shall X'.

Notice how similar the structure of the Dworkinian argument is to that of conflicts of belief. The ultimate goal is coherence. Regarding conflicts of belief, Williams says that 'conflict is basically adventitious, and a resolution of it disembarrasses one of a mistaken view which for a while confused the situation' (1973: 175). Dworkin is proposing something similar to conflicts in the realm of practical reason. When facing an apparent conflict, I must interpret the values involved looking for the all-things-considered best interpretation of them, the interpretation that dispels their conflict, and this interpretation is taken by Dworkin as the

[7] Domselaar points out that much of legal theorising is under the spell of the opposite idea, namely, commensurability, the claim that there are ways of comparing different decisions in order to find out the best one (Domselaar 2022: 226–31). Among the defendants of commensurability, Domselaar points out Dworkin (the focus of this chapter) and – perhaps more influential in the Civil Law world – Robert Alexy.

right one. Now, if Dworkin were to be right on this score, the result would be that the many issues I just pointed out (underdetermination by reasons, incommensurability, matters of regret) would be no-issues at all.[8] The first two would be solved in the course of our interpretive endeavour, whereas the last one would be the emotional hangover of our former, irreflective, understanding of value.[9]

At this point, something starts to feel wrong. It is useful, I think, to turn to a distinction made by Williams in 'Ethical Consistency', in order to see what is it that feels wrong in the Dworkinian account.[10] Williams distinguishes between conflicts of beliefs – we have already seen those –, conflicts of desires, and moral conflicts. There are a couple of differences between conflicts of beliefs and conflicts of desires. Firstly, says Williams, conflicts between beliefs naturally point out to their solution, so to say, because by the moment I acquire a pair of inconsistent beliefs, one of those beliefs tends to lose its grip (Williams 1973: 169). We can see this in the theatre case. As soon as I have the pair of beliefs 'I saw you at the theatre' and 'you were working that day', one of them will start losing credibility. As Williams points out, this is so due to the relationship between beliefs and truth.

When it comes to desires, however, conflict by itself will not make any of them weaker, at least not necessarily, and this is so because desires do not have the same relationship with truth that beliefs have. The second difference is related to the aftermath of conflict. After a conflict of beliefs, the defeated belief simply ceases to be a belief (Williams 1973: 169–70). My reaction, after realising that you were not at the theatre, is likely to be 'Oh, I guess I was mistaken then!' and that will be the end of it. With desires, matters are different. A desire can (but not necessarily will) survive conflict, as anyone going through a diet knows well. The fact that I decide to not have dessert does not mean that I stop desiring it, and as Williams suggests, sometimes this desire can reappear in different forms at a later moment. Desires can be recalcitrant in a way that beliefs cannot (unless, of course, we have a desire to believe in something) (1973: 170).

What Williams calls moral conflicts in 'Ethical Consistency' is related to what I've been referring to as our engagement with practical reason and to what Dworkin refers to as moral reasoning (I will say more on this in a moment). Williams defines moral conflict as 'cases in which there is a conflict between two moral judgments that a man is disposed to make relevant to deciding what to do' (1973: 170). Dworkin, it seems, treats those conflicts as similar to conflicts between beliefs. He explicitly says, about apparently conflicting values, that 'we are drawn to each of the rival positions through arguments that, *if we were finally to accept them as authoritative, would release us from the appeal of the other one*' (Dworkin 2001a: 82 – my emphasis). Now, this does not seem to be the case. In the second scenario post-PhD I presented, it makes sense to

[8] See also what Dworkin has to say about the difference between uncertainty and indeterminacy (2011: 88–96).

[9] To be sure, Dworkin does not mean that remorse, regret and the like do not happen, but he does play them down (2011: 200–202).

[10] For a useful summary of Williams' argument on 'Ethical Consistency' and its developments in the hands of other writers, see Iris van Domselaar 2022: 221–26.

think that I can feel a sense of regret or loss for the path not taken. If I go back home, I can daydream about the career that never was, or if I stay abroad, I can sorely miss my loved ones and lament the fact that I am not with them. In our engagement with what we shall do, with practical reasoning, it makes more sense to leave space for those recalcitrant feelings than to put them away as unwanted by-products of interpretation. In this aspect, what Williams calls moral conflicts, conflicts of desires and what I am loosely referring to practical conflicts are closer to each other than they are to conflicts between beliefs.

There is more to be said about conflicts between desires that sheds light in our current analysis. As I will try to show, both conflicts between desires and moral conflicts are instances of practical conflicts, although this is sometimes murky. Desires play a role in the explanation of action. This is fairly uncontroversial, but how they do that is trickier, notably, the relationship between desires and reasons for action is the subject of much philosophical controversy. A thesis usually associated with David Hume and that Williams himself sometimes writes as if that were the case, holds that desires *are* reasons for action. This is inaccurate, at least as it is usually presented, for reasons that I cannot detail here. The gist of the argument against the simpler Humean thesis – and in this I am borrowing a bit from Raz – is that *intelligible* desires are backed by reasons of some sort, reasons that point out to some good or value in satisfying that desire (we should be careful here to not read good or value as necessarily entailing moral qualities). This is what distinguishes desires an agent can properly recognise as her own from those that she identifies as external to her or even pathological (Raz 1999b: 54–62). Someone with an urge to wash her hands every five minutes can point this out: that her washing her hands every five minutes it not really her, but her OCD. This person sees that there is nothing of value in acting out of that urge, but she can't help herself.

This means that, when it comes to desires, we have margin to reason our way out of some of them. If by chance I stop seeing that anything good or valuable will result from pursuing a given desire, this might make the desire weaker or even make it vanish. If a person has a desire to cheat on her partner, after some deliberation she can conclude that it is not worth it, that no good is achieved by cheating. After her deliberation, the desire is likely to be weaker (of course, desires can take different forms after deliberation. Their psychology is more complex than what I can address). Williams points out that much ancient philosophy, Stoicism for instance, revolved around the idea that a person can train herself to have the fewest possible amount of desires or only the right desires. This is intelligible as a claim because desires are not definitive in practical deliberation. Nonetheless, there are important limits to this capacity of abandonment of desire, since some desires can be connected to a person's sense of self, and of course, a person without any desires at all would not be (really) human (Williams 1973: 177–78).[11]

[11] This is also the reason why some desire-negation goals (such as nirvana or apatheia) have so little appeal to some people (to me, for instance).

The main point is that desires can lose their grip on us (or, conversely, become stronger) depending on how they relate to the reasons we have. This is why I think that we can treat conflicts between desires as a case of practical conflict. We find out what we *really* desire when we deliberate about what we shall do. We are back to reasons for action.

Let me organise the train of thought a bit before moving on. I started the chapter pointing out that there are at least two forms of reasoning, theoretical reasoning and practical reasoning. Theoretical reasoning is mostly concerned with what is the truth about a given matter, whereas practical reasoning is about the question 'what shall I do?'. Following that, I pointed out that Dworkin divides things in a slightly different way: science and interpretation. The confusion starts because those two pairs are not mapping the same territory. Notably, Dworkin puts our engagement with normative matters in the realm of interpretation, but interpretation itself looks a lot more to theoretical reasoning than to practical reasoning as it is usually conceived. In the last couple of paragraphs, I've been trying to show how the relationship between desires, reasons for action, beliefs, and so on is murkier than on first impression, and that moral conflicts and conflicts of desires at the end of the day are about reasons for action.

We can now put the issues in a sharper way. One plausible way to understand Dworkin's claim is to see Dworkinian interpretation as a method of practical deliberation, that is, as a version of what Williams has called a 'sound deliberative route'. A sound deliberative route, says Williams, explains how an agent can get from her subjective motivational set to the reasons for action that apply to her (Williams 1995). Understood in such terms, Dworkinian interpretation would hold that what an agent has reason to do is what the best interpretation of her values and so on tells her to do, where best interpretation is understood as the most coherent one. I must reinterpret all my values, attachments and so on in order to turn them into Dworkin's 'geodesic dome' (2006: 160–61).[12] Dworkin's approach bears much resemblance to what we saw about Hare at the Introduction, and what Williams says about the latter also applies to the former:

> This is inadequate on two counts. First, the only focus that it provides for retrospective regret is that I arrived unprepared, and not that I did not do the thing rejected in the eventual choice. Second, there must surely be something wrong with the consequence that, granted I do not go back on the choice I make on this occasion, no similar situation later can possibly present me with a conflict (Williams 1973: 176).

[12] I do not think that, at this stage of the argument, Dworkin is committed to what Williams refers to as reasons externalism, that is, the view that there are reasons for action that are independent of one's subjective motivational sets (Williams 1981c). As I understand Dworkin's point, we can get to internal reasons for action through an exercise in constructive interpretation, reasons that are for him objective in an important sense. I will come back to externalism and internalism later in this chapter. For a subtle discussion of Williams' reasons internalism (one that I tend to endorse), see Gerald Lang's contribution to this volume in chapter three.

Let us unpack this a bit. The first point Williams makes is about regret. Cases like the PhD scenario are ones in which no matter the choice I make, I am likely to feel some sense of regret, even if I take the choice I believe to be correct. A theory like Hare's or Dworkin's might suggest that the locus of regret is my lack of vision before the conflict, whereas the real locus of regret is the *decision I made*. The second point is the most important one. This kind of theory supposes that, once I have figured out the best interpretation in a given case, then I will have no sense of conflict (and its accompanying feelings of regret) when facing the same situation in the future. This flies in the face of the phenomenology of conflict. There is little reason to think that – let us assume – already at home after the PhD, I will not feel conflicted again when someone offers me an excellent professional opportunity abroad.

Underlying those two points is the fact that practical reasoning starts from whom we are, from our personal resources as attachments, values, projects, and so on. The meaning of those resources is not (only) a matter of interpretation but also a matter of cultural and historical contingency. What we come to understand as privacy or freedom (to recall the values discussed by Johnny and Dio) depends on what Williams has called 'contingent historical deposits' (2001: 94–95; 2005b: 75). This means that the materials that make up my motivational set are not as plastic as Dworkin needs them to be. Of course, there is margin for refinement and reinterpretation, but I cannot do that to an indefinite extent. If I keep reinterpreting those values or goods beyond that margin in which they are recognisable as the values or goods that I endorse, I might get to a coherent interpretation in which they do not conflict anymore, but they will not be the values I recognised as *mine* anymore. If I stop the exercise of interpretation at a point in which the values are still recognisably mine, then it might be the case that they will still be in conflict, and in that case, choosing one option over another will be ground for regret and similar notions.

My arguments can be labelled phenomenological, since I was concerned with how we – as concrete agents – engage with matters of practical reasoning, and the conclusion so far is that, as Williams said, 'Moral conflicts are neither systematically avoidable, nor all soluble without remainder' (1973: 179). Like Hare's account of moral reasoning, Dworkin's interpretive theory misplaces the idea of regret. The reason for this is that Dworkin's interpretive theory attributes way more flexibility to the materials it interprets than they have. Because practical reasoning starts from whom we are, the Dworkinian model ends up presenting interpretations of values and the rest that cannot be accepted by the concrete agents. At the end of the day, the model resembles theoretical reasoning, with its emphasis on coherence and truth. This means that the model cannot explain (all) practical reasoning.[13]

[13] For a similar conclusion, although through a different path, see Veronica Rodriguez-Blanco (2016). The argument she puts forward is that 'constructive interpretation and its conception of "imposing meaning, value or purpose" on practice is a theoretical perspective that neglects and misunderstands action and practical reason' (Rodriguez-Blanco 2016: 431).

For sure, there are instances in which we do interpret in the terms proposed by Dworkin, but there are limits to that.

## IV. Dworkinian Replies and a Matter of Philosophical Temperament

A Dworkinian might avail herself of two different replies. Firstly, they might reply that I've been answering to the wrong question from the start. In *Justice for Hedgehogs*, Dworkin makes much of Hume's principle, and a Dworkinian could avail herself of the following move inspired by it: when we engage in constructive interpretation of our values, goods, and so on, we are trying to seize their *true meaning*. That agents feel regret (or any other emotion) in concrete cases is of no importance to the truth-value of interpretations. If we want to know what freedom *really* is, says the Dworkinian, we need to engage in interpretation and present freedom in its best light, supported by all other values we have. Indeed, Dworkin himself recognises that a full account of value is beyond human grasp, as none of us have the time, resources, and intellectual power to lay bare the full net of value. Nonetheless, if you want to know what freedom, or familial loyalty, or religion *really* means, you need to take your shot at the interpretive endeavour.

In a nutshell, the first Dworkinian reply is that my Williams-inspired criticisms miss the mark because they are not *really* about the normative. This seems to me a mistake. Practical reasoning is about what we, concrete agents, do in the world. Each one of us engages in it all the time, and our engagement is always from our standpoint, from whom we are. It is not that we cannot attempt to produce the sort of all-things-considered interpretation that Dworkin talks about, but that such interpretation, even if produced by ourselves, will not have the power to demand our allegiance *unless* it can be recognised by us as binding. That will be the case only if this interpretation does not take our values, goods, and so on beyond what we can recognise as our understandings of them.[14] To keep with the Dworkinian jargon, the interpretative character of our concepts allows for ample margin of resignification (and Dworkin is right in claiming that we can sharpen our own understanding of them when we engage in their interpretation). However, the resulting interpretations must still be recognisable by us as interpretations of *our* concepts.

What if a Dworkinian abandons the presumably uncontroversial starting point that practical deliberation starts from ourselves? That is unlikely to be a move endorsed by Dworkin himself, since he emphasises the need for conviction in our interpretations (and conviction about an interpretation only comes if this interpretation speaks to us),[15] but let us entertain it for a moment. A Dworkinian that

[14] A point pressed by Williams many times in his criticism of Dworkin. See also Williams 1981b: 80–81.

[15] See Dworkin 2011: Chs 2–5.

forfeits the idea that practical deliberation starts from ourselves would need to argue for the existence of reasons for action that apply to agents but that are independent of their subjective motivational sets. This is the position that Williams calls reasons externalism (1981c). According to externalism, there can be reasons for action that apply to an agent even if such agent fails to recognise them *after proper deliberation*. This later qualification is important: agents can deliberate defectively (i.e. they might have misinformation or engage in wishful thinking and so on) and so miss reasons that they themselves would come to recognise had their deliberation gone well. This is why Williams claims that any plausible account of practical deliberation will have room for corrections of both facts and reasoning (Williams 1995). What the externalist claims is stronger, they claim that there can be reasons for action that are independent of an agent's motivations whatsoever.

An in-depth analysis of externalism is beyond the scope of this chapter, but it faces two main challenges. Firstly, a reasons externalist must explain from where external reasons come from. This is likely to take the shape of an ethical theory such as utilitarianism or Kantian morality (e.g., the grounding of ethical reasons on considerations of utility or rationality).[16] Secondly, and more important for our purposes, there is need for an explanation of how those external reasons can be recognised by concrete agents as binding on them, as being reasons *for action*.[17] It is hard to tackle this second challenge. If the externalist claims that those external reasons are recognised as binding because they are about things that the agents care about (values, goods, etc) then those reasons are at the end of the day *internal*, that is, an agent could come to recognise them from her subjective motivational set. This has the cost of bringing back all the limitations we have seen: the need to accommodate conflict, regret, and so on. Dworkin's own insistence that our interpretations must speak to us suggests that he was no externalist (or, at least, that he was ambivalent about it), but such insistence should also point out the limits of our interpretative endeavours.

What about the second reply? This one is more interesting to my mind. To understand this reply, let us take a look at an interesting exchange that happened between Williams and Dworkin, in the context of a tribute to Isaiah Berlin:

> Mr. Williams: … Do you think there is a sense in which, if values are properly understood, then it cannot be the case that one of them rightfully asserted leads to the sacrifice of the other?
>
> Mr. Dworkin: I haven't made that strong a claim. I've said that we should concentrate on finding the most attractive conceptions of our political values, and only then ask whether, on those attractive conceptions, these values conflict (Dworkin et al 2001b: 126).[18]

Dworkin proceeds to recognise that there might be cases in which the most attractive conceptions of our values will show them as being in conflict (that is, their

[16] See, in general, the criticism made in Williams (2011).
[17] As suggested by S.G. Chappell and N. Smyth (2018).
[18] I am thankful to Damian Cueni and Matthieu Queloz for bringing my attention to this exchange.

interpretation in their best light will present the conflict) (Dworkin et al 2001b: 127)[19] and he also recognises that he 'didn't mean to claim that our lives were always free from dramatic, even tragic, conflicts in personal values' (2001b: 136). The second reply, then, would be to say that Dworkin's claim is more modest. This more modest claim is made of two parts. Firstly, it is not that values *never* really conflict, but that we cannot take conflict for granted. Since values are not found out there in the wild but are constructed interpretively, there is no reason to assume conflict as default. Secondly, '[w]e shouldn't buy failure in advance' (2001b: 127), rather, Dworkin's suggestion is that first we should try our hand in the exercise of articulating integrated conceptions of our values before assuming irresolvable conflict.

This second reply seems to me correct, but it dissolves many of the important differences between Williams' outlook and Dworkin's (and to be fair, there is nothing wrong in that! It is a mistake of much philosophy to think that its practitioners are playing some sort of *battle royale*). What do I mean by that? Regarding the first part of the modest claim, we have seen that there is indeed space for reinterpretation and refinement of our values one in the light of the other, but there are important limits to this, limits granted by what can count as a value that is recognisable as mine. So, there is nothing wrong with the suggestion that we should first see if we can make our values integrated before declaring them to be in conflict. We actually do that when we stop and think 'what is it that justice or liberty really demands from me?'. Insofar as those values can still make a claim on our allegiance, refining them is not only plausible but possibly the most sensible thing to do as well. It is true that many conflicts might be unavoidable, but this is no reason to not avoid those that can sensibly be avoided.[20] As Dworkin himself stressed several times, we should not allow moral pluralism to become moral laziness. Insofar as this is all that Dworkin means, then his view and then one I've been defending in this chapter might very well supplement each other.

The last remark takes us to the second part of the modest claim. It seems to be an exhortation in favour of optimism of some kind. There is nothing wrong with that, granted that optimism does not degenerate into wishful thinking. On this point, the difference between Williams and Dworkin might be better described as one in 'philosophical temperament', to use William James' famous expression. A difference in temperament between an American legal philosopher that shaped his thinking during the liberal optimism of the Warren Court and an English moral philosopher that was first and foremost a reader of the Greeks and Nietzsche.

## Bibliography

Chappell, SG & Smyth, N (2018) 'Bernard Williams' in N Zalta (ed), *The Stanford Encyclopedia of Philosophy* (Fall 2018 Edition), available at https://plato.stanford.edu/archives/fall2018/entries/williams-bernard/.

[19] See also Dworkin 2011: 118–20.
[20] This point was raised to me by both Stephen Bero and Christopher Tollefsen.

Domselaar, I (2022), 'Law's Regret: On Moral Remainders, (In)commensurability and a Virtue-Ethical Approach to Legal Decision-Making' 13 2 *Jurisprudence* 220.

Dworkin, R (1986) *Law's Empire* (Cambridge, Harvard University Press).

—— (2001a) 'Do Liberal Values Conflict?' in M Lilla & R Dworkin (eds), *The Legacy of Isaiah Berlin* (New York, New York Review of Books).

—— (2006) *Justice in Robes* (Cambridge, Harvard University Press).

—— (2011) *Justice for Hedgehogs* (Cambridge, Harvard University Press).

Dworkin, R et al (2001b) 'Discussion – Pluralism' in M Lilla & R Dworkin (eds), *The Legacy of Isaiah Berlin* (New York, New York Review of Books).

Raz, J (1999a) 'When we are Ourselves' in J Raz, *Engaging Reason* (Oxford, Oxford University Press).

—— (1999b) 'Incommensurability and Agency' in J Raz, *Engaging Reason* (Oxford, Oxford University Press).

Rodriguez-Blanco, V (2016) 'Action in Law's Empire: Judging in the Deliberative Mode' 29 *Canadian Journal of Law & Jurisprudence* 431.

Williams, B (1973) 'Ethical Consistency' in B Williams, *Problems of the Self* (Cambridge, Cambridge University Press).

—— (1981a) *Moral Luck* (Cambridge, Cambridge University Press).

—— (1981b) 'Conflicts of Values' in B Williams, *Moral Luck* (Cambridge, Cambridge University Press).

—— (1981c) 'Internal and External Reasons' in B Williams, *Moral Luck* (Cambridge, Cambridge University Press).

—— (1995) 'Internal Reasons and the Obscurity of Blame' in B Williams, *Making Sense of Humanity* (Cambridge, Cambridge University Press).

—— (2001) 'Liberalism and Loss' in M Lilla & R Dworkin (eds), *The Legacy of Isaiah Berlin* (New York, New York Review of Books).

—— (2005a) *In the Beginning was the Deed*, edited by G Hawthorn (Princeton, Princeton University Press).

—— (2005b) 'From Freedom to Liberty: The Construction of a Political Value' in B Williams, *In the Beginning was the Deed*, edited by G Hawthorn (Princeton, Princeton University Press).

—— (2011) *Ethics and the Limits of Philosophy* (London, Routledge).

# 15

# A Williamsian Account of Jurisprudence as Conceptual Morphology

MIODRAG JOVANOVIĆ AND BOJAN SPAIĆ*

## I. Introduction

Apart from sporadically and indirectly tackling legally relevant issues (e.g., the idea of equality), law was not in the focus of Bernard Williams' philosophy. However, his understanding of what it means to philosophise and what are the central tasks of philosophy can be of the utmost importance for meta-jurisprudential debates regarding the proper methodology of legal philosophy. By methodology, we mostly mean a way of doing things in the philosophy of law, modalities of going about one's job when one does jurisprudential research. A cursory look at the methodology of jurisprudence shows that conceptual analysis in one or the other of its forms has been the staple of jurisprudential inquiry. However, the method that is preferred by legal philosophy has been subject to criticism from both philosophers of law and general philosophers. At times, these criticisms were joined with proposals for alternative methodologies that might be able to solve the issues identified with conceptual analysis. This chapter aims to identify one of those alternatives in the work of Bernard Williams.

In the first part of the chapter, we explain the use and problems of conceptual analysis in jurisprudence, along with some sceptical jurisprudential views about conceptual analysis. In the second part, we elaborate on Williams' understanding of conceptual analysis, as well as his criticisms and alternatives. We argue that a Williamsian understanding of legal philosophy would be closer to a moderate, 'down-to-earth' analysis of law as a distinctive social practice, albeit one that does not insist on the sharp distinction between analytic and synthetic judgments. More specifically, we argue that Williams does not solve the tension between analytical and historical philosophical methodology. Still, he offers a convincing way of thinking about the criteria for evaluating philosophical inquiries by assessing its

* This chapter results from research conducted within the Horizon Twinning project 'Advancing cooperation on The Foundations of Law – ALF' (project no 101079177). The project is financed by the European Union.

ability to help us understand the law in our time and our relation to it. We label this approach 'conceptual morphology' and in the third part of the chapter we try to demonstrate that the contours of this distinctive approach to jurisprudence can be illustrated on his treatment of human rights.

## II. Conceptual Analysis and its Discontents (in Jurisprudence)

The dominant approach of contemporary legal philosophy is conceptual analysis. Philosophical analysis examines and clarifies concepts, ideas, arguments, and theories in philosophy. It involves breaking down complex philosophical concepts into their constituent parts, analysing their underlying assumptions, and evaluating their logical coherence and consistency. Philosophical analysis is often used to clarify and resolve philosophical debates, identify and solve philosophical problems, as well as to develop new philosophical theories and perspectives. Analysis is used by philosophers across various fields, including metaphysics, epistemology, ethics, and political philosophy.

Jurisprudence has embraced philosophical analysis to clarify the nature of law, legal concepts, legal reasoning, and any other legal problem. It is, however, far from obvious what exactly the method of 'philosophical analysis' amounts to in philosophy or jurisprudence. For one, throughout its history, analysis 'has been understood and practised in many different ways' (Beaney 2016). Secondly, in the development of modern analytical philosophy, Timothy Williamson (2014) notices that what was 'a species of philosophy with so much anti-metaphysics in its gene pool' has, in the last decades, witnessed 'the growth and flourishing of boldly speculative metaphysics' within its tradition. This has led to various positions regarding the content and the applications of philosophical analysis and significant confusion in branches of philosophy that use it. Needless to say, legal philosophy has not stayed unaffected by this trend.

A prominent strand of legal positivism, with slight differentiations, favours the so-called '*metaphysically driven conceptual analysis*'. According to Joseph Raz (2005), a theory of law 'consists of necessary truths, for only necessary truths about the law reveal the nature of law'. In Kenneth Himma's words, explicating the nature of law in terms of claims that are necessarily true is 'the hallmark of metaphysical inquiry' (2015: 83). In that respect, '[t]he metaphysical character of conceptual analysis, traditionally conceived, is logically connected to the view that the epistemology of conceptual analysis is *a priori* in character' (2015: 83). Finally, the necessary and essential features of law 'are those found not only in all existing and historical legal systems, but in all possible ones – or all humanly possible ones – and those are numberless and unobservable' (Green 2013). Philosophical analysis has been considered an invaluable tool for understanding legal systems, the meaning of legal concepts, and the nature and principles of legal reasoning in the tradition called 'analytical jurisprudence'. The method of philosophical analysis has not been confined to the descriptive strand of contemporary jurisprudence championed by Hart. Some prominent representatives of non-positivism think of the method of analysis in the same terms. Hence, Murphy states that 'natural law jurisprudence … takes seriously the task of providing what Raz calls a "theory of law"' (Murphy 2015: 124), while Alexy notes that the question on the nature of law may be substituted with the one on the necessary properties of law (Alexy 2008: 290).

Williamson rightly points out that

> [a]nother main strand in the development of the analytic tradition, ordinary language philosophy, tended to be almost equally suspicious of the ways in which metaphysicians made free with ordinary words, far from the everyday contexts of use on which their meaning was supposed to depend' (Williamson 2014: 7).

Metaphysically driven conceptual analysts readily meet this challenge, by arguing, along with Frank Jackson (1998), that theirs is a *modest* version of metaphysics, which 'seeks to understand the nature of a thing as it is defined by the conceptual framework we impose on the world through shared linguistic practices'.[1] In doing so, this approach to the method of philosophical analysis tries to emphasise that 'it is not overly abstract or insufficiently connected to the social realities of law as it operates in people's lives in law-governed societies' (Dickson 2022: 53).

However, not all are persuaded by this argument. Leiter (2021) dismisses this approach by calling it 'the current fad in analytic philosophy'.[2] Chiassoni (2016: 69) goes a step further, arguing that this trend 'constitutes a very serious threat to philosophical progress in jurisprudence', insofar as it represents 'the return to a pre-analytical theory of concepts'. Bix sides with them, raising the voice against this newly found 'metaphysical focus' of jurisprudence.[3] In his last book, Schauer also acknowledges that he departs from the dominant methodological search for 'properties that define law in all possible legal systems in all possible worlds'. Instead, he proposes to focus on 'typical', rather than 'necessary' features of law, because just as we

> can understand important aspects of the history and chemistry of wine by focusing on the fact that wine is typically but not necessarily made from grapes, so too might we learn a great deal about law in general … from law's typical but not necessary features' (Schauer 2015: 4).

According to these authors,[4] abandoning the metaphysically driven conceptual analysis pushes us toward an analytical work with 'a more down-to-earth

[1] In contrast, the immodest version 'seeks to understand the nature of a thing as it really is independent of any such conceptual framework that we impose on the world' (Himma 2019: 33).

[2] In particular, Leiter criticises Shapiro's Legality for popularising 'a strange and unproductive way of framing the problems in general jurisprudence … in terms of metaphysical grounding relations'. See Leiter 2021: 753.

[3] Thus, Bix argues that 'legal philosophers should remove metaphysical language which serves only to distort or distract from the true underlying issues'. See Bix 2021.

[4] For a criticism of Himma's employment of the 'metaphysically driven conceptual analysis' in his book *Coercion and the Nature of Law*, see Jovanović 2021. For a more comprehensive application of a prototype theory of concepts in the analytical exposition of international law, see Jovanović 2019.

ambition', the one that is commonly associated with Hart, and aimed at '"explanatory elucidation" of the structure of legal phenomena' (Chiassoni 2016: 64).

What is problematised by these authors is the intricate relation between analytical and empirical methods of research. The most radical step, in that respect, is suggested by Leiter, who favours a Quine-inspired naturalism, which is sceptical about the analytical approach and takes philosophy to be continuous with empirical science (Leiter 2007). The 'naturalization' of jurisprudence is generally welcomed by the 'third branch of jurisprudence', which is in Tamanaha's words, composed of both traditional schools of historical and sociological jurisprudence and legal realism, as well as new proponents of socio-legal studies, who all heavily rely on the empirical method in studying law (Tamanaha 2017).

## III. Williams and Philosophical Analysis – A Historical Alternative

The entire conception of ethics developed by Bernard Williams was prompted by a rejection of the claim that linguistic analysis can be used to solve the most important issues of moral philosophy. Linguistic philosophy, as elaborated by J.L. Austin, was applied in moral philosophy by Richard Hare for the development of a conception of ethics named 'universal prescriptivism'. Universal prescriptivism advanced the idea that the entirety of morality can be derived from a linguistic analysis of the concepts of 'ought' and 'good'. When we start from this position, Hare claimed, we can arrive at an explanation of moral utterances as prescriptions about how we think things ought to be. These prescriptions are distinct from other prescriptions because agents are willing to make the same prescriptions apply to them and other moral agents (Chappell & Smyth 2023).

The clarifications of some of the concepts offered by linguistic analysis are praiseworthy. In earlier writing, Williams was adamant that analytic philosophy is the only serious contender in the contemporary philosophical landscape, with other currents coming and going while analytic philosophy 'remains the only real philosophy there is' (Williams 2006: 168). Still, even at these early stages of thinking, the claim involved significant caveats. Namely, in ethics, political philosophy, and legal philosophy, linguistic analysis is failing to 'deliver that what might be expected of it', namely, a theory that can guide our reasoning and action (Moore 2003: 337). However, this is not only true of analytical philosophy; it is also true of any philosophy. The reasons for our reasoning and actions do not come from rational inquiries. For something to exist as a reason for action, it has to be based on some motivation – values, desires, commitments, etc. (Williams 2008b).

In this sense, analytic philosophy doesn't fare any better than any other philosophy that is unaware of its own limits. As a result, Williams did not repudiate analytic philosophy or try to alter its methodology from within. He famously claimed that he is both deniably and undeniably an analytical philosopher.

Deniably, because he was prone to deny that what he did was conceptual analysis. Undeniably, because very few people would be ready to accept his arguments for denying his belonging to the analytical tradition. In the Preface to the *Ethics and the Limits of Philosophy*, he says that '[t]he philosophy of this book can no doubt be called on some broad specification, "analytical"'. For him, '[w]hat distinguishes analytical philosophy from other contemporary philosophy … is a certain way of going on, which involves argument, distinctions, and … moderately plain speech'. Accordingly, the main 'aim of analytical philosophy … is to be clear' (Williams 2006: viii).

Still, he was intent on differentiating clarity from simplification. In fact, the accounts of ethics simplified the ethical life rather than enriching it, which has been an important target of his criticisms (Koopman 2010: 7). In this sense, Williams had issues with what it means for a philosophy to be analytical. In practical terms, he greatly valued the enterprise of analysing concepts with clarity while at the same time trying to determine the reach and limits of analysis in the totality of philosophical approaches to problems. As far as it confines itself to its main task – clarity – there cannot be many objections to the analytical way of doing philosophy. However, the aim of clarity has, for some reason, resulted in technicality and narrowness. As a follow-up, the analytical tradition has parted ways with the humanist goals of philosophy and entered close relations with scientism – a philosophical belief that science is the only valid way of understanding the world and solving problems. This view holds that all other forms of knowledge, including philosophy, religion, and art, are either irrelevant or inferior to scientific knowledge. Analysis, or conceptual description, is only part of the job. He argued:

> Philosophy has to learn the lesson that conceptual description (or, more specifically, analysis) is not self-sufficient; and that such projects as deriving our concepts *a priori* from universal conditions of human life, though they indeed have a place (a greater place in some areas of philosophy than others), are likely to leave many unexplained features that provoke philosophical enquiry (Williams 2006: 192).

Williams believed that the analytic tradition had become too narrow and technical, which led to a disconnection from the concerns of everyday life and practical matters. He argued that philosophy should return to its roots as a discipline that engages with human concerns and emotions and should not shy away from exploring the historical and cultural contexts in which ideas are embedded.

Williams understands the allure of scientism. Science has grown to have intellectual authority that philosophy can only dream about (2006: 188). The authority is earned and deserved by science's technological and predictive successes. Philosophy fails if it tries to deny this success. It fails, however, even if it tries to reproduce this success by insisting on the ideal of a neutral description of phenomena because it incorporates itself in a narrow and limiting view of the world. With scientism, philosophy ignores the complex and subjective aspects of human experience. In the spirit of scientism, the cardinal vice of conceptual analysis, especially the one understood as 'metaphysically driven', is that it treats all concepts as a-historical. Philosophical concepts, along with philosophical problems of those concepts, are abstracted from the point in time in which they are analysed for the sake of arriving at necessary and sufficient criteria for something to count as a determinate concept. For Williams, the scientific inquiry model is the best approach to understand the world independently from subjective experience, local phenomena, and bias. However, the same approach is not suitable for all aims.

What was, thus, Williams' addendum to analytical philosophy? In a world of labels, it is difficult to provide one for Williams' philosophical position, particularly as he seemingly could not care less about the classification step. Nevertheless, in carving out a distinctive philosophical position (e.g., by criticising both deontology and utilitarianism as ethical theories or arguing that both analytic and continental philosophy have some serious flaws), Williams was ready to acknowledge that he ultimately considered philosophy a humanistic discipline. More precisely, philosophy is taken as a 'general attempt to make the best sense of our life, and so of our intellectual activities, in the situation in which we find ourselves' (2006: 182). In that respect, the main question of philosophy of various disciplines is to explain how a specific portion of human activities figures in making sense of ourselves and our activities.

In pursuing this task, philosophy, according to Williams, has to rely on history. In a series of papers culminating with his final book *Truth and Truthfulness: An Essay on Genealogy*, Williams developed an account of analytic philosophy that embraced historical inquiry. He writes: 'History is central to my argument not just because history is central among humanistic disciplines, but because … philosophy has some very special relations to it' (2006: 180). In other words, historical understanding, the 'genealogical' approach, is a necessary part of philosophising about virtues and values. In the contemporary philosophy of law, we struggle between philosophising about the law to make sense of it within the entirety of the practical human life and philosophising about law as a discrete object of inquiry suitable for scientific inquiry. Our general inclination towards one or the other object drives our philosophical research. Authors who understand the law as an integral part of our practical life have adopted a stance in which analysis is important only insofar as it assists in explaining our practical reasoning. Authors who understand the law as a discrete object of inquiry have taken the philosophical grounding of law as the main task of their philosophical efforts.

Understanding human practice needs concepts from culture, history and local practices that others may not share. Unlike concepts of science, the concepts that arise from local practices are historical. This does not simply mean, as some authors claim,[5] that these concepts have a history and others do not. This means that the

[5] See Mordacci 2016: 74.

history of the concepts arising from human practice is something added to the concept, which cannot be eliminated without much being lost in understanding. History is an integral part of the content of those concepts in such a way that in order to comprehend cultural, moral or legal concepts, it is necessary to reconstruct their history.

Following this line of thought, Williams emphasised the importance of engaging with the history of philosophy, which he saw as a valuable resource for understanding the development of ideas and the problems philosophers grappled with over time. He criticised analytic philosophers for their lack of historical awareness and tendency to approach philosophical problems as if they could be solved in isolation from their historical context. Thus, Williams argued in favour of a genealogical account of analytic philosophy. This kind of narrative is especially important for concepts that are of importance for him – the ethical ones (Williams 2002).

Of what use is this narrative? Firstly, it helps us understand the source and development of our concepts and ideas. Secondly, it focuses on the practical functions that the concepts (mainly values) have in the society in which they emerged. Thirdly, it allows us to reflect on these ideas more broadly, given that some concepts might be contingent, but they might prove valuable and worth pursuing from a genealogical perspective. The first form of inquiry might be called *descriptive*, the second can be called *functional*, and the third can be called *critical* (Koopman 2010: 13).

All these motives for adopting a form of historical inquiry can be identified in authors that come to be identified as the main contemporary philosophers of hermeneutics and genealogy. Gadamer's account of hermeneutics revived a defunct discipline as a specific ontology of our existence and comprehension of the social world. Foucault's genealogies emphasised the roots of our concepts and practices with the aim of reforming them. At the same time, Williams is more conservative in adopting a historical perspective in philosophy than those authors and more radical in historical questioning of the contemporary philosophical beliefs that are thought unshakable (Koopman 2010: 15–16).

We could then say that the main preoccupation in Williams' late work was to develop a philosophical methodology that would incorporate historical inquiry into a specifically understood analytical style of philosophising. In describing it, concepts that do not relate to reality are synchronically and diachronically dependent on context and conceptualisations. In this sense, philosophy is, in his understanding, using what can be called the method of *conceptual morphology*.[6]

[6] Morphological approaches to terms, concepts, conceptions, and even ideologies are rare but existent. For example, in his *Philosophische Terminologie: zur Einleitung* (unfortunately not translated to English), Theodor Adorno argues that a proper introduction to philosophy is inconceivable as a series of analytical definitions of philosophical terms. Accounting for changing the content of terms and concepts is necessary to understand the very concept in question (Adorno 1973). In his influential

On the most basic level, conceptual morphology entails the study of the formation and change of philosophical, legal and other concepts.[7] This does not say much by itself, for the formation of concepts can be studied with different pretences. For one, concepts are formed individually due to cognitive and intellectual factors that might be idiosyncratic. However, concepts are usually formed based on certain cultural, historical, social, and pragmatic factors. A similar issue is created by the common content of a concept and the philosophical content of a concept. The philosophical content of a concept often deviates significantly from the common content of the same concept, expressing subtle, often technical nuance that is not present in the ordinary use of concepts.

While we can provide some rational, ahistorical elaboration of certain legal concepts and concepts related to law, we are usually unable to comprehend the reasons for their content without understanding the history of their emergence and development. The basic intuition supporting such an approach is that the conceptions of concepts that emerge in our ordinary communication, science or philosophy is not random. On the contrary, it is a consequence of practices related to the concepts being discussed. By discussing those practices that give rise to concepts and their theoretical formulations and reformulations that often reflect again on those practices, we can better grasp the content of a concept by engaging in conceptual analysis.

Indeed, many legal terms cannot be explained or justified without an explanation of how they came to be, how they developed, and why they are still used. Concepts that are often taken for granted, like 'fiction' and 'presumption', along with the technical terms of the likes of 'disposition', 'plaintiff', and even 'norm', are very hard, if not impossible, to grasp without an account of their morphology. Williams take 'human rights' as an illustrative example of the necessity of the morphological approach to concepts.

account of ideology, Michael Freeden argues for a morphological approach to establish and explain the structure of political ideologies. By focusing on political concepts that are at the centre of ideological thinking, their changes and relations, Freeden aims to formulate a method for 'investigating and decoding the internal structure of ideologies … offering and revealing insight into the ways ideologies consequently construct the political and navigate through it' (2013: 115). The general account of conceptual morphology we present here does not closely follow any of the above-mentioned, but it is used to explain Williams' approach.

[7] In that respect, it is possible to differentiate between it and related methods of history and genealogy. The former is interested in an adequate representation of certain factual events, both individual and social, which raises a number of interesting issues belonging to 'philosophy of history', such as what does history consist of and how do we categorise or periodise respective factual units; does history have meaning, or direction, beyond the individual events that make it up; what is involved in our knowing, representing, and explaining history, etc. (Little 2020). The latter method is explained by Williams himself. It is 'a narrative that tries to explain a cultural phenomenon by describing a way in which it came about, or could have come about, or might be imagined to have come about'. Hence, this method partly relies on 'real history', but partly also on 'a fictional narrative, an imagined developmental story, which helps to explain a concept or value or institution by showing ways in which it could have come about in a simplified environment containing certain kinds of human interests or capacities, which, relative to the story, are taken as given'. See Williams 2022: 20–21. Unlike genealogy, morphology is not relying on a fictional element of a historical analysis of the concept.

## IV. Towards a Williamsian Jurisprudence – The Case of Human Rights

After exposing the specificities of Williams' style of analytic philosophy, we will try to sketch what a Williamsian task of jurisprudence, understood as conceptual morphology, would look like. In his paper 'Human Rights and Relativism' (2008c), one can find all the ingredients of his distinctive style of philosophising. First, he reiterates that philosophers should strive towards the goal of making unclear clearer. The paper on human rights is a paradigmatic case of Williams' down-to-earth analysis, much like the one on the idea of equality, in which he explicitly states that analytical clarity is in the function of 'sav[ing] the political notion of equality from … extremes of absurdity and of triviality' (2009: 231). In discussing human rights, Williams aspires to do the same thing, even if that requires 'emphasiz[ing] reality at the expense of philosophical abstraction' (2008c: 64).

The focus on political reality signals that this style of philosophical analysis requires thinking of human rights, especially the blatant cases of their abuses, in political terms. Put differently, instead of coming in the form of some aprioristic claims, philosophical abstractions should emerge as 'ineliminable consequence' of 'thinking politically' (Williams 2008c: 64). For that reason, Williams' starting point is 'the "first" political question', the one which Thomas Hobbes recognised as pertaining to 'the securing of order, protection, safety, trust, and the conditions of co-operation'. Its logical and conceptual primacy is reflected in the fact that 'solving it is the condition of solving, indeed posing, any other political question' (2008c: 62). At this point, Williams makes an immediate dismissal of an ahistorical approach to the subject matter by noting that while 'a solution to the first political question is required *all the time*, the character of the solution is affected by historical circumstances' (2008c: 62). That is, some such solutions have always been intricately connected to our thinking about what the legitimate exercise of political power requires. The response to this question has never been unequivocal – throughout history, a number of different legitimation strategies have been employed.

This has a direct implication for the discussion of human rights as a distinctively liberal response to the first political question. Namely, Williams abandons *a*historical, foundationalist doctrine of 'liberal universalism' – or any other disputable 'particular ideology', for that matter. Williams is, however, focused on 'liberal universalism', insofar as it claims

> that if certain human rights exist, they have always existed, and if societies in the past did not recognise them, then that is because either those in charge were wicked, or the society did not, for some reason, understand the existence of these rights' (Willliams 2008c: 65).

According to him, such an attitude is unwarranted for various reasons, most obviously due to the lack of 'theory of error' in the presumed framework of correct moral reasoning. Namely, if all the people in the past were wrong/blind about not seeing the moral correctness of liberal views, then one would need a resounding reason why this was so. Not only do liberal universalists fail to offer any meaningful explanation, but they also do not realise that imposing present-day moral horizons on people in distant historical societies confuses between being actually 'presented *with such a society*' and being presented 'with the *description* of such society' (2008c: 65–66). Williams says: 'Of course, one can imagine oneself as Kant at the court of King Arthur, disapproving of its injustices, but exactly what grip does this get on one's ethical or political thought?' (2008c: 66). Hence, the only right way to go, methodologically speaking, is a genealogical endeavour that will clarify what is the status and role of human rights in our, present-day world.

At this point, it is interesting to draw a parallel with Raz's more recently developed conception of human rights. In a couple of articles dedicated to this topic, he also launched an attack on the so-called 'foundationalist' human rights doctrine, which commonly grounds this type of rights in some aspect of our humanity. According to Raz, this account leads to the absurd conclusion that cave dwellers in the Stone Age also had those rights (2010a: 40). Hence, '[t]he more plausible claim is that human rights are synchronically universal, meaning that all people alive today have them' (2010a: 41). A claim of this sort is also assumed in the contemporary human rights practice.[8] This practice, and not some abstract foundation, is what singles out human rights from other types of rights. They are dominantly 'trump-over-sovereignty' rights,[9] that is, 'those regarding which sovereignty limiting measures are morally justified' (Raz 2010b: 329). In the human rights literature, this view has become known as a 'political conception' of human rights.

Although rarely, if ever, discussed among human rights theorists, Williams' treatment of the subject-matter might easily go under the aforementioned label. His analysis in political terms has led him to conclude that 'our conceptions of human rights are connected with what we count as … the mode of justifying explanation or legitimation' (Williams 2008c: 63) as opposed to the 'unmediated coercive power' of state. Again, very similarly to what will be Raz's stance, Williams is concerned only with 'the most basic human rights'. Despite not qualifying them explicitly, Williams primarily has in mind Isaiah Berlin's negative liberties.[10] He particularly singles out one of them – freedom of expression and communication. On Williams' account, this human right is basic on instrumentalist grounds, insofar as it 'mak[es] effective any criticism of what a regime is doing, in relation to any reasonable conception of the individual's interests' (2008c: 74).

[8] Some other human rights theorists follow in these footsteps. Charles Beitz, for instance, argues that '[m]odern human rights doctrine cannot plausibly be regarded as seeking to articulate protections of timeless significance; it speaks to what might be described broadly as the conditions of modern life'. See Beitz 2009: 30–31.

[9] This was also Dworkin's standpoint. See 2011: 333–34.

[10] At one point, he mentions examples of 'torture, surveillance, arbitrary arrest, and murder', which were all characteristic of 'the world of Argentina under the junta'. See Williams 2008c: 69.

On the other hand, Williams is highly suspicious of the possible human rights status of 'so-called positive rights, such as the right to work'. Actually, for him, it was doubtful whether they could be called rights at all:

> Since in many cases governments cannot actually deliver what their peoples are said to have a right to, this encourages the idea that human rights represent simply aspirations, that they signal goods and opportunities which, as a matter of urgency, should be provided if it is possible. But that is not the shape of a right' (2008c: 64).

The possibility of institutional enforcement was also, for Raz, one of the necessary conditions for something to count as a human right. In his words, 'where there is no possibility of fair and reliable enforcement, there is no human right' (Raz 2010a: 44).

A final Williams' analytical clarification concerns the question of whether rejecting the universalist foundations of human rights implies endorsing the meta-ethical stance of moral relativism. While discharging 'standard relativism', according to which 'if "we" think X right and "they" think X wrong, then each party is right "for itself"' (2008c: 68), Williams favours the so-called 'relativism of distance'. Not only does it tell us about certain judgements that we need not make about past societies, but it also opens the room for tolerating some contemporary non-liberal justificatory practices as 'decent cases' of legitimation of coercive power.

When it comes to the first point, Williams wants to emphasise that '[t]he relativism of distance … applies to the past … because the past is not within our causal reach'. At the same time, 'there are some judgements we can make about the past' and they concern the very first question of politics. Namely, '[t]he categories of an ordered as opposed to a disordered social situation, disorder which is at the limit anarchy, apply everywhere; correspondingly, so do the ideas of a legitimate political order'. Put differently, '[e]verywhere, universally, at least this much is true, that might is not per se right: the mere power to coerce does not in itself provide a legitimation' (Williams 2008c: 69).

However, this does not imply that our judgment about what we count now as a legitimate political order can be imposed on some past societies. However, what about present-day societies which depart from the liberal standard of human rights protection as a source of legitimate political power? Williams devises a two-step test, which includes three distinctive yet interrelated questions. In the first step, we ask ourselves: What is going on in that society – and in relation to it – and how is it to be interpreted? In the second step, we are faced with the question of what, if anything, we can do about it. The crucial step for Williams' analysis is the hermeneutical one, insofar as not everything that would, from the standard liberal perspective, count as a violation of human rights would necessarily end up as an unacceptable ground for the legitimation of power.

It is hard to resist the analogy with Rawls' idea of tolerating non-liberal peoples and their 'decent hierarchical societies' (2000: 64 ff). Williams is obviously not so detailed, but he makes a rather general point:

> Up to a certain point, it may be possible for supporters of the system to make a decent case … that the coercion is legitimate. Somewhere beyond that point there may come

> a time at which the cause is lost, the legitimation no longer makes sense, and only the truly fanatical can bring themselves to believe it' (Williams 2008c: 71).

It is difficult to tell what exactly that point is, and, hence, Williams offers only a general guiding idea:

> It is a mark of philosophical good sense that the accusation should not be distributed too inconsiderately, and in particular that our theories should not lead us to treat like manifest crimes every practice that we reject on liberal principle and could not accept here – especially if in its locality it can be decently supposed to be legitimated' (Williams 2008c: 27).

To this, he adds that '[i]t is also a question of *political* sense, how widely the accusation should be distributed' (2008c: 72), particularly if one has in mind the second step of political action. Some sort of intervention, according to Williams, would be justifiable in those cases that are 'nearer to the paradigm [of human rights] violations' (2008c: 73).

## V. First Steps Towards Conceptual Morphology as a New Method in Legal Philosophy

A generalisation of Bernard Williams' approach to all jurisprudential issues in a way that can displace conceptual analysis is doubtful for various reasons. Firstly, Williams' interest in jurisprudential issues arose mainly from his interest in ethics. Human rights theory is closely associated with ethical discussions on values. Secondly, law is not just about moral rights. Thirdly, new developments in law do not easily yield themselves to a historical analysis.

However, these points are not in any way fatal to the possibility of incorporating elements of a Williamsian approach to legal philosophy. In fact, it would be contrary to the very ideas of philosophy endorsed by Williams to use his approach as a revolutionary methodology of any philosophical discipline. In this sense, one cannot really claim that what we labelled as conceptual morphology is a fully-fledged alternative to conceptual analysis. Still, one can find some remedies to conceptual analysis in jurisprudence that might have a beneficial effect on the discipline. In this sense, the basic tenets of the approach to philosophy championed by Bernard Williams can be considered a first step towards the development of conceptual morphology as a new method in legal philosophy. This method can be summarised in the following way.

### A. Analysis without Simplification

According to Williams, philosophical analysis that is not conducted for the sake of clarity deviates into technicality and narrowness. In ethics, this meant, for example, including luck,[11] tolerance,[12], and politics,[13] in his discussions about morality, with the aim of understanding the entirety of the human ethical life (Koopman 2010: 7–8).

Likewise, jurisprudence has its fair share of technicality, narrowness and simplification. With an over-emphasis on jurisprudential problems that have limited bearing on general philosophical issues and even less bearing on practical concerns of subjects of law, it has painted itself as uninteresting, even boring,[14] reaching a dead end.[15] In contemporary philosophical thinking, relevance and appeal relate to a discipline's ability to keep a keen eye on developments in empirical sciences. This might, however, be a temporary fad that typically coincides with times of forceful scientific developments. Williams had other ideas. He was clear that philosophy should aim for social understanding, with historical understanding being a special kind (Koopman 2010: 11).

## B. Dialogue without Dialectics

Williams engages in a productive dialogue with past philosophy without postulating any overarching idea of the development of philosophy or philosophy of history. The dialogue he engages in is aimed at elucidating the content of the concepts elucidated by his predecessors based on knowledge about the actual societies in which these concepts are used.

We might say of contemporary jurisprudence the same thing that Williams claimed of the philosophy of its time: It was hopelessly anachronistic and without tools to deal with issues of the modern world. So, our dialogue with past philosophers of law is valuable if we undertake it with the aim of understanding our contemporary legal practices, changes, and problems in the living world of law. To better understand and justify our present concepts and practices, Williams does not propose dialectics in a methodological or ontological sense. The mistake of other historically minded philosophies is precisely the absolutisation of the development of concepts. The method is a conversation, a productive dialogue with past events and ideas that gave rise to the present ideas and practices.

## C. History without Historicism

Historicism is the stance that social and cultural phenomena are determined by the processes by which they came about. Williams is adamant that making sense of

[11] See Williams 1981.
[12] See Williams 2006b.
[13] See Williams 2006c.
[14] See Enoch 2019.
[15] See Hershovitz 2015. Needless to say, not everyone agrees: see, e.g., Dickson 2017.

ourselves and the social world that we live in is premised on a historical approach like the one advanced in various historicisms. However, he rejects the idea that individual agency is determined by history or that history should substitute philosophical inquiry. In fact, his view could be characterised as a 'historically-engaged analytic philosophy'.[16]

With clarity as an aim and history as an aid, the approach that would be closely connected with Williams' efforts in the domain of the philosophy of law can be, as we suggested, alternatively termed *conceptual morphology*. In this sense, the concepts that we use to carve up our legal and ethical lives do not have immutable ahistorical contents. In fact, their very essence, so to speak, is determined by their history and the changes that they underwent during their use. The term conceptual morphology emphasises the fact that the very content of concepts is determined by the use of the concept in the historical changes of a society that uses the concepts so diachronically. The term, furthermore, highlights the changes and differences in the understanding or conceptions of a concept both synchronically and diachronically. Needless to say, this is not a position endorsed by Williams explicitly, but it can be derived from the Williamsian approach to legal problems, such as, for instance, human rights.

The relevant meaning of history is not factography, doxography, or any other retelling of real or imagined sequences. It is the 'understanding of the specific way in which certain of our practices and concepts have developed over time' (Koopman 2010: 11), a diachronic, developmental, genealogical perspective on human matters. The aim of a historically enriched analysis is most certainly the adoption of a critical stance, without which 'various of our ideas and procedures can seem to be such that we cannot get beyond them, that there is no conceivable alternative' (Williams 2006a: 195). In the lack of this critical perspective in jurisprudence, our contemporary legal practices might seem fixed and immutable. Even worse, they become self-explanatory and natural, impervious to change, both for the better or for the worse.

## D. Science without Scientism

A Williamsian account of jurisprudence would entail it being a humanistic discipline that tries to make sense not only of the object of the inquiry but also of the very subject that participates in a practice that constitutes an object of inquiry. Making sense of ourselves would be, to Williams, the ultimate goal of philosophy, with the philosophy of law aiming to make sense of our practical relations to legal rules, legal practices, and legal authority. In order to do so, jurisprudence 'should certainly be interested in the sciences' (2006a: 182), or even rely on scientific

[16] In 2010, Koopman writes: 'Analytic philosophy … largely proceeds today with strongly ahistorical assumptions about the practice of philosophy itself' (2010: 4).

inquiry in some areas. This might hold true for philosophy of mind or ontology, given that there is a strong conviction that modern empirical science might represent reality independently of perspectives, to give 'the absolute conception of the world' (2006a: 184–85).

While science can inform the enterprise of philosophy and philosophy of law by providing it with the latest factual knowledge, the legal and ethical philosophies are focused on making sense of our positions within the practices that we call law, ethics and science. Making sense of our intentional activities requires a first-person approach that explicates how we, humans, interact with the world and how we approach it (Williams 2006a: 187).

## VI. Conclusion

As we suggested, conceptual morphology might be an approach to jurisprudence that does justice to these main ideas. Understanding the dynamic interaction between social changes, crucial legal concepts, and their theoretical reformulations in a diachronic, developmental perspective could enrich our understanding of the practice that we are particularly fond of. But even without a methodological shift, a Williamsian perspective in jurisprudence legitimises a broader set of issues than the one currently discussed by philosophers of law. The incorporation of international law, state, alternative normative orderings, artificial intelligence, and data in our jurisprudential discussions would bring us closer to the philosophical and legal audiences that we rely on. It might even bring us closer to sounder accounts of normativity, authority and law itself.

## Bibliography

Adorno, TW (1973) *Philosophische Terminologie: zur Einleitung* (Frankfurt, Suhrkamp).

Alexy, R (2008) 'On the Concept and the Nature of Law' 3 *Ratio Juris* 281.

Beaney, M (2016) 'Analysis' in E Zalta (ed), *The Stanford Encyclopedia of Philosophy* (Summer 2016 edn).

Beitz, C (2009) *The Idea of Human Rights* (Oxford, Oxford University Press).

Bix, B (2021) 'Against Jurisprudence's New Metaphysical Focus', JOTWELL (2 August), available at https://juris.jotwell.com/against-jurisprudencesnew-metaphysical-focus

Chiassoni, P (2016) 'Supporting The Force of Law: A Few Complementary Arguments Against Essentialist Jurisprudence' in C Bezemek and N Ladavac (eds), *The Force of Law Reaffirmed – Frederick Schauer Meets the Critics* (Cham, Springer).

Chappell, SG & Smyth, N (2023) 'Bernard Williams' in E Zalta (ed), *The Stanford Encyclopedia of Philosophy* (Summer 2023 edn).

Dickson, J (2017) 'Why General Jurisprudence is Interesting?' 147 *Crítica: Revista Hispanoamericana de Filosofía* 11.

—— (2022) *Elucidating Law* (Oxford, Oxford University Press).

Dworkin, R (2011) *Justice for Hedgehogs* (Cambridge, Massachusetts, The Belknap Press).
Enoch, D (2019) 'Is General Jurisprudence Interesting?' in D Plunkett, S Shapiro & K Toh, *Dimensions of Normativity* (Oxford, Oxford University Press).
Freeden, M (2013) 'The Morphological Analysis of Ideology' in M Freeden, LT Sargent & M Stears (eds), *The Oxford Handbook of Political Ideologies* (Oxford, Oxford University Press).
Green, L (2013) 'The Morality in Law' in L Duarte d'Almeida, A Dolcetti & J Edwards (eds), *Reading HLA Hart's The Concept of Law: The Morality in Law* (Portland, Hart Publishing).
Hershovitz, S (2015) 'The End of Jurisprudence' 124 *The Yale Law Journal* 1160.
Himma, KE (2015) 'Conceptual Jurisprudence: An Introduction to Conceptual Analysis and Methodology in Legal Theory' 26 *Revus* 65.
—— (2019) *Morality and the Nature of Law* (Oxford, Oxford University Press).
Jackson, F (1998) *From Metaphysics to Ethics – A Defence of Conceptual Analysis* (Oxford, Clarendon Press).
Jovanović, M (2019) *The Nature of International Law* (Cambridge, Cambridge University Press).
—— (2021) 'On Law and Coercion – Once Again' 3 *Jurisprudence* 417.
Koopman, C (2010) 'Bernard Williams on Philosophy's Need for History' 1 *The Review of Metaphysics* 3.
Leiter, B (2007) *Naturalizing Jurisprudence: Essays on American Legal Realism and Naturalism in Legal Philosophy* (Oxford, Oxford University Press).
—— (2021) 'Back to Hart' 4 *Annals – Belgrade Law Review* 749.
Little, D (2020) 'Philosophy of History' in E Zalta (ed), *The Stanford Encyclopedia of Philosophy* (Winter 2020 edn).
Moore, AW (2003) 'Williams on Ethics, Knowledge, and Reflection' 78 *Philosophy* 337.
Mordacci, R (2016) 'From Analysis to Genealogy. Bernard Williams and the End of the Analytic-Continental Dichotomy' 4 *Philosophical Inquiries* 71.
Murphy, MC (2015) 'Two Unhappy Dilemmas for Natural Law Jurisprudence' 60 2 *The American Journal of Jurisprudence* 121.
Rawls, J (2000) *The Law of Peoples (With The Idea of Public Reason Revisited)* (Cambridge, Harvard University Press).
Raz, J (2005) 'Can There Be a Theory of Law?' in MP Golding and WA Edmundson (eds), *The Blackwell Guide to the Philosophy of Law and Legal Theory* (Oxford, Blackwell Publishing).
—— (2010a) 'Human Rights in the Emerging World Order' 1 *Transnational Legal Theory* 31.
—— (2010b) 'Human Rights Without Foundations' in S Besson & J Tasioulas (eds), *The Philosophy of International Law* (Oxford, Oxford University Press).
Schauer, F (2015) *The Force of Law* (Cambridge, Harvard University Press).
Tamanaha, B (2017) *A Realistic Theory of Law* (Cambridge, Cambridge University Press).
Williams, B (1981) *Moral Luck: Philosophical Papers 1973-1980* (Cambridge, University Press).
—— (2002) *Truth & Truthfulness: An Essay in Genealogy* (Princeton, University Press).
—— (2006) *Ethics and the Limits of Philosophy* (London, Routledge).
—— (2006a) *Philosophy as a Humanistic Discipline* (Princeton, Princeton University Press).
—— (2006b) 'Political Philosophy and the Analytical Tradition' in B Williams, *Philosophy as a Humanistic Discipline* (Princeton, Princeton University Press).
—— (2006c), 'Tolerating the Intolerable' in B Williams, *Philosophy as a Humanistic Discipline* (Princeton, Princeton University Press).

—— (2008a) *In the Beginning Was the Deed: Realism and Moralism in Political Argument* (Princeton, University Press).
—— (2008b) 'Internal and External Reasons' in E Jonathan and LJR Adler (eds), *Reasoning: Studies of Human Inference and its Foundations* (Cambridge, Cambridge University Press).
—— (2008c) 'Human Rights and Relativism' in B Williams, *In the Beginning Was the Deed: Realism and Moralism in Political Argument* (Princeton, University Press).
—— (2009) *Problems of the Self: Philosophical Papers – 1956-1972* (Cambridge, Cambridge University Press).
Williamson, T (2014) 'How Did We Get Here from There? The Transformation of Analytic Philosophy' 27 *Belgrade Philosophical Annual* 7.

# INDEX

A
**'Absolute conception of the world',** 4, 234–5, 299
**Agency**
Aristotelian-Irwin theory, 45
connections between Williams' Shame and Necessity and constitutional theory, 129, 132
lessons from moral luck
the responsibility dilemma, 31–2
strongest argument against the hegemony of MRV, 27–30
*The Man Who Shot Liberty Valance*, 152
moral luck as applied to tort law, 113
morality system, 2
politics of control, 46–7
problem for reasons internalism, 80–1
reasons internalism
essentials of Williams' position, 68
recognition of crimes which are not committed voluntarily or intentionally, 37
responsibility beyond MRV, 38
role and importance of superficial concept of voluntariness, 34
separation thesis, 42–3, 46
subjective motivational sets, 275, 278–81
summary of Williams' views, 5–6
unifying interpretation of Williams' argument, 35–6
ways in which concepts may fail the test of conceptual strength, 262
**Agent-regret,** 7, 27, 81, 262, 275
**Aristotelian-Irwin theory,** 43–5

B
**Basic demands of justice,** 48–50, 60–4
**Blame and blameworthiness**
*see also* **Praise**
absence of intention, 25
analogy between humanistic middle-range theories and Williams' philosophical work
concluding remarks, 209–10
middle-range general orientation, 208
middle-range generality of the explanandum, 205–6
middle-range isolation of the explanans, 206–7
middle range normativity, 208–10
middle-range perspective linking the micro and the macro level, 207–8
overview of key points, 204–5
discussion of responsibility, 23
intrinsic luck, 43
lessons from moral luck, 27, 38
morality and law
concluding remarks, 121–3
introductory remarks, 103–6
legal luck problem in tort law, 107–11
moral luck and forms of blameworthiness, 117–21
moral luck as applied to tort law, 111–15
moral luck scepticism, 106–7
overview of Zipursky's key points, 10–11
return to blameworthiness and the topic of moral luck, 115–16
overview of Cueni's key points, 14
overview of Zipursky's key points, 10–11
proleptic blame mechanism
advantage of the Motivational Interpretation of reasons internalism, 77–9
overview of Lang's key points, 9–10
Williams' morality system, 2, 17

C
**'Cab rank rule'**
Bar Standards Board, 95
dominant justification for restriction, 95–6
failure to pass moral muster, 98
protection against the internal costs of dealing with ethical conflict, 96–8
**Cause**
lessons from moral luck, 27

voluntariness, 32
Williams' writings on responsibility, 25–6
**Civic maturity**
and the politics of justice
concluding remarks, 63–4
the demands of justice – undermining Williams' key statements, 48–50
introductory remarks, 41–2
maturity and learning to be good, 50–60
response to 'the basic demands of justice', 60–3
Rodriguez-Blanco's key points, 9
Williams' arguments and their implicit premises, 42–8
**Common sense**
making philosophy accountable to common sense
Austin's approach, 250
political action, 253–4
a safeguard against frivolity, 250–1
William's response to Austin, 251–3
metaphor of microwave-resistant concepts, 258–60
overview of Queloz's key points, 15–16
relationship with tort law, 249–50
that Williams was a sage and cultivated man, 229
ways in which concepts may fail the test of conceptual strength, 261, 264
why law is an ideal testing ground for common sense
cost allocation and compensation, 256–7
difference between Austin and Williams, 257–8
key features of Anglo-American tort law, 254–6
quasi-evolutionary pressures, 254, 256
survival of concepts distinguished from the survival of legal principles, 257
**Constitutional theory** *see* **Liberal constitutional theory**
**Control principles**
fairness control principle, 108, 111–12
general control principle, 106–7, 112
moral luck as applied to tort law, 111–15
**Criminal punishment**
law modelled on Williams' treatment of truth and truthfulness, 182
objections to Williams' approach, 36–7
recognition of crimes which are not committed voluntarily or intentionally, 37
role and importance of superficial concept of voluntariness, 34–5
**Culpability manifestation argument,** 106–8, 112

D
**Dworkin, R.**
Dworkinian replies and a matter of philosophical temperament
abandonment of uncontroversial starting point, 280–1
answering to the wrong question, 280
challenges to reasons externalism, 281
Dworkin's claim is more modest in two respects, 282
on interpretation and morality
bare truths, 272
general theory of interpretation, 272–4
science and interpretation distinguished, 271–2
interpretation and practical deliberation
conflicts of belief, 275–6
conflicts of desires, 276–8
contingent historical deposits, 279
Dworkinian interpretation as a method of practical deliberation, 278–9
limits to Dworkin's interpretive theory, 279–80
moral conflicts, 276–7
matters of plain fact, 244
moral rights must be called from the vasty deep, 222
overview of Murata's key points, 16
William's rejection of 'a claim in liberty,' 143–4

E
**Emotion**
connections between Williams' Shame and Necessity and constitutional theory, 130–3
Williams' model of internal reasons, 150
**Ethical perspectives**
connections between Williams' Shame and Necessity and constitutional theory
conception of the will, 129–30
conceptions of intention and responsibility in Ancient Greek tragedy, 128–9

introductory remarks, 125–6
juxtapositioning of will and intention, 127–8
resisting a heavily moralised psychology, 130–3
William's resistance to heavily moralised psychology underpinning modern moral philosophy, 126–7
importance to Williams of Nietzsche and Wittgenstein
fundamental insight in reappraising modern moral philosophy, 231–3
Williams as a Left Wittgensteinian, 235–44
Williams' critique of morality, 234–5
law as a humanistic discipline, 210
*The Man Who Shot Liberty Valance*
Ford and Williams on legitimation narratives, 154–7
transition from the partially political condition to State, 151–2
many ethical resources, 3
moral luck
concluding remarks, 121–3
introductory remarks, 103–6
moral luck and forms of blameworthiness, 117–21
moral luck as applied to tort law, 111–15
moral luck scepticism, 106–7
overview of Zipursky's key points, 10–11
return to blameworthiness and the topic of moral luck, 115–16
morality system
'a deeply rooted and still powerful misconception of life', 2
concept of the voluntary, 261
continuing role in our ethical lives, 3
legal decision-making, 220
*The Man Who Shot Liberty Valance*, 156–7
overview of Owen's key points, 12
overview of Voyiakis' key points, 10
responsibility, 6, 262
utilitarianism and Kantianism, 2
William's contrast between 'thick ethical terms and 'thin' terms of moral theory, 224
Williams' critique of morality, 234
moving beyond the positivism versus anti-positivism debate in legal theory
introductory remarks, 219–21
law's uneasy relation to morality, 221–3
overview of Kutz's key points, 14
William's contrast between 'thick ethical terms and 'thin' terms of moral theory, 223–7
philosophy as a humanistic discipline
a model philosophy that lies in between facts and norms, 200–1
as a response to moralism, 199–200
practical reasoning
Dworkin on interpretation and morality, 271–4
interpretation and practical deliberation, 275–80
professional morality
'cab rank rule' as protection against internal costs, 94–8
concluding remarks, 99–100
ethical conflicts and their costs, 89–94
introductory remarks, 85–9
overview of Voyiakis' key points, 10
shifting perspectives on others, 55–7
Williams' ethical philosophy, 126
**External reasons**
Dworkin's approach, 278
essentials of Williams' position, 68–70
externalist response to Williams' position, 71–2
law and lawfulness, 194

F
**Fairness control principle,** 11–12, 108

G
**General control principle,** 106–7, 112

H
**Human action,** 2
**Human rights**
association with with ethical discussions on values, 296
example of the necessity of the morphological approach to concepts, 293–6
law as the primary way in which to ensure respect, 192
understanding or conceptions of a concept, 298
Williams' genealogical method, 17
Williams' view about the BLD, 189
**Humanistic middle-range theory**
analogy between Williams' philosophical work on truthfulness, blame, and voluntariness
concluding remarks, 209–10

middle-range general orientation, 208
middle-range generality of the explanandum, 205–6
middle-range isolation of the explanans, 206–7
middle range normativity, 208–10
middle-range perspective linking the micro and the macro level, 207–8
overview of key points, 204–5
introductory remarks, 197–8
law as a humanistic discipline
analogues with scientism and moralism, 210
answering why the law does or doesn't work, 210–11
approach to basic rights, 211–13
overview of Cueni's key points, 14
philosophy as a humanistic discipline
a model philosophy that lies in between facts and norms, 200–1
as a response to moralism, 199–200
as a response to scientism, 198–9
problems with focus on political realism, 213–14
theories of the middle range in sociology
generality, isolation, and the defining characteristics of middle-range theories, 203 *f*10.1
Hedström and Udehn's analytical notions of middle-range, 202–4
link between the micro and the macro level, 204
Merton's work to identify the features of such theories, 201–2

I

**Intention**
*see also* **Voluntariness**
connections between Williams' Shame and Necessity and constitutional theory
conceptions of intention and responsibility in Ancient Greek tragedy, 128–9
juxtapositioning of will and intention, 127–8
overview of White's key points, 11–12
moral luck, 24
political freedom, 37
responsibility beyond MRV, 38
the responsibility dilemma, 31
state's intention does not forcibly become one's own intention, 36–7
support for Williams' approach
role and importance of superficial concept of voluntariness, 34–5
way to scepticism, 32
unifying interpretation of Williams' argument, 36
voluntariness defined, 32
Williams' writings on responsibility, 25–6
**Internalism** *see* **Reasons internalism**
**Intrinsic luck,** 43

J

**Justice**
basic demands of justice, 48–50, 60–4
role of self-knowledge and civic maturity
concluding remarks, 63–4
the demands of justice – undermining Williams' key statements, 48–50
introductory remarks, 41–2
maturity and learning to be good, 50–60
response to 'the basic demands of justice', 60–3
Rodriguez-Blanco's key points, 9
Williams' arguments and their implicit premises, 42–8

K

**Kantianism**
blameworthiness, 103
classical universalism and classical relativism contrasted, 240
ethical and political thought, 294
importance of history for philosophy, 232, 234
misconceptions, 252
moral motivation, 6
moral responsibility, 26
progressivist picture of ethical thought, 128
view on morality, 11
why we should do right, 224
the will, 129, 137
Williams' approach, 2

L

**Language-games approach,** 50–1, 53, 61, 230, 244
**Law**
connections between Williams' Shame and Necessity and constitutional theory, 138–9
Dworkin on interpretation and morality, 274

as a humanistic discipline
analogues with scientism and moralism, 210
answering why the law does or doesn't work, 210–11
approach to basic rights, 211–13
jurisprudence as a conceptual morphology
concluding remarks, 299
introductory remarks, 285–6
overview of key points by Jovanovic and Spaic, 16–17
possibility of incorporating elements of a Williamsian approach to legal philosophy, 296–9
use and problems of conceptual analysis in jurisprudence, 286–8
Williams' understanding of conceptual analysis, 288–93
methodology of jurisprudence
internalisation and the internal point of view, 170–4
introductory remarks, 161–3
lawfulness and the emergence of law, 174–8
overview of Bero's key points, 12–13
Pettit on the genealogy of primary rules, 164–8
Williams on the genealogy of truthfulness view of justice, 168–70
modelling based on Williams' treatment of truth and truthfulness
denial of authority to law, 183
Hart's conception of the nature of law, 182–3
introductory remarks, 181
overview of Tollefsen's key points, 13
parallels between truth and law, 182
political realism – legitimacy and law, 188–95
problem with a naturalised and de-mythologised world, 183–6
state of nature as a linguistic community, 186–7
two contemporary attitudes toward truth and truthfulness, 181–2
virtue of sincerity, 187–8
moral and legal luck
concluding remarks, 121–3
introductory remarks, 103–6
legal luck problem in tort law, 107–11
moral luck and forms of blameworthiness, 117–21
moral luck as applied to tort law, 111–15
moral luck scepticism, 106–7
return to blameworthiness and the topic of moral luck, 115–16
moving beyond the positivism versus anti-positivism debate in legal theory
introductory remarks, 219–21
law's uneasy relation to morality, 221–3
overview of Kutz's key points, 14
William's contrast between 'thick ethical terms and 'thin' terms of moral theory, 223–7
Pettit on the genealogy of primary rules
expansion of Hart's story, 165–7
Hart's *The Concept of Law*, 164–5
internalisation as a significant development, 167
primary rules of conduct, 167
ratification of primary rules, 167–8
possibility of incorporating elements of a Williamsian approach to legal philosophy
analysis without simplification, 296–7
dialogue without dialectics, 297
history without historicism, 297–8
science without scientism, 298–9
relationship between legal authority and the citizen, 46
relationship of law and politics
concluding remarks, 157–8
Ford and Williams on legitimation narratives, 154–7
forms of classic Western which are salient, 145–6
introductory remarks, 141
overview of Owen's key points, 12
political realism, law and the legitimation demand, 141–5
synopsis of *The Man Who Shot Liberty Valance*, 146–9
transition from the partially political condition to State, 149–54
Williams' contention that philosophy might learn from the law
his search for independent test of conceptual strength, 276
making philosophy accountable to common sense, 250–4
metaphor of microwave-resistant concepts, 258–60

ways in which concepts may fail the test of conceptual strength, 261–4
why law is an ideal testing ground for common sense, 254–8

**Lawyers**
'cab rank rule'
Bar Standards Board, 95
dominant justification for restriction, 95–6
failure to pass moral muster, 98
protection against the internal costs of dealing with ethical conflict, 96–8
chaos on the tracks – *Palsgraf v Long Island*, 219–21
meaning of law, 226
pressure to reach a determinate answer, 258
professional morality
'cab rank rule' as protection against internal costs, 94–8
concluding remarks, 99–100
ethical conflicts and their costs, 89–94
introductory remarks, 85–9
overview of Voyiakis' key points, 10
real-world significance of tort theory, 110
role of lawyer-philosophers, 226
specialised conceptual repertoire, 254

**Learning**
analysis of Murdoch's mature agent, 61–2
Aristotelian-Irwin theory, 45
downranking of emotion, 137
law as a test of conceptual strength, 261–4
maturity and learning to be good, 50–60
narratives in transition, 12

**Legal luck**
*see also* **Moral luck**
alleged conceptual incoherence, 115
concluding remarks, 121–3
introductory remarks, 103–6
legal luck problem in tort law, 107–11
overview of Zipursky's key points, 10–11
return to blameworthiness and the topic of moral luck, 115

**Legal realism,** 220, 288

**Legitimacy**
law modelled on Williams' treatment of truth and truthfulness
normativity of law, 182
overview of Tollefsen's key points, 13
parallels between truth and law, 182
political realism – legitimacy and law, 188–95
political realism
Ford and Williams on legitimation narratives, 154–7
political realism, law and the legitimation demand, 144–5
voluntarist accounts of political legitimacy, 134

**Liberal constitutional theory**
conceptions of intention responsibility in Ancient Greek tragedy, 128–9
introductory remarks, 125–6
juxtapositioning of will and intention, 127–8
legal theory, 138–9
overview of White's key points, 11–12
peculiar will in the foundations of liberal constitutional theory, 133–8
transition from the partially political condition to State, 149–54

**Luck** *see* **Legal luck**; **Moral luck**

M

**Maturity** *see* **Civic maturity**

**Middle-range theory** *see* **Humanistic middle-range theory**

**Moral luck**
*see also* **Legal luck**
introductory remarks, 23–4
lessons from moral luck
the responsibility dilemma, 31–2
strongest argument against the hegemony of MRV, 27–30
*The Man Who Shot Liberty Valance*, 154
morality and law
concluding remarks, 121–3
introductory remarks, 103–6
moral luck and forms of blameworthiness, 117–21
moral luck as applied to tort law, 111–15
moral luck scepticism, 106–7
overview of Zipursky's key points, 10–11
return to blameworthiness and the topic of moral luck, 115–16
Williams' writings on responsibility, 24–5

**Moral Responsibility View (MRV)**
objections to Williams' approach
responsibility beyond MRV, 38
restriction of criminal justice to voluntary agency, 37
the responsibility dilemma, 31–2
unifying interpretation of Williams' argument, 35–6

Williams' approach to voluntariness
role and importance of superficial concept, 33–5
way to scepticism, 32–3
William's argument against the hegemony of MRV, 26–7
**Morality system**
'a deeply rooted and still powerful misconception of life', 2
concept of the voluntary, 261
continuing role in our ethical lives, 3
legal decision-making, 220
*The Man Who Shot Liberty Valance*, 156–7
overview of Owen's key points, 12
overview of Voyiakis' key points, 10
responsibility, 6, 262
utilitarianism and Kantianism, 2
William's contrast between 'thick ethical terms and 'thin' terms of moral theory, 224
Williams' critique of morality, 234
**Motivations**
analytic philosophy, 288
concept of moral obligation, 135
gap in the motivations to truthfulness, 170, 172
how 'the dispositions of trustworthiness are secured', 169
law and lawfulness, 194
overview of Lang's key points, 9–10
practical reasoning, 29
reasons internalism
Agency Problem, 80–1
considerations favouring the Motivational Interpretation, 74–7
essentials of Williams' position, 68, 70
fundamental motivations for Williams' internalism, 79–80
Motivational and Procedural Interpretation distinguished, 72–4
Promiscuous Influence Problem, 78–9, 82
treatment of blame and the proleptic mechanism, 77–9
State of Nature story, 185
subjective motivational sets, 275, 278–81
summary of Williams' views, 6
Thucydidean 'impartiality', 5
Williamsian philosophy, 5–6

N
**Naturalism**
law modelled on Williams' treatment of truth and truthfulness
introductory remarks, 181
political realism – legitimacy and law, 193
problem with a naturalised and de-mythologised world, 183–6
state of nature as a linguistic community, 186–7
moral luck, 120
search for an 'absolute conception', 4
use of non-moralised, or less moralised, psychology, 127
Williams' ethical philosophy, 126
**Necessity**
claims of rational necessity, 226
connections between Williams' Shame and Necessity and constitutional theory
overview of White's key points, 11–12
'human rights' as an illustrative example, 292
meeting our obligations, 224
*Shame and Necessity*
conceptions of intention and will, 125
history as essential dimension of genealogical approach, 232
moral philosophy, 233
Thucydidean 'impartiality', 5
Williams' views about responsibility, 8
**Nietzsche, F.**
importance for Williams
concluding remarks, 244–5
fundamental insight in reappraising modern moral philosophy, 231–3
introductory remarks, 229–31
overview of Macedo Jr's key points, 14–15
Williams' critique of morality, 234–5
will seeking to align its actions with principle, 223
William's comparison with Thucydides, 5
William's shared view of philosophy, 17
**Non-Enforcement Thesis,** 82–3

P
**Political freedom**
recognition of crimes which are not committed voluntarily or intentionally, 37
restriction of criminal justice to voluntary agency, 37
state's intention does not forcibly become one's own intention, 36–7
unifying interpretation of Williams' argument, 35–6

voluntariness and political freedom
role and importance of superficial concept, 33–5
'voluntary' defined, 32
way to scepticism, 32–3
**Political realism**
concluding remarks, 157–8
Ford and Williams on legitimation narratives, 154–7
forms of classic Western which are salient, 145–6
introductory remarks, 141
law modelled on Williams' treatment of truth and truthfulness, 188–95
*The Man Who Shot Liberty Valance*
concluding remarks, 157–8
Ford and Williams on legitimation narratives, 154–7
forms of classic Western which are salient, 145–6
introductory remarks, 141
overview of Owen's key points, 12
political realism, law and the legitimation demand, 144–5
synopsis, 146–9
transition from the partially political condition to State, 149–54
overview of Owen's key points, 12
political realism, law and the legitimation demand, 141–5
problems with focus on political realism, 213–14
synopsis of *The Man Who Shot Liberty Valance*
arrival in in Shinbone, 146–7
flashback, 147–8
flashback returns to present, 148–9
transition from the partially political condition to State, 149–54
Williamsian account of law and lawfulness, 188, 213
**Politics**
Dworkin on interpretation and morality, 273–4
liberal constitutional theory
conceptions of intention responsibility in Ancient Greek tragedy, 128–9
introductory remarks, 125–6
juxtapositioning of will and intention, 127–8
legal theory, 138–9
overview of White's key points, 11–12
peculiar will in the foundations of liberal constitutional theory, 133–8
liberty as a political value, 211–12
making philosophy accountable to common sense, 253–4
relationship of law and politics
concluding remarks, 157–8
Ford and Williams on legitimation narratives, 154–7
forms of classic Western which are salient, 145–6
introductory remarks, 141
overview of Owen's key points, 12
political realism, law and the legitimation demand, 141–5
synopsis of *The Man Who Shot Liberty Valance*, 146–9
transition from the partially political condition to State, 149–54
role of self-knowledge and civic maturity
concluding remarks, 63–4
the demands of justice - undermining Williams' key statements, 48–50
introductory remarks, 41–2
maturity and learning to be good, 50–60
response to 'the basic demands of justice', 60–3
Williams' arguments and their implicit premises, 42–8
three levels of politics, 46–7
**Practical reasoning**
the demands of justice in terms of rights and duties
Aristotelian theory, 44
the demands of basic justice, 60–1
how the demands of justice are presented to practical reasoners, 48–50
introductory remarks, 41
Dworkin on interpretation and morality
bare truths, 272
general theory of interpretation, 272–4
science and interpretation distinguished, 271–2
Dworkinian replies and a matter of philosophical temperament
abandonment of uncontroversial starting point, 280–1
answering to the wrong question, 280
challenges to reasons externalism, 281
Dworkin's claim is more modest in two respects, 282

Finnis's *Natural Law and Natural Rights*, 193
how law figures in the agents' practical reasoning, 6
interpretation and practical deliberation
conflicts of belief, 275–6
conflicts of desires, 276–8
contingent historical deposits, 279
Dworkinian interpretation as a method of practical deliberation, 278–9
empirical disagreements, 274
limits to Dworkin's interpretive theory, 279–80
moral conflicts, 276–7
paradigmatic aspects of practical reasoning, 274–5
subjective motivational sets, 275
introductory remarks, 269–71
overview of Murata's key points, 16
a 'sound deliberative route' from given motives, 29
transition from raw exercise of coercive power to an initial attempt at legitimacy, 195
**Praise**
*see also* **Blame**
bare truth, 272
linguistic analysis, 288
moral luck, 27
political realism, 153
Williams' morality system, 2
Williams' praise of Thucydides, 233
**Private language,** 53–4, 58, 60
**Professional morality**
'cab rank rule' as protection against internal costs
Bar Standards Board, 95
dominant justification for restriction, 95–6
failure to pass moral muster, 98
protection against the internal costs of dealing with ethical conflict, 96–8
concluding remarks, 99–100
ethical conflicts and their costs
case for giving protection against social or reputational costs, 91
comparison of four different professional profiles, 92–3
constraint on institutional power, 90–1
exercise of power by legal profession, 90
importance of varying internal costs, 93–4
issue of conflict between ordinary and professional morality, 89
standard conception of legal ethics., 89–90
introductory remarks
the ethical quandary, 87–8
three alternative conceptions, 86
'tortured co-existence', 88–9
Williams' working premise, 85–6
*'Lawyers Are Responsible'* Declaration, 94–5
overview of Voyiakis' key points, 10
**Proleptic blame mechanism**
advantage of the Motivational Interpretation of reasons internalism, 77–9
overview of Lang's key points, 9–10
**Promiscuous Influence Problem,** 78–9, 82
**Punishment** *see* **Criminal punishment**

R
**Reasoning** *see* **Practical reasoning**
**Reasons internalism**
*see also* **External reasons**
Agency Problem, 80–1
alternative interpretations
considerations favouring the Motivational Interpretation, 74–7
Motivational Interpretation, 73–4
Procedural Interpretation, 72–3
Dworkin's approach, 278
essentials of Williams' position
actual motivation, 69–70
dismissal of externalism, 70
explanation condition, 69
external reasons distinguished, 68–9
rational deliberation condition, 69
externalist response to Williams' position, 71–2
fundamental motivations for Williams' internalism, 79–80
introductory remarks, 67–8
law and lawfulness, 194
lessons from moral luck, 30
*The Man Who Shot Liberty Valance*, 150
methodology of jurisprudence
internalisation and the internal point of view, 170–4
internalisation as a significant development, 167
Motivational Interpretation
considerations favouring the Motivational Interpretation, 74–7
Procedural Interpretation distinguished, 72–4
treatment of blame and the proleptic mechanism, 77–9
Murata's discussion on Williams' work, 163

Non-Enforcement Thesis, 82–3
overview of Lang's key points, 9–10
Promiscuous Influence Problem, 78–9, 82
Self-Understanding Thesis, 79–82
summary of Williams' views, 5
treatment of blame and the proleptic mechanism, 77–9

**Reflection**
Aristotelian theory of practical reason, 44
ethical experience, 253
legitimation narratives, 155–7
Locke's reflections, 149
modern conception, 52
for Murdoch, 54–5
myth of the substantive reality, 45–6
relation to ethical knowledge, 243
thick ethical concepts, 224–5
transformative impact, 58–9, 63
truth and truthfulness, 181, 187
understanding relativism, 242
voluntariness condition, 32

**Relativism**
'absolute conception of the world', 4
Cambridge tradition of philosophical pragmatism, 225
importance to Williams of Nietzsche and Wittgenstein
concluding remarks, 244–5
introductory remarks, 230–1
Williams as a Left Wittgensteinian, 235–43
Williams' approach to human rights, 295

**Relativism of distance,** 230, 239–44, 295

**Responses**
lessons from moral luck, 27
Moral Responsibility View, 27
responsibility beyond MRV, 38
the responsibility dilemma, 31
retribution, 35
role and importance of superficial concept of voluntariness, 33
unifying interpretation of Williams' argument, 36
Williams' writings on responsibility, 25–6

**Responsibility**
Aristotelian-Irwin theory, 45
connections between Williams' Shame and Necessity and constitutional theory
conception of the will, 129–30
conceptions of intention and responsibility in Ancient Greek tragedy, 128–9
introductory remarks, 23–4
*'Lawyers Are Responsible'* Declaration, 94–5
lessons from moral luck
the responsibility dilemma, 31–2
strongest argument against the hegemony of MRV, 27–30
objections to Williams' approach
political freedom, 37
recognition of crimes which are not committed voluntarily or intentionally, 37
responsibility beyond MRV, 38
state's intention does not forcibly become one's own intention, 36–7
overview of Heuer's key points, 8
separation thesis, 46
summary of Williams' views, 6
unifying interpretation of Williams' argument, 35–6
voluntariness
defined, 32
support for William's approach, 32–5
Williams' writings on responsibility
cause, intention, state of mind, and response, 25–6
moral luck, 24–5
moral responsibility, 26–7

S

**'Scepticism without reductionism',** 3–4

**Self-knowledge**
concluding remarks, 63–4
the demands of justice – undermining Williams' key statements, 48–50
introductory remarks, 41–2
maturity and learning to be good, 50–60
response to 'the basic demands of justice', 60–3
Rodriguez-Blanco's key points, 9
Williams' arguments and their implicit premises, 42–8

**Self-Understanding Thesis,** 79–82

**Separation thesis**
concluding remarks, 63–4
the demands of justice – undermining Williams' key statements, 48–50
introductory remarks, 41–2
maturity and learning to be good, 50–60
response to 'the basic demands of justice', 60–3
Rodriguez-Blanco's key points, 9

three key statements, 48
William's arguments and their implicit premises, 42–8
**Shame**
awareness of of our deprived or lacking position, 60
connections between Williams' Shame and Necessity and constitutional theory
conception of the will, 129–30
conceptions of intention and responsibility in Ancient Greek tragedy, 128–9
introductory remarks, 125–6
juxtapositioning of will and intention, 127–8
legal theory, 138–9
overview of White's key points, 11–12
peculiar will in the foundations of liberal constitutional theory, 133–8
resisting a heavily moralised psychology, 130–3
William's resistance to heavily moralised psychology underpinning modern moral philosophy, 126–7
drive to self-destruction, 151
*The Man Who Shot Liberty Valance*, 154
one of many many ethical resources, 3
*Shame and Necessity*
ethical language of Greek tragedy in, 152
viability of political realism, 157
Thucydidean 'impartiality', 5
truth and truthfulness, 168
**Social events,** 5
**Socratic question,** 42
**State of mind**
humanistic middle-range theory, 206
law as a test of conceptual strength, 263–4
Moral Responsibility View, 27
unifying interpretation of Williams' argument, 36
voluntariness, 32
Williams' writings on responsibility, 25–6

T

***The Man Who Shot Liberty Valance***
concluding remarks, 157–8
Ford and Williams in legitimation narratives, 154–7
form of classic Western which is salient, 145–6
introductory remarks, 141
overview of Owen's key points, 12
political realism, law and the legitimation demand, 144–5
synopsis
arrival in in Shinbone, 146–7
flashback, 147–8
flashback returns to present, 148–9
transition from the partially political condition to State, 149–54
**Theoretical perspectives**
Aristotelian-Irwin theory, 43–5
connections between Williams' Shame and Necessity and constitutional theory
conception of the will, 129–30
conceptions of intention and responsibility in Ancient Greek tragedy, 128–9
introductory remarks, 125–6
juxtapositioning of will and intention, 127–8
legal theory, 138–9
overview of White's key points, 11–12
peculiar will in the foundations of liberal constitutional theory, 133–8
resisting a heavily moralised psychology, 130–3
William's resistance to heavily moralised psychology underpinning modern moral philosophy, 126–7
human rights theory, 296
humanistic middle-range theory
analogy between Williams' philosophical work on truthfulness, blame, and voluntariness, 204–10
introductory remarks, 197–8
law as a humanistic discipline, 210–13
overview of Cueni's key points, 14
philosophy as a humanistic discipline, 198–201
problems with focus on political realism, 213–14
theories of the middle range in sociology, 201–4
liberal constitutional theory
conceptions of intention responsibility in Ancient Greek tragedy, 128–9
introductory remarks, 125–6
juxtapositioning of will and intention, 127–8
legal theory, 138–9
overview of White's key points, 11–12
peculiar will in the foundations of liberal constitutional theory, 133–8
transition from the partially political condition to State, 149–54

moving beyond the positivism versus anti-positivism debate in legal theory
introductory remarks, 219–21
law's uneasy relation to morality, 221–3
overview of Kutz's key points, 14
William's contrast between 'thick ethical terms and 'thin' terms of moral theory, 223–7
**Tort law**
legal luck in torts
challenges to two core arguments, 111–15
and its defenders, 107–11
linking tort theory and moral theory, 104–6
metaphor of microwave-resistant concepts, 258–60
overview of Queloz's key points, 15–16
*Palsgraf v Long Island*, 219–21
recklessness and negligence as part of the criminal law, 37
relationship with common sense, 249–50
return to blameworthiness, 115–18
standards of legal liability, 122
variety of different ways of reasoning about blameworthiness, 123
ways in which concepts may fail the test of conceptual strength, 261–4
why law is an ideal testing ground for common sense
cost allocation and compensation, 256–7
difference between Austin and Williams, 257–8
key features of Anglo-American tort law, 254–6
quasi-evolutionary pressures, 254, 256
survival of concepts distinguished from the survival of legal principles, 257
Williams' interest in *Palsgraf v Long Island*, 220
**Truth and truthfulness**
analogy between humanistic middle-range theories and Williams' philosophical work
concluding remarks, 209–10
middle-range general orientation, 208
middle-range generality of the explanandum, 205–6
middle-range isolation of the explanans, 206–7
middle range normativity, 208–10
middle-range perspective linking the micro and the macro level, 207–8
overview of key points, 204–5
bare truth, 272
changes in our thinking, 54–5
Dworkin on interpretation and morality, 273
importance to Williams of Nietzsche and Wittgenstein, 232–3
law as grounded in truth, 221
law modelled on Williams' treatment of truth and truthfulness
denial of authority to law, 183
Hart's conception of the nature of law, 182–3
introductory remarks, 181
overview of Tollefsen's key points, 13
parallels between truth and law, 182
political realism – legitimacy and law, 188–95
problem with a naturalised and de-mythologised world, 183–6
state of nature as a linguistic community, 186–7
two contemporary attitudes toward truth and truthfulness, 181–2
virtue of sincerity, 187–8
*The Man Who Shot Liberty Valance*, 154, 156
methodology of jurisprudence
internalisation and the internal point of view, 170–1
Pettit on the genealogy of primary rules, 167
overview of Cueni's key points, 14
Williams on the genealogy of truthfulness view of justice, 168–70

U
**Utilitarianism**
classical universalism and classical relativism contrasted, 240
ethical knowledge, 137
ex-ante deliberations, 42
misconceptions, 252
morality system, 234
Rawls' *A Theory of Justice*, 134
Williams' *A Critique of Utilitarianism*, 232
Williams' approach, 2
Williams' philosophical position, 290

V
**Voluntariness**
*see also* **Will**
analogy between humanistic middle-range theories and Williams' philosophical work
concluding remarks, 209–10

middle-range general orientation, 208
middle-range generality of the explanandum, 205–6
middle-range isolation of the explanans, 206–7
middle range normativity, 208–10
middle-range perspective linking the micro and the macro level, 207–8
overview of key points, 204–5
defined, 32
objections to Williams' approach
restriction of criminal justice to voluntary agency, 37
state's intention does not forcibly become one's own intention, 36–7
overview of Cueni's key points, 14
support for William's approach
role and importance of superficial concept, 33–5
way to scepticism, 32–3
unifying interpretation of Williams' argument, 35–6
ways in which concepts may fail the test of conceptual strength, 261–2

W

**Will**
*see also* **Responsibility**; **Voluntariness**
connections between Williams' Shame and Necessity and constitutional theory
juxtapositioning of will and intention, 127–8
peculiar will in the foundations of liberal constitutional theory, 133–8
dominant feature in modern ethical theory, 125
intrinsic luck, 43
language-games, 54
overview of White's key points, 11–12
thoughts and imaginative thinking, 55
ultimate author or gate-keeper, 2–4
will seeking to align its actions with principle, 223

**Williams, B.**
'absolute conception of the world', 4
criticisms of the morality system, 2–3
distinct way of doing philosophy, 6–7
importance of Nietzsche and Wittgenstein
concluding remarks, 244–5
fundamental insight in reappraising modern moral philosophy, 231–3
introductory remarks, 229–31
overview of Macedo Jr's key points, 14–15
Williams as a Left Wittgensteinian, 235–44
Williams' critique of morality, 234–5
jurisprudence as a conceptual morphology
concluding remarks, 299
human rights as conceptual morphology, 293–6
introductory remarks, 285–6
overview of key points by Jovanovic and Spaic, 16–17
possibility of incorporating elements of a Williamsian approach to legal philosophy, 296–9
use and problems of conceptual analysis in jurisprudence, 286–8
Williams' understanding of conceptual analysis, 288–93
one of the most prominent moral philosophers of the 20th century, 1
possibility of incorporating elements of a Williamsian approach to legal philosophy
analysis without simplification, 296–7
dialogue without dialectics, 297
history without historicism, 297–8
science without scientism, 298–9
summary of his views
how 'situations appear to agents', 5–6
jurisprudential theory, 6
need to relate human actions to motivations, 5
responsibility, 6
we should not attempt to reduce human affairs to physical or natural facts, 5
understanding of philosophy's business, 4–5
unifying themes in his work, 3–4
way of doing philosophy, 1–2
what counts as 'an intelligible and typically human motivation', 6

**Wittgenstein, L.**
criticism of private language, 53–4, 58
importance for Williams
concluding remarks, 244–5
fundamental insight in reappraising modern moral philosophy, 231–3
introductory remarks, 229–31
overview of Macedo Jr's key points, 14–15
Williams as a Left Wittgensteinian, 235–44
Williams' critique of morality, 234–5
language-game, 51, 61

**World** *see* **'absolute conception of the world'**

www.ingramcontent.com/pod-product-compliance
Ingram Content Group UK Ltd.
Pitfield, Milton Keynes, MK11 3LW, UK
UKHW020240290926
15470UKWH00002B/638

9 781509 976133